THE OUTRAGEOUS JERRY SPRINGER

THE OUTRAGEOUS JERRY SPRINGER

IAN MARKHAM-SMITH
AND LIZ HODGSON

BLAKE

Published by Blake Publishing Ltd,
3 Bramber Court, 2 Bramber Road,
London W14 9PB, England

First published in harback in 1999

ISBN 1 85782 3311

British Library Cataloguing-in-Publication Data:
A catalogue record for this book is available
from the British Library.

Typeset by BCP

Printed in Great Britain by
Creative Print and Design (Wales), Ebbw Vale, Gwent

1 3 5 7 9 10 8 6 4 2

Acknowledgements

First and foremost we would like to thank our dear friend and publisher John Blake without whom this book would not have been possible. John's continuous belief in us and encouragement is always gratefully received and much appreciated.

Second, we would like to thank all the people we met in Cincinnati who showed us immense kindness and went out of their way to be helpful. In particular, our thanks and heartfelt appreciation goes out to Ray Zwick, Cheryl G Swartz, John Kiesewetter and everyone else who helped us at the *Cincinnati Enquirer*; Bob Hahn and Greg Paeth at the *Cincinnati Post*; Laura Chace of the Cincinnati Historical Society; the staff of the Cincinnati Public Library and John Pahlgren, Edwin A Pfetzing and Robyn Carey Wilson.

Third, our thanks also go out to Alan Aldaya, Ron Britton, Albert Coombes, Rosalia de Guzman, Robert J Harbottle, Wade P Huie III, David A Jones, Barry Kernon, John Polsue, Jack Roth and Murray Rudomin.

About the Authors

IAN MARKHAM-SMITH has been a journalist, writer and broadcaster for more than 30 years. Originally from Farnham, Surrey, he has worked for numerous publications including the *Sunday Telegraph*, *Daily Mail* and *Sunday Mirror* newspapers in Britain.

In addition, he has held positions on the US magazines the *Globe* and the *National Enquirer* and the prestigious *South China Morning Post* in Hong Kong. He was also editor of Hong Kong's leading social magazine the *Tatler*.

For many years a freelance, he has covered stories in Europe, Africa, the Far East and North and South America. His articles appear in newspapers and magazines around the world. When not writing about the activities of celebrities and international events, he is also a widely published writer on wine, food and travel.

Based in Los Angeles, California, he spends his time between America's West Coast, the Far East and France.

LIZ HODGSON is a well-known and respected journalist whose articles appear in newspapers and magazines around the globe.

Originally from Wingate, County Durham, she has held positions on the *Sunday Mirror* and the *Daily Mail* in Britain and the *South China Post* in Hong Kong. She has also edited a number of consumer and general interest magazines in the Far East.

A specialist on the entertainment industry and celebrity circuit, she also writes about human interest, travel, wine and food. She has homes in Los Angeles, London and Chamonix, France.

The First Amendment

The 1st Amendment to the Constitution of the United States is the best-known provision of the Bill of Rights. It guarantees freedom of religion, speech and of the press, and the right to gather peacefully and to complain about injustice to the Government. Written in 1789, ratification of the Bill of Rights was completed on 15 December 1791 after two years of debate. It reads:

> Congress shall make no law respecting an establishment of religion, or prohibiting the free exercise thereof; or abridging the freedom of speech, or of the press; or the right of the people peaceably to assemble, and to petition the Government for a redress of grievances.

Prologue

Jerry Springer is TV's undisputed Titan of trailer trash trauma. The 'talkmeister's' recipe of freaks, frumps, fornicators, fantasisers and fanatics serves up a deliciously tasty menu of spicy life that most people have not — and would not even want to have — sampled, but that his army of famished fans around the world greedily devour and happily savour.

The bespectacled master chef of titillating TV dishes up a daily diet of screaming fights, on-stage brawls and angry confrontations that is worshipped by a mainly young audience. With fists flying, hair pulled and the air filled with obscenities, the only thing his guests can agree upon is that Jerry's rage-filled show is a smash hit.

Despite his strait-laced appearance in his immaculate Armani suits, which he claims are rented, and horn-rimmed glasses, he has an astonishing ability to encourage people to reveal the most dysfunctional details of their indiscreet lives.

His programme was for a long time considered a sideshow act rather than prime-time fodder before it rocketed to the top of the ratings in the USA. With its newfound success, Jerry suddenly became the undisputed ringmaster of emotional mayhem in the circus of human life, presenting a forum for cross-dressers, drag queens, nudists, strippers, pornography addicts, psychics and sickos.

Many of his guests walk the high wire of emotional instability while demonstrating astonishing acrobatic passions for peculiar behaviour that seems impossible to believe.

Widely criticised for presenting an unpalatable programme filled with bleeped-out profanities, no show in the history of TV has sunk so low searching for its subject ingredients. Jerry's outlandish mix cooks up such themes as *Hey, I've Slept With Your Husband*; *Sorry Honey, I'm Gay*; *I Am Pregnant by a Transsexual*; *My Sister Slept With My Three Husbands*; *I'm Pregnant and Have to Strip*; *I Slept With 251 Men in Ten Hours*; *My Girlfriend Is a Man*; *Prostitutes v Pimps*; *I Cut Off My Manhood*; *My Teenager Worships Satan*; *Mistress Attack*; *My Man Wears a Dress*; *I Want Your Man*; *I Stole My 12-Year-Old's Boyfriend*; and *Paternity Test: I Slept With Two Brothers.*

He had recorded some 1,400 episodes of his show by the end of 1998 and, in doing so, has become one of the most popular and notorious TV personalities in the world. His programme earns more than $400 million in advertising revenue a year in the USA alone.

As a result, this sultan of salaciousness signed a new multi-million dollar contract in 1997 to continue doing his scandal-packed show for a further five years, which means that his particular brand of brash provocation and mind-boggling revelations will have a lasting effect on TV long into the new millennium. His show is aired on more than 150 stations in the USA five days a week and soon to be six, and is seen in some 50 countries around the world.

In addition to his own top-rated show, he has made guest appearances on many other popular series and talk shows, has produced a top-selling series of videos of out-takes from his programmes, *Too Hot For TV!*, has recorded an album of country songs, has written a book about his programme and is starring in a comedy movie about himself.

The son of German Jewish refugees who fled the Holocaust three weeks before the Nazis invaded Poland to settle first in Britain before finally making their home in the USA, Jerry Springer appears to celebrate the most excessive lifestyles in his new homeland, welcoming them with open arms onto his show and presenting them on a plate for all the world to see.

He often jokes that his internationally popular show should be saving the US working public millions in taxes that the Government does not need to spend on defence. He says, 'When people in other countries see our show, all of a sudden they lose interest in taking us over!'

However, there is far more to this fascinating figure than meets the eye of the fans who tune in daily to *The Jerry Springer Show*. Intelligent, articulate and with a dry, self-deprecating sense of humour, he has recreated himself repeatedly in public while remaining an intensely private person. Few people outside his adopted hometown of Cincinnati had ever heard of him before his show started hitting the headlines, but he was a quiet player on the national and international political stage in his younger days, and still regards politics as his first love.

As a small boy growing up in the New York borough of Queens, Jerry, who was born in London in 1944, quickly embraced the USA as his home and everything American as his culture of choice. An avid baseball fan, he loves to strum his guitar and sing country and western and rock and roll songs.

A natural scholar, he excelled at school and university and become a lawyer. However, in his earlier years, his greatest passion was politics. He campaigned for Robert Kennedy to become President before he was tragically assassinated, ran for the US Congress when he was just 26, became a councillor in Cincinnati by the time he was 28 and, despite a major political setback when he became embroiled in a prostitution scandal, he made a spectacular comeback as the city's most popular politician and became its mayor when he was just 33, making him one of the youngest-ever mayors of a major city in the USA.

After unsuccessfully attempting to become governor of Ohio, he switched careers to become the most successful news presenter in Cincinnati, the city he called home for more than two decades, before moving on to his current position as the wizard of wham-bam TV.

The totally devoted father of a handicapped daughter, who has bravely fought her disabilities, Jerry has remained married to a long-suffering 'secret' wife who has witnessed his infidelities and love for strippers, porno stars and brassy women, many of whom would fit in as guests on his show.

Cigar-puffing Jerry has always been a dedicated doer, who has had to sample life's experiences first-hand. When he was a councillor, he went undercover to experience what life was like in jail and, as a news presenter, he spent a week posing as a tramp to discover what it was really like to be homeless. He travelled to Ethiopia to help deliver much-needed medical and food supplies to the famine-ravaged African nation, and visited the Middle East as an envoy for President Jimmy Carter days after the Israel–Egypt peace accord.

His critics call him the most loathesome man on TV who has successfully lowered the standards of talk shows to their most base and debauched.

Jerry takes it all in his stride. He stresses that his programme is nothing more than entertainment and should not be taken seriously. Instead of wanting to be remembered for the startling impact he has had on TV, the most talked-about man in the entertainment business hopes that in 50 years he will be long forgotten.

CHAPTER 1

'JER-RY! JER-RY! JER-RY!' the audience scream enthusiastically. As he walks onto the stage in his trademark Armani suit, clutching in his hand a microphone and a small prompt card with his name printed on it for the viewers to see, the chants of 'JER-RY! JER-RY! JER-RY!' reach an almost hysterical crescendo.

The ringmaster of this circus of human extravagances, Jerry Springer, has arrived. The king of TV talk shows is in his element, holding court before his millions upon millions of devoted subjects around the world.

He purposefully strides around the set, among his worshipping audience, with more energy than the average power company. To his critics he is no more than the king of sleaze TV but to jovial Jerry he is the clown prince, marvelling at the fact that people enjoy his 'silly show'.

Jerry is totally unapologetic that his talk show topics are the raciest in the business, dealing with such issues as *Porno Saved My Marriage* and *Granny Works In A Brothel*. He admits: 'I'm the ringmaster of a circus. My show isn't a talk show. There's no talking. There's just yelling, cursing and throwing whatever's at hand. Some people would be less upset if we didn't call it a talk show, if we said it's professional wrestling.'

It is certainly amateur wrestling; on almost every show fists or chairs fly, punches are thrown, hair is pulled, until the audience is stirred into a frenzy of cheering and jeering approval, and the burly security guards pull the irate guests apart. The soundtrack has more high-pitched beeps than words on many occasions, as participants spit curses and obscenities at each other.

Jerry confesses: 'I have no idea why it's successful. It's crazy. I think viewers at home with remote controls get to our show and suddenly stop and say, "What's going on? What's that about?" Young people get it. They are not sitting there watching the show and saying, "Maybe this is how I should live?" No. They've been in class all day, they want to free their minds for an hour. When I was in law school, we used to get out of class and run home to watch *Batman*. I can't tell you that we thought we would one day put on capes and race around town. OK, maybe some of us did.

'I think the attraction of the show is that you realise these are the people that live down the block from you, or maybe you wish they didn't. The format is supposed to be outrageous. There will always be outrageous things in the world and we'll always be fascinated by them Not for one second do I believe the average American is like this. But it's what viewers want.'

Jerry and his team agree that there is one simple philosophy to producing one of the most popular and successful shows on TV. He says: 'There are no orders to follow; we all agree that our show is about outrageousness. As long as the subjects are outrageous and the guests are outrageous, I don't interfere. It's escapism. It's entertaining.

'This is entertainment, pure and simple. It has to be entertaining because we are in showbusiness. I make no apologies for the show. Heck, I'm not mayor of Cincinnati any more. I don't have to conform to that mind-set.'

Jerry, the man who takes dysfunction to new and ever-lower depths was, in a previous life, a serious politician and a good one at that. Although he spends his working life listening to guests cursing each other, he really does say 'Heck'.

He reflects: 'I want to say the show is interesting rather than entertaining. While most of our shows are entertaining, occasionally we have a serious subject, and no one out there is laughing. The show has to be interesting. It has to grab you. You have to say, "Whoa, don't hit the remote, what was that?" And sometimes what's interesting is silly.'

It may be hard to believe, but *The Jerry Springer Show* has rules — among them, no swearing and no fighting. A printed list is handed out to all the guests before they appear, but none of the production staff expect people to abide by them. But at least most of them abide by another rule — a ban on chewing gum.

Jerry shrugs off the flagrant rule-breaking: 'Sure we tell

them that, and we mean it, but they do it. That's the price of a totally open show without a script. If we told people what to say we wouldn't have that. But if we told people what to say we'd be a soap opera. We might as well hire the actors. Everyone on our show has seen our show many times before. They see how people behave on the show so when they come on they probably think they can do it.'

In any case, he says, 'It's still tame compared with the rest of TV, where murders, robberies and rapes are routine. I've seen more violence in hockey games. On my show, most of the fighting is done by the security guards who run onto the stage to stop the shoving or to get someone out of a headlock.

'There's nothing on our show that's attractive, nothing that would induce people to say, "This is how I'm going to behave, this is good." I would argue that they make violence look attractive on soap operas and even on prime-time TV, where everything is made to look exciting. The people on those shows are attractive, even the music is enticing. Nothing on our show is enticing, we're obviously a cultural cartoon. OK, it's kind of dangerous, but that's the price we pay for the First Amendment.'

Despite the violence Jerry jokes, 'More people have died from watching our show than from being on it.'

The Jerry Springer Show hit TV screens outside the USA as a full-blown freak show, noisy and noxious and addictive from the first. It was not always that way and, although Jerry shakes his tousled head in wonder at his success, there is little accidental about the way it developed. Jerry has trod a twisting path to get to where he is now — and he has loved every minute of it.

The show today is a very different animal from the one unleashed on just five local TV stations in the USA in 1991. Jerry, then a TV anchorman in Cincinnati, Ohio, offered staple talk show fare such as family reunions, the plight of battered women, fashion tips and straightforward interviews. He was a well-known and popular figure at home and doing the show was not much of a risk because he kept his news job to have something to fall back on if he was a flop.

Only two things have always remained constant — Jerry's 'Final Thought', which was born out of a nightly commentary he had been doing for years during the late-night news and has now become a brief sermon that ends each *Jerry Springer Show*, and his familiar sign-off, 'Till next time, take care of yourself, and each other'.

Jerry was offered the job because Multimedia Entertainment,

who owned the local WLWT-Channel 5 TV station where he worked, was keen to expand its lucrative talk show empire, which already included Phil Donahue, the longest-running daytime chat host in the USA, and Sally Jessy Raphael, one of the most original. Genial Jerry, who had honed his public persona during more than 20 years in the spotlight as a local politician and TV star, had a pleasant and engaging screen personality and Multimedia thought he had potential. They were right.

In the USA many TV programmes are made by independent companies who try to sell them in different markets. The nationwide networks — established giants like the American Broadcasting Company known as ABC, Columbia Broadcasting System, CBS, and the National Broadcasting Company, NBC, and more recent arrivals like Fox Television and Warner Bros' The WB — are affiliated with local stations around the country, and order major drama or comedy series like *ER*, *NYPD Blue* and *Friends* for their whole network. However, that leaves many hours of the day when the stations have to provide local shows or buy other material. Still other stations are privately owned or part of smaller, regional groups. To fill these thousands of hours stations turn to syndication companies, which sell re-runs of old series like *M*★*A*★*S*★*H*, *Hill Street Blues* and *Cheers*. They also buy original programming. In the 1970s and 1980s the staple original programmes were game shows and soap operas; by the 1990s talk shows were taking over.

Production companies were scrambling to get new chat hours on the air. The shows were cheap to make, with a seemingly endless stream of guests willing to talk about divorce, adoption, cancer, death or alcoholism, for no payment other than an air fare, a ride in a limousine and a night in a hotel. Politicians and authors were equally keen to plug their latest ideas and books, and there was no shortage of experts on every subject to offer on-air advice or explain people's actions. As the legion of talk shows increased, no subject, however intimate, seemed to be taboo — rape, incest, sex-changes, fetishes, all found their share of advertising dollars and a place in American living rooms every day.

This was the climate into which *The Jerry Springer Show* was launched. By the beginning of its second season, in September 1992, it had been bought by stations in nearly 100 cities and looked set to become an established hit. However, although talks shows were already being criticised for trashy content, no one could have dreamed how Jerry was to take the genre and mould it in his own special way.

Perhaps the first hints came that second season, when the show moved to Chicago, where it is still made, though Jerry continued to commute back to Cincinnati to present the evening news for several months after it was relocated to the much bigger TV production centre. Along with topics like courageous amputees, teen gamblers and gays raising children together, he increased the number of strippers, drag queens and fetishists, while still managing to attract serious guests like Irangate figure Colonel Oliver North and civil rights leader the Rev Jesse Jackson.

The mix seemed to work, the all-important viewer ratings, on which advertising rates are based, began to climb and more stations expressed an interest in buying the show. Executive producer Rick Dubrow insisted that Jerry was going to take the high road: 'The niche is more of a focus on Jerry, with Jerry as an advocate for women, Jerry fighting for those issues,' he declared in February 1993.

One early show featured a woman called Debra Babula, who shot and seriously wounded her live-in lover when he threatened to kill her parents if she left him. She was sentenced to four years in prison. The subject fascinated Jerry, who organised a successful petition to win her a pardon by the Illinois Governor Jim Edgar.

He recalled: 'After the show I said, "There must be thousands of women who are watching our show and worry that their husbands could come home at six o'clock and could kill them."'

That concern prompted a three-part series on battered women, including segments shot at a Wisconsin safe house and in a Florida jail where 75 women were serving sentences for killing abusive lovers and husbands. Sitcom stars Roseanne and Charles Dutton and *LA Law* actress Susan Rutton taped special public service announcements that were aired during the show, urging women to call special hotlines if they needed help.

His show was also credited with reuniting two mothers, Jeanne Cvetkovich and Nancy Lindler, with children who had been kidnapped by their fathers after they appeared on a segment called *My Husband Was Brainwashed By A Radio Talk Show Host.*

Jerry was thrilled at the response and the potential of his show. But even then he acknowledged that not every show would be serious.

'This forum is so powerful and you can use it, once you've got the viewer's attention, to do some very serious topics from time to time,' he told *Cincinnati Enquirer* TV critic John Kiesewetter, who followed his career throughout much of the 1980s and 1990s. 'We're still going to have big-breasted women, of course. This is entertainment. But this serious direction is where we want to go.'

So he did shows about race, shows about sex equality, segments about domestic violence. He was particularly pleased with a show on the Waco stand-off in Texas, when a siege of the headquarters of the religious cult the Branch Davidians by federal agents from the US Bureau of Alcohol, Tobacco and Firearms — who believed sect members had a stockpile of illegal weapons — ended in a fiery tragedy that killed 80 people, including sect leader David Koresh and many children.

True, he did go on featuring big-breasted women, including a segment about a blonde exhibitionist who got her thrills flashing at people in shopping malls, but he was gaining a reputation as someone who could present the serious and the sensational with equal aplomb.

When his longer-established rival Geraldo Rivera announced his show was leaving Channel 5 in Boston for Channel 7 in the same city, Channel 5, WCVB, not only snapped up Jerry to replace him but also threw a party to introduce him to their viewers. Over chicken and chocolate mousse pie, he acknowledged his crazy shows but reiterated his commitment to real issues.

'I am not defensive at all about what I do for a living,' he told the crowd, but added, 'We're trying desperately to take the high road. We want to keep the show issues-oriented.'

The reporters fell for his charms. Monica Collins of the *Boston Herald* commented: 'In the talk show *demi-monde* Jerry Springer could shine some rays of intelligence. He does, after all, have a few standards. When asked if there was any show topic he would refuse to do, the answer came easily, "Necrophilia".'

Executive producer Dubrow added that the show would resist plumbing the depths of sleaze during the all-important advertising 'sweeps'. Viewer figures in the USA are carefully monitored by a number of companies, the most important of which is the Nielsen Organisation. Three times a year, in February, May and November, the figures from the 'sweeps' period are used to set advertising revenue for the next few months and the more viewers, the more cash producers can demand. Naturally stations hold back their most attractive shows for those weeks, whether that means the first TV run of a major feature film or an obscenity-laced slug-fest on *The Jerry Springer Show.*

True to their word, Jerry and Dubrow continued to hunt down serious subjects and by the beginning of 1994 the show was seen on 145 stations around the country. Jerry, who had long since given up the short commute between Chicago and Cincinnati and his job reading the news, now found himself flying from coast to coast interviewing subjects and promoting the show. He was also invited to take part in events not related to the show, such as hosting a seminar on youth violence at the Dr Martin Luther King Jr Centre in Atlanta, Georgia.

For the sweeps week of February 1994 they turned to what they thought would be a sure-fire winner. Jerry flew to Los Angeles to meet up with a 21-year-old homeless man called Tweaky Dave. Jerry had interviewed him two years earlier, in his first season, and the show had been very well received.

'I'm going to walk the streets with him at night, from 10pm to 5am, in a rough area near Hollywood with lots of street kids,' Jerry explained. 'Then we're going to tape a second show at a diner where they all hang out. Dave is helping other kids get off the streets, trying to get them some help.'

Also in the line-up for February was an interview with New York City Mayor Rudolph Giuliani.

'When we've done the hard issues, that's when ratings jump,' he told the *Enquirer*'s Kiesewetter. 'The staff now knows I'm not comfortable doing the makeover stuff.'

Jerry's contract had just been renewed for two more years, at a time when other talk shows were being taken off the air. Despite all his flamboyance and the way he calmly brushes off critics, Jerry has always been very unassuming about his achievements: 'It's unbelievable! I'm really lucky. I know how lucky I am. If we'd started out with 150 cities, we might be off the air by now. But we started out slow. I was able to learn how to be a host. We were all trying to see what works.'

Sadly for Jerry, he discovered he was not so much taking the high road as driving down a cul-de-sac. His ratings began to fall and that always means danger in the cut-throat world of TV. So he decided to concentrate on the back alleys and dark streets for future shows with the help of a new executive producer, Richard Dominick, after Dubrow was promoted within Multimedia.

Dominick — a bearded, dark-haired former tabloid journalist, joke writer for Jay Leno and one-time English teacher who smokes cigars in his large office, which is decorated with lamps whose bases are busts of Elvis Presley — immediately changed the direction of the show by tapping in to a totally new audience — has shaped it ever since. He recalled: 'Basically, I'm told "You take over the show now, April 1994. You have until November 1995 to get the numbers up, otherwise you're cancelled." Ricki Lake was going after the teenage kids. Everybody else was going after the mom at home. Nobody was going after the college kids. My idea was to turn the show into a spectacle, so if you clicked it on at any moment, you'll stop and watch the show. I told my producers, "Don't bring me a show unless it's interesting with the sound off." The day I took over, the first show was *I Want to be a Nude Centrefold*.'

More of the same followed. Along with a clutch of other shows they tried and failed to win an interview with a 16-year-old girl who told a friend she was willing to pay $60 to have her mother murdered, preferably by use of a substance that would trigger a heart attack.

That did not work out, but shows like *I Caught My Husband Having An Affair With My Aunt*; *I Strip With My Family*; *I'm Raising My Daughter To Hate Men*; *The Woman I Love Is A Man*; *Honey, Please Don't Join The Klan*; *Newlyweds On the Verge Of Divorce*; and *Couples Make A Fantasy Home Video* turned the show around.

The ratings were also helped by an even more bizarre story — a woman who swore she had been born on Venus.

The show increasingly featured confrontations between guests. This was not a new technique, but one that Dubrow had developed on another Multimedia programme, *The Sally Jessy Raphael Show*. With confrontation came shouting matches and scuffles, which were edited out to start with but which brought to prominence the now-familiar, well-muscled security guards. The security squad, headed by burly, 6ft 3in Steve Wilkos, has expanded as the show has become more outrageous. Today there is one guard per guest on stage.

Jerry made no excuses about his change of direction. 'You reassess all of the time,' he shrugged. 'We're now a far more entertainment-oriented show than a political one. I may love having Oliver North and Jesse Jackson on, but I was the only one watching. Look, people watch TV during the day to be entertained. It has to be entertaining and interesting. I always have to remind myself that this isn't my platform.'

His stance was more surprising because talk shows were coming under heated criticism and repeated calls to tone down their subject matter in early 1995 after a man who appeared on the rival *Jenny Jones Show* later shot and killed another male guest who revealed on the programme that he had a gay crush on him.

'Talk shows will never be in trouble because of the subject matter,' Jerry insisted. 'The more controversial, the bigger the shows get.'

His prophecy proved to be true, at least as far as *The Jerry Springer Show* went. The more outrageous the subjects he chose, the more the critics, both professional and political, lambasted him; the more the guests swapped insults and punches, the wilder the studio audience became. All the while more and more viewers tuned in and his ratings shot up.

'Each day's non-issue is seized upon hungrily by Jerry's guests, a crop of wailers, louts and showoffs put on the stage in a line-up of club chairs,' harped *Associated Press* critic Frazier Moore. 'Thus does the tackiness unfold, and Springer receives it with his dull but solicitous gaze. Gender-benders and adulterers are big with Jerry. But even bigger is the female bosom. If his show is any indication, Springer has a breast fixation that rivals Maidenform's.

'For instance, one recent *Springer* posed the questions, "Who is sexier? Large-breasted women or small-breasted women?" In a multi-event competition, comely specimens of both body types vamped onstage in teddies, and less, for the whooping studio audience. Then Springer mounted his stool to deliver a 'Final Thought', his daily bid to redeem the hour's rot with a pro-social sermonette. This time he piously told viewers that "a guy who sees a woman only for her breasts is really the biggest boob of all".'

Greg Paeth, who has written about Jerry and his show for the *Cincinnati Post* for many years, said: 'Springer makes no apologies for a show that typically wallows in the muck, providing at least an hour of notoriety for people who seem to have a masochistic need to pre-soak, wash and dry their soiled linen on national TV. From Springer's point of view, TV writers who have blasted the show since its debut just don't get it.'

Jerry has a routine rebuttal to people who slam his show, call it a bad influence on the young and accuse him of being cynically exploitative. First, the people who look down on the show and the people who appear on it are snobs who think everyone should subscribe to their values; second, although the topics are lurid the studio audience always jeer the bad guys, the two-timers, the neo-Nazis and self-confessed sluts; and third, everyone who appears is there voluntarily and knows, if not exactly what to expect, that they could be in for a rough ride.

In sentiments he has expressed dozens of times before, not so much defending his show as insisting it does not need to be defended, he says: 'American TV is so upper white middle class. On mainstream TV, that's the only perspective we see. And so here you have a show that just defies all these traditions, where the people on it don't speak the King's English, they're not rich or powerful and most of them don't have an education. But the critics don't want to see that. A lot of the criticism of talk shows such as ours is that deep down we are not too crazy about "the kind of people that are on these shows" and that's pretty elitist.'

He also insists, 'Though our show is produced primarily for entertainment, if you're concerned about values, these shows are wonderful morality plays.' And he fires back at the earnest media folk who call him intrusive: 'Look what you do when you jam a microphone in the face of people who don't want to be on TV, without worrying if it will ruin their career, embarrass their children, humiliate them. You run to a family that has been involved in a horrible tragedy and you just fire off your questions, having no regard for their privacy.'

Jerry was in his element making the increasingly wilder show, even to the extent of warming up the studio audience himself with one-line jokes and humming pop classics. Among his standard, deadpan lines, were, and still are, 'Some years ago my best friend ran off with my wife ... I still really miss him,' 'I've been seeing this beautiful woman for about six weeks now ... I got a telescope for my birthday,' and 'I've just done a new cable deal ... they come to install it next Thursday.' They may be corny, but the studio audience, which is overwhelmingly made up of young and culturally diverse people, reflecting what was the make up of his TV audience for many years until he gained wider acceptance and popularity as his fame grew, love it. They line up to shake his hand after the show, ask for autographs and have their picture taken with this unlikely folk hero almost old enough to be their grandfather.

The audience's reaction can be gauged by people like Stacy Smith, who was a 22-year-old student and aspiring stripper from Chicago when she went to see the show being taped in the studio. She said: 'Jerry is so sweet, he's down-to-earth and considerate. I like the way he interacts with people.' While Alan Brown, a then 26-year-old who had travelled from Birmingham, Alabama, to watch the production, said that he especially respected Jerry for his 'Final Thought'. He added, 'But I really like the fights.'

Jerry has become such a cult hero with college kids across

the USA that they even skip classes to watch his show. The more conscientious record it to watch later. Many meet up in bars so they can watch the show in a group. It has become a college fad — from the Friends Sports Bar and Restaurant in Kenosha, Wisconsin, to bars like Bennigan's and KC's Cove in Tampa, Florida, young people get together and enthusiastically shout their lungs out watching Jerry and his goofy guests.

As Jerry climbed in the ratings, especially among young adult viewers, still more TV stations added him to their line-up, and the show began to be sold overseas. In the UK satellite TV viewers were already familiar with tamer hosts like Oprah Winfrey and Phil Donahue and, at first, Jerry was regarded as just another American talking head. As the months went by the show was sold to stations in Australia, Belgium, New Zealand, Taiwan and assorted Middle Eastern countries, and is now aired in some 50 nations.

However, executive producer Dominick was frustrated because he felt the show was not reaching its full potential, not because of Jerry, or the guests, or the subject matter, but because of constraints imposed by the owners of the programme.

He explained: 'They weren't happy with the fact that we had a lot of sex on the show; we stopped being an issue-oriented show and became a wild and crazy show, but they couldn't get over the fact that the numbers were going up. It was, "edit this out," "edit that out," "that strip is too long". The show could never take off because it was better in the studio than it was on the air.'

All that changed in the beginning of 1997 when the show was sold to Universal Television. Dominick said: 'They said, "What can you do to make the show take off?" And my answer was, "Let's air the show we tape."'

So was born the no-holds-barred show of today, one which audiences freely admit they watch more in the expectation of a punch-up or a catfight than from concern or interest in the subject matter — even if the subject is a blonde breast-feeding porn star who makes 'lactating bondage videos' and sashays on to the stage carrying a champagne glass full of milk, which she offers to share with her indignant husband, already on stage telling tales of woe about their bizarre marriage.

'Everyone knows why they're here,' justified Dominick. 'Yes, these are real problems but they are temporary problems. No one comes on with a *real* problem. It's about who's dating who, who's going out with who, and viewers can relate to it. The people who come here fought before, they'll fight tonight on the show, and they'll be fighting tomorrow after they get home.'

The show brings in extra security for Ku Klux Klan segments, which are always popular and give liberal Jewish Jerry good material for a tongue-lashing in his 'Final Thought'. But although one Klan appearance prompted the worst-ever fist fight, with chairs flying and people being rugby-tackled to the floor, the most vicious confrontations tend to be between hair-pulling, face-scratching women.

'The women fight dirtiest,' said Steve Wilkos, who says his team break up about 30 fights a week. 'They claw, they grab the air, they're kicking each other when you're breaking them up. They don't want to let go.'

Jerry tapes two shows, three days a week in the NBC Tower on Columbus Avenue in the heart of Chicago. Each show takes many days of work by the six production teams to set up, lining up guests, checking their stories, bringing them to Chicago and preparing them to go on the show.

There is no shortage of potential guests — between 4,000 and 5,000 people call a free phone number every week, offering themselves as sacrifices on the altar of TV ratings. Every call is analysed; although staff reckon three-quarters of the calls are genuine, most are dismissed immediately. If a story sounds interesting and potentially provocative TV, they get a call back and are quizzed about details of what they want to say. The assistant producers whose job it is to weed out the wheat from the chaff are on the alert for any discrepancies in telling a tale a second time — any hint of a lie and the caller is dropped. If they are accepted, they are asked to provide proof of identity and provide any back-up documents to support their story — marriage and divorce certificates, rental agreements to prove addresses and so on.

Assistant director Brenda You, who as a producer grilled her share of potential participants, says it is impossible to define precisely what makes a great guest: 'They have to have a point to come on the show. If they say, "I want to be on TV" we don't want that. If they say, "I want a free trip to Chicago" we don't want that. When they say, "I want to confront him on TV and talk about this", then they're going to be passionate.'

Many potential guests back out before they are taped. After initially agreeing to go on the show they will get cold feet and give any number of reasons, even the most trivial, to wriggle out of their agreement. Not everyone who makes it to the studio makes it on to the air on national, and eventually international, TV. If

Dominick or other key members of the team suspect a guest is a phoney, they do not air the segment. That happened in the case of a lesbian couple who appeared on the show because one wanted to tell her girlfriend she had made porn movies. Production staff simply did not believe the second girl's reaction to the news.

'You take a big risk when you deal with secrets shows,' said producer John Gleason. 'I didn't know if they were telling the truth. I didn't think it belonged on the show and my boss agreed so we took it off. It's obvious it's acting. You just can't fake this stuff.'

About 10 stories a year are scrapped because they simply do not ring true, and the production teams say they have developed gut feelings to tell the truly bizarre from the fake bizarre.

Despite this confidence, however, the show has been fooled at least once, by a team of Canadian comics who staged a confrontation show, and on another occasion when a number of former guests claimed they had been coached in what to say and encouraged to fight.

On taping days, the soon-to-be studio audience queue up outside the NBC Tower, where they are searched for weapons and made to go through an airport-style, metal detector security gate. Meanwhile, Jerry arrives in his chauffeur-driven limousine at the back door, dressed casually, usually in jeans and a sweatshirt, before changing into his immaculate Armani suit behind his desk in his small, cluttered office, decorated with photographs of his beloved, disabled daughter, Katie, who is a regular visitor to the set, and his childhood baseball heroes.

'I get up at seven in the morning, put the radio on, get ready and come to work,' he says of his routine. 'I write my commentary, go into make-up and tape my first show.'

Perhaps surprisingly, Jerry does not know the subject of his show until the day of the taping when he is sent a summary of the programme before taping commences so he can write his commentary — hence the prompt card listing the names of his guests and the topics they want to talk about.

The topic is discussed at a pre-show meeting in Dominick's office. As a representative of the production team responsible for that day's show outlines the premise, chubby Dominick sits in his chair with his hands neatly folded over his large belly and Jerry stands listening, holding a baseball bat, which he occasionally cuts through the air with a gentle swing. At the end of every meeting, Jerry says, 'This show is good for America. Let's make this the greatest show we've ever done,' as the staff file out of the office to prepare for taping.

Jerry is unconcerned about his lack of involvement in lining up shows before the event, content to crack his ringmaster's whip only when he is standing there among the audience. 'I have no particular skill in that area, what do I know what works?' he says. 'I never would have dreamed that this would work. I take charge when I'm out there because I have to. Then it is me. No one can send me signals.'

In fact, he believes that not knowing much about the guests in advance helps give the show its winning edge. 'I'm as fascinated by what's on the stage as anyone watching at home,' he says. 'So maybe that's why it works. I'm asking the questions the viewer would ask.'

Before Jerry goes out there stage manager Todd Schultz gingers up the audience to give the right reactions — jeers for the bad guys, *oooohs* for the shocking secrets. Production staff go over stories with guests who have already signed a statement that what they say is true, authorising Jerry to sue them for the $80,000 production cost of the show if they are caught lying, and signed a list of 21 possible surprises that could confront them on the air. If they mark any one of them as unacceptable, even if it does not apply to their story, they are rejected.

With high-minded critics looking down their noses at Jerry and his show, he ran into a major controversy in 1997, when the Chicago TV station, WMAQ, that aired his show, invited him to do political commentaries on their evening news broadcast. There was a storm of protest and one of the station's main news anchors quit rather than share the screen with him. Jerry himself gave up his new job after less than a week, saying he did not need the aggravation.

The row, which was followed all over the USA, showed how, love him or hate him, it was impossible to be indifferent to this unlikely cultural icon. Perhaps thanks to all the extra exposure in serious-minded newspapers and magazines, even more viewers tuned in to Jerry in its wake. His viewership leaped 14 per cent in the first week of May sweeps, the biggest increase among daytime talk shows.

By November the figures were even better. He leapfrogged over Rosie O'Donnell with a 70 per cent increase over the previous year, and found himself in second place, behind only Oprah Winfrey, acknowledged queen of daytime TV. In the all-important category of adults aged from 18 to 49 he was actually ahead of Oprah. Wherever *The Jerry Springer Show* aired at the same time as Oprah or Rosie, he beat them. By now his name was a byword, even among people who had never seen the show. The words 'Jerry Springer' were increasingly being used as an adjective, a shorthand for bad behaviour. America was becoming 'Springerised'.

Jerry, who attributed the increase largely to the commentary row, was cock-a-hoop. 'Geez, it's unbelievable,' he said. 'Since all the flak last spring, the show has been on an absolute surge. It's totally out of control. You can make a timeline from that week on and we've grown literally every week. And it's not just kids watching. You can't get numbers like this with just kids. A year ago everybody thought it was awful. Now that we've got a great audience, it's suddenly fashionable.

'We've become, for better or worse, the symbol of the crazy talk show. It's silly, stupid, crazy. It's obviously outrageous and people finally know what it is. It's crazy, outrageous entertainment. And as soon as people realise what it is, they figure out if they want to choose to watch.'

In February 1998 his triumph was complete. He knocked Oprah from the number one slot for the first time in 11 years. The May sweeps the same year still saw him at the top, despite controversy over a show about bestiality — which never aired because of massive public outcry and the refusal of many TV stations to accept it — called *I Married A Horse* and demands from the show's owners to crack down on the violence, or at least edit it out.

The kinder, gentler Jerry Springer maintained his lead in the ratings, although his viewing figures dropped, and it was soon back to business as normal.

While critical commentators bemoaned his incredible success as proof of the 'dumbing down' of America, and warned that his 15 minutes of fame must soon be up, Jerry fever showed no sign of abating. He appeared on a host of other TV shows, wrote a book, made a movie and generally made the most of his good fortune.

So who is this genial, mild-mannered, bemused-looking man, who appears more like a friendly bank manager than the evil incarnate his critics describe? A liberal lawyer, passionate politician, devoted dad, Jerry Springer has ridden a roller-coaster from obscurity as a refugee in the dark days of World War II to a superstar for the brave new world of the next millennium.

CHAPTER 2

Gerald Norman Springer entered the world on a cold and damp winter's morning in war-torn London, England, on 13 February 1944. He was the only son and second child of his Jewish refugee parents, Richard and Margot Springer, who had fled their native Germany to avoid the terror of Adolf Hitler's Third Reich just before the outbreak of World War II in 1939. Richard had been forced to sell his Berlin shoe business to save himself and his young wife. The SS had marched in one summer's day and arrested Jerry's grandparents, uncles and aunts while his mother was luckily hiding at the back of the building. The Springers left their homeland with only a few possessions, as they rushed to escape the tyranny of the Gestapo and save their lives.

They arrived in Britain just two weeks before the Nazis goose-stepped into Poland and war was declared. As it was to turn out, Richard Springer would be the only member of his immediate family to survive the horrors of the Holocaust. Both of Richard's parents, his brother and Margot's mother all died in Auschwitz. Many more uncles, aunts, cousins and assorted relatives also perished in other Nazi concentration camps. They had all been bundled onto trains, never to be seen again. The guilt and grief of losing most of their relatives and the dreadful memories of life under Hitler's regime, plus recollections of having to watch how they spent every penny to survive in Blitz-battered London, were to haunt the Springer family for the rest of their lives. Even today, what his family endured has left a significant and everlasting effect on Jerry.

'It was understood in our house that it was too painful to

talk about,' he remembered. 'My grandparents, aunts, uncles, cousins were killed in the camps. I lost five direct relatives.'

It wasn't until the early 1980s, a few years before his parents passed away, that Jerry truly realised the full extent of the pain and suffering his mother and father had endured. His elderly dad had become a dangerous driver and his 'mom' — Jerry always called her mom even though he spent his first five years in the UK, where it is more usual to say mum — begged her husband to sell the family car. His father adamantly refused.

'Dad just calmly said to me, "I don't drive it any more, but I can't get rid of it because you never know when you have to get away",' Jerry said. It shocked him to realise that his father was still so terrified from his experiences more than 40 years before that, even in the USA all those miles away and all that time later, he felt he might still need to make a quick getaway.

Referring to his family's flight from Germany and the Holocaust, Jerry said: 'That's been the major influence on my life — nothing else is even close to that. It was something that was always there, a part of my parents' life that shaped all of us. Six million people were destroyed simply because they were Jewish. If that isn't a fundamental lesson of life, nothing is. So the fundamental fact of life in our family was that we must never judge people based on who their parents are or how they pray or the colour of their skin.'

By the time Jerry was born, the Springers had already been blessed with a daughter, Evelyn, who is four years older than her brother and now teaches French in the USA. In London the Springers found refuge in a four-storey block of flats when they moved in with a distant cousin on Lyttleton Road in Hampstead Garden Suburb, a respectable and quiet, predominantly Jewish community in north London. Today, life is very pleasant for most of the people who live in the hilly community with its tree-lined streets just to the north of Hampstead Heath, a large park where people walk their dogs and go jogging, and close to such pubs as Jack Straw's Castle and The Spaniards Inn.

However, in those early days, life was tough for the Springers. There was Government-ordered rationing throughout Britain, meaning quantities of food were sparse, the quality unpredictable and the choice limited. All available resources were going to the War Effort. Because they had had to run for their lives — the Springers had escaped Germany with just the clothes on their backs and what they could get into their suitcases for the week-long rush across Europe — they were broke. They also had the handicap of speaking virtually no English. To survive, Richard Springer started making stuffed toys, which he sold on the streets of London while Margot took a job as a shop assistant. They struggled with the language and life in a strange land but were determined to make a better future for themselves and especially for their children. Even though the Springer parents never truly grasped the English language well themselves, they were determined their children would. So despite the fact that they were economically struggling, they still hired a nanny to give their children English lessons and eradicate any hint of a German accent.

England was not to be their home for ever. Despite the persecution against Jews they had witnessed in mainland Europe, while living in London they never felt threatened because of their creed or felt the need to hide that they were Jewish. But they always dreamed of an even better life.

Jerry said, 'They felt safe and they didn't hide their Jewishness. There were many Jewish refugees living where they did. But they had in mind to get some money together and go to America. Having lived through two world wars they thought there would always be wars in Europe.'

It took the Springers almost a decade from the time they had sought sanctuary in London to realise that dream, but finally, by January 1949, Jerry's family had managed to save enough money for them to go in search of yet another new life, this time in the USA. They had longed to move to New York where Margot's sister lived. It had taken them all those years but eventually, by hard work, saving and going without, they had scraped together the cash to buy four one-way, third-class tickets to cross the Atlantic on the newly refurbished *Queen Mary*, arguably the greatest ocean-going liner of all time, which had been taken out of commercial service at the beginning of World War II to become a British troop carrier. Unbeknown to the Springers at the time, young Jerry was indeed embarking on a voyage that for him would truly live up to the American dream of finding fame and fortune in the New World.

It was a lifestyle change that was to have an awesome effect on the small boy. Jerry still vividly remembers sailing up the mighty Hudson River that bitterly cold winter's afternoon and seeing the magnificent Manhattan skyline for the first time. Setting his eyes on the Statue of Liberty and entering the USA through the famous gates on Ellis Island — as millions of other persecuted immigrants searching for a better life had done before him — has had a lasting impact on Jerry.

Years later, on 3 July 1986, as Americans prepared to celebrate their most important public holiday, Independence Day, which is held on 4 July every year, Jerry opened his heart on the TV station where he was then working as a newscaster to tell his viewers how important the USA was to him.

He said: 'A five-year-old could perhaps be forgiven for not understanding the full significance of the moment, which is what I was when Mom awakened me from an afternoon nap. "Come on, Gerald," she said. "We're going up on deck. We're going to see the Statue of Liberty. We're in America."

'And there we stood, my parents, sister and I, along with virtually everyone else on the *Queen Mary*, gazing quietly at the first visible evidence of a new world. It's funny what you remember of such moments but what I remember most was the absolute silence of it all. Thousands of us crammed together on this ship and nobody said a word, and then silence was unsettling, because even at the age of five, I knew Mom and Dad were scared, and at some point I asked Mom, staring at the statue, "What does it mean?" And she said in the German she spoke, responding to the English she barely understood, "*Ein tag, alles.*" "One day it'll mean everything."

'Well, I am now at the age that they were then and I can tell you, they had reason to be scared. The first half of their lives had ended in Hitler's concentration camps and then an escape to England. Everything they had, everyone they knew — family and friends — gassed into oblivion. So they saved up enough money to buy four tickets to America and start life over. They believed the Lady who stood so majestically in the New York harbour. They believed the promise. After all, that's all they had. Two kids, a little luggage, no job, no place to live. Just the promise of Miss Liberty. And somehow, like the millions who came before them, and since them, that was enough.

'The rest, they just figured out. Dad would make stuffed animals and sell them on the sidewalks of New York and the beaches of New Jersey. Mom would count and work and never miss a day in 20 years, and she got a job in a bank, and the subways were tough, and the language was tough, and making ends meet was tough, but after Hitler everything was a piece of cake. And this was America and their kids would have it all. And you know what? They did — because Mom and Dad gave it their all and the Lady kept her promise and she kept it until the day they died. And until the day I die I'll remember that.'

Ellis Island, immortalised in numerous books and movies, was established in 1892 as the point for processing the huge tide of immigrants seeking a new life in the USA at the end of the 19th and beginning of the 20th centuries. During the 62 years that it operated as the main immigration entry point into the USA more than 16 million people fleeing poverty and persecution and searching for a better life stood on American soil for the first time there as they were being processed. In those days most people came by sea. First- and second-class passengers were processed by immigration officials on board the ship after they arrived in port, but third-class passengers, or 'steerage' as they were also known, were ferried to the island, where they underwent often humiliating medical examinations and intense questioning in the cavernous main building before passing through Ellis Island's famed gates of freedom. Many arrivals from Eastern Europe, especially those who did not speak English, had their names arbitrarily Anglicised by immigration officials who could not understand, or spell, their original names, a fate the Springer family were able to avoid. In 1954, which was ironically the year that the Springers all became naturalised American citizens, the USA closed its operation on Ellis Island and today it is a museum.

From sedate Hampstead Garden Suburb in north London, little Jerry found himself in bustling New York where the buildings were tall, the streets busy, the people noisy and the taxis weren't the familiar black cabs he was used to but yellow sedans. Nevertheless, Jerry embraced America and everything American.

'My parents had a real plan to Americanise me and I loved every bit of it,' Jerry said. 'We were immigrants coming to the greatest country in the world, a place where freedom was everything.'

Special American holidays such as Independence Day and Thanksgiving have become emotionally immensely important for him to honour and he has become an ardent, almost obsessive, baseball fan. This refugee child who was born in Britain of German Jewish parents has grown into a most patriotic American who wishes to be seen as just one of the common people in a country where equality is supposed to be a God-given right. As a first-generation American from such humble beginnings, Jerry now says that he feels an affinity with the very people who come onto his TV show, albeit to yell, fight, cry, and often to feel humiliated.

'The lesson of the Holocaust is you never, ever judge someone based on what they are,' he said. 'You only judge them based on what they do. We Jews cannot turn around and suddenly discriminate against others. We have to be the most liberal of all faiths. I think that's where I got my political liberalism from.'

Thanks to help from a New York Jewish refugee organisation, the Springers were able to find a home in the Kew Gardens neighbourhood of the New York borough of Queens, near to where Margot Springer's sister was living. They lived in a four-roomed rented apartment costing $120 a month. Jerry's sister Evelyn slept in the dining area, and he slept in a partitioned-off corner of his parents' bedroom.

Like the Springers, most of their neighbours were also Jewish refugees, displaced from Eastern Europe because of the War, who had sought the protection and freedom that America had to offer as promised by Lady Liberty standing proudly welcoming newcomers. It was a close-knit community where everyone was friendly and neighbours knew each other. The area was safe and people were all chasing the American Dream.

For the second time in 10 years Richard and Margot were starting a new life in a new land, only this time they had their two beloved children to think about. They were determined to fulfil their dreams after having lived through the nightmare of the Nazi years. To make ends meet, Jerry's father once again turned to selling handmade stuffed toys on street corners but this time it was on the avenues of Manhattan and the beaches of nearby Atlantic City and Asbury Park, New Jersey, and inland at Rockaway. In New York terminology he worked as a 'jobber'. His mother found employment as a bank clerk.

'We were never rich but I had a perfect childhood,' Jerry said. 'I can't remember anything bad.'

Richard Springer, who would eventually expand into wholesale marketing of his goods, would often take his young son, who spoke much better English than he, along with him during the tedious days in the blistering, humid heat of summer or the bone-chilling cold of an East Coast winter as he attempted to sell his cuddly tigers and bears. Jerry loved every minute of it.

'It was the quintessential American dream,' Jerry remembered. 'An immigrant family working to the point of exhaustion so that my sister Evelyn and I could have this great life. My dad made stuffed animals and sold them on the street, on beaches, on the boardwalks, and a lot of times he'd take me along.'

It took no time at all for young Jerry to adopt his new environment as home and his proud parents were delighted to witness his Americanisation, which they greatly encouraged. He quickly became an avid fan of America's favourite sport, baseball, brought about mainly because of a need to survive in school, and was soon a fervent supporter of his local team, the New York Yankees.

Soon after Jerry arrived in the USA it was time to begin his formal education. To this day, he remembers the tears that poured down his young face on his first day at tough Public School 99 in Queens. He recalled: 'My mom dressed me in blue shorts, a jacket, a bow tie, a beret and knee-high socks. Boys in England didn't wear long trousers until they were 16. Plus I was small and had this British accent. The kids beat the hell out of me! There was even a girl called Phoebe who beat me up.'

The second day, his mother dressed him in a new but similar outfit and again he was beaten and the other kids even ripped his suit. By the third day, he was running out of smart clothes.

His mother soon realised her young son was going through an ordeal at school so she visited her neighbours in the upstairs apartment, whose son, David, was a playmate of Jerry's, to discuss the problem. She asked her friends how Jerry might better fit in in this strange new environment. By the time she came back downstairs she had learned a lot about an alien game called baseball that Jerry would have to take up — a sport which is a national obsession in the USA — to be accepted by his peers in America. She also found out that it would be best to support the local team, the New York Yankees.

'So she goes to Gertz department store and buys me a Yankees uniform,' Jerry later remembered. 'I wore it to school and the kids loved it. I wasn't sure at the time what it was, or why I was wearing it, I just knew that I didn't get beat up that day. I actually started to make friends. I remember wearing it until I got quite gamey and nobody wanted to sit next to me. Soon the other kids started showing up in Dodgers and Yankees uniforms and we started our own little ball clubs.' Jerry rapidly became fanatical about the Yankees after that.

Then came the first day that school was closed. Jerry asked his mother why he and his sister weren't going to school that day and she told him it was because it was George Washington's birthday. 'Oh, are we invited to his party?' Jerry, who was six, asked. He now laughs, 'It was then that my mother gave me my first history lesson.'

Jerry, always a happy child, adapted well to life at school, which he loved, and he excelled at his studies. Even though he was a precocious joker in class, he was popular in school with both his classmates and the teachers. When he was 14 a teacher wrote in his report, 'We expect great things of Jerry.' He said, 'Maybe I had a couple of bad days but I was totally loved and I loved everything I was doing.' Referring to one of the many American TV shows he came to enjoy, Jerry added, 'I lived a *Brady Bunch* kind of life.'

Like any typical American boy, Jerry became a member of his local Little League baseball team and was soon an enthusiastic player. He also joined the Boy Scouts, working diligently to earn his merit badges, learned to play the guitar and the tuba, enjoyed singing and hanging out at the local soda fountain drinking egg creams, which don't actually contain any eggs or cream but are, in fact, a mixture of milk and soda water, flavoured with syrup, and talking about the New York Yankees.

During the school holidays, he went off to summer camp. He loved all-American sports and is still an ardent sports fan. To this day he has the ability to recite a blow-by-blow description of the 1959 boxing match in which Floyd Patterson lost his heavyweight title to the Swede Ingemar Johansson. He regularly goes to watch the Chicago Bulls basketball team, but it is baseball memorabilia that dominates the walls of his office and, with the exception of his daughter whom he idolises, is the great love of his life.

However, as far as his parents were concerned it always had to be work before pleasure. His mother recalled before her death, 'We were very strict with him. It was always work before play. I guess it's the German in us.'

In spite of his precociousness, Jerry remembers himself as the sweetest, nicest, most peace-loving of youngsters. He never got into trouble, never received as much as a spanking, never argued with his father, was never rebellious, never smoked marijuana or sniffed cocaine and never even once drank so much that he made himself sick. 'I honestly don't remember a sad day in my whole childhood,' Jerry said. 'I was a diehard Yankees fan. My heroes were Yogi Berra and Mickey Mantle. A bad day was when the Yankees lost. Real bad.'

Perhaps it is because so few of his family survived the Holocaust and he never knew an extended family, or perhaps it is because he and Evelyn were given so much love and support by Richard and Margot, that Jerry's family ties have always meant a great deal to him. He said: 'My parents were great. Dad was the head of the house but Mom was really in charge. There was no yelling, no fighting. It was nice. The house was not like my show.'

The Thanksgiving holiday is the most family-orientated of all national holidays in the USA. It is the day set apart for a public acknowledgement of God's goodness and mercy. Always held on the fourth Thursday of November, it dates from 1621, when the Pilgrim Fathers, newly settled in New England, celebrated their first harvest. However, over the years it has taken on a greater meaning, recognising how the survivors of the *Mayflower* voyage from England, where they were being persecuted for their religious beliefs, found freedom in the New World. It has been observed nationally throughout the US since 1863. Nowadays the day is especially important for family reunions. People travel thousands of miles across the States to be together on this day and dine on a traditional meal of roast turkey and sweet potatoes. To Jerry it has become immensely important as a symbol of what he and his family achieved in their new homeland.

He remembered his happy childhood and his loving family when he gave a commentary on the Thanksgiving Holiday and what it meant to him to his viewers as he ended his nightly newscast for the WLWT–TV station, in Cincinnati, Ohio, on 24 November 1987.

He said: 'My lasting childhood memory of the Holiday Season is Mom listening to Perry Como's version of "There's No Place Like Home for the Holidays", while putting the finishing touches on a turkey we would inevitably be eating for the rest of the week. We would sit around the table and talk about the things we were thankful for, a list not much different from most folks lucky enough to enjoy good health and sufficient food. But, in retrospect, I can now see that what we really were engaged in during this litany of thankfulness was a celebration of family, the one entity where love was a "given", that Mom and Dad loved us kids, not because of what we did or what we might become but simply because we were.

'Indeed, after our parents, all relationships would have to be earned, affection and respect a function of what we achieved or how we behaved or whether or not we were in a position to be helpful. But with family, there were no such strings. We were simply loved. That security enabled us to face a world where the news isn't always good, where the burdens aren't always fair, where interpersonal dealings aren't always what they seem to be. For whatever assaulted us in life, there was always home and unconditional love. There was always Mom humming along with Perry Como ... "There's No Place Like Home for the Holidays".'

But, possibly aware that his mother and father were getting older and would not always be with him, Jerry was in a sombre mood that night. He added: 'And, of course, there wasn't and isn't. Yet, each year it gets tougher to be home. Careers and marriages and lifestyles have chased us to different parts of this globe, forcing us to love each other by letter and phone more than by shared experiences. It's the sadness of this season that each holiday increases the odds that someone you love won't be able to make it next year, won't be able to be "home" for the holidays, to feast and wallow in turkey and laughter and pictures and love.

'Knowing that, believe this. All gifts are secondary. Family is first.'

And whatever Jerry was to achieve during his career, nothing has ever been more important to him than his family, whatever the trials and tribulations he encountered as he was marching purposefully down life's highway to become one of the world's Titans of TV.

Despite his great love of American holidays, being Jewish while growing up in the USA, which these days embraces many religions but was then overwhelmingly Christian — while then, as now, worshipping anything commercial — presented one problem: Christmas. Why did he, as a young Jewish boy unconcerned with Christmas carols, Nativity plays, Santa Claus and the other religious and secular trappings surrounding the holiday, get presents for a Christian holiday? Margot Springer gave her inquisitive son an explanation that seemed to appease him, at least for a while.

Jerry said: 'As she told me, Santa Claus's real name was Saul Claustein. He just had it changed for business reasons and he had reindeer pulling his sleigh because, of course, it was improper to eat or ride pork. If I was good and would stop looking under Phoebe Nelaboff's dress in kindergarten, Saul, or rather Santa, would indeed come toting my share of presents, perhaps on Christmas Eve, but in any event, sometime during the eight days of Chanukah. You never knew exactly when because, for security reasons, Santa never revealed his travel plans ahead of time when coming into New York. I was always afraid that my neighbourhood was so tough that if Santa stopped to ask someone how to get to my house they'd say, "I don't know. No one's ever made it before."'

However, as he got older Jerry began to doubt his mother's

explanation. He went on, 'I first started having my doubts about this whole thing when I kept seeing Santa in every store to which my mom took me. Why would he always be where I was? At first she seemed stumped by the question, but then told me, with the assurance only mothers can muster, that these were just Santa's helpers... that the real one was in Macy's. I believed her because she was my mom. But somehow in the back of my mind, I harboured the thought that if Santa was really Saul Claustein, wouldn't he be in Miami Beach this time of year?'

Although Jerry adored his mother, and she certainly adored him, he joked that she wasn't a particularly good cook. Jerry recalled: 'When it came to food, what my mom made best was reservations.' Despite her alleged inability to produce exciting food for Jerry, Margot Springer was fanatically houseproud and protected all of the best furniture in their house with plastic slipcovers. 'The only time I ever saw her take them off was for our rabbi,' Jerry laughed.

Although not an Orthodox Jew, Jerry has throughout his life had a total belief in God and follows the Jewish traditions from the dietary restrictions to the rules of Passover and fasting on the Jewish High Holidays. He said: 'I am identifiably Jewish. I'm not sure any one religion has cornered the market, but I don't think that's important. What's important is to be humble enough to believe that our lives are gifts from God. And whatever traditions you were raised in, follow that tradition to show your appreciation.'

Money was always a problem for the Springer family and it wasn't until the same year that they became American citizens, 1954, when Jerry was 10, that they finally scraped together the cash to buy their first TV set, a large box with a small screen, showing snowy, black-and-white images that suffered from poor reception.

However, it became the focal point of the family's evening entertainment and they would gather around the set at night to watch the popular shows of the period. Jerry quickly became a fan of cowboy shows and loved to watch Roy Rogers, Gene Autry, William Boyd playing *Hopalong Cassidy* and Clayton Moore portraying *The Lone Ranger*, with Jay Silverheels co-starring as his trusty sidekick Tonto.

'Then as I got older I loved *The Dick Van Dyke Show* and *My Little Margie*,' Jerry said. 'I liked sitcoms, I guess, when I was a kid.'

My Little Margie was first shown in the US in 1952 and remained on the air until August 1955. It revolved around the womanising antics of a widower played by Charles Farrell and his meddlesome daughter, played by Gale Storm, in the title role of Margie Albright. *The Dick Van Dyke Show* ran for five years in the early 1960s and turned the actors playing the two main characters — Dick Van Dyke as Rob Petrie and Mary Tyler Moore as his wife Laura — into international stars of TV and the movies. The show is still aired in re-runs around the world.

Jerry got his first taste of true politics watching the 1956 Democratic and Republican political conventions on TV and he was soon hooked on politics as well as TV. He remembered: 'With our background politics wasn't just a hobby. Politics had wiped out our family.'

The truth of Jerry's remark often came back to haunt the Springer family. When the now classic movie *The Sound of Music*, which was a big-screen version of Rodgers and Hammerstein's musical based on the true story of the Austrian von Trapp family and their escape from the Nazis just before World War II, was released in 1965 with Julie Andrews and Christopher Plummer in the starring roles, Jerry's parents could not bring themselves to go to watch the movie all America was rushing to see. For them, seeing this uplifting family film would have brought back memories that were too painful, and the sense of grief and loss they still felt deep inside would have swelled up to the surface and have been too much for them to bear.

Jerry was always encouraged to take an interest in politics. Even as a teenager he harboured political ambitions and his parents always encouraged him to be liberal and see the underdog's point of view. He said: 'My family just always seemed liberal. My parents were Stevenson Democrats. Whatever heroes we had, even in the music world — Pete Seeger, Peter, Paul and Mary, Joan Baez — always seemed to be avant-garde, caught up in that whole civil rights milieu.'

Jerry had first caught sight of then Democratic candidate Adlai Stevenson during the 1956 presidential race when he became fascinated by the political debates being shown on the Springer family's new TV set. Stevenson, a US statesman and diplomat celebrated for his elegance and wit, was twice the unsuccessful Democratic candidate for the US presidency. In 1952 and 1956 he was beaten by Republican nominee and great American war hero Dwight D Eisenhower. However, the speeches he gave during both campaigns attracted worldwide attention and praise for their idealism. Stevenson, a lawyer turned politician, had already gained a reputation as a reformer in areas such as health, education and highway construction during his years as governor of Illinois. Young Jerry and his family were captivated by him and his style.

At night the Springers would sit around the dinner table discussing politics. It was a grounding that would serve him well later in life when he took a stand against the Vietnam War and entered into political life in Ohio. Jerry was to refine his liberalism in the early 1960s when he first attended Tulane University in New Orleans, where he earned an undergraduate degree, majoring in political science, and later at Northwestern University in Illinois, where Adlai Stevenson was also educated.

'I really feel like a child of the 1960s because all those incredible, unimaginable things really affected me,' he recalled in 1977, when he was first the Mayor of Cincinnati, Ohio. 'I got involved in some civil rights and anti-war marches. And the Kennedy assassinations, Martin Luther King's killing, the Chicago Democratic national convention — it was impossible to be on a college campus and be oblivious to that.'

It was his studies that set him in the direction first of a political career and then to move on to TV. However, very early in his public life Jerry learned that his love of ladies could and often would get him into trouble. His first kiss, which he alleges came from a rather plump girl in his class, cost him his first bid at politics — the third grade presidential election. A teacher had told the class to be nice to the unfortunate girl because she was heavy-set and young Jerry figured that he might get some votes from his classmates by kissing her. However, his scheme backfired. He admitted, 'The kiss didn't go well. I lost the election by one vote.' It was the first, but definitely not the last, time that his libido would cost him dearly.

Like the plump girl in Jerry's story, so little Phoebe Nelaboff, whom he claims was the object of his affections in kindergarten, also appears in many of Jerry's recollections of his formative years. It appears that every encounter he had as a boy was with a girl called Phoebe, and she was often plump, leaving one to think that Jerry — always an articulate showman — may have learned from his mother's tales of old Saul Claustein and invented a mythical Phoebe to suit every occasion. Particularly as it is difficult to find a single Nelaboff listed in any telephone directory in the entire USA.

Despite his love of baseball, young Jerry didn't play sports at high school because he was too short. Jerry's father was only 5ft 2in tall and Jerry appeared to be taking after him. It was not until he got to college that he sprung up a foot in height — he's now 6ft tall — but by that time his sporting abilities were not considered good enough to make him eligible to play.

One of Jerry's strongest memories of his days at Forest Hills High School was the prom, always a significant event for American schoolchildren because it marks their preparation to move on to college.

According to Jerry, he took Phoebe — that familiar female character — to the dance in his senior year. By now, he claimed, she had grown into a hefty girl. A sceptic might wonder whether the Phoebe who was his sparring partner on his first days at school, the fat girl he kissed, and now the big girl who escorted him to the dance were all one and the same girl or the product of an over-zealous imagination.

Remembering the prom night with amusement, Jerry said in another of his TV commentaries: 'My date wore a dress to the senior prom. Of course, she was a girl, but it still caused quite a stir. You see, Phoebe was big, really big, and this bright yellow dress she was wearing, well, everybody kept saying it looked as if I had taken a taxi to the prom. We laughed a lot that night.'

In fact, Jerry may not have been a great sportsman at school but he was a good sport who could always make people laugh. Right from the beginning he was a performer with a desire to please and to be liked. He said, 'I was the class clown.'

Today, it is the class clown who is laughing all the way to the bank.

CHAPTER 3

Despite the upheaval of his younger years and having to learn to adapt to a new culture, Jerry did so well at Forest Hills High School that he graduated at 17, a year younger than usual. To the delight of his parents, he was accepted at university, and he prepared for the long trip from New York to the very different world of New Orleans, home of Tulane University.

The day he left home for the first time to go to college and in search of adulthood has remained vividly in Jerry's mind. Years later he recalled in one of his TV commentaries: 'I remember the first time I left for college. I remember, the night before I left, thinking more about what I was leaving than what lay ahead.

'At the age of 17, I knew pitifully little about life, but I knew enough to know that when I left home the following morning, it would never be the same. I would still love my parents, but it'd be by letter and phone. The guys on the block with whom I grew up, with whom I spent 12 years playing ball in the schoolyard — and sharing lies about girls we were too scared to ask out! — these friends that are friends as only kids can be friends, all this was about to change, and I knew it.

'I didn't sleep much that last night at home, staring at my pennants from camp and mementos from school, my walls plastered with pictures of the Yankees, cars and Annette Funicello, with Annette getting most of the attention. For I knew once the morning came and I left my room for the life of college, things would never be the same. And I'm not sure I liked the idea. Indeed, in the privacy of my room, I was scared to death and I cried. But the tears were for naught, for college became life's finest moment.

It was an invitation to test the world, to learn about it and shape it.'

Jerry adored Annette Funicello, a child actress in the popular 1950s American TV show *The Mickey Mouse Club*, who went on to become a popular singer and starred in a series of lighthearted 1960s surfing movies opposite crooner Frankie Avalon. Tragically she was diagnosed with multiple sclerosis in 1992 and has been bravely battling against the disease ever since, mainly confined to a wheelchair.

Jerry was to admit that his remembrance of that night seemed pretty naïve because the world has changed so much since his college days. He added, 'But that was 1961 and all was possible. At least that's what we thought. Our imagination was our only limitation. A president, who looked as young as we did, spoke to us of new frontiers and shared burdens, and we bought the whole package.

'But our puritanical social conscience was tempered by a less-than-serious view of campus life. We were the last generation of collegians that could listen to Peter, Paul and Mary and Frankie Avalon and not be embarrassed. Fraternities were "in", campus violence was a panty raid and college football was king. We were the last freshmen class before the loss of innocence. By the time we graduated, our president would be shot, our campuses would be in turmoil, our cities would burn and Vietnam would bury our classmates. College, much like life, would never be the same.'

The terrible violence that struck America as the 1960s progressed made those innocent 'panty raids,' when college freshmen would invade girl students' dormitories and steal their underwear, look pretty tame even though these days the act would certainly be regarded as politically incorrect and those who carried it out might even find themselves the subject of tabloid TV programmes such as *The Jerry Springer Show: Men Who Steal Women's Knickers*. But back then it was just innocent fun.

Jerry has always maintained that his first girlfriend was that young lady who turns up in so many of his childhood memories, Phoebe. He said: 'I had a crush on her when I was 12. We went to the same school, and I took her to the milk and cookies dance that we had every Friday afternoon. I learned about the facts of life in the school playground. It wasn't something I ever talked about with my parents.'

However, it was really at the age of 17 that Jerry was not only learning about life but also about love. It was then that he had his first real kiss: 'It was when I was 17 with a girl called Barbara. I kissed her at the end of a date on the way home. She was the first girl I had kissed full on the lips.'

Once he had made that monumental move, Jerry, who has subsequently become a legendary lady's man, ambitiously and enthusiastically set about learning more about love and as a result got his heart broken for the first time. He said: 'A girl called Linda whom I was also going out with when I was 17 broke my heart. She found someone else and broke it off none too gently. I was heartbroken for at least the ride home.'

Jerry also lost his virginity the same year: 'It was when I was 17 with another steady girlfriend. It wasn't a relationship that could sustain marriage, but for that age it was fine.' But he admitted, 'Let me just say it was as clumsy as you would expect from someone totally inexperienced.'

The year he learned about love and went to college, 1961, was also an important year for baseball-barmy Jerry because one of his boyhood heroes, Yankees ball player Roger Maris, was chasing to beat the home-run scoring record set by another legendary Yankees player, Babe Ruth.

'Roger Maris was my boyhood hero,' Jerry said. 'He dominated the walls of my room, with his picture-perfect swing, and the summers of my adolescence, as I took on the neighbourhood with my self-proclaimed certainties. Maris was the best, I would yell, in a city with lots of alternatives... Micky Mantle, Willie Mays and Joe DiMaggio among them. He would break Ruth's record, I argued vehemently. Indeed, heroes were uncomplicated then, and Roger was mine.'

Jerry was reminiscing about his hero in December 1985, after his death at just 61, sharing his memories with his TV audience in Cincinnati. At the time he admitted: 'Now, a quarter of a century later, it still hurts when I hear that my childhood idol, who lived in the shadow of the Babe, or at least his record, died like him, too, of cancer, too young and too painfully.'

The death of a man Jerry never knew but loved as a kid prompted him to say the week after Maris's death: 'His assault on the Babe, in the summer of '61, still stands as the most exciting record chase of our lifetime. That's not to say that it will never be broken or other achievements are less worthy, but understand the moment and what he faced. You see, America had never had a sports hero like Babe Ruth. Indeed, the Babe made baseball the national pastime and then became bigger than the sport itself. All legends paled in comparison. Yet Roger Maris, of insignificant note, from a place called Fargo, North Dakota, put on the same uniform as the Babe, in a town already in love with legendary teammate

Mickey Mantle, and dared to break the magic "60", to hit more than 60 home runs in one season. The idea was sacrilege. The media hounded him, fans booed him and the commissioner of the sport said that the record would have an asterisk because the season was now a little longer.

'The nation became obsessed with the chase. Roger Maris, up against a legend and time, each at bat high drama, his hair literally falling out under the pressure. And then, on the final day of the season, he did it. Number 61, into the right field seats, and Roger Maris had done what nobody had ever done.'

Ironically, the Maris record-breaking achievement came back to haunt American baseball in 1998 when two new giants of the game, Mark McGwire, of the St Louis Cardinals, and Sammy Sosa, of the Chicago Cubs, both slugged their way past the old record to make that season even more spectacular than Maris's feat had made 1961.

Fans in that summer of 1961 were unhappy that Maris, a relatively unimpressive player throughout his career, was threatening the great Babe Ruth's place in history. Maris even received death threats and he was regularly booed by some Yankees fans as he came onto the pitch, even at home games in New York's Yankee Stadium. The stress got so bad for Maris, who was only 26, that his already grey, crew-cut hair started to fall out in chunks. After he achieved the pinnacle of his career — breaking the record — the then Baseball Commissioner Ford Frick, who happened to be a friend of Ruth's, put an asterisk by Maris's name in the record book, pointing out that he achieved a score of 61 in a season that was eight games longer than when the Babe scored 60 in 1927.

The strain destroyed Maris, who quit the Yankees and ended his days in Florida selling beer. It was not until 1992, seven years after his death, that the asterisk was removed. To add further insult to the original injury, Maris was not inducted into the Baseball Hall of Fame.

That was not a fate facing McGwire or Sosa, who were both worshipped by the fans, and cheered whenever they played. Even though Jerry realised that Maris' record would fall in 1998, it still brought a tear to his eye when McGuire became the first man to hit number 62. On that record-breaking occasion, after making the strike, McGuire ran into the spectators and hugged Maris' by-now-grown-up children.

Jerry confessed, 'That choked me up a bit. I was really surprised by my reaction. I was sad the record was going to be broken, but I didn't realise it was going to be so emotional.'

Years after Maris achieved his record, Jerry accomplished a boyhood ambition to meet many of his childhood heroes. In 1988 Jerry revealed that inside this grown man still beat the enthusiastic spirit of a little boy when he attended the 'Yankees Dream Camp', a reunion in Florida of all the great surviving Yankees players. It was a week-long chance for grown men to dress up in baseball uniforms and play with their heroes, fulfilling youthful fantasies. Jerry recalled: 'There they were: Mickey Mantle, Whitey Ford, Bill Skowron, Hank Bauer, all those greats in Ford Lauderdale for one week. You got your own Yankees uniform, you had a locker next to theirs, you ate all your meals with them and you played a double-header every day. You got your own baseball card, and on the final night you played against the all-time Yankees.

'I was a catcher. In high school, I always wanted to be Yogi. I was too small then. So here I am now, catching for Whitey. I'm behind the plate when all of a sudden everyone in the little stadium — maybe 10,000 fans — gets on their feet because out from the dugout comes Mickey Mantle. Mickey steps into the batter's box, Whitey's on the mound and I'm behind the plate. I've got tears in my eyes and I'm shaking, I'm so excited. I call time-out and I rush to the mound because my whole life is flashing in front of my eyes. So I get to the mound and Whitey asks, "What are you doing?" "I can't stop shaking," I say. He puts his arm around me like I'm a little boy in front of all these people. "Get behind the plate," he says. "Mantle hasn't hit in 20 years." So I'm all right. I get behind the plate again and it was great. Mantle flew out to left. Deep left.'

Getting to play with the Yankees was one of the great moments of Jerry's life. To this day he says that he would happily give up his job if the team would offer him a job as an announcer at Yankee Stadium.

Despite Jerry's love for baseball he was never destined to become involved in sport, even as a college player. As far as his parents were concerned he was going to become a successful professional. Even though money was always tight, the Springers were determined that their only son would get a college education and not go through the privations they had suffered to provide a loving home with food on the table.

Jerry said, 'I grew up in a home where I knew I was either gonna be a doctor or a lawyer. Having lost everything during the Holocaust, education meant the world to my parents. They said, "The one thing they can't ever take away from you is what's in your mind. Be smart."'

It was more by accident than good judgment that Jerry ended up enrolling as, quite predictably, a political science major at Tulane University in New Orleans, the Southern American state of Louisiana's most vibrant and exciting city, where the French influence and Cajun culture rub shoulders with the still-ingrained beliefs of the Deep South. A city that rests between the mighty Mississippi River and Lake Pontchartrain near the Gulf of Mexico, it earned a reputation for glamour and wild living during the 19th century, which lasts to this day. The jazz music that originated in the city in the late 1800s from black musicians still blasts out from the bars of the city's world famous French Quarter. New Orleans was a wonderfully wicked city for young Jerry to gain his first experiences of life alone.

He had been allowed to apply to only five universities, because Forest Hills High School, where he was attending in New York, was so enormous — it had 5,200 pupils — that the administrators could only process application forms to five colleges from each student.

Recalling the application process, Jerry said: 'I was fairly sheltered at the time. It was a family decision that I should go out of town to college.' He decided to cast his net wide across the country, so he applied to Tulane, the University of California, Los Angeles, better known as UCLA; the prestigious Ivy League college of Cornell in Ithaca, New York State; a university in Wisconsin; and one in New York City, in case he or his parents had second thoughts about him leaving home after all. 'I got accepted to all of them,' he proudly boasted. 'I just said, "New Orleans, what an exciting place to go!"'

But he admitted, 'Today 17-year-olds are much more worldly than back then. I was book-smart, not worldly. I remember having my eyes wide open, immediately learning about civil rights and thinking, Wow! New Orleans! This was my first experience with cultural diversity. I mean, really being close to people who had completely different life experiences. I had grown up with people from the same background. So this was really an eye-opening experience for me.'

Just as Jerry had adapted to life in the USA with ease and embraced his Americanisation with open arms and a smile on his face, he took to Tulane and college life as a duck takes to water. He said, 'I loved college. I was not one of those students who couldn't wait until school ended. I enjoyed class. I enjoyed the academics of it.'

As well as studying, Jerry also got immense pleasure out of

the social life that university offered him. After growing up in the over-protection of Jewish family life, for the first time he was out on his own and could be as wild and as bad as he wanted. In the USA colleges and universities have organisations called fraternities and sororities, social clubs that link students of similar interests, often criticised for indulging in heavy drinking and bizarre, often painful and dangerous, initiation ceremonies which are disapproved of by the university authorities. These organisations are known by Greek letters.

While excelling at his studies, Jerry also became an enthusiastic member of the University's Tau Epsilon Phi fraternity, which had the creed of practising friendship, chivalry and service each day. It appealed to Jerry because its members seemed to share sentiments he had grown up respecting. Its rules stated that members should, 'Judge our fellows not by their rank, not wealth but by their worth as men.' He was to excel within the group and was eventually elected the organisation's chancellor.

Rooting for the university's sports teams, late night drinking with his buddies, performing on his guitar and in a couple of plays, and midnight expeditions into the French Quarter — especially the world-famous Bourbon Street with its strip clubs, jazz bars and sleazy watering holes where people party by day and definitely all night — became important ingredients of Jerry's social calendar.

However, by now, playing baseball or any other sport was not part of the agenda. Jerry, who shot up a full 12 inches taller while at Tulane, said, 'I wasn't good enough to play sport in high school and by the time I'd arrived at Tulane my interests had shifted a bit, too. I became a typical college kid. It was a very innocent time. We didn't know anything about drugs. I mean, nothing. Oh, we used to "dex it" [take Dexedrine to stay up studying for exams] but I don't remember anyone ever saying, "Gee, this would be fun for recreation."

'There was great activity with panty raids. The girls had an 11pm dorm curfew. So if you had a date, you had to take her home by 11.00 or 12.00, then you'd go down to Bourbon Street. It was unfair on the girls. I think we were the last class of innocents.'

At Tulane Jerry was certainly destined to lose his political innocence pretty quickly. In the early 1960s there was still segregation in the Deep South. Jerry was shocked by the racism that he discovered still widely existed there. This is not what first-generation American Jerry had expected in the country he had so willingly adopted as his homeland. It was Jerry's first experience of bigotry and it brought back haunting memories of the stories his parents had told him about pre-World War II Germany. He related the way that black people were being treated in the South to the persecution of the Jews by the Nazis.

There was a move to place black and white students in the same schools, which caused an outcry among many white families who did not want their children to study with black pupils. Jerry quickly found himself wrapped up in the turmoil of the times. 'They were integrating the local schools, so I got involved in that. The parents were involved and that was the first time I actually saw people screaming. It's one thing to watch it on the news, but to be there is kind of scary.' Watching people screaming and shouting was obviously a good grounding for what was facing him in the future.

Almost immediately Jerry became a dedicated and energetic civil rights activist. As with so many other things in his past, what he witnessed and what he did about it has had a permanent effect on what he has become today. His civil rights activities were just the embryo of what was to develop within him.

It was always his destiny, because of the way he had been brought up, to become a staunch supporter of all liberal causes. No matter how small or obscure to other people, they were important to him, and he became an ardent and outspoken opponent of America's involvement in the Vietnam War. His parents' experiences and heartaches had already moulded him.

After successfully obtaining his political science degree from Tulane in 1965, Jerry enrolled at Northwestern University in the Chicago suburb of Evanston to read law. Once again, he eagerly and diligently buckled down to his studies, while embracing the social life he discovered there with equal enthusiasm.

While at law school as part of his work experience, he was appointed to represent poverty-stricken people in Federal Court. He was one of ten students selected for this programme in the Midwest.

In his spare time, Jerry sang with a folk music group called Springer's Stringers. Later, when he moved to Cincinnati, he performed in a duo with a girlfriend under the group name Linda and Gerry. During those early years, Gerald N Springer obviously had an identity crisis, at least, as far as his name was concerned. Sometimes he'd be Gerry with a G, while more and more he became Jerry with a J. He obviously didn't realise that as the years passed his fans would decide Jerry the performer should actually be called 'JER-RY! JER-RY! JER-RY!'

However, long before that would happen, a history professor friend introduced Jerry to then US Senator Robert F Kennedy, the younger brother of assassinated President John F Kennedy, in 1967. It was a meeting that would lead to yet another turning point in Jerry's complicated life.

Until that chance meeting, Jerry had seemed destined for a high-level government job in Washington, DC. But the following year, when Kennedy made a late entry into the 1968 US presidential race, Jerry took leave of absence from his studies to campaign for Kennedy and aid his bid to follow in his brother John's footsteps. Until Kennedy entered the race, the youth vote appeared to be going overwhelmingly to Eugene McCarthy, who was challenging incumbent President Lyndon Johnson, who had replaced JFK after his assassination, for the Democratic nomination.

McCarthy, a Midwesterner and a staunchly religious man, was campaigning on one issue — opposition to the Vietnam War — and came close to toppling Johnson in the all-important New Hampshire primary. Jerry and other Kennedy supporters were sent to campaign on college campuses, trying to recruit young voters. In Indiana, he was one of 12 young people hand-picked to work on the Kennedy campaign. Jerry, who was passionately committed to Kennedy, worked tirelessly in support of the crusade.

However, RFK's presidential bid came to an abrupt and tragic end when on 5 June that year, after winning the Californian primary election that night, he was shot by 24-year-old Jordanian-born immigrant Sirhan Sirhan as he left the now-defunct Ambassador Hotel in Los Angeles through the basement kitchen. He died in hospital the following day. McCarthy eventually lost his bid to rival incumbent Vice-President Hubert Humphrey — Johnson dropped out of the race — at the Democratic convention in Chicago later that year.

Kennedy's death, at an early age like his brother, sent Jerry into a deep depression. He described it as 'the worst day' of his life. He returned to university to complete his law degree but was uncertain about what he wanted to do with his life.

After passing his degree Jerry was preparing to take the bar exam to practise law when he went into Chicago to watch the Democratic convention. The convention was overshadowed by massive protest rallies which would stun the world when they turned horribly violent. Inside the convention hall, delegates debated the party's position on the Vietnam War, which began in 1959 and wasn't to end until 1975. Outside, supporters of the anti-

Vietnam War movement clashed with the Chicago police in the streets. Millions of Americans, watching the battles outside the convention on their TVs, were shocked by the bloody conflicts they witnessed. Jerry was even more shocked because he was actually in Chicago's Grant Park with thousands of Vietnam War protesters when they clashed with the riot police.

Jerry, who ironically has never enjoyed being involved in physical conflicts, said: 'It was a strange turning point in my life. I had just graduated from law school, and so I had the bar to think about, in terms of not getting arrested, because then they were being very careful about who they were accepting into the profession of law. There was one part of me that was this anti-war protester and anti-establishment and the other part of me that said, "Wait a second, I can't blow my whole career here!"'

Once his degree was obtained he returned to live with his family in Queens where he floundered in a series of dead-end, odd jobs. But just as he had ended up at Tulane University almost by chance, so it was that he arrived in the southern Ohio city of Cincinnati equally coincidentally.

While studying law in 1967, he had been recruited from Northwestern for a summer job as a clerk with the Cincinnati law firm of Frost & Jacobs. He said: 'I enjoyed the summer but I can't say I had any concrete plans to return to Cincinnati.' When the firm offered him a full-time position in the spring of 1969, he jumped at the chance. Jerry recalled: 'I was just sitting around in New York. I had to do something to get my life moving again.'

He had a haircut which cost him $2, studied and passed the Ohio state bar exams so he could practise law in that state, and he set off for a new life.

Jerry recalled: 'I was exactly your image of what 1960s kids were — very active in the civil rights movement in college and later, in law school, the anti-war movement. I was too Jewish and too much of a long-haired liberal to go far in Cincinnati.'

How wrong could he have been. It was a decision that certainly got Jerry moving from would-be lawyer to quickly becoming probably America's youngest mayor of a big city and eventually, arguably, the most popular yet most decried TV star of today.

CHAPTER 4

Jerry set about his new job as an attorney with the Cincinnati law firm of Frost & Jacobs industriously and with enthusiasm, anxious to make a name for himself, but his love of practising law exclusively was not to last long. He started to make new friends and get to know the respectable Midwest city he now called home.

Within weeks of moving to Cincinnati, which nestles by the banks of the great Ohio River, a friend in the same law practice, Thomas Luebbers, who went on to become Cincinnati's city solicitor, invited him to attend a local democratic party steering committee meeting.

Already deeply politically motivated and always fascinated by what went on around him, Jerry was pleased to go to the meeting which, in addition to his political interest, he also saw as a possible way to meet eligible girls. At the gathering he discovered a local campaign was being organised in Hamilton County, which covers a large part of Cincinnati, for Vote 19, a statewide referendum on whether to give 19- and 20-year-olds the right to vote in Ohio. The voting age in the USA, both for federal and local elections, was 21 at the time, although it was subsequently lowered to 18.

'Because I was the oldest one there, I wound up as the local chairman for Vote 19,' Jerry, who was 25 at the time, recalled.

He was pleased to be embarking on his career as an attorney, but right from the start Jerry showed more interest in down-to-earth street politics than practising law. Through his hard work and tireless campaigning, Jerry galvanised the youth in the community as no other politician had done before and, in the process of the campaign, displayed a keen and natural ability for grass-roots political organising.

Jerry's appointment as coordinator of the campaign in Hamilton County to get the voting age lowered in Ohio was announced by Pat Keefer, southwest Ohio's director of the Coalition for Vote 19, early in September 1969, when he was still very much a newcomer to Cincinnati.

New to public office, Jerry was prepared to call on anyone and everyone to achieve his task. He told the *Cincinnati Enquirer* newspaper: 'We want this to be as broad-based a campaign as possible, with people of all political persuasions participating.'

To reflect that sentiment, Jerry was joined by Randolph J Stayin, who also worked in the Frost & Jacobs law firm and was a vice-president of the Cincinnati Young Republicans, and Warren Dennis, vice-president of Cincinnati's West End Community Council, to mastermind the drive in the county. The proposed amendment to the Ohio Constitution would extend the vote to around 300,000 young adults across the state if passed.

During his campaign Jerry said: 'At issue is whether we think enough of our system of government to extend it to the young. Giving them the vote will give them one more alternative to violence. The young of this state have asked us for the vote. What would the consequences be of telling them "No"? We would have asked the young to be committed, yet have made no commitment ourselves. We would have asked the young to be responsible yet denied them responsibility.'

The election was to be held on Tuesday 4 November 1969, so Jerry proclaimed the Saturday before, 1 November, as Vote 19 Day and organised campaigners to swarm through shopping centres and other public places calling upon people to vote.

Jerry complained during the campaign: 'Unfortunately this issue is not being decided on its merits but rather the image of young people that has been presented to the public.'

The argument he pushed strongest was that the 'young, silent majority' had no decision in the issues that effected them very directly. The 19-year-old's tax money, work, ideas and blood were being used to oil the US democracy, he argued. He asked, 'Should these 19-year-olds have a say in how this machine affects them? Despite all of these responsibilities that our young people have, it is only the two per cent that protest and riot, it is only they who have a political voice.' He told anyone who would listen, 'The time has come to offer the young silent Americans, the 98 per cent, a political voice also. And, we can do this if we give them the vote.'

His opponents countered that 19-year-olds were not mature enough or responsible enough to vote and surely, they added, wouldn't the drinking age have to be lowered — it was and is 21 — if the vote was given to them?

Jerry quickly responded: 'My only answer to this is that we are in more trouble than we know if we start confusing the right to drink with the right to vote. It is possible that one is never old enough to drink, but if you have completed a compulsory education, as 19-year-olds have; if you are considered adults before criminal court, as 19-year-olds are; if you can die for your country, as too many 19-year-olds have already done, then indeed you are old enough to vote. Maturity does not concern chronological age. Responsibility breeds maturity. If young people are given the responsibility of voting, the evidence is that they will demonstrate the maturity of exercising that vote wisely.'

His opponents claimed that the young were too idealistic but Jerry countered that this was, in fact, an asset. 'What can be better than to refuse to accept a less than perfect government?' It was not to be too many years later that he was striving for more perfect government, at least at city level, from the inside.

During the campaign, journalist Kathy Lang, who covered the war of words for the *Cincinnati Enquirer*, described Jerry as a 'dynamo of nervous energy', who paced as he spoke. He told her: 'We can talk in terms of whether 19-year-olds are mature enough, intelligent, or committed enough to vote, but the real issue is whether we, who can vote, have sufficient faith in our system of government to think it strong enough to include the young.' Jerry spent all his spare time touring high schools in a bid to get the young politically motivated and demanding that their elders support their call for the vote.

'Jerry Springer was a genius when it came to organising election campaigners,' said John Pahlgren, who worked for Jerry on a later campaign. 'Even when the election was over Jerry would insist that his campaign workers went around the neighbourhood taking down campaign banners and that they visited everyone they'd canvassed to thank them for voting, even if they hadn't voted for Jerry or his cause. He was very insistent that we did that.'

Although Vote 19 was defeated statewide by a narrow majority in Ohio, it was successfully carried by a large majority, some 10,000 votes, in Hamilton County, making the local

Democratic party leaders realise immediately that in baby-faced Gerald Norman Springer they had a potential winner in their midst. Ironically, the next year the US Congress lowered the voting age to 18. The Supreme Court later upheld the reduction for federal elections, but ruled Congress did not have the power to order individual states to comply. Then, in 1971, the 26th Amendment to the USA Constitution brought in a universal voting age of 18.

Jerry enjoyed the fight and particularly his political glory, however local it might have been. He had been well and truly bitten by the political bug. Now Jerry regarded politics as a disease from which he did not want to be cured. So after the fight to gain voter approval for Vote 19, Jerry set his political sights far higher.

In October 1969, Jerry had attended a Democratic fund-raising dinner in Cincinnati where Indiana's Senator Birch Bayh was the main speaker and Jerry had been given two minutes at the podium to speak on the Vote 19 issue. Bayh later recalled it was the most eloquent discourse he had ever heard on the subject. Audience response to Jerry's speech was extremely positive and favourable. The local Democratic party leaders all came to talk to Jerry at the end of the meeting to learn more about him. In those days he wasn't so much a politician but rather a personality, a counter-culture kid who somehow was managing to wedge his foot in the establishment door.

Shortly after that fateful speech, he decided he wanted to run for public office. Jerry modestly said, 'It was a good speech.'

He had been living in Cincinnati for less than six months when on 25 November 1969, he launched a bid to run for the US Congress against the Second District's incumbent Republican US Representative Donald D Clancy. It would be an uphill battle. Jerry was running in a district where Republicans outnumbered Democrats by almost two to one, and he was up against a former Cincinnati councilman and mayor who was serving his fifth consecutive congressional term for the Second District. Jerry was the first candidate from either the Democrats or the Republicans to announce he was running for the public office.

At a press conference at the Terrace Hilton Hotel to announce his candidacy, Jerry proved his eloquence from the outset. He said: 'I run because it has become increasingly evident that unless some new alternative, some new initiative, some new approach is injected into the political life of our community, we are destined to lose here at home the very prize we seek to defend abroad — the politics of participation.

'We hear today much talk about the silent Americans. Let me suggest that a community or country of silent Americans is as unhealthy for a democracy as is the existence of lawlessness and violence. We should take no comfort in being called silent Americans. For our silence young men shed blood in foreign lands and our cities crumble around people too poor to eat, in air too polluted to breathe, amidst hopes long since shattered by reality.'

Timing was on Jerry's side because a candidate for a Congressional place had to have lived in the constituency where he or she was standing for a minimum of a year before the election, which was to be held in November 1970, so he qualified by just a few months.

The Second District covered western Cincinnati and most of Hamilton County, with the exception of four townships which were in the 24th District. At the time, Jerry was living in a cramped flat in the Clifton Colony Apartments building at 714 Julia Ann Street.

Pat Keefer, who had announced Jerry's appointment to run Vote 19, was briefly considered the front-runner to be Jerry's campaign manager but she took a job as associate director of the Youth Franchise Coalition, a pressure group pushing for the voting age to be lowered, in Washington, DC and, in the end, another unknown entered the Cincinnati political scene.

While campaigning for Vote 19, Jerry had visited Cincinnati's Xavier University where he met Mike Ford, who had joined the university in 1966 with the intention of playing American football and hopefully becoming a college sports star. Unfortunately for Ford, before tryouts ended that season, an aggravated old injury ended his athletics career.

During Jerry's campus visit the two hit it off. Ford, who left Xavier with a bachelor's degree in government studies, was heading a student group interested in changing the drug laws. They heard each other speak and decided that they shared many ideas and were philosophical kindred spirits.

So when Jerry decided to run for Congress he invited the 6ft 1in, 250 pound would-be football team centre, who was four years younger than him, to be his political campaign manager. It was the beginning of a close friendship and a long-running political alliance — Jerry the aspiring public servant and Ford a professional political activist.

'I guess I sort of backed into politics,' recalled Ford, who became Jerry's administrative aide when, in 1977, the still relatively young Springer was appointed mayor of Cincinnati. 'Jerry's 1970 race was largely considered to be a joke. There wasn't anybody around to manage the campaign. Anybody who had the interest could get the job.'

Jerry's bid to unseat Clancy was a classic liberal versus ultra-conservative confrontation — idealistic, young anti-Vietnam War activist Jerry Springer against Clancy, a hawkish House Armed Services Committee member. No one gave Jerry a serious chance in the race.

Rather tongue-in-cheek, while on a visit to Washington, DC in May 1970, Jerry told a journalist, as he dined on a stuffed veal lunch at the National Press Club, that he had to admit that his opponent was the front-runner in their Congressional race. But he added quickly, 'I think he can be beaten — he's never had a real campaign against him.'

Jerry was aware that he must not come over as weak when compared to Clancy, a right-winger who supported then-President Nixon's commitment to fighting communism in Southeast Asia. So Jerry, who had protested the Vietnam War while at university, was at pains to point out that, although he was opposed to sending American troops into Southeast Asia, he most certainly was not a pacifist.

When questioned about Nixon's decision to dispatch still more American troops, this time into Cambodia, Jerry said: 'I believe the President is sincere, I even believe his policy in attempting to wipe out the Cambodian sanctuaries will succeed. But I do not believe that this is the point — I do not think we can forever hold these governments from Communist takeover, so why spend another American life trying?'

His comments were particularly poignant in view of recent bloodshed in the Vietnam conflict, this time on American — Ohio — soil. An anti-war demonstration at Kent State University on 4 May ended in tragedy when National Guardsmen opened fire on a group of students, killing four of them.

Always trying to stress that his parents had fled the repressive regime of the Nazis, Jerry explained: 'I believe there could come conditions under which we must fight and I would not favour a pull-out of American troops from Germany. The difference is that our presence in Southeast Asia is the only force that unites the Communist countries there while in Europe our presence is a stabilising force that keeps Communism from spreading.'

Jerry's campaign was hampered by Clancy's reluctance to debate him in public. The Springer camp complained that Clancy constantly ducked and dived attempts to get the two candidates on the podium together. Clancy either refused, or accepted and then cancelled or sometimes just failed to turn up. Clancy's response was, 'When I've been unable to make an appearance it's because I've been tied up in the business of Congress.'

After Clancy made an official visit to South Vietnam, Jerry accused him of ignoring the 'gross mistreatment of war prisoners' by the Thieu-Ky regime in Saigon. Jerry was particularly concerned about the so-called Con Son 'tiger cages' where civilians and soldiers were subjected to torture without trial. He believed that all the time suspected Viet Cong and North Vietnamese sympathisers were kept in cages without sufficient food, water and health care while being interrogated by the South Vietnamese at the Con Son island camp, it jeopardised the possibility of American servicemen being held by the North Vietnamese being freed and, possibly, resulted in them being mistreated.

He sent Clancy a telegram offering to buy five minutes of TV time so the two candidates could debate the issue on air. He accused Clancy, who had visited Vietnam as a member of the Select Committee on the US Involvement in Southeast Asia, of walking out on a student who had been released from the Con Son prison where the cages were used after listening to him for only 10 minutes.

Asked what he expected to achieve on TV for just five minutes, Jerry said: 'I can bring out the fact that it is an issue. These atrocities are going on and the people don't know it. The reason we send Congressmen in there is to find out what's going on and then they are to inform the people.' Jerry said that the tiger cage issue brought out the fundamental question 'What kind of government are we supporting in Vietnam? We have spent $110 million on the penal system in South Vietnam so it is not a matter of us interfering in the internal matters of a sovereign state.'

Jerry was particularly incensed because, when he was asked about the use of the cages and conditions at the Con Son prison on his return to the USA, Clancy had said: 'This is something I know nothing about.' Jerry believed that Clancy and some other members of the visiting team who supported the Saigon government had allowed themselves to be led around by the nose by the US military in Vietnam, and that they tried to suppress information about the full atrocities of the famed tiger cages.

Even though he had announced his intention to run against Clancy in November 1969, Jerry had to delay starting his campaign. Three days after making his decision known, Jerry, an army reservist, was called to active duty. He had had to fulfil a four-and-a-half-month Army Reserve training stint at Fort Knox, Kentucky.

While on active duty, one day Jerry was summoned to the commanding general's office; Senator Bayh wanted Jerry to attend Senate judiciary hearings on a constitutional amendment to roll back the voting age to 18. Jerry was flown to Washington at the Army's expense, where he spent five days testifying before Bayh's committee.

After his stint at Fort Knox, Jerry was later appointed as a specialist in the 135th Judge Advocate General's Detachment of the US Army Reserves headquartered in Sharonville, Ohio.

Finally he was released from duty on Friday 27 March 1970, leaving him with only a few months to campaign for his election bid. Nevertheless, at the start of his campaign he split his time between campaigning for Congress and mustering his old Vote 19 supporters to back a Congressional bid lowering the voting age nationwide to 18. The bill which had passed comfortably in the US Senate (64–27) met stiff opposition in Congress and eventually failed, only to be quickly revived.

Jerry's attempt at a smooth election campaign was further confounded when briefly another candidate wished to challenge him for the Democratic nomination. Vernon D Bible planned to oppose him but his candidacy was disapproved by the Hamilton County Board of Elections because he had voted in the Republican primary four years earlier which was against the rules. A would-be political candidate could only vote for the party he wished to represent in the four years prior to an election in which he wished to be a candidate. As a result Bible was not qualified to run as a Democratic candidate. Jerry was delighted and joked that it would have been hard to stand against a person called Bible to gain the nomination.

Jerry was so anxious to make a success of his political ambitions that he quit his job as an attorney with Frost & Jacobs less than 12 months after joining the law firm so he could devote all his efforts to local politics.

The young, affable candidate, with endless ambitions for his generation, was always nattily dressed throughout his campaign with his hair neatly trimmed, giving him the appearance of being rather square for a child of the swinging 1960s and 1970s. But Jerry defended his appearance, telling people that if it took a square-like physical appearance to make headway in 'the system', then he was all for it. 'I tell young people to cut their hair, to bathe, to do the things they have to do if they want older people to listen to them on the issues. Blame for the things that are going on in our society falls with the younger as well as older generations. It's so essential to have rapport between both.'

Jerry loved the feel of Washington, DC right from the first time he went there to publicise his run for office. It was as if he had discovered his element. As he ambled through the massive complex of federal architecture he looked up and sighed, 'My, all these buildings make me want to campaign all the harder.' It wasn't the architecture but the idea of being in Washington, at the heart of the action and power, that really appealed to the young would-be politician.

'So many people I meet, young and old, have copped out, saying they've had it with taxes and all the rest,' he said. 'But I tell these people I see in the Second District that they've got to put up with politics a little longer if they want to do something about hunger and all the problems that confront us.'

Jerry had a plan to even up the odds against his well-seasoned opponent. He tried to drum up some support by persuading Democratic party bigwigs to come into his district and campaign on his behalf.

'Can you imagine the people who would show up if they heard Ted Kennedy was to be a speaker on a programme with me?' pondered Jerry, who had, of course, campaigned on behalf of Senator Kennedy's late brother Robert. 'Even those who do not like him would come.'

Among the Washington power brokers whom Jerry did manage to get to support him at one of his fund-raisers was Sargent Shriver, a Kennedy clan family member by marriage and the then chairman of the Congressional Leadership for the Future. Shriver was director of the US Peace Corps under President John F Kennedy, head of President Lyndon Johnson's campaign against poverty and ambassador to France under Johnson and President Richard Nixon. And, of course, he is the father of Arnold Schwarzenegger's wife, Maria Shriver.

However, when Shriver turned up at the $50-a-plate fund-raiser that October at the Hotel Netherland Hilton, the audience of more than 200 who dined on ham-stuffed chicken, brussels sprouts and carrots, followed by brandy and crème de menthe, wholeheartedly agreed that the seasoned politician's speech was upstaged by the words of the young candidate he had come to Cincinnati to support.

At a press conference before the dinner, Shriver described Jerry as 'a breath of fresh air', sorely needed in Congress as a replacement for Clancy, whom he said was 'distinguished for doing nothing for his constituency or, for that matter, the rest of the nation'.

However, it was Jerry's speech to the assembled supporters that won them over. Shriver was first to the podium after dinner, followed by Jerry who told his audience: 'I am a young man growing up in a nation whose history has secured for me the right to be free and whose future demands that my sacrifices be no less.' He said Clancy's congressional record revealed him as 'insensitive' to problems in education, housing, health and labour. 'The only thing we can seem to get Mr Clancy to vote "yes" on is an appropriation regarding a military expenditure,' he said.

Jerry brought down the house at the end of his speech when he said that the 3 November vote, no matter who won, would not be a victory. 'That will come only when we have borne witness to the silencing of the guns, and the end of hunger and the eradication of disease,' he concluded.

Charles Bailey, who was the *Cincinnati Enquirer*'s political reporter at the time, attended the dinner. In his subsequent report, he said: 'It wasn't much of a contest. The best thing that could have happened for Shriver did — he didn't have to follow Springer to the podium.' And, he added, 'Springer-on-the-podium can outshine almost any big name, a political no-no.'

Jerry was a guest speaker at a fund-raising dinner for John J Gilligan, the then Democratic nominee for the governorship of Ohio. The young bachelor spoke far longer than he was supposed to but no one seemed to mind.

In his speech, Jerry told his audience: 'We are here tonight, two generations — those who created today and those of us who will inherit tomorrow. Because of an act over which I had no control, I am a member of the youth generation, a generation fortunately born too late to wait in the breadline and unfortunately too early to witness the silencing of guns, the cure of disease, the last of hunger.

'Our generations are divided only by your experiences and our energy. Yet we are united by the indisputable fact that both these virtues are needed if we are ever to see the America we have a right to expect, the America we have the duty to seek. And it is only when we learn to respect each other, it is only then that we can hope to have the future respect us.'

Very quickly and justifiably, Jerry acquired a reputation as an excellent platform speaker and crowd pleaser. He had good timing and could mix humour and dead seriousness without losing a beat. He could be fiery, fierce, friendly, frivolous, funny or any combination of them depending on the moment when he spoke. When he spoke at the convention of the Ohio State Building Trades, he declared: 'America is not dead or dying. It is merely experiencing the growing pains of a society well on its way to becoming what Abraham Lincoln referred to as the last best hope of mankind.' He castigated the brand of politics that took to the streets and raised voices and he called for, 'A commitment to our political processes that will last as long as we are concerned about the state of the country we live in today and the country our children will inherit tomorrow.'

When the Nixon Administration proposed a 'no knock' provision in a controversial anti-crime bill that was being pushed in the summer of 1970, Jerry was outraged. The 'no knock' provision would have allowed a policeman with a warrant to force his way into a building or home without announcing his presence or identifying himself if there was reason to believe evidence inside would be otherwise destroyed. Jerry could see shades of Nazi Germany in the suggestion. He argued that people should be concerned about the quality of police protection they were getting and that this would not be enhanced by letting officers enter their homes without warning. Passionately, he said: 'Sanctity of the home must not be diminished on the excuse that law enforcers would be paralysed were they required to announce their authority and purpose, and be denied admittance before breaking down the door.'

However, he was equally determined to show himself to be pro law and order. When police officer Edmund Schinder was shot and seriously injured as he sat alone in his patrol car, the young candidate was quick to come forward to call for action. He told a meeting of the 25th Ward Democratic Club that the shooting put Cincinnati square on the list of American cities reaching a crisis in law enforcement. He said that 'Unless action was taken to restore faith in American justice this sorry incident may be repeated'. He told his enthralled audience that the police were charged with carrying out the will of society and, if there was weakness in law enforcement, 'Then these failings also must be claimed by society'. He told the gathering that there were three areas in which police forces needed help maintaining the social order: enactment of legislation directed toward eradicating urban conditions that breed lawlessness and despair; upgrading of the judicial system to provide sufficient and unequivocal judgment of wrongdoers and to restore respect for the courts; and increased public support for police departments.

To get more funding, Jerry proposed that cities and regional governments be allowed to impose progressive local service taxes that could be deducted in full from an individual's federal income tax bill. He said that such a system would 'combine the beneficial aspects of local control with a national balancing of total personal tax expenditures'. He concluded, 'Only when Americans are willing to pay the price of social and judicial reform can there be a return to social stability.'

He was learning very quickly how to capitalise on events around him to gain publicity for himself and get his point of view covered.

With only two months to go to the impending election, Jerry proposed a six-step plan to achieve better use of healthcare dollars. Speaking at the opening of a health clinic he told the gathering that government should subsidise the training of medical students so that no one qualified would be barred for lack of funds; medical school facilities should be expanded to train all those qualified and interested; less expensive technical personnel should be trained to take over routine chores that at the time needed to be done by a doctor; the construction of community health clinics should be increased; education in preventive medicine, aimed at informing people about how to avoid illness, should be stepped up; and a national health insurance programme to allow all people, regardless of income, to get access to quality medical attention, should be considered.

In some ways young Jerry Springer was years before his time. In the nearly 30 years since he made that speech, many of those suggestions, including the controversial idea of a national health plan, are still being discussed.

During his campaign, Jerry did the usual round of meetings, picnics, church socials and bingo games that political candidates are supposed to do. He joked: 'If I ever get run out of politics, I think I can always get a job as a bingo caller.' He found himself going to meetings prepared to discuss issues but finding that people mostly wanted to know who he was and talk generalities. Jerry even took to the air in a helicopter to gain publicity for Cincinnati's traffic congestion problems and resulting air pollution and used it as an opportunity to promote his views for improving the city's mass transit services and attack his opponent's record on environmental issues.

David Sternoff, the president of the Young Democratic Clubs of America, visited Cincinnati to promote Jerry's congressional bid and described him as 'the first meaningful Democrat to run in years'.

Jerry fought his campaign on a platform of cutting military spending, stopping American involvement in the Vietnam War and his idea of having voters draw credits on their federal income tax returns for taxes paid locally to run schools and other municipal services. Clancy was pro-war and pro-military spending. Jerry portrayed him as a big spender on defence items that pushed up inflation.

As the election date approached speculation grew about whether underdog Jerry could actually pull off the David-like feat of felling a Goliath of Cincinnati politics and defeat Clancy. A few months earlier, Jerry had been dismissed as an outsider but as the day approached some people in the community realised that Jerry had, through his tireless hard work and endless energy, indeed got some momentum going and established himself in the community.

'Two more unalike in their approach to issues would be hard to find anywhere,' Robert Webb, the *Cincinnati Enquirer*'s Washington, DC bureau chief, wrote just five days before the election. He speculated that Clancy would keep his seat but that Jerry had definitely emerged as a 'comer'. Jerry had brought zing to the ring where Democrats had fallen five times before to Clancy's punch. Webb pointed out, 'Audiences, even those hostile to his views, have applauded the sharp wit of the one-time campaign aide to the late Senator Robert F Kennedy.'

Jerry's repartee was never more pointed than when he told a woman's group meeting: 'I have an idea how we can end hunger in this country. Make every poor man a candidate. He would be well fed; this is my 103rd luncheon of the campaign.'

Considering that Jerry's campaign got off to a late start due to his commitment to military service, that he got distracted with other issues in the early days of the campaign and that he was definitely the underdog in conservative Cincinnati, it came as a considerable surprise that, although he lost, Jerry made a remarkably strong showing, receiving 46 per cent of the votes cast. Incumbent Clancy had been shaken more than stirred by his young adversary.

'He has a personal connection with the voters that frankly baffled a lot of us,' said campaign manager Ford, who is now a political consultant in Washington. 'He had a work ethic that was incomparable and a gift for relating to every person he met. He'd say, "When people wonder why I spend so much time walking the streets and knocking on doors, the answer is, "Ask my parents".' And the place would go nuts.'

Jerry said: 'The whole campaign was more important than just electing Jerry Springer. We wanted to bring new people into the political arena. A lot of people, particularly young people, are turned off by politics. We wanted to bring them back into politics, to get them involved.'

That Jerry's candidacy had attracted young people to politics could not be questioned. With one exception, everyone on his campaign staff was under 30. Jerry predicted: 'You're going to hear from these people. Their experience and influence is going to be felt.'

Kerry Klumpe, youth writer for the *Cincinnati Post*, wrote as the dust began to settle: 'Jerry's campaign was more than a children's crusade. It was everything American democracy is all about. It was a group of political novices taking on a seemingly invincible politician and giving him more than a good run for his money.'

Like the Terminator, Jerry vowed to be back. 'If we wait 20 years to try to solve the problems of 20 years from now, it will be too late. I think people want to listen to issues. I wasn't always of this opinion. But I found out no one is going to win a campaign on a sign.'

Jerry and his workers, many of whom campaigned between college classes and high school homework, proved that at least one theory worked. He said: 'We stuck close to the basic theory that I had to meet as many people as possible. We followed the textbook strategy of going door-to-door, and working at the polls. There was no aspect of campaigning we left out. We tried a little of everything.'

His hard work had paid dividends. Two years earlier Clancy had beaten his Democratic opponent in the 15th Ward by more than 1,000 votes. In that ward, he beat Jerry by just over 100 votes. The same was true all over the Second District.

Although Jerry always professed never to have expected to

beat Clancy, renowned Cincinnati columnist Frank Weikel discovered one occasion when the young wannabe politician had a delusion of grandeur. Weikel, who wrote a well-read and highly respected column in the *Cincinnati Enquirer* for three decades before retiring to Florida, discovered that on a 1970 Anti-Vietnam War petition Jerry had signed, he listed his occupation as 'Congressman'. Jerry told Weikel that he had signed many anti-war petitions but did not recall ever listing Congressman as an occupation.

It was unfortunate, therefore, that when Jerry ran for a place on the Cincinnati Council in 1971, Weikel discovered in biographical literature the Springer campaign office had supplied to the Cincinnati League of Women Voters, Jerry's occupation was listed as 'presently on leave from the Cincinnati law firm of Frost & Jacobs'. Weikel, who was never one of Jerry's greatest fans, took delight in pointing out that by then Jerry had long ended his association with the law firm. Jerry explained that it was an 'honest mistake' made by a staff worker who picked up an old résumé.

Throughout his political career, Jerry was to be dogged by inconsistencies that he always insisted were mistakes or misunderstandings.

A month after losing to Clancy, Ohio Governor-elect John Gilligan invited Jerry to run for the first year an Ohio volunteer youth corps he was organising. The job required Jerry to get the project — whose prime purpose was to create an army of young volunteers to do such things as work in state mental hospitals or recreational centres and help local police departments by doing clerical jobs — off the ground. Jerry saw the programme as a way for young people to get involved directly in government and to be able to lobby for the things they were interested in. It was to be patterned after the national Volunteers in Service to America programme, better known as VISTA.

Despite his defeat, Jerry had laid the groundwork for his forthcoming political career which, throughout the 1970s, would make him one of Cincinnati's most colourful and successful political figures.

CHAPTER 5

Lawyer-turned-dedicated-politician Jerry Springer's appetite was whetted. By the end of 1971, at the age of 27 and having lived in Cincinnati for less than two years, he ran for a place on the City Council, with his good friend Mike Ford as his campaign manager once again. Astonishingly, he was elected on his very first attempt, a feat that had been accomplished by only a handful of other would-be Cincinnati politicians in the previous 20 years. He had momentum. Those closest to him thought it was only a matter of time until it would be Congressman or, perhaps, even Senator Springer.

Although his time with Robert F Kennedy had been brief, his contact with the late Senator, whom he always referred to as Bobby, played a major role in the evolution of his liberal ideology. Jerry's speeches were laced with quotations from Kennedy but it was always his parents and their experiences that had the most effect on his opinions and outlook on life.

Cincinnati seemed to suit Jerry, although he hadn't realised it would when he first took the summer job as a clerk with Frost & Jacobs back in 1967. But by 1971, Jerry had laid the foundations to build a solid career and life in the city. He was growing into a big fish in a small, but comfortable, pond.

Often voted one of the most pleasant US cities to live in, Cincinnati is one of Ohio's largest, with a population of around 400,000 in those days. The metropolitan area, which also takes in parts of Indiana and Kentucky as well as Ohio, has more than 1.8 million residents. The climate is moderate and living costs low. It is the most important industrial city in southern Ohio, with the population employed in the manufacture of soaps and detergents, machine tools and playing cards, as well as brewing and meat-packing. It is the headquarters for such giants as Proctor & Gamble and Chiquita Bananas. The port of Cincinnati is busy. Much of the cargo it ships is soft or bituminous coal.

For Jerry to accomplish political success so young in life was an astounding achievement, especially considering he was an immigrant Jew in an area that was regarded as both staunchly WASP (White Anglo-Saxon Protestant) and ultra conservative, and was also pioneered by conservative German Catholics, who made up a quarter of the city's population during its formative years. Even today there is a suburb called Over-the-Rhine, now a trendy area north of downtown but home to thousands of German immigrants in the 19th century.

When asked some years later by reporter Barry Horstman of the prestigious *Cincinnati Enquirer* to explain the secret of his overwhelming political success soon after he was appointed the city's mayor, Jerry was uncharacteristically at a loss for words. 'I don't know. When you look at it on paper, it really doesn't make any sense. I guess all you can say is, I've touched a nerve here.'

But strangely Jerry did fit in to the city, which was founded in 1788 but not named Cincinnati until two years later by General Arthur St Clair, governor of what was then known as the Northwest Territory. It became a thriving port in the 1800s, supplying produce and goods to the American South via the Ohio-Mississippi River system. With the influx of German immigrants beginning about 1840, the city became a centre of grape culture and a wine market. It also became a major brewing centre around that time.

During America's pre-Civil War decades, it was a major Underground Railroad station — a term that meant it was a hub for helping escaping slaves fleeing the South to find freedom and safe shelter in the free states of the North or Canada — as it is situated on the northern side of the Ohio River and was, therefore, one of the first cities that escapees could reach in the slave-free North.

The city has enjoyed many nicknames including the Queen City of the West and the less flattering Porkopolis, due to the astonishing number of slaughterhouses that were based there at one time. It had become America's chief pork packing centre by 1835 and would later become the largest such centre in the world.

Booming Cincinnati was fully expected to become the

largest city in the USA but short-sighted city leaders failed to plan adequately for the introduction of the railroads and the effects they would have on it and their commercial operations. When river transport was replaced by the 'iron horse', Cincinnati quickly found itself being bypassed for cities like St Louis and Chicago.

Although Cincinnati was a border town between North and South during the American Civil War, it was not nearly as affected by the conflict as other nearby cities. Only once was the city in grave danger of a Confederate invasion, and then General Law Wallace — better known for writing the novel *Ben Hur* — mustered 72,000 squirrel hunters and ordinary citizens to its defence.

Cincinnati is noted for its symphony orchestra, established in 1895; the Cincinnati Art Museum; Historical Society, now housed in the old, magnificent art deco former railroad terminus; Cincinnati Zoo and Botanical Garden; and Riverfront Stadium, now known as Cinergy Field and located on the Ohio River, which accommodates the city's professional football and baseball teams.

Perhaps what attracted baseball fanatic Jerry to Cincinnati most was that it was the home of the Cincinnati Reds baseball team, the first professional team in America, and the birthplace of their renowned but now disgraced player Pete Rose. Rose, like Jerry, is definitely a legend in his own lifetime who has known highs and great lows in his career. Unlike Jerry he has never managed to bounce back although, in Cincinnati, at least, he has managed to achieve forgiveness.

Always regarded a great player, on 11 September 1985, Pete Rose got his 4,192nd hit, becoming baseball's all-time hits leader, and the city renamed the road leading to Riverside Stadium Pete Rose Way. During his career, he went on to make 4,256 hits, which far surpassed the great Ty Cobb's record of 4,191 during a 24-year career spanning the first three decades of the century, a mark once thought unapproachable. However, four years after he beat Cobb's record, Rose's exploits were tarnished when Baseball Commissioner A Bartlett Giamatti banned him from the sport for life for betting on baseball games, some of which involved the Reds, the team that he not only played for but also managed. Rose was jailed for five months after pleading guilty to filing false income tax returns and underpaying his income tax on gambling profits by $162,000. The street named after him was allowed to remain.

It was not just Jerry's career that was going well in Cincinnati; so was his personal life. Not long after joining Frost & Jacobs full-time as a lawyer in 1969, he received a telephone call one hot and humid summer's day in August asking him whether he would be willing to go on a blind date. Flirtatious Jerry never turned down the opportunity of meeting a new girl. Margaret Velten — Micki to her friends — was a secretary working for Proctor & Gamble, one of the biggest employers in Cincinnati. She was going to the cinema with one of her sisters and her brother-in-law and didn't want to be the odd one out, so she asked a friend at work to find her an escort. The friend, who had met new-kid-in-town, eligible young attorney and bachelor Gerald N Springer, called him and Jerry was only too willing to help. Micki later said: 'It was the best blind date you could ever imagine. He was totally uninhibited. I guess it impressed me because I'm so worried about what people think. Now I realise that's just Jerry.'

She soon began to worry about what her new boyfriend must have thought when, on the way home from the movies, she was violently sick in his car. But it didn't put Jerry off and the two started dating. By 1971, their relationship had blossomed into a full-blown romance.

While Jerry was fitting in to political life in Cincinnati his old adversary, veteran politician Donald Clancy was reeling at his near defeat at the hands of the young candidate. Hamilton County's Republican organisation was so amazed by the narrowness of the margin by which Clancy had won that in mid-January its executive members commissioned a study of Jerry's campaign and the involvement of young people in it.

The study, carried out by a 12-member committee of the county's Young Republican Club, attempted to discover what had brought so many young people into Jerry's campaign organisation and how the Springer campaign made use of its army of youth. The idea for the study came from Guy Guckenberger, a newly appointed Republican Cincinnati councilman who was 26 at the time and hoped to motivate young people into his campaign organisation when he was up for re-election.

Meanwhile, Jerry was chuckling at his new nickname of 'King Kid' because of his appointment to head Ohio's proposed youth movement. Governor John Gilligan's plan was for Jerry to head his administration's department that would organise a viable corps of youthful volunteers who wished to give time and energy for bettering the community. Jerry moved into his own office in the state capital of Columbus, Ohio, although his heart remained 111 miles down the road to the southwest in Cincinnati.

He said: 'We'll leave it up to the kids to decide what programmes they want to tackle. We'll be travelling around the state to find out what programmes and projects Ohio youth want to become involved in.'

Although Jerry had his own ideas about how the department should be set up and run, he wanted to discover what type of schemes his hoped-for troops wished to undertake before he set up the structure of the organisation: 'It's their programme and they should be the ones to decide what it will be.'

Jerry decided to concentrate on recruiting high school pupils so that both college students and other young people who went straight into the workforce after leaving school would be involved in the programme years down the line. He said: 'We'll not overlook anyone that way.' In one of his first interviews about his new job, Jerry told Nancy Logue of the *Cincinnati Post*: 'The youth corps concept is an attempt to find some way young people can have a greater voice in influencing their environment. They are not just limited to throwing rocks and carrying signs. Youth is a state of mind and not a time in life. This generation has seen only one victory and that was when man stepped on the moon. They still have war, they still have race problems. They need to see some victories. We're not expecting to save the world, just improve a little part of it.'

Jerry, an amateur folk singer who idolised entertainers of the 1960s and 1970s such as Bob Dylan, Joan Baez and the Beach Boys, echoed the sentiments they sang about in his speeches. He was truly a child of the halcyon American Flower Power days.

By April that year, Jerry was giving serious consideration to running for a place on the Cincinnati Council in the autumn. Administration observers regarded Jerry as the hottest thing politically to have hit Cincinnati in years. But he still struggled with his decision. Unusually lacking in confidence, he spent many sleepless nights trying to decide whether he would make a good councilman. He told friends that, although he was well versed on national affairs, he was not yet well acquainted with local issues in Cincinnati. The second thing that worried him was whether or not he wished to have another run for Congress when the elections came around again in 1972. He told his friends that if the Vietnam War worsened between then and the end of 1971, he would definitely have a second go at unseating pro-war, right-wing Republican Clancy.

Democratic leaders in Cincinnati prayed that Jerry would decide to run for the council. They felt he would add flair, youth and excitement to the ticket.

Jerry was becoming increasingly disillusioned by his $12,000-a-year job attempting to establish the youth corps but it took him until the middle of June before he finally decided to quit to run for a council seat. He announced his decision on 17 June and said he was giving up the reins of the youth organisation on 9 July. He devoted his last few days at work writing up the report on how he proposed the youth corps should be set up and run.

Nevertheless, by the end of June it was obvious the idea of a youth corps was rapidly falling to pieces. One report called the creation of a Youth Department 'an obscene waste of time, a needless waste of energy and an organisationally ass-backwards effort'. Even Jerry was opposed to creating a separate Youth Department in Ohio. Instead he favoured having one person in each of eight state departments to represent youth. He saw the creation of a Youth Department as 'too easily becoming another bureaucracy, another institution so complex in its functioning that it is incapable of dealing either with the needs of youth or the needs of the community'. He thought 'nothing would turn kids off faster than another board, another task force, or another hearing'.

The idea of galvanising the young of Ohio into a viable task force doing good deeds around the state was in total disarray. Sounding like a man whose dream had turned into a nightmare, he said: 'I don't know what Gilligan will do with my proposal, but he has it now and my job with the Youth Corps is completed.' He turned his back on it and walked away to concentrate on his effort to secure a council seat in his beloved Cincinnati.

Jerry promised the people of Cincinnati that, if elected to the $8,000-a-year position, he would definitely not give up his seat in mid-term to run for Congress in 1972, although he did not rule out a possible congressional bid in 1974 or later. At a press conference he called to announce his intention to stand for council, he was surrounded by 35 youthful campaign workers, indicating that once again he intended to mobilise an army of young helpers to canvass on his behalf.

Outraged by the staggering sums of money Republican party candidates had spent on their campaigns in previous years to secure a seat on the council, Jerry wanted each candidate for city council to sign an agreement not to spend more than $16,000 —

'the sum of the salary for the two-year council term' — on campaign expenditure. Jerry accused the Republicans of spending more than $200,000 on their campaign in the 1967 elections. He saw it as the virtual 'purchase' of public office by the rich. What Jerry failed to say was that the previous autumn he had spent $16,781 on his bid to run for Congress, almost twice the $9,468 his incumbent opponent Clancy spent to retain his $42,500-a-year job representing the Second Congressional District.

Jerry hit the ground running with his aggressive campaign, first attacking the council for not trying to prevent cutbacks in public bus services being introduced by the Cincinnati Transit Company then calling for the council to set up an office in Washington, DC to represent Cincinnati and keep in touch with agencies controlling federal grants for housing, education, transport and environmental pollution. He capitalised on the bus service debacle, using it as an example of the council failing to keep in touch with federal agencies that could have halted the cutbacks. He accused the city of being 'out of touch with important federal agencies'. Despite his earlier apprehensions, Jerry quickly adapted to small town politics and grasped the issues with both hands.

Mayor Willis D Gradison Jr found himself forced to go on the offensive against this aggressive new politician in the council's midst. He criticised Jerry for making what he called 'puzzling' and untrue statements over the city bus service cuts issue. Jerry had claimed to have personally travelled to Washington to meet with John Simpson, a lawyer in the Office of Emergency Preparedness, in a bid to aid Cincinnati's efforts to reverse an OEP ruling that bus cuts did not violate a wage-price freeze that was in effect nationwide at that time.

In a letter Gradison sent to Jerry and made available to the press, he said that Simpson's office 'has informed me you did not, in fact, meet with him and that your statement that you did is not true'. Gradison said that he had learned that Jerry merely talked with Simpson by telephone. Gradison disputed Jerry's assertions that the council had not done enough to get the cutbacks reversed. Jerry dismissed Gradison's accusations as 'petty bickering'.

Within days, Jerry came under attack from Councilman Guy Guckenberger, who took offence over comments he made about a proposed public housing development in the Price Hill area of Cincinnati, a middle-class, hillside suburb west of downtown where many families had owned Victorian houses for generations. Some residents opposed the public project, and at a meeting to discuss the controversy Jerry was asked why there are always some people who are against public housing in their neighbourhoods. Jerry listed a number of possible reasons, including, 'Some people just don't like blacks living near them.'

Guckenberger interpreted this as Jerry accusing the Price Hill residents of being racist, and challenged him to appear in Price Hill and repeat the allegations. Jerry countered that Guckenberger's assertions that he accused the residents of being racist were 'absolutely false' and declared he would be perfectly happy to go into any part of the city and repeat whatever statements he made.

The gloves were off and war had been declared but it was the young would-be councilman who was landing the punches and making the successful, headline-grabbing skirmishes. Not a day went by when Jerry didn't seem to be dominating the pages of the two major local newspapers, the *Enquirer* and the *Post*.

Jerry was among the Democratic candidates calling for better jails, streets and hospitals, more federal money for local needs and a mayor who stayed home in Cincinnati more than the globe-trotting incumbent, Gradison. Once again, he was pressing his idea that people should lobby Washington, DC for federal legislation that would permit up to 10 per cent of an individual's federal income tax to be paid locally to help finance a priority item, such as health, education, housing or mass transit. He firmly believed that if they could get the legislation through, the city would be able to afford many programmes that would improve the quality of life in Cincinnati. He accused the Republican majority on the sitting council of deliberately misleading the public about what it could achieve against crime in the city. He recalled that in 1967 the Republicans had promised to 'lift the shadow of fear from our streets' but that since that election crime in Cincinnati had gone up 84 per cent. 'In 1969–70 crime here increased 30 per cent faster than the national average for cities the same size,' he stressed.

However, the main thrust of Jerry's platform was that there were no more important or immediate issues in Cincinnati than health and hunger. He said that the city had to change its list of priorities and insisted: 'Some of the luxurious items will just have to wait.' Opposing a plan to link all the downtown city buildings by a series of first floor covered bridges over the streets, he said: 'The building of a sky-walk downtown is very pretty but it isn't pretty to the 26,000 persons in our city who eat on less than 28 cents a meal. Nor is it pretty to the thousands of people who live in dilapidated housing and face inadequate health service.'

Jerry was concerned that all Cincinnati's city fathers really cared about was the prestigious downtown business district: 'In Cincinnati, we tend to be building a six-block area in downtown. As soon as you step north of Sixth street, the city begins to crumble.'

He was opposed to increases in either personal property tax or income tax, instead promoting his own tax scheme to get back 10 per cent of federal taxes people paid and use it for local projects. Dismissing politicians as not being experts on mass transit systems, he wanted the city to obtain a grant for a one-year study by transport specialists to help solve the city's public transport service problems.

When Jerry was not energetically pacing the campaign trail, singing his own praises — as well as still singing and telling jokes in local nightclubs — and spouting off his own political agenda, he was happy to raise his voice to support other Democrats running for public office. One night he turned up at a benefit dance raising funds for E Winther McCroom, who was a Democratic candidate for Municipal Court judge. Although the benefit was being entertained by the Dee Felice Trio, a local jazz group, much to the dance crowd's surprise Jerry took over the microphone to give a creditable rendition of 'Blowing in the Wind'. The audience, made up of staid political supporters of the would-be judge, were taken aback to discover that their clean-cut, youthful-looking prospective councilman was no novice at entertaining. Jerry showed the crowd that night that if his voice was to be heard in the council chambers, at least it would be in key.

No music could have been sweeter to Jerry's ears than when, at the beginning of November, he was one of six members of a coalition made up of Democrats and Charterites — the third Cincinnati political party — voted into office, overthrowing the Republican majority and ending their 14-year control over Cincinnati City Hall.

The election night itself wasn't without high drama. The polling took place on Tuesday 2 November but the count was not actually announced until Sunday 7 November because a fault in the counting machines botched the election night tally and technicians had to write a new programme for the antiquated machines.

When the first-time candidate for council office finally learned he had received a healthy 56,225 votes, he could not conceal his joy. Amid cheers and applause from happy supporters at the victory headquarters in the Ohio Room of the Terrace Hilton,

Jerry leaped about congratulating his fellow councillors.

Willis Gradison, a Republican, who held on to his seat with 65,325 votes but was destined to lose his position as mayor, which he had held only for eight months after the previous mayor resigned, said from his home: 'It looks like the people want a change.'

Jerry described his election victory as 'very gratifying'.

He took his seat on 1 December 1971 and later that month he became an associate with the Cincinnati law firm of Wiesen, Rosenberg and Wagner. By the end of the month, he was already livening up otherwise dull council meetings with exchanges with his old adversary, councilman Guckenberger.

Jerry infuriated Guckenberger when, in a lengthy statement, he deplored the US bombing of North Vietnam. He then called upon the city solicitor, William A McClain, to search out any legal means open to Cincinnati to prohibit residents from participating in military combat unless a war had been constitutionally declared.

It was like a red rag to a bull as far as Guckenberger was concerned. Guckenberger remarked that he shared Springer's distress about what was going on in Vietnam but added: 'I wish he'd spend as much time on city business as federal business.' Guckenberger complained that Jerry had only been a councilman for a month and yet every week he had called for a resolution on federal business. Observers noted that Guckenberger had once asked for a resolution deploring Soviet atrocities against the Jews — and had requested copies be sent to the highest officials in the Kremlin. The two of them had only been sitting around the same council table for a month and the grudge match had already begun.

CHAPTER 6

While the escalating Vietnam War raged in Southeast Asia at the beginning of 1972, Jerry was fighting his own war in Cincinnati and taking almost as much flak from some quarters as the troops were in the hostile rice paddy fields along the Ho Chi Min Trail.

An editorial in the *Cincinnati Enquirer* called Jerry's attempt at banning the city's residents from taking part in the war as 'Springer's Folly'. It said: 'There are two possible ways to view Councilman Gerald N Springer's attempt to find legal means to prohibit Cincinnati residents from participating in an undeclared war (i.e. Vietnam). One can interpret this ill-advised dalliance with foreign policy either as failure on the part of Mr Springer to do his homework or as a cynical grandstand play in full knowledge of the unconstitutional nature of his proposed ordinance. Either way, it doesn't reflect much credit upon Mr Springer.'

The newspaper regarded Jerry's demand that Cincinnati City solicitor William A McClain should investigate legal avenues by which the council could prohibit citizens from taking part in the war as 'a total waste of time and effort better spent on the city's "domestic" problems'.

The *Enquirer* pointed out that two years earlier — in 1970 — the state of Massachusetts had passed legislation quite similar to Jerry's 'pipe dream'. The Massachusetts statute authorised servicemen from the New England state to refuse combat duty in the absence of a congressional declaration of war. One of Jerry's gripes was that Americans should not be fighting in Southeast Asia because the US Government had not declared war on any enemy.

The Massachusetts statute was nullified by three Federal Court decisions, the newspaper stressed. Tearing into Jerry, the paper stated: 'In addition to the court ruling on the Massachusetts law, a reading of the Constitution and of the nation's history shows the folly of Mr Springer's proposal. The Constitution forbids states (and, by implication, cities) from exercising any power in foreign affairs or to make or declare war, except to repel invasion. As far as the constitutional power vested in Congress to declare war there is ample *de facto* precedent in our history for wars that lacked a formal congressional declaration. American fighting men have been sent abroad to armed combat at least 160 times. In only five of these instances has there been a congressional declaration of war.'

Plunging the editorial dagger deep into Jerry's chest, the paper concluded: 'We realise, of course, that the making or unmaking of foreign and military policy is much more glamorous than the workaday wrestling with such mundane city problems as transportation, law enforcement or public health. But the voters have, in two succeeding years, given Mr Springer two mandates. In 1971, they told him they wanted him to work for the betterment of Cincinnati as a member of city council. In 1970, they told him they thought the war in Vietnam could best be handled by someone else. Mr Springer should heed those twin mandates.'

The job of a Cincinnati councilman was only part-time with part-time pay. The $8,000-a-year salary had been set in 1953 and not increased since. So by the end of January, in addition to his legal work, Jerry was exploring the possibility of getting a job as a teacher. Word of his plans quickly reached his constant critic, columnist Frank Weikel who took delight in reporting that he understood 'Councilman Jerry Springer, who for a long time had no steady job, is attempting to get on another public payroll. Word is that Councilman Springer is seeking a teaching post at the University of Cincinnati.' The University confirmed to Weikel that Jerry had expressed interest in joining the staff but the administrators would not reveal which department he was interested in joining.

The political hot property was scoring low marks with the Cincinnati establishment. To take his mind off his critics, after attending a political meeting in the Delhi Township suburb of Cincinnati one night, Jerry and some friends went 10-pin bowling but Jerry couldn't hit the pins well and ended up with a low score card. Jovial Jerry laughed off his poor playing by telling his pals that he never did well in anything he tried in Delhi.

Jerry even managed to run foul of famous, ultra-liberal author Jessica Mitford, a transplanted member of the British aristocracy who made her home in San Francisco and became famous as the scourge of the undertaking business in the USA with her best-selling documentary book *The American Way of Death*. Mitford, who went by the nickname Decca, visited southern Ohio in February 1972 to give a speech to the Cincinnati's Women's City Club. She took issue with young Councilman Springer over a statement he had made in which, in effect, he said, 'If we want to deal with the problems of prisons what we have to do is pay for it.' Mitford, who was widely regarded as an expert on the penal system, told her audience: 'Pouring money into the old institutions is like pouring money down the same old drain. You've got to be jolly sure you're not giving the vast bureaucracies all the money they can absorb, which is endless, you know.'

Stung by her criticism, Jerry said that more action and less talk would help improve jail conditions and might help ease the conditions that put men and women in prison. He said that 'Speakers who seek to prod our people into a more sensible humane and just approach to corrections become somewhat misleading when they imply that society will not have to pay for it. I am not saying that we should simply pour more and more money into the same old institutions. What I am saying is that it is not enough to just put away someone who commits an act of violence. If we are to do something about the life situation of those who inhabit our institutions, if we are to do something about their employment possibilities, education, housing, etc., we are just not telling the truth if we say that this won't cost.'

Jerry was finding himself coming under attack from all sides and quickly discovering that life in the public eye was not always enjoyable.

Long before the criticism had reached a crescendo, Jerry had realised that he needed to turn the situation around and gain some positive publicity. So he came up with a scheme to spend the night in the Cincinnati Workhouse, the local jail, which would give him the opportunity of talking first hand about what life really was like in prison and, hopefully, it would get him some publicity he could manipulate.

After much effort and sweet-talking persuasion over a period of a month, against the odds he got Henry Sandman, the safety director, William McClain, who was acting city manager at the time, and George Studt, the Workhouse superintendent, all to agree to allow him to carry out his scheme.

On the afternoon of 28 February at 3.30pm he entered the Victorian-style building, which had been built at 3208 Coleram Avenue to house Confederate prisoners during the American Civil War, to begin his ordeal as an inmate for the night. Studt was one of the few people in the prison who knew that prisoner Springer was in fact a councilman and not a genuine inmate.

After spending a sleepless night he emerged to tell the press the story of his 'absolutely terribly depressing' experience. Recounting his night in the cells as an incognito inmate, Jerry said: 'I was taken to the room where prisoners are given physical check-ups. They didn't give me one. The room was small, but fairly clean. There were a couple of medicine cabinets along the walls, and a doctor's table.' He was issued the dull inmates' uniform and given the number 00000. Then he was taken by a guard to the Workhouse hospital section in which there were about 20 to 25 patients. For security reasons, Studt did not want his charlatan prisoner to be placed in the cell block, although he did allow him to tour that section the following day. It was a hungry night for the novice inmate because he missed the last meal, which was served at 3pm.

In the hospital, prisoner Springer was assigned a bed, where he was to spend the night with the other men who were sentenced to jail for a variety of crimes. Jerry watched the guard walk away, go through the only door in the room and slam it shut. Now he was on his own and there was no turning back.

He reported: 'At first the prisoners were silent. I had the feeling they were looking me over, but soon the guy next to me struck up a conversation. I told him I was here for three days on a second speeding violation.' One of the inmates had been designated ward leader. He was responsible for passing out towels, blankets and linen. The men in Springer's ward were suffering from a variety of medical problems: 'There were two inmates with hepatitis off in a room by themselves. There were some guys on crutches, some had chest infections and one or two were suffering from the DTs.'

During the evening, Jerry was unable to get much of a conversation going about conditions in the Workhouse other than hearing prisoners' complaints about medical care being inadequate and in some instances almost non-existent. One man pointed to his foot, puffed out and purple, and told Jerry that it had been like that for a long time. Jerry told the press: 'The man complained that medical treatment on his foot was inadequate. Others complained there was no dental care. Inmates are told to go to the dentist when they get out of the Workhouse. There is no full-time doctor at the Workhouse, so many inmates are told to get treatment when they are released.'

Jerry found himself in trouble the morning after his long night behind bars when news of his exploits was leaked to a local radio station, which broadcast that young Councilman Springer was in the Workhouse posing as an inmate. One prisoner had a small radio and heard the news item. Jerry, who listened to the broadcast, shuddered: 'I was sitting there turning purple. I was thinking that all of a sudden this project was such a bad idea. The inmates started to suspect me. They kept asking where Springer was. Then the word started to spread to the guards and I think everyone started to figure out who I really was.' By 8.15am he was forced to confess his true identity to his fellow inmates. He delicately explained that he wanted to find out what kind of problems inmates had at the Workhouse and he wanted to take the message back to Cincinnati City Council.

Amazingly, his fellow inmates seemed to open up rather than shut up even though they now knew that he wasn't a genuine inmate. He learned that after 8pm each cell in the main prison was issued a pail to be used as a toilet. His fellow inmates told him that 250 men were assigned to one shower: 'One inmate said the shower was a slimy sort of thing. And since there are too many persons for one shower, many prisoners don't take showers.'

Jerry told the assembled press that there was no talk about police brutality and that, in fact, the subject was never brought up by the inmates. Besides the universal complaint of poor medical care, the inmates complained about the physical structure of the building and the lack of educational and rehabilitation programmes. He said: 'When a man is sent to the Workhouse he almost immediately gets a feeling of hopelessness. I was really depressed, and I knew I was getting out.'

Unlike Jerry, who was returning to his job as a councilman, the other inmates had nothing waiting for them when they were released. 'There is no way they can get a job. Two men were released today and everyone said, "See you Monday." We talk about law and order but we do nothing about rehabilitating prisoners so they won't come back on Monday. Every time we want to spend money on rehabilitation, the cry goes up that we are coddling criminals. It is absurd to think that jail is a deterrent to crime. I think the University of Cincinnati can really help out by supplying doctors, rehabilitation programmes and volunteers to work with the inmates. We have to start giving inmates an identity and a chance to do something with their lives when they get out of prison. I saw a man about 60 years old who has been in and out of the Workhouse since he was 20. What a human life.'

The last Tuesday of February 1972 was a leap year day and that 29 February Jerry made a quantum leap as a career politician in Cincinnati. He had turned all the public criticism to his advantage and, long before TV tabloid journalism had been invented, Jerry had quickly learned how a stunt could grab him the headlines and get people to listen to his point of view. Headlines like HE CHECKS INTO JAIL TO CHECK IT OUT and SPRINGER TO URGE WORKHOUSE REMEDIES meant that Jerry had come up with a remedy of his own to make sure the checks and balances were once again in his favour.

Jerry announced that he would ask the council to take immediate action to improve medical facilities at the jail and to expand its rehabilitation and counselling programmes. He proposed that the council should hire a full-time doctor, at a cost of $25,000 to $30,000 a year, for the facility. He emerged from the Workhouse advocating a 'new approach to the problem of corrections, such as smaller facilities and more half-way houses where we can make a serious attempt to rehabilitate the criminal'. He called for the 100-year-old Workhouse to be demolished and replaced by a modern jail providing the recreational facilities and educational programmes he was suggesting. 'We have to rehabilitate inmates so they can be productive persons after they are released,' he announced. 'The inmates live just like dogs. That's the way one inmate described it to me.' It might have made the topic of a *Jerry Springer Show: Incognito Con Cons Cons And Finds Rehabilitation.*

Weikel attacked Jerry's overnight stay in the Workhouse. 'Mr Springer learned what most people already know ... conditions are deplorable.'

Not surprisingly, Cincinnati's two youngest council members were quickly at each other's throats. Their animosity towards each other stretched back to the election campaign the previous autumn. Guy Guckenberger, who sat next to Jerry in the Council Chamber, criticised Councilman Springer's self-imposed stay in the jail as a publicity stunt. When Jerry retorted that his comments were 'damn sneaky', Guckenberger asked Robert Sullivan, the council clerk, to see that an ordinance against the use of profane or indecent language in City Hall be enforced in the council chamber. Jerry countered: 'I guess you get to expect things like that from Guckenberger. But it probably would be somewhat better for Cincinnati if, instead of simply trying to be cute, he'd start spending some of his time helping the rest of us deal with the real problems of our city.'

The attacks by Weikel and Guckenberger didn't matter. Jerry had successfully grabbed the headlines and was once again the hottest political potato in Ohio.

Weeks after his night in jail, Jerry made a special guest appearance on the popular *50-50 Club* TV show hosted by Bob Braun. On the show he sang several songs with the Apple Butter Band, which had previously been the resident band at the Playboy Club.

Around that time Jerry went into the studios to record a song written by some fellow Cincinnatians, 'Save the Union Terminal', a plea from the heart to put new life into the Cincinnati train station. The song was part of a million dollar fund-raising effort to revitalise the building. The station subsequently was turned into a magnificent museum and headquarters for the Cincinnati Historical Society and a prominent city landmark.

Jerry also made an appearance on the then *Nick Clooney Show*, singing his 'Save the Union Terminal' song along with Bobby McGee. Clooney, who is now a host on the American Movie Classics station in the USA that airs old films, is the brother of veteran entertainer Rosemary Clooney and the father of *ER* TV series and movie heart-throb George Clooney. Ironically, in the 1980s Nick Clooney and Jerry would become TV rivals in Cincinnati.

Jerry's single, with its B-side song 'Faded Photos Just Won't Do', started getting air play on the radio in Southern Ohio that early summer. When old adversary Frank Weikel heard of Jerry's recording, he wrote, 'I haven't heard Springer's voice but I have viewed some of his political work ... I hope he makes it as a singer.'

It wasn't just Weikel with whom Jerry always found himself crossing swords. He soon found himself clashing with former mayor Willis Gradison Jr, who had been relegated to the ranks of a mere councilman after the 1971 elections but was still the leading Republican voice on the council. Jerry had come up with a scheme to help solve the city's public transport problems by proposing that the council buy out Cincinnati Transit Inc., which ran the bus system. Gradison was adamant that Jerry's proposal to exchange city revenue bonds for CTI stock and ownership would not work.

But while the two councillors were rowing about the proposed scheme in the council chambers, it was another transport situation that was causing Jerry a personal problem. Weikel discovered in late March that police records revealed the owner of Ohio driving licence 89760 — one Gerald N Springer — had six outstanding unpaid fines for a variety of traffic violations dating back to the previous October. Weikel wrote in his Tuesday column: 'If the tickets aren't paid Councilman Springer, who received a lot of publicity when he voluntarily spent a night at the Cincinnati Workhouse, could be back at the old jail ... and not as a visitor.'

Within hours of the column appearing the City of Cincinnati was $206 richer as Jerry paid his fines, or, at least some of them. Although Weikel had reported that Jerry owed six outstanding fines, mostly for parking offences, when the councilman turned up at the police station that morning, officers checked their records and found five more traffic fines he hadn't paid, making a total of 11. Jerry paid all but one, the one he had been given the previous day. He had a week to come up with the cash to settle that and cash-strapped Jerry did not intend to part with a penny he didn't have to.

Whatever affable Jerry achieved, at the same time he was constantly making blunders that put him on the spot and gained him more criticism. Jerry Springer, the politician who looked to the youth of Cincinnati for inspiration, even managed to run foul of a 16-year-old supporter whose comments in his school newspaper were quickly picked up by the Ohio press.

Steve Stein, a member of the student council and debating team at Walnut Hills High School, was not impressed by Jerry so he wrote about him in the school newspaper, the *Chatterbox*, and, in the process, found himself a star journalist when the *Cincinnati Enquirer* got permission to reprint his comments.

Steve wrote: 'City Councilman Gerald Springer held a meeting recently to inform his campaigners about his goals for 1972 and to raise some support for his programmes. The meeting was not successful. Of the hundreds of people who campaigned for Mr Springer, only 20 came to the meeting. Mr Springer himself almost forgot to come, arriving over half an hour late.'

The young scribe quoted comments made by Zev Nathan, who attended the meeting: 'As Zev Nathan remarked, "Mr Springer gave a poor speech and many of the 20 campaigners were completely disenchanted with his programme by the end of the evening."' Steve added: 'The councilman made his usual statement that he is "above party politics" and is only interested in "the good of the people of Cincinnati". His programme indicated just the opposite. What Mr Springer did was to propose a gigantic neighbourhood publicity programme designed to make Jerry Springer a household word and then claim it was for the benefit of the people of Cincinnati.

'Mr Springer described the programmes that he is working on in City Council. He has been concentrating specifically on the public purchase of the transit company and the improvement of it. Mr Springer also stated, "I would like to improve conditions in the Workhouse so that they do not use pails any more for bathrooms." He was especially interested in providing counselling and drug rehabilitation. He said that he favoured moving toward a halfway-house system and abolishment of the Workhouse.'

At the disastrous meeting, Jerry's co-workers had announced their campaign's new programme. Each neighbourhood was to receive a committee, including a chairman, publicity director, transportation officer and others to spearhead the effort.

Winding up his attack on Jerry, the young author wrote: 'Their job is to publicise Mr Springer to the neighbourhood residents and to relay their complaints to City Council. Mr Springer hopes council will take a more personal role in helping individual citizens, like placing "No Parking" signs in front of stores. As one person who attended the meeting commented: "We realised that politician Springer is not the idealist he claims to be and the campaigners, mostly high school students, are not the politically interested people they claim to be."'

The boy's comments showed that not all young people were enamoured by living under the reign of the politician once called 'King Kid'.

It appeared that for everyone who loved Jerry there was another who loathed him. His flamboyant style and spellbinding way of delivering speeches was annoying local Republicans who were so concerned that his public utterings wandered from the path of accuracy that they proposed forming a 'truth squad' to follow his speech tours.

Soon after joining the council, Jerry was appointed chairman of its Inter-Governmental Affairs Committee, and used his position to pick up support for his scheme for Cincinnati to have a full-time representative in Washington, DC to work for the city to get federal grants and other financial assistance.

Despite his critics, Jerry was rapidly expanding his political empire. By now he was also chairman of the Emergency Citizens Transit Committee, pushing his opinions to overhaul the city's transport system. He was eventually successful in getting the committee to recommend the Cincinnati Transport Inc. purchase and the introduction of a 0.3 per cent tax increase to pay for it and he finally managed to get that recommendation placed on the November ballot that year.

Usually keen to be seen and heard, Jerry uncharacteristically disappeared off the local political scene in early September. The reason was that he was having a bad hair day, a very bad hair day. As part of his duties to the US Military Reserve, he was obliged to attend summer camp where his curly long locks had been shorn. On his return to Cincinnati, Jerry announced to his friends that he was going into hiding until his hair grew back to normal. But it didn't take him long to return to being Cincinnati's favourite renegade.

However, his military duties did cost him a place on the council's transit campaign committee. It was widely speculated that then Mayor Thomas Luken had conveniently used Jerry's absence on military service as an excuse to forget to give him a place on the powerful body. Luken, who often reprimanded Jerry for talking too much to the press, had appointed himself as the Democratic Council member on the committee. Nevertheless, Jerry's scheme did get voter approval in the elections of 7 November.

The ballot approved Jerry's plan to transfer ownership from private to public, ending 150 years of Cincinnati's tradition of privately owned transport operations, in a bid to solve the city's worsening public transport problems. Cincinnati Transit Inc. was destined to become Queen City Metro by mid-summer 1973.

Despite the controversies he had caused and the criticisms he had faced during his first year in public office, Jerry's rise to political power was meteoric. On 1 December 1972 Theodore Moody Berry was installed as Cincinnati's 47th and first black mayor. At the same inaugural ceremony and, in front of possibly the largest inaugural audience ever to crowd into the City Council Chamber, Councilman Gerald N Springer was installed as vice-mayor. Berry and Jerry replaced Luken and William Chenault as mayor and vice-mayor, respectively, under an unusual political arrangement. Usually the mayor and vice-mayor served a two-year term but this council had decided that the positions should be for only one year and new people would be appointed to the offices in the middle of the council's term.

Jerry announced that he intended to use his new office as a

liaison between the council and community organisations to give people a greater voice in local government decisions affecting their neighbourhoods.

He was on top of the world, his career and personal life couldn't be better. Early in the New Year, the new vice-mayor and only bachelor on Cincinnati City Council had proposed to girlfriend Micki, who was two years younger than him, and much to his delight she had accepted. He would later joke that he realised she was the right girl for him when he discovered 'she was a Democrat'.

Micki, who was born and brought up in Kentucky, had moved to Cincinnati in 1964 after finishing high school and landing a secretarial job with Proctor & Gamble. She had decided she wanted more out of life and, in 1971, enrolled at the University of Cincinnati. By the time of her engagement she was studying to gain a Bachelor's degree in elementary education with the intention of becoming a primary school teacher, while still working part-time in administration for Proctor & Gamble. In a later interview, she said: 'Secretarial work was all right but I had sat behind a typewriter for seven years. I wanted to work with people instead of paper and machines.'

At the end of March 1973, Mr and Mrs Joseph G Velten of Cynthiana, Kentucky, officially announced their daughter's engagement to Gerald N Springer in the local newspapers.

Normally a committed self-publicist, Jerry pledged to keep their wedding 'out of the political world'. Jerry, who was an active advocate of the Equal Rights Amendment on giving women equality, joked: 'I'm not giving her equal rights. She has earned them by being a human being. The question is, will I be a good husband? I don't know. I've had no experience.'

They were married by Rabbi Solomon T Greenberg on 16 June in a small, quiet ceremony in front of their family and friends at Cincinnati's Valley Temple Synagogue. However, they delayed their honeymoon to Hilton Head, South Carolina, for several weeks until the council recessed for a summer break.

Jerry was enjoying his new role as vice-mayor and when he had to sit in for Mayor Berry, who went to Israel as a guest of the Hebrew Union College, he took full advantage of his elevated position as acting mayor. In advance of the council gathering, Jerry predicted he would conduct a meeting that would last no longer than two hours. With Berry at the helm, council meetings generally lasted around three hours. The first item on the agenda was the swearing in of a deputy clerk of council. When it was finished, Jerry said, 'Congratulations and now back to work.' The meeting lasted one and a half hours and when he asked for the council to vote for an adjournment, referring to Mayor Berry, joker Jerry said, 'OK, Ted eat your heart out.' Jerry continued his pace as the fastest mayor in the Midwest at the next council meeting when for the second straight week he concluded it in less than two hours.

However, Jerry's haste left him with a red face when he and the city manager went to Washington, DC to find out what they could about a proposed federal budget and how it could affect federal programmes in Cincinnati. Jerry returned on the Monday without his car keys, so he was forced to leave his vehicle at the Cincinnati Airport running up a large car parking bill. He found himself having to walk around the city or cadge rides from friends until the manager was due back on Wednesday night. Unfortunately for Jerry the city manager missed the plane and didn't make it back until Thursday, meaning his parking bill was even bigger!

A month rarely went by when Jerry didn't come up with a new scheme to get publicity and promote himself and his council work. So it should have come as no surprise when he decided that, if the people weren't coming to City Hall, then City Hall must go to the people.

He borrowed an old red and white mobile home van and hung a banner proclaiming it Vice-Mayor Springer's Mobile City Hall. Each week he would take it out into the community so he could listen to the complaints and concerns of people who might never take their problems to City Hall. It was more than just a political gesture that ended with a jot in a notebook and a handshake. Once the problem was explained and recorded by Jerry and one of his aides in the van, it was then tracked down and presented to the appropriate city council official. Jerry insisted that his staff respond to all of the citizen's complaints either by post or telephone, with good news or bad, within two weeks of his community visit. It was an expression of interest that was not lost on local residents. 'People want to know you're concerned, that's why this is so good,' one resident, Fred Miller, told Jerry. Not only was Jerry a hot politician he was also becoming a very popular one with the people. In him they saw there was someone from the city who would actually listen — to them he had become Jerry Springer, Man of the People.

Jerry took delight in solving city problems. Surrounded by

his enthusiastic young aides, Jerry managed to generate a community-wide reputation that his office was like an 'unofficial ombudsman' trying to cut through bureaucratic red tape and that he got things done for people. At the time Jerry's legislative assistant Timothy Burke said: 'We try to serve in this capacity, not so much in an advocacy role as in the role of facilitator, trying to see that the right information gets to the right place. It doesn't mean we win every time, but at least the complaint or request of a citizen will get to the place where the final decision should be made.' As the reputation of Jerry's office spread so, too, did the workload.

In August man-of-the-people Jerry introduced an ethics ordinance into the council that required the disclosure of financial holdings by all city councillors, all city officials earning more than $15,000 a year and all legislative employees earning more than $8,000 a year. He said the people had a right to expect public officials to have 'the utmost of integrity, honesty and fairness in all of their dealings. Our representative form of government is founded on a belief that those entrusted with the offices of government have nothing to fear from full public disclosures of their financial and business holdings. The public's right to know of the financing of political campaigns and the financial affairs of public officials and candidates far outweighs any right that these matters remain secret and private.' His proposal would later run into difficulties because it was discovered to be in conflict with an Ohio state law and also the Cincinnati City Charter but it sounded good at the time.

With his popularity so came the death threats. A phone call from what sounded like a well-spoken man to his headquarters claimed a bomb had been placed in his office, although nothing was found by the police who rushed there. Despite the bomb hoax, Jerry was on a roll and it looked as if nothing was going to stop him.

That summer Jerry's dream of having a city-run public transport system came true. On Wednesday 15 August 1973 with the flourish of a pen CTI became Queen City Metro and Cincinnati taxpayers became the owners of a bus company that would only charge passengers 25 cents to go anywhere in the city. Less than two hours after the city-owned bus line officially came into existence the new organisation had its first bus hijack — and the mastermind behind the crime was none other than Vice-Mayor Springer.

Sporting a driver's cap, Jerry boarded the lead bus of two waiting outside City Hall to take officials and dignitaries from the official signing of transfer papers for the new company over to the nearby Fountain Square, one of the major landmarks in Cincinnati, for a day-long celebration party. He jumped into the driver's seat and began playing around with the levers. With Mayor Berry and other city officials fuming at the curb, Jerry and five hapless passengers — Councilmen Thomas Luken, Willis Gradison and William Chenault among them — disappeared around the street corner. When after about five minutes, the wayward bus did not reappear, Berry and the other officials boarded the second bus and headed for Fountain Square without Jerry and the other councillors. The 'hijacked' bus, with a real driver behind the wheel, turned up at the Square later. Jerry recalled: 'It was a big fight the whole way, most of these politicians had been against it. Now comes the big day of the takeover and we're all going to Fountain Square for this ceremony, where we're all going to get on a bus and take a ceremonial ride. Suddenly all these politicians show up who had fought against it. And I'm thinking "What a load of ..." So I get on the bus. I didn't plan it. I climb into the driver's seat and I'm just playing around and pretty soon the bus starts rolling forward. So I close the door and pull away from the kerb and these politicians realise they're being left behind. And I'm watching their faces in the rear-view mirror. It was stupid to do, because of the insurance concerns and I could've killed 20 people. But it was fun.'

Jerry always seemed to be at the centre of a controversy over transport. A few days later, police issued a warrant against him for not paying yet another traffic fine that had been issued against him back on 16 April. Jerry immediately announced that he was unaware of being issued with the ticket and would pay it straight away. With the interest that had accrued, the oversight cost him $30. Ironically a warrant was issued the same day for fellow councilman Luken for failure to pay a parking fine. Luken was unable to clear his record that day because he was away on holiday.

When not bathing in the political spotlight, Jerry was still padding out his councilman's salary working as a lawyer. In late September he joined the newly established law firm of Smith & Kircher, who had taken offices in Cincinnati's Kroger Building. The firm's intention was to concentrate primarily on labour law issues, which was a new field for Jerry who had formerly focused mainly on juvenile cases.

As 1973 came to an end, Jerry was back in the thick of arguing against the Vietnam War again. He was giving speeches on national issues attacking the Nixon Administration and calling for a 'less militaristic' America. On the home front, he had firmly established himself as Cincinnati's most charismatic politician and was being talked about as the most likely candidate for mayor the following year.

CHAPTER 7

The year 1974 was set to be a banner one for Jerry. As it began, he and Micki were redecorating his bachelor flat for family life, although they were shortly to move to a more spacious detached house on Shirley Place in the Covedale area of Cincinnati, and they were thinking about starting a family.

Jerry was riding a wave of popularity, having become the second biggest vote winner in his second council run at the end of 1973.

When the biggest winner, Thomas Luken, resigned to run for Congress early in 1974, the majority coalition of Democrats and Charterites, the city's third political party, appointed Jerry, who was already vice-mayor, to become leader of his adopted hometown the coming December, when the office was due to change hands. Jerry was appointed a week after his 30th birthday, making him probably the youngest politician ever to achieve that rank in a major American city.

His rapid rise, which he modestly ascribed to luck and being in the right place at the right time, was noted in higher quarters. State Democratic Party Chairman William Lavelle called him, 'One of the brightest in the galaxy of stars we have in the Democratic party here in Ohio. Because of his youthfulness and popularity in the Cincinnati area, he is being watched very, very closely.'

Although the role of mayor was largely ceremonial, with the real power being wielded by a professional cty manager, Jerry was looking forward to making a difference. At a time when many big cities were falling prey to crime and violence and residents were moving out to the suburbs, he wanted to encourage a greater sense of community in local neighbourhoods.

'We have not reached the state of deterioration so many other large cities have,' he reflected shortly after his new position was announced. 'If Cincinnati is going to save itself from going the way of so many other cities in this nation then we have got to recognise that people relate to the eight or ten blocks around their homes much more than they do to the city as a whole. I view the job as an excellent vehicle for moving ahead in the area of neighbourhood development and neighbourhood control over their own priorities. We have a chance here to show a big city can survive, can be a viable place to live and to raise a family, to hold down a job. We have a chance of setting up Cincinnati as a model for other cities. The situation isn't hopeless at all. Crime is one of the major reasons people get up and leave the city. It is important and vital to this city to do something about curbing crime. Unless we are ready to start dealing with the lives of people who are committing crime, we're not doing anything about cutting down crime.'

Not all his plans were so serious, however. He proposed that the city should buy a surplus US navy ship as an attraction for the new Riverside Park the city was opening on the banks of the Ohio. And he made no apologies for the lighter side of his nature: 'I can be very serious about the issues but I am what I am as a person. It's almost trite to say but we all have to accept people for what they are.'

Jerry did admit to a certain amount of apprehension about his year in office, due to start on 1 December 1974, partly because of his youth and status as a relative newcomer to town. 'You know, a lot of experienced people have gone before me. People who were kind of like pillars of the community. Highly qualified people. There's the precedent they set in making Cincinnati such a well-governed city. I'm not interested in being like every other mayor, of course. But I do nevertheless recognise the success they had. I'd hate to ruin our winning streak. In the end, people are going to judge me on whether or not I was a good mayor, not on when I was born.'

Micki, a student alternating teaching at Peaslee Elementary School with classes in education at the University of Cincinnati, was even more nervous at the prospect of being pushed into the spotlight as a politician's wife. Although she had campaigned with her husband and made public appearances during his re-election run, she was due to graduate at the same time as Jerry would assume office, and was looking forward more to working full time than being lady mayoress.

'To me, being the mayor's wife just means the husband is a mayor,' she said in March, shortly after his appointment. 'I can see myself in a situation where I could speak to small groups but I am petrified of large groups. I've received several invitations to join women's clubs in the city and I'm flattered. But I don't have time to be an active member and I think it would be selfish of me to join if I don't.' Jerry completely understood her reaction; he was the flamboyant, outgoing half of their partnership and enjoyed the limelight, and she did not.

'She's her own person with her own interests,' he said. 'She doesn't expect anything particularly of me because she's a teacher, so I don't expect anything particularly of her because I'm a councilman. We're just two people in love.'

As it happened, however, their anxieties about the perils of office were soon to be overshadowed. Jerry's term as vice-mayor seemed unremarkable, with him concentrating on non-controversial local issues like bus passes and calling for a halt to building new petrol stations to ease air pollution.

Then the local Democratic party became embroiled in a squabble over who should replace Luken on the council. At the time there were only three Democrats —Luken, Jerry and William Chenault. Under the council system in Cincinnati, councillors designate a colleague to name a replacement should the councillor resign or for some other reason be unable to complete his or her term of office. The other members of the councillor's political party then have to ratify this appointment. This way of choosing a replacement avoids the trouble and expense of holding a full-blown public election. In the case of Luken, Jerry had been chosen by him to name a replacement. He was supporting one candidate while Chenault was backing another, consequently causing a potential political impasse.

But then Jerry dropped his own bombshell by suddenly resigning!

On the morning of Monday 29 April *Cincinnati Enquirer* columnist Frank Weikel — consistently a dedicated critic of the young councilman — wrote: 'A well-known Cincinnati political figure is currently the subject of a VICE investigation that is underway in both Ohio and Kentucky.' That afternoon, at 3.30pm, after having had a secret at-home meeting with his closest advisers, Jerry issued a terse statement from his office in City Hall, a handwritten note read by his aide Timothy Burke.

It stated: 'It is with deep personal regret that I am announcing today my resignation from City Council. I understand what I am giving up, an enormous opportunity to share in the leadership of this great city. However, very personal family considerations necessitate this action. My family must and does come before my own political career. Thank you for all you have given me. I hope that I have offered something positive in return.'

The city and the Democratic Party were stunned. As rumours and speculation spread and Jerry refused to elaborate, Ohio Governor John Gilligan described him as 'a brilliant young man' and echoed State Democratic Party Chairman Lavelle's sentiments. Lavelle himself had no idea what was going on and said, 'We regret any misfortune he may have had.'

Astonished Mayor Theodore Berry announced that the council might not accept the resignation. 'A resignation tendered is not a resignation accepted,' Berry said. 'He is a member of a legislative body and my preliminary investigation shows that it is the legislative body which must act on any resignation.' Mrs Bobbie Sterne, a Charterite like Mayor Berry, said, 'It's just a shame. I have no idea what his reasons are. He was a very intelligent and capable young man, and a good member of council.' Even his political enemies were dismayed. Republican Helen Hinckley said, 'I know of no one who enjoyed working in council as he did. Whatever his personal problem is it must be a major one. I am honestly sorry it will take him out of council. I did not always agree with him but I respected him in the things he gave to the council.'

The story completely overshadowed the other news of the day — a report from City Manager Robert Turner that Jerry's plan to buy a Navy vessel was too expensive.

By the next day the *Cincinnati Post* was reporting that Jerry had been given an ultimatum by Hamilton County prosecutor Simon Leis — resign or go to court on vice charges. He was accused of visiting 'health clubs' in Cincinnati and Northern Kentucky, over the Ohio River, and paying by cheque for services rendered. Jerry denied everything.

The *Post* asked him whether Simon Leis had told him he could be charged with aiding and abetting prostitution — a misdemeanour carrying a penalty of up to 60 days in jail and a $500 fine — but that he would not take the case to the grand jury if Jerry resigned and testified to a grand jury.

'I have never talked to Si Leis about this,' he stated flatly. 'I know nothing about any grand jury. I have never been before a federal grand jury or a county grand jury. I am resigning for family and personal reasons.' As for the timing of his abrupt departure from public life, he said, 'The date of my resignation was unfortunate. It coincided with the report. Again I say my resignation is for purely personal and family reasons. It has nothing to do with any of these things.'

However, by that afternoon he had changed his mind about his denials. He called a press conference to make the dramatic confession that as a newly wed and apparently devoted husband he had, indeed, visited brothels masquerading as health clubs. It was the sort of announcement that, years later, would be routine on *The Jerry Springer Show*, but this time it was Jerry in the hot seat, with the audience — the citizens of Cincinnati — looking on curiously to see how his wife would react.

'When I resigned yesterday I did so because I believed then as I believe now that there are some problems which are better faced as a private citizen,' he told the crowd in a second-floor meeting room at City Hall. 'I am currently confronting such a problem. On two occasions I have been a customer of a "health club" in northern Kentucky and engaged in activities which, at least to me, are questionable. These actions have weighed heavily on my conscience. Early last week I contacted the FBI and voluntarily answered all inquiries of what I had done and of what I had knowledge. I am continuing to cooperate in any way that I can. I have visited health clubs in Cincinnati on a number of occasions. To the best of my knowledge no club in Cincinnati which I visited was engaged in any improper or illegal activities. It is my fondest wish to re-enter public life but I believe the interest of the public is best served by my resignation until such time as the air has been cleared.'

Clearly shaken and embarrassed, he stammered through questions for the best part of an hour, at first being coy about what exactly he had done in the 'health club', and explaining why he had gone to the FBI in the first place and why he had then tried to cover up the reason behind his decision to quit. Although he was evidently chastened, whether because of what he had done or because he had been caught out, he was already talking about a possible return to public life; after all, the city council had still not accepted his resignation.

'That club was under investigation,' he explained. 'It was across the river and it's been in the newspapers and on TV. I was publicly known and as soon as it became publicly known to me I went in. I went to the FBI. I volunteered myself. I said I was a customer over there. As much as people have been very nice to me there have been some incredible, incredible stories about me being involved in some kind of ring, hearings before grand juries, just ridiculous rumours that are totally untrue.

'My involvement has been as a customer. I find that unsatisfactory enough. The public has a right to expect a very high standard of its officials and I feel I have violated those standards. Particularly, I have been fairly outspoken in things that I believe in and I have set standards and, in frankness, I have violated a standard that I would expect other people to follow. And I must accept the consequences. There's no way you can possibly understand what it's like unless you've been through it. My thought was, the prime responsibility was to the city and I didn't think the city, and I still don't think the city, and the running of our government ought to be burdened by my personal situation.

'This behaviour, this particular incident, sets a bad example for anybody else to follow and one which I'm obviously not very proud of. I hope that at least in my public service I've set a good example. If I am affected as a human being that affects how well I can perform in public office and it's tough to separate the two.'

But he hinted that that would not always be the case: 'For those of you who know me, know the incredible passion I have for what I do in public life, obviously I would like to return something to Cincinnati. I have no desire to leave this community which has given me so much. But I've got this situation which I think is best dealt with, and not to place a burden on anybody else.'

He concluded: 'I wish to express my deepest gratitude to those who have stood by me during this ordeal. My wife, my family and so many friends, both those in public life and private citizens, have given me strength when I needed it most. It's a question of how much embarrassment you can accept for yourself and your family.'

Micki, who wore the same dress as on the day Jerry was sworn in for his second term on the council, five months earlier, was in tears for much of the press conference. Despite her admitted timidity about public speaking, she stepped forward to stand by her man: 'While what Jerry did was wrong, it's nothing to throw your life away for. Politics, council, has been Jerry's life and to give that up would destroy him. It's his whole life. He loves it and he's worked so hard for five years that I can't stand to think of him throwing it all away. I've never been very political but I know what Jerry needs to stay alive. I just love him and I can't bear to see him broken like this. It means a lot to me that people realise that whatever Jerry admitted has nothing to do with our relationship and our life together.'

The seedy saga had actually started the previous year, when Jerry drove across the Ohio River, which divides Ohio from Kentucky, to the President Motor Inn on Dixie Highway in Fort Wright, Kentucky, one of a cluster of towns on the south side of the river that boast massage parlours, tattoo shops, pawnbrokers and cheap booze. Three rooms in the motel were rented out to the Leisure Health Club, and that was where he headed. There he met up with Pamela Jean Knight, 21, for what he later termed an 'act of prostitution' (generally believed to be oral sex) and paid her with a personal cheque for $25 drawn on the Fifth Third Bank. She showed it to club boss George Lewis, who told her she could accept it but warned her not to tell his partner, Monty Emery, who it was from. On 10 January 1974 Jerry once again headed for the now defunct President Motor Inn, this time for a tryst with a black hooker, Norma Jean Hall, 26. He paid her with a cheque for $50.

Unfortunately for him, the very next day a team of 11 armed FBI agents raided the health club and arrested six people — Knight, Hall, a third prostitute called Linda Webb, Lewis, Emery and a man named Don Hubbs, on federal charges of prostitution and white slavery. They learned the club accepted cheques and credit cards and started checking bank records. Somehow, it was later revealed, there was a leak, because Jerry's City Hall office started receiving anonymous phone calls hinting that he was a customer of a dubious health club. Then a lawyer friend told him that Pamela Knight had been with a lawyer to talk to Hamilton County prosecutor Leis. That was when he decided to bite the bullet and admit his involvement, at least in private, in the vain hope of avoiding a public mess.

'I thought, "Oh Jesus, I'm going to be blackmailed,"' he recalled later. 'I realised that I couldn't live my life with that hanging over my head. I had seen in the newspapers that the club had been raided. I'd been thinking about it for some time, and decided to contact the FBI and tell them what happened. Besides being a tremendous burden on my personal conscience, I had the public responsibility to contact the FBI. I told them I would be standing by if needed. I told my wife and my family, and then I told her family.'

Before making any confessions, however, Jerry discussed his problem with Democratic Party co-chairmen John Wiethe and Sidney Weil, who urged him to see the FBI, which he did on 22 April. The next day he confessed what he had done to Micki, who was horrified but said she would stand by him. For a few days they were said to have considered packing up and leaving town, but instead braced themselves for the storm. Ironically, on the day Weikel's article appeared, Jerry had already made the decision to resign. He had spent the weekend at home with his closest advisers, pacing backwards and forwards, working out his resignation strategy.

Remarkably, after Jerry made his public confession, his fellow councillors asked him to reconsider his resignation, and passed a formal resolution putting the matter on hold for a week. The public supported him, too, with 30 of 35 people who called the mayor's office to discuss the affair on day one of the scandal in favour of Jerry staying on the council.

But the sex talk was not over. Lewis, 50, Emery, 25, and Hubbs, 23, had gone on trial the day after Jerry's resignation, on charges of conspiracy and prostitution in the Federal Court in Covington, Kentucky.

The three girls arrested at the President Motor Inn had been given immunity from prosecution in return for their cooperation and were called on to give evidence. Jerry was a witness, too, though he was there voluntarily, 'to clear my conscience'. Although he had told his press conference he had paid only two visits to the Leisure Health Club, and that his visits to similar establishments in Ohio had been innocent, the picture the girls painted in court suggested that he was almost a regular customer. FBI Special Agent William Dillon believed that he was. He told the court that Knight's explanation for taking a cheque was that it was from a 'regular customer' but added, 'I don't know if "regular" was her word or mine.'

Knight, a single mother who turned to prostitution to make ends meet while she was going through a messy divorce, and who later claimed she was on the game for just six weeks, told the jury Jerry had indeed been a customer on 18 December 1973 and identified the cheque, which Jerry had voluntarily handed over to the FBI after it had been cashed and returned to him by his bank, which is the usual practice in the USA. But she also said that this was not the only time she had seen him. 'This was the only cheque I took from him,' she said. 'I got money from him, maybe two other times.' On those occasions, she said he gave her $20 cash. According to evidence from a security guard, who investigated the club on behalf of the hotel owners, he received a straight massage for $20, which he paid up front to Lewis — but for an extra $10 in cash, paid direct to her, Knight performed oral sex and also masturbated him. Knight also said she and the other girls were not paid by the club, but kept all but $25 a month of what they made privately 'turning tricks'. Emery collected the $25 as a kind of legal fund in case they needed a lawyer, she said. 'Monty told us what would be a good price to charge but the money was ours,' she went on. 'If business was slow I'd make $90 a week but averaged about $300.'

When Hall was brought into the courtroom for identification Jerry paused for a moment before saying, 'Yes, she is one of the girls,' and again identifying the cheque he gave her. Hall told the jury that when she was working she called herself Shawn Taylor. 'I didn't want my customers to know my real name,' she explained. However, Jerry's cheque to her was made out to Norma Jean Hall. She confirmed that the girls did not get a cut of the $20 fee to enter the club and added, 'Whatever we made was by turning tricks in the back room.' At one point defence lawyer Louis Sirkin asked her, 'Did you have relations with him in Cincinnati?' She replied, 'Yes, I did.' However, because she had been granted immunity from prosecution on Ohio state charges as well as the federal counts she was not pressed on this. Jerry insisted he had never had any sexual encounters in Cincinnati health clubs.

After his day of testimony, Jerry told a throng of reporters: 'I wanted to get it over with so I can start sleeping again. I have no regrets about what I did, coming here, because what I did, my actions were wrong.' His name featured heavily in the summing up of the case the next day. Prosecutor James Arehart said he had not subpoenaed Jerry but had telephoned him the previous day to ask him to give evidence, and that Jerry had voluntarily handed over the two cheques. Defence lawyer Sirkin also praised Jerry for giving evidence, and both he and Arehart played down Knight's and Hall's evidence about seeing Jerry more than once. 'Springer had more to lose than anyone,' said Sirkin. 'I believe that he told the truth.' Arehart said there were simple inconsistencies in the evidence, and that girls who had worked there for three or four months, turning tricks at the rate of three or four a day, could not be expected to remember all their customers.

However, years later Knight told an American TV show that

Jerry — by now a TV star himself — had paid for sex more than twice, and that she bitterly regretted ever meeting him. 'I remember two, three visits, then another lady told me he'd been there,' she recalled of her days at the club. Using the name Marsha, she said the first time she met him he used a phoney name but she quickly realised who he was. 'He was nervous. He was friendly. But I thought he was stupid to risk his career. I think he thought he was untouchable, unbreakable.' And she was in no doubt that from the moment of the raid that Jerry would be involved. 'They said did I know Jerry Springer,' she recalled. 'Then they mentioned the cheque and I said, "Well, I guess you got it." They had the cheque. I don't think he's ever stopped to think about me, the girl who took the cheque and what happened to her. He apologised, but it kept my life torn up.' Jerry, asked to comment about the encounter for the same show, laughed, 'She never writes, she never calls!' More seriously, he added, 'I certainly hope her life wasn't ruined. It certainly didn't do me any good.'

Retired Kentucky police officer William Minnick recalled that Norma Jean Hall had repeated to him that Jerry was a regular client. 'The prostitute Norma Jean said he was nice, and even cried for him when he was brought into court,' he remembered. 'She also said he was a regular customer.'

The charges against Hubbs were dismissed by Judge Mac Swinford on the grounds of insufficient evidence on the second day of the three-day trial. Emery was convicted of conspiracy and three counts of prostitution and given four concurrent jail sentences of a year and day. Lewis was convicted of conspiracy and one count of prostitution and given two concurrent jail sentences of a year and a day.

Jerry still had to learn what sentence, if any, he would receive from his fellow council members and the public of Cincinnati. Encouraged by support from Mayor Berry and the rest of the council he withdrew his adamant resignation on the Wednesday of that week and wrote the council a second letter accepting their idea of postponing a decision on his future for a week. 'No matter what the ultimate outcome of this,' he wrote in the note received the day he gave evidence, 'I am deeply grateful for the public support and understanding I have received from all members of council.'

The next day he went one step further, and formally withdrew his notice to quit. At his second press conference of the week he said he had told the other council members that what he had done was wrong. But he added, 'Based on their support I decided the best thing to do was to return to my seat in council.' He also said Micki had urged him to reconsider his decision. 'I cannot condone what I did and I'll pay for it for the rest of my life,' he went on. 'But I will work hard to do the best job I can and to restore public confidence in me.' After a meeting with his colleagues, the mayor announced that Jerry would formally resign from the council and be reappointed the following week.

'We accept his public statements as being truthful,' Berry said in a statement issued on behalf of the council. 'Council members do not condone Mr Springer's conduct but feel that it should not force abandonment of his career, since he has performed his duties well and diligently. We felt his decision to tender his resignation was made under pressure of circumstance and in haste. Our delay on accepting his resignation was to provide time for him to consider his action carefully. We do not feel we have the right or responsibility to urge Mr Springer to resign. The responsibility for this decision rests with Mr Springer.'

Jerry gratefully, even humbly, accepted his reprieve: 'I realise I am returning as less a person than many people thought I was but I will work hard to restore that confidence. I have told you the whole truth, the entire truth, of my involvement. I am prepared to take the consequences of what I have done wrong. It is a highly embarrassing situation and it has, as I have said, weighed heavily on my conscience. But the initial public response has been that I should not throw away my public responsibility because of it. After meeting with members of council I have decided now that I shall not. The support of family and friends, which has been so tremendous, has convinced me that the best thing to do is to return to my seat on city council and work hard to do the best job I can for as long as the people of Cincinnati want me.'

It looked as if Jerry was going to escape any penalty for his indiscretion. Even his position as the next mayor looked secure. But the tide of public opinion turned against him, with new letters and phone calls to City Hall calling for him to resign again. He hung on for reappointment, hedging his bets by announcing that if he retained his seat he would not serve as mayor. 'I don't know if I'm going to be appointed to council,' he admitted. 'It's up to the council members now. I publicly stated the truth of what I have done and I can't do any more than that. If I am appointed I'm going to ask that I not be considered for mayor, for reasons having to do with my own conscience.'

His fellow Democrat on the council, William Chenault, the man formally charged with reappointing Jerry or naming a successor under Cincinnati bylaws, was reluctant simply to rubber-stamp his return without testing the opinion of people throughout the city. He told a sombre council meeting that, while the Friday after Jerry's confession he received 35 calls in favour of him staying on and only three against, on the following Tuesday he had 20 calls, 18 of them against Jerry. The council clerk had received 306 phone calls and 28 letters against him, versus 148 calls and eight letters for him, while the mayor's office had 135 calls and 61 letters demanding he go opposed to 114 calls and 23 letters for him to stay. Jerry still had other popular support, with three women arriving at a Wednesday council meeting with a petition signed by 70 people asking him to stay on. But the council voted to accept his resignation, and Chenault did not reappoint him.

Jerry was shaken and bitterly upset. Even though he was clearly down, he refused to consider himself out for the count. Ever the politician, he accepted the decision without bitterness, taking care to promote the good he had done in office, to distance his private life from his public performance, and to lay the groundwork for his eventual return. He ruled out completely his plans of fewer than 14 days earlier to leave the city he had made his home.

'I have absolutely no regrets about my performance in public office,' he insisted, his voice breaking up with emotion. 'I have always fought for what I believed in and in some way I will continue to do that. I don't fault council for considering their own interests. Everyone has a right to do that. I don't want to remain or be reappointed at the price of impairing the work of the whole council, dividing the coalition or losing my own self-respect. I am not going to beg. What I did was wrong but I still have a certain amount of pride and self-respect left. I will miss it terribly. I loved my work. It was my life. But I committed a serious indiscretion, to my way of thinking, and I guess I must now pay for it dearly. Maybe in retrospect I should have stuck to the original resignation and saved myself the last eight days. I have not given that much thought to what I am going to do. Right now I think I should be concerned about picking up the shattered pieces of my life. The only thing I have now is my wife and the fact that I have told the truth. The city ought not to be asked to bear my problem. The only way to ever settle a public reaction would be if an election were held today.'

Even as he bowed out, he reminded the public of what he had done in his two and a half years as a councillor. 'I am somewhat proud of my contributions in the area of transit, the initiation of the Mobile City Hall and, in general, my responsiveness to the everyday problems of the average citizen,' he said. 'I would hope that you view me as someone who stood up and fought for what I believed in, but also as a human being, and one clearly not without sin, but one who had the courage to stand up and tell the truth about his mistakes.'

Ironically, while Jerry was under fire in Cincinnati, he knocked much bigger politicians on the world stage out of the local headlines. During his 10-day domination of Cincinnati news, President Richard Nixon was publicly issuing 1,308 pages of edited transcripts of the notorious Watergate tapes, which would ultimately lead to his downfall. And the day it was announced that the Cincinnati Bar Association would look into Jerry's conduct, 3 May 1974, Nixon's disgraced former vice-president, Spiro Agnew, was barred from practising law in the USA by Maryland's Court of Appeals, after he admitted tax evasion.

There was an amusing postscript to the whole sorry affair, amusing to everyone except the unfortunate man concerned. The phone number 513 481 8941, listed in the phone book under the name of Gerald N Springer at 3026 Harrison Avenue, started ringing off the hook as soon as the news broke. Jerry, however, had changed his phone number since the telephone directory was published, and his new number was ex-directory. His old number was assigned to a new resident who had only arrived in Cincinnati two days after the scandal broke. 'I had never even heard of Jerry Springer when I moved into town on Wednesday,' he complained to one of his dozens of callers. 'At first the phone calls didn't bother me. Most of them were from people calling up to express sympathy or to tell me they were behind me, or really Springer. But then I received some nasty calls and some hostile ones.' He promptly had his number changed.

Although prostitution is a crime for the customer in most US states, Jerry was never charged, though he was punished by being forced out of public life. He turned down a job offer at the local Office of Economic Opportunity and joined the law firm of Ronald Lee Grinker. He remained a staunch Democrat and was well received at political functions. But at the end of 1974, when he should have been mayor of Cincinnati, he admitted he was ambivalent about running for office again, because of what had become known throughout southern Ohio and northern Kentucky as 'the cheque incident' and had already passed into local folklore, although he wanted to serve the community where he lived and worked.

'I'm convinced that in order for me to survive as a human being of any particular worth, I've got to do something with my life which is more than making money,' he told Bill Furlow, who interviewed him for the *Cincinnati Post*. 'Now, whether that translates into elective office is a separate question. But I've been raised to believe that political participation, government participation, issue-oriented participation, is the noblest thing you can do with your life. There has to be some justification to why I'm alive and that's it for me. I'm not necessarily sure that means you have to run for political office. But do you have to be involved? Yeah.'

He prevaricated on his plans to run for the council again, because of the events of the previous spring. 'They vary from day to day,' he went on. 'One day I'm certain I want to run, then other days I say, "This is crazy. I'm 30 years old. What am I in such a hurry for?" Recovering from these scars is going to take time, you know. The way I cope with this is just by deciding that I'm not making any decision about that now. I cry a lot on the inside. It was a horrendous personal situation and I must have been scarred by it. It did some damage to me as a person. Whether or not the wounds have sufficiently healed in my own person to face all that again, that's what's so difficult. And it's just a decision I'm going to one day sit down and make.' Tellingly, he added, 'That's a decision only I can make, my wife and I. If she has the final decision, then I'd be running. But there's a lot of emotion involved in that.'

Jerry had ridden a roller coaster during the past year, as he would many times in years to come. Despite her heartbreak at his betrayal, Micki was still enjoying the ride with him.

When he said, 'It sounds blatantly immodest but I think if my prior election showed anything, it showed that there was generally a feeling in the community, even if a person didn't particularly like me, it was the general consensus of the community that I was a hard-working, effective public servant.' It seemed pretty clear that Cincinnati had not seen the last of Jerry Springer, public figure.

CHAPTER 8

Jerry was gone from public life but by no means was he forgotten. However ambivalent he was about the prospect of running for the council again, he had legions of supporters who wanted to see him re-elected sooner rather than later. A Democratic Party poll in April 1975 placed Jerry fourth out of nine potential candidates. Fellow lawyer John Peck formed a fund-raising committee that spring, before Jerry had even reached any decision about whether he would run for office again, and commissioned a survey to gauge public support for a proposed campaign.

Encouraged by these results Jerry approached the Democratic Party and asked whether he could run on their ticket, and was disappointed to be turned down. However, having gone that far he decided to go for it anyway, and after discussing it with Micki and his parents in New York, he threw his hat into the ring as an Independent candidate that August.

He set up a 'Springer for Council' office in the heart of downtown Cincinnati and wrote to his former Democratic supporters asking them to attend a campaign meeting and press conference. In the letter he made no attempt to duck the possible embarrassment he and Micki faced from opponents raising 'the cheque incident', admitting they both faced 'potential abuse' because of it, and said he believed he could be 'a hard-working, efficient, innovative leader in the public workings of the city'.

Two of his former campaign aides, Michael Ford and Eugene Beaupre, threw themselves into full-time campaigning, even taking leave of absence from their jobs. With Jerry's typical exuberance he was unconcerned about entering the race late, just a week before the deadline, saying he did not need a long campaign because most voters already knew him and his politics, and already knew whether they would vote for him.

Hand in hand with Micki, he walked into a crowded room at the Terrace Hilton Hotel on 2 September 1975 for his first press conference since his resignation more than a year earlier. Again he acknowledged the scandal, and said deciding to run had been an agonising choice. But he insisted that to let the past keep him out of the public arena would be, 'running away from a job that needs to be done'. However, he did not dwell on the incident and asked voters to consider the good and the bad in both his personal life and his past performance as a councilman.

His main campaign theme was familiar — increase the power of local communities by lessening the influence of the central council. He called for an increase in council size from nine to fifteen members and for the introduction of a ward system under which local neighbourhoods would directly elect local representatives instead of having a city-wide vote. He also wanted to establish mini-council meetings where local residents could discuss local issues, and proposed that the central council should give neighbourhoods a share of the city revenues to spend within the community.

As he campaigned he warmed to his theme: 'We must find out why people are leaving the city and attempt to correct it. One way to help control the problem is to give people more power and control over their own neighbourhood.' Referring to Cincinnati's dual system of both an elected council and a professional administration, he went on, 'There should be more involvement of council in the preparation of the budget. It should be council, not the city administration, preparing the budget.'

Micki campaigned for him and with him. She recalled: 'In 1975 I was, for the first time since our marriage in 1973, really active in Jerry's campaign. Jerry's staff didn't pick what I should do. I found out what interested me the most and did that. Some of it was clerical, some was telephoning, sometimes it was dropping off literature.'

It was evident that many of his former supporters were ready to give him a second chance. But one opponent, businessman Charles Keating, was so incensed at his running again he bought full-page adverts in the *Cincinnati Enquirer* and the *Cincinnati Post*, denouncing him. Ironically, at the end of the 1980s Keating faced a far bigger disgrace than Jerry, when a savings and loan bank — the US equivalent of a building society — he owned in California went broke, losing $288 million for its investors. He was charged with looting the bank for his own profit, deceiving investors about risky 'junk bonds' he was selling, and setting up phoney land deals to make it appear as if his company was solvent. He was convicted of both California state and federal offences and served four years and nine months before both convictions were overturned.

Looking back on that election race 20 years later, when he was getting ready to leave Cincinnati after half a lifetime there, Jerry told the *Cincinnati Post*: 'I had to run. My father's advice at the time was that I should make sure the cheque business wasn't the last thing people knew of me. Because people will remember you for the last thing you do. So I decided I had to stay in Cincinnati. I didn't want there to be a place in America where I couldn't go. I took the jokes and the abuse. And for a year it was awful.

'Then I ran again and it got ugly. The party wouldn't endorse me. Charlie Keating took out a full-page ad in both newspapers. It was just one sentence. "Jerry Springer is singularly the most despicable person ever to run for public office in the history of Cincinnati," signed Charles Keating. It was two days running. On the third day I held a press conference. I said, "OK, I'll give you maybe the top 10. But the worst *ever*?"

'I wound up in hindsight having done the smart thing, which was admitting what I'd done, resigning and then coming back and letting the voters decide. I am forever indebted to this town. These people saved me.'

Considering how hard he had fallen from grace, the election was a triumph for Jerry. He finished fourth in the nine-way race, beating all three of his former Democratic allies who were also elected. And in a crowning irony, not only did the Democrats immediately begin wooing the man they had refused to endorse, he also took on the mantle of king-maker, as a deciding factor in who would become the city's next Democratic mayor.

The two majority parties, once again the Charterites and the Democrats, each would choose a councillor who would serve as mayor for a year in the two-year council session. The trouble was that all three Democrats — James Cissell, James Luken, and David Mann — wanted the job and would vote for themselves. If Jerry were brought back into the Democratic fold, he would have the deciding vote.

Luken, a long-time friend, laid the groundwork for his

return in the days immediately after the November election in a letter to Hamilton County Democratic co-chairman Sidney Weil in which he wrote, 'It was and is my suggestion that the four elected Democrats meet as soon as possible, and obviously I include Jerry Springer in that group.' A few days later he said, 'My feeling is that whatever Jerry's problems have been in the past, the voters elected him.'

Jerry, not surprisingly, found the whole situation amusing and was actually able to lay claim to the moral high ground by pointing out that while his colleagues were squabbling over a largely symbolic title, he had no interest in it and wanted to tackle the issues. 'They are interested in being mayor,' he said wryly. 'And I am interested in some basic issues; neighbourhood and things like that. It's an interesting position to be in after being non-endorsed!'

Looking back on his fall from grace and his remarkable re-entry into public life a couple of years later, Jerry admitted how depressed he had been: 'They were beginning to write my obituary and I was beginning to believe it. And I did feel more dead than alive. Words aren't sufficient to describe how terrible that period was.' After his re-election, he said, 'I began to feel whole again. I was back doing what I loved. Things were looking bright again.'

He threw himself straight back into council work, fighting to prevent police and fire officers and rubbish collectors being laid off because of budget cuts and challenging conventional wisdom. 'We have constantly assumed the way you cut the budget is to fire people,' he said. 'We say, "Let's see what happened with the wage negotiations then we can determine how many people we have to fire." That's backwards. First you should decide what programmes you want, how many people are needed to run them and what is left is for wage increases.'

Despite his conviction of the importance of local actions, however, he nevertheless took an interest in wider-ranging issues. A month after New York City Health Department banned the transport of most radioactive materials through the city in January 1976, he called for a similar ban on land and air shipments of lethal nuclear substances through Cincinnati, especially because a consortium of three companies, Cincinnati Gas and Electric, Dayton Power and Light and Southern Ohio Electric Co., were on the verge of completing the Zimmer Nuclear Power Station at Moscow, some 35 miles southeast from Cincinnati, upstream on the Ohio River.

'Vital questions of safety, in terms of pollution, security and transportation of materials still need to be answered fully,' he told a council meeting. 'We cannot control what happens in Moscow; we can in Cincinnati. Transportation of nuclear materials through our streets creates the potential for catastrophe. The absence of adequate security opens us up to hijackings or even terrorist sabotage, not to mention accidents. This country has not fully analysed its nuclear power situation. Dangers exist and critical questions must be answered. Considering the consequences of a nuclear accident, we cannot afford to make a mistake.'

Residents of rural Clermont Council, who expected a massive boost to their finances when the plant opened, dismissed big-city fears of water and air pollution. But Jerry responded: 'The reason we put nuclear plants in low density areas like Moscow in Clermont County is to protect people in high population density areas from catastrophes. That same logic applies to transporting nuclear fuel and water.'

He looked again at the example of New York to try to prevent traffic chaos during the two-year closure of a major road bridge for renovations, proposing that businesses and the University of Cincinnati should stagger their working hours to spread rush hour over a longer period, as was done in the Big Apple during a bus and subway strike.

Cincinnati, as Jerry had often pointed out, was not facing the kind of urban decay and inner-city violence that many American cities had to deal with, but no city is crime-free and serious trouble can erupt in even the most peaceful communities. As crowds gathered in Fountain Square, the heart of the city, to celebrate a major victory by the local baseball team, the Cincinnati Reds, fights broke out, a gun was fired and two people were injured. When the mêlée calmed down, a juvenile was arrested and charged with the shootings.

Partly in response to that, and in a bid to crack down on juvenile crime in general, Councilman Walter Becklord launched a petition to impose a curfew on children under 18, from 11pm to 6am on school nights and from 1am to 6am at weekends and holidays. He collected sufficient signatures for the proposal to be included on the ballot for that November's local elections.

Jerry immediately leaped into action. He was still young enough to remember vividly his teen years and the value teenagers place on the freedom to enjoy staying out late or having all-night parties. With the energy he had devoted to campaigning for the right to vote at 19, he wholeheartedly opposed the plan. He attacked it as being unfair to the teenagers who would be the obvious targets, and as a waste of police time. It would be expensive, costing probably half a million dollars a year, money that would have to be obtained by raising taxes or cutting services. Worse, he said, it would have little or no effect on crime figures. 'I oppose it not only because a curfew bears no relationship in curbing crime, but also because of recent information my office has received from the safety director detailing the cost of legislation in terms of police protection and response time,' he stormed. 'With each juvenile detained for curfew violations, two man-hours of police time would be lost to other, more important activities. This would take police off more serious matters and turn them into babysitters. They don't want it either.'

He gave his fellow councillors the latest figures from the Cincinnati Committee on Youth, which showed that 78 per cent of juvenile crimes, including the Fountain Square shootings and associated fighting, took place out of the curfew hours in any case, and that the police already had weapons like anti-stalking laws that enabled them to arrest suspicious-looking people of all ages, day or night. He also pointed out that overall, 39 per cent of crimes were committed by juveniles, with adults committing the other 61 per cent. 'There is no relationship between the curfew and the crime being committed,' he went on. 'If a curfew is going to reduce crime, then why not have a curfew for everybody?'

In addition, he urged the people who would be most affected by the curfew, teenagers, to sway the election results even though they did not have a vote, by talking to their parents, their parents' friends, teachers and any other adults they came into contact with, asking them to vote no on the curfew measure, Issue 12 on the ballot. 'You have the greatest impact on adults,' he told a school gathering. 'The influence you have is fantastic.' His ardour paid off, and the proposal was defeated.

Not all Jerry's headline-making exploits were so favourable to him. Problems over his driving record continued to dog him. He became involved in a row between the police and City Hall when he ignored two parking tickets, tickets he later claimed he did not know had been issued. Police doing a routine review of parked cars in a search for unpaid tickets ran a check on the number plate of Jerry's 1974 Oldsmobile Cutlass Supreme, which was parked outside City Hall while he was at a council meeting, and discovered two tickets that had been outstanding for three months. Officer Tom Lind promptly called for a tow truck to impound the car until the fines were paid. But as the truck driver was getting ready to drive off, Deputy City Manager Henry Sandman came rushing out of City Hall and ordered him to leave the car where it was.

Officer Lind later recalled the incident. 'The tow truck driver had the car hooked up and hoisted into the air when Mr Sandman and another man came running out of City Hall,' he said. 'They told me they had previously written a letter to the police chief saying it was legal to park properly identified council members' cars in official spots around City Hall when they were in council meetings. My partner told him that the car was parked legally but had two delinquent tickets outstanding against it. "Drop it," Mr Sandman told my partner. "Are you saying that we're not allowed to impound this car?" I asked. He replied that through his experience he knew that cars sometimes got on delinquent lists that didn't belong there. "What you're saying," I replied, "is that Mr Springer gets preferential treatment."' Lind did not get the car towed, but filed an official complaint against Sandman.

Sandman explained the story differently. 'First of all Mr Springer was in a late council meeting,' he said. 'His car was parked legally in a spot reserved for official cars. It was pouring down rain and I just felt we ought to extend the courtesy of seeing whether Mr Springer knew anything about the tickets. It was a matter of discretion. In fact, there is a standing order that policemen should check with someone on the first floor of City Hall prior to tagging of cars outside in light of the difficulties.'

Jerry, who insisted he was not involved in the mini-débâcle at all, promptly paid his tickets.

A minor run-in with the law at that time was the least of his worries, however. While Jerry was enjoying his life back in the limelight, his mind was on a lot more than politics when he first returned to the ugly, red-brick City Hall on Plum Street. He and Micki had just learned the good news that after three and a half years of marriage, and the inevitable strain 'the cheque incident' had put on their relationship, Micki was pregnant.

Kathleen Suzanne Springer, soon to be nicknamed Katie, checked into the world at Good Samaritan Hospital at 6.26am on 7 July 1976. Sadly for the proud parents, their beloved daughter was born disabled. Breathing passages in her nose were not completely opened and she was put straight into intensive care. The day after she was born, she underwent an operation to widen them and have tubes inserted to keep them open until they healed — if they healed. The baby was listed in 'fair' condition the next day. This was a heartbreak that went beyond public life but both Jerry and Micki were determined right from the start to give their cherished daughter the best they could.

Jerry announced the bad news to friends, family and the city, and political friends and foes alike wished the family well. The baby was kept in hospital for a further five weeks before her smiling parents were able to take her home and begin learning about the realities of bringing up a handicapped child. One of them was that Micki put her career on hold to be a full-time mum, at least for the first few years, deciding to assess the situation when the baby was older. Katie's handicaps also meant that she was even more work than most babies; among other things Jerry and Micki had to clean out Katie's nose with a special tube each night to help her breathe.

Years later Jerry relived the trauma of those first days. 'What was to have been the happiest day of our lives turned into the scariest just seconds after Katie's birth,' he said. 'She started turning blue. There were no holes in the back of her nose, so she couldn't breathe when her mouth was closed. Doctors rushed our baby into surgery before either of us even had a chance to hold her.'

Three months after her birth the news became worse, Katie was blind. The bad news came as the Springers were preparing for a family celebration, when a routine check-up put parties out of the question. 'It appears to be a situation that cannot be corrected with surgery,' the young councilman reluctantly and soberly announced. 'But we're still consulting with specialists. We're hopeful that sometime in Katie's life something will be developed. We are obviously crushed, but we're determined to give her the fullest life any child can have in the meantime.'

Later he talked about that dire day: 'My parents were coming in from New York. It was my mother's 70th birthday. I remember I kept asking myself, "Why doesn't the doctor hurry up so I can get to the airport?"' When they finally got to Covington International Airport, which is actually in Northern Kentucky, they broke the sad news to Katie's grandparents, who were naturally heartbroken. But Micki recalled later, 'It was good to have family around at a time like that.'

After the grim discovery, Katie underwent yet more tests, which revealed she was suffering from a condition called coloboma, in which the optic nerve is damaged beyond repair. The doctors explained the problem to Jerry and Micki, and sadly reiterated their first verdict: surgery would not help. But that, of course, was in 1976 and the family hoped that future medical developments might make a difference. 'It wasn't easy to hear someone say, "Excuse me, your daughter can't see,"' Jerry went on. 'We all have blind spots in our eyes, but hers are much larger.'

Following the initial heartache, Jerry and Micki were delighted when, a few months later, the specialists became cautiously optimistic. Katie was not totally blind; she could not see through the abnormally large blind spots in her eyes, but the undamaged tissue surrounding them would give her limited vision. However, they could not tell precisely what she could see. That would have to wait until she learned to talk and could try to describe what she could see. Micki recalled, 'We were told that she was blind. We weren't optimistic. It was a real shock but we were able to handle it. Then the doctors told us she would be able to tell between light and dark but they didn't know what else.' Added Jerry, 'The doctors are amazed. She's not totally blind by any means, she sees things. How much, we can't tell for sure. She has some developmental problems but we're encouraged. It's been like a miracle. At least we have hope now.'

Right from the start Jerry doted on his daughter. He was to tell friends over the years that he learned a lot from her, and that the way she fought to overcome her problems inspired him to distinguish between the trivial things in life and the really important ones.

Devoted though he was to Katie, Jerry still had his constituents in Cincinnati to consider. He did not allow his private sorrow to intrude on his work on the council, as he continued to campaign for a better life and government for residents of the city.

The American Midwest is no stranger to extremes of climate, from baking heat in the summer to bitter cold and drifting snow in winter, and destructive floods and powerful hurricanes are regular visitors. The people who live there are used to the changing moods of Mother Nature, but however prepared they are for the next wave of weather, there will always be times when regular provisions do not work. Early 1977 was one of those periods, when a bitter cold snap and deep snow confined many frail or elderly Cincinnatians to their homes and prompted power cuts as people turned up the heat.

As City Hall thermostats were turned down and staff bundled up in warm clothing to set a good example, Jerry proposed a city ordinance to compel everyone to set their heating to a chilly 65 degrees Fahrenheit. He then called a televised press conference to announce 'Operation Deep Freeze', a plan to distribute food and other help, including medical care, to people shut in by the appalling conditions. His plan called for volunteer groups to deliver supplies to the needy. The city applauded, but his colleagues in the Charter–Democrat coalition were appalled. For two days earlier Charterite councillor Charles Taft, a low-key figure who tried to avoid the headlines as much as Jerry enjoyed courting them, had outlined a virtually identical plan to the council, with the backing of party colleague Bobbie Sterne and Democrat David Mann, pledging that their three offices would be manned round the clock to take calls from people who needed emergency help. In announcing his scheme, Jerry made no mention of his fellow councillors and took all the glory.

Remarkably, however, a couple of days later his *Cincinnati Enquirer* nemesis, Frank Weikel, offered him a rare and effusive piece of praise. 'A tip of the "town cap" to councilman Jerry Springer for his Operation Deep Freeze. I talked with Springer Monday and the programme had fed about 100 persons. With the snow emergency gone, Springer has now turned the operation of the programme over to the Community Chest. The only "sour note" on the whole programme were complaints from fellow council members that Springer was getting all the publicity. He got the publicity because he did a good job.' The Community Chest, an institution throughout the USA, is a collection of local charity groups who work together for the good of the community.

From the welfare of the old and infirm, Jerry next turned his attention and boundless energy once again to concerns of the young — rock music. Conservative Cincinnati in those days was not seen as a natural venue for rock concerts, so when it was announced that Led Zeppelin would play at the city's Riverfront Coliseum, the two concerts quickly sold out at $9 a ticket. When Tuesday 19 April, rolled around, however, thousands of fans who had not been able to buy tickets turned up anyway. Police set up security checkpoints near the entrance and the ticketless crowd became an angry mob, gathered on the west side of the stadium.

Shortly after 8pm bricks and bottles started flying through the air, hitting police officers and smashing five glass doors leading into the auditorium, as well as two windows. Assistant Police Chief John McLaughlin was hit on the head by a rock and police community relations expert Randy Anderson took a blow to the shoulder. An usher suffered a head cut in the mêlée. There was still more confusion inside the Coliseum, because there were no pre-assigned seats and people with tickets were fighting to get through the doors first to grab the best positions.

The 40 police on duty were desperately outnumbered and found it hard to make headway against the mob. There were dozens of arrests, with police vans hauling the fighting fans first to the local police station, District One, then to the Central Station in City Hall when District One became overcrowded. Still other, younger, kids were taken directly to the Juvenile Detention Centre. The youths were charged with a variety of offences, including disorderly conduct, assaulting police officers, resisting arrest and public intoxication.

Despite the chaos the police also found time to make several arrests of people selling memorabilia without a city licence, and there was one case of criminal damage. It took 90 minutes of non-stop activity to clear the crowd; fortunately this was done in time for the legitimate concert-goers to be able to leave without problems.

The next day the miscreants lined up in court, where most of their cases were adjourned and, in preparation for that night's concert, security was beefed up. The police presence was doubled, and officers set up a barricade in the middle of the afternoon, checking tickets and only letting ticket-holders through. They also confiscated all bottles and cans, to prevent them being used as missiles if there was more trouble. The plan worked reasonably well. People without tickets were kept further from the previous night's trouble spot, although there was an outbreak of bottle throwing shortly after the concert started. At that, the police simply marched everyone without tickets away from the scene, back to downtown. Even so there were 18 arrests, but that was better than 58 the night before.

Ironically, some of the trouble was worse on night two; an 18-year-old boy was rushed to hospital after falling 20 feet on to a concrete ramp when he was trying to climb over a wall, and three others were treated for drug overdoses. Another teenager was held up at knifepoint and relieved of his ticket for the concert and $25.

After two days and nights of disturbance, there were calls to ensure that this would never happen again by banning rock concerts from the area. This was not the first time that music fans had caused trouble at Coliseum concerts, though nowhere near as serious as these disturbances. The previous year 15 people had been arrested after an Elton John performance, mainly for disorderly behaviour, eight people were injured by fireworks at a Fleetwood Mac concert, one fan was arrested for throwing fireworks when the Eagles played there and nine fans were arrested for throwing rocks and bottles during a show by REO Speedwagon and Aerosmith.

There had already been talk of staging a show at another venue, Riverfront Stadium, just along the banks of the Ohio River from the Coliseum. It had a much bigger capacity — up to 60,000 as opposed to the 18,000 seats available at the Coliseum. Now the city authorities were having second thoughts. Perhaps it was because Jerry was a month younger than Jimmy Page, leader of Led Zeppelin, that he immediately leaped into the fray, firmly on the side of youth. Just as he had fought the teen curfew, he now fought for teenagers' rights to have fun. 'I hate to say it, but I honestly feel we have a feeling in these areas that there is a fear of young people,' he stormed in a May council meeting, two weeks after Led Zeppelin left town. 'I'm angry about it. It's an example of the administration thinking that they know what's best, rather than the elected officials. I think it's an example of particular people deciding they don't want a concert here.' He also poked fun at a report from public safety director Joseph Rochford, which called for a ban on concerts that year and made provision for just one in 1978, because there was too much planning involved. Part of his report declared, 'The difference between soft and hard rock is that soft draws generally a younger crowd.' Jerry, a rock fan more in tune with teenagers than their elders, countered: 'The opposite is true!'

Riverfront Stadium, then the home of the Reds baseball team and the Bengals American football squad, was already a hot political issue, with the city administration and council fighting over how it should be run. The bureaucrats wanted to have the major say, with the council expected to subsidise the stadium without asking too many questions. However, Jerry led a council protest when management announced they needed more than half a million dollars to repair a computerised scoreboard and he called for other means of financing it, including a rock concert. 'I think we should search for alternatives to see whether we can get a board for half that cost, especially at a time when the city finances are short,' he added.

The management had already hired William Cunningham, general manager of the highly successful Oakland Stadium in California as a consultant and he more or less said the council should keep its collective nose out. 'The council, in the opinion of the consultant, becomes too involved in too many stadium operating and management matters, often without any real background and ignoring detailed staff advice,' he wrote. 'Negotiations in public forums are no way to run a stadium.' In addition, based on Cunningham's report, the city's safety department announced that logistically it would be impossible to stage such a show at the stadium until the following year.

Not unexpectedly, Jerry was furious. 'The city's policy on what kind of entertainment should be held at Riverfront Stadium should be set by elected officials, not one person in a department,' he protested, calling for the dismissal of safety chief Joseph Rochford. 'The conclusion that city council should stay out of the stadium operation is ridiculous. It is the people and their elected officials who should decide where tax money is spent, not some kind of bureaucrat. If the council had not "interfered" as Cunningham calls it, the stadium would be vacant 280 days a year. Taxpayers have to pay for it even while it is vacant. At a time when police services are cut, streets go unrepaired, taxpayers should not be supporting an empty stadium. One single rock show at the stadium will bring in more revenue than any other single event in the stadium and this includes the Reds' World Series games. I think this is a chance for the city to make money and at the same time provide entertainment that young people like.'

Simultaneously he attacked another report by the city's Public Utilities Department, which had been asked to draw up a plan for improved handicapped parking and access but which instead offered drop-off and pick-up points for the disabled, but no guaranteed parking. Jerry, who was, after all, the father of a disabled little girl who would one day be a teenager wanting to go to concerts herself, was again incensed. 'The report is ridiculous,' he complained. 'It isn't a question of whether we will provide the parking. We asked the administration to figure out a way to do it, not to tell us how it couldn't be done. Council has decided it cannot deny some citizens the right to have the kind of entertainment they enjoy to be held at a public stadium. The administration's instruction was to figure out a way to do it, not to tell us they didn't want to do it. If we can't get cooperation then I suggest we remove that person from the department and get someone else.'

Perhaps as a nod to the sensibilities of concert critics, he also proposed a new bylaw to control noise levels including concerts throughout the city. 'Cincinnati is one of the few large

American cities not to recognise the need for a comprehensive noise ordinance,' he told the council. 'Living in an urban environment we have to tolerate a certain amount of noise. However, there are noise levels that all of us can agree are unacceptable.'

Not everyone shared Jerry's enthusiasm for putting Cincinnati on the music map. Columnist Frank Weikel complained: 'The rock concert that has received the city of Cincinnati's blessing for Riverfront Stadium continues to be a concern for many who remember past problems caused by such concerts. However, Councilman Jerry Springer looks at the $100,000 the city will get for renting the stadium and assures the public all will be well ... HUMBUG.' Even Jerry's old friend, now mayor, Jim Luken, was against the plan, especially because the stadium was not proposing pre-assigned seats, offering instead so-called 'festival seating', despite the problems this had caused at the Led Zeppelin shows: 'We've had enough trouble with festival seating at rock concerts at the Coliseum, which is not under the city's control, but we should not approve festival seating for a rock concert with a potential of 50,000 in Riverfront Stadium.'

In the end, however, all Jerry's efforts went for nothing, for mundane reasons that had nothing to do with potential trouble or rioting youth. The first date selected, 20 August, turned out to be tentatively reserved for a Reds baseball game, as a fail-safe in case a regularly scheduled game was rained out, and that booking took precedence over any other function. Secondly, because of all the political rows over the concert and the uncertainty of whether it should go ahead, promoter Ross Todd had not actually got around to booking an act!

With less than a month to go the controversial event was cancelled. Jerry was, naturally, infuriated and demanded a full inquiry into the fiasco. 'We are talking about a large sum of money that is lost to an already badly strained budget, simply because an administration or the promoters selected failed to do what they were told to do,' he announced.

At the same time as campaigning for the concert that never happened, Jerry did not neglect his next campaign, his run for re-election at the end of 1977. Never afraid of speaking out on his beliefs, he took a remarkably liberal stance for such a conservative city, invoking the name of then California Governor Jerry Brown, who was dating pop singer Linda Ronstadt at the time and was popularly known as 'Governor Moonbeam' because of what many people regarded as his unrealistically idealist views. Jerry rejected Republican calls for reducing city services and therefore tax, as people moved from the city centre to the surrounding towns and villages in the Ohio countryside. Instead, he said, the city should be improving services and providing more resources for the people at the bottom end of society to make the city a better place for all residents.

'The people who have left the city are the more affluent who can afford to live in the suburbs,' he repeated in campaign speeches from spring to late autumn. 'That leaves Cincinnati with a higher density of low-income people who have a great need of services. So you can't propose to offer less services in the face of that fact. It was Jerry Brown who coined the phrase "More is not necessarily better". I do not dispute that contention but it is only half the story. For if more is not necessarily better, neither is less. I reject the notion that government is doing too much. In fact, in light of all the poverty, all the inequality that still exists in today's world, to agree to do less is morally unacceptable. If we are prepared to say that the time has come to cut back, then we must first ask, "For whom shall we do less?"'

At the start of his official campaign he followed a time-honoured liberal track of visiting down-and-outs to report on their plight. But he was such an effective, emotional, speaker, that when he brought the subject up at a fund-raising dinner, it came across as a matter of genuine concern rather than a trite political cliché, resonating with the implication that if society abandoned those at the bottom it would make it easier for the government to harden its heart against other people in need.

'Earlier this week I visited the Alcoholic Drop-in Centre in downtown,' he said. 'If hopelessness were visible, it was there in its purest form. Seventy-five men, homeless, hungry and helpless, stumbling in at all hours of the night. They ask the city for help. Just a place to bed down, even a floor. What should we tell them? Are these the people for whom we shall do less? What about our kids? Shall we close their schools? And what about our traditional middle-class family? All of a sudden out of a job with a heavy mortgage and large medical bills hanging overhead? Are these the people for whom we shall do less? Let's not get involved in the argument that, "I made it on my own, why can't they?" We will not do less. We cannot do less. I will not be a party to it.'

Jerry's passionate campaigning served him well. When the citizens of Cincinnati went out to choose nine representatives from a field of 24 on 8 November 1977, they resoundingly voted for Jerry, who was not only the top vote-getter but outstripped his nearest rival by some 8,600 votes, collecting 75,000 votes, nearly 30,000 more than in his previous race. He was astonished and made no secret of the fact he was proud and overjoyed. He was determined to make his comeback complete by becoming mayor, the role he had lost three years earlier because of 'the cheque incident'.

'I was absolutely shocked how well I ran,' he told *Cincinnati Enquirer* reporter Bob Weston the day after the election. 'It was a weird sensation for me as the results came in and my lead steadily widened. I was pretty confident I would be re-elected but I had no illusions about leading the field. Right now I am most interested in becoming mayor. I'm not hiding that fact. After that, I really don't know about my future. There are attractive parts about holding either federal or state office. I love what I do as a councilman and that obviously communicates itself to the public. I know it's self-serving, anything I say about my job, but I think the public knows I work hard at it, dealing with constituent problems and providing services. If I can't get their streets fixed, they're not going to care whether I'm a liberal or much about what my political views are.'

He touchingly paid tribute to his beloved daughter Katie and the influence she had already had on his life. 'Her eye problems have helped me to see better what is important and what isn't,' he said.

Katie might have been legally blind, but she had helped to give her father a vision of the future he wanted to see for Cincinnati.

CHAPTER 9

For the second time in three and a half years Micki Springer was nervously getting used to the idea of becoming lady mayoress. This time around, however, it was a surprise; she was not spending a year easing her way in as wife of the vice-mayor who had been picked to become the next mayor.

As TV crews, reporters, friends and political cronies headed up the driveway of their detached house on Western Hills Avenue, less than a mile from their previous home on Shirley Place, Micki, caught out casually dressed in green cords, frantically cleared Katie's toys from the living-room floor and tried to tidy up and make space for the people crowding in. Jerry, greeting all comers, was in his element, shaking hands, smiling for the camera, chatting on the phone. Micki, on the other hand, tried to dodge the photographers as she muttered, 'You don't know how much I hate this.'

Jerry's appointment as mayor was by no means a foregone conclusion, despite his stunning victory at the polls. Once again the city had a Democratic–Charterite coalition and it was assumed, inside and outside the council, that the tradition of splitting the mayor's duties between the two for a year each would continue.

As far as incumbent Mayor Jim Luken was concerned, that meant he would stay on in office. He recalled past precedents where, under the power-sharing agreement, the mayor who had served for the second year in the council term would keep the office for the first year of the next term, assuming the coalition retained power. Furthermore, although he ran second to Jerry, he had won a respectable 62,000 votes, nearly 20,000 more than he had two years earlier and claimed this proved that the voters actually preferred him after they had seen his performance as mayor.

He also pointed out that he and his predecessor, Charterite Mayor Mrs Bobbie Sterne, were generally regarded as having been a successful team and added, 'Therefore I think this should be the leadership in the next two years.' Diplomatically, Jerry avoided criticising his friend and colleague. 'Yes, I would like to be mayor and I am sure every other council member would like to be,' he said as he left for New York on a family visit three days after the election. 'I think my strong finish puts me in a good position. I have demonstrated that I have great popular support. I hope I can get that kind of support from council members.'

The Democrats were anxious to avoid the appearance of a public split and popular sentiment was certainly behind Jerry. Even columnist Frank Weikel predicted that Luken would not be able to hold on and that Jerry would not only become mayor but that the following year he would run as lieutenant governor of Ohio. The four councilmen, Jerry, Luken, James Cissell, Luken's vice-mayor and David Mann, met for hours without being able to reach a decision. Then, suddenly, Luken changed his mind. On Monday 28 November he announced he was holding a press conference at 9.30. Jerry and Micki thought he was talking about 9.30 the following morning. Instead, the meeting went ahead that same evening, which was why Micki was tidying the house and welcoming visitors when she would normally have been getting ready for bed.

Luken did not simply withdraw from the race. He specifically said he was yielding in favour of Jerry, to prevent a rift in the party. 'I'm very grateful to him,' Jerry immediately said. 'I think if he is right and I turn out to be the choice, he has set a very high example of what the mayor should be and I hope I can be as good a mayor as he is. I think I'm in a good position, but there has never been a formal vote taken.'

Once again Micki was questioned about how she saw the role of the mayor's wife. 'I don't think this makes me more a politician,' she said, adding that she would not follow the example set by the wife of former Mayor Theodore Berry, who used to appear at functions and make speeches on his behalf if he was double-booked. 'Certainly I wouldn't be as active. I'm just not the kind of person who can speak before large groups.' More reflectively, she went on: 'I don't know that I thought he would be coming this close to mayor again. But I knew he would be successful. I have confidence in him.' Then she had to break off to stop her over-enthusiastic husband, who had just sung a song into a TV microphone, from calling his parents in New York. 'They'd probably be in bed,' she reminded him.

Jerry was voted mayor by his colleagues with no fuss on the evening of 30 November, and took office the next morning. When he arrived at City Hall for his swearing-in ceremony, he was in high spirits and admitted he had been out celebrating and had not gone to bed until 4.30 that morning, then realised with a start that he had forgotten to write a speech. 'I spent from 5am to 9.30am writing it,' he admitted. He set the tone for his term as mayor as soon as he accepted office, making a sly reference to the sex scandal by joking as soon as he was sworn in, 'Whew! It wasn't easy getting here!' Then, in an acceptance speech that was surprisingly graceful and gracious considering the conditions under which it was written, he returned to his favourite political theme of local control, and was generous in his praise for both the new blood in city government and the veterans to whom he was a young whippersnapper of a mayor at just 33.

'Neighbourhood decisions must be made by the people living there,' he told a crowd of about 400 people in City Hall. 'This is more than a philosophical imperative. It is, I believe, the only way our cities can survive.' Welcoming the other eight members of the council to the new session, he went on, 'To those of you who are young, come on in. There is room here for all of us. To those who have already invested their years of sweat and toil to making our town the very liveable city it is, thank you. Thank you for letting this son of refugees from the Nazi Holocaust make it in America.'

He also thanked Luken for making his new position possible. 'Your magnanimous decision of three days ago to let me share in the leadership of our community has not only presented me with a great honour but also a significant challenge and that challenge is to be as good a mayor as you were,' he said. Then he walked into his new office, sat down in the mayoral chair and said, 'Bring on the Rolling Stones!'

One of his first official acts as mayor was to welcome Vice-President Walter Mondale to Cincinnati, ferrying him around the city in his official limousine. It was one of only a handful of times he used the limo; for all his flamboyance, he preferred to travel in a more low-key style.

The city expected great things of Mayor Springer. He had

scarcely got his feet under the table when the *Cincinnati Enquirer* began speculating where his political career would take him next. Editorial writer Robert Clerc declared: 'Jerry Springer, at age 33, is not going to spend the remainder of his active political life on Plum Street. He's a natural — bright, personable, in love with public life and, recently, more settled in his approaches to public business. Given that, and recalling comments he has made at various times over the past several years, one has to wonder where Springer's road is leading him.' Congress was out, Clerc concluded, because Jerry's old friend and former council colleague Tom Luken had just unseated a Republican, but like Frank Weikel, he raised the possibility of Jerry running for Lieutenant Governor. 'It would be naïve indeed to expect that Mayor Springer of Cincinnati will not be sampling, testing and probably influencing some of the decisions to be made by Ohio Democrats,' he concluded. Ohio Democratic Chairman Paul Tipps and Hamilton County Democratic Co-chairman John Wiethe also announced after a party central committee meeting, attended by Jerry soon after he took office, that they would back him as either lieutenant governor or Secretary of State for Ohio the following year.

Jerry admitted he did have greater ambitions, but insisted he wanted to serve Cincinnati well before moving on to higher things. He made no excuses about his plans to be outspoken on issues he thought were important, even at the risk of being criticised for being a populist jumping on soap-boxes for the sake of self-publicity. 'One of my duties as a public official is to focus attention on issues I believe to be important. If I learned one thing from the 1960s, it's to get on the six o'clock news. Civil rights and anti-war activists show that you could influence public opinion by getting on the news.'

As for the future, he knew that any political opponents would dredge up the cheque incident in an attempt to discredit him. But he said, 'I'm tougher than I look. I'm not just a wide-eyed kid gazing round in amazement. I'm aware of my political possibilities in the future. By this time I suppose I've heard all the Jerry Springer jokes. So, personally, I know I can face that again. Politically I don't see it as a big obstacle. The point is, they can't talk about 1974 without talking about what's happened since then — leading the ticket, getting to be mayor. The more they talk about 1974, the more remarkable the comeback appears.' As things turned out, however, when Ohio Lieutenant Governor Richard Celeste announced his short-list of running mates in his bid to become governor of Ohio in 1978, Jerry's name was missing. It appeared to be a last-minute decision of Celeste's to drop him from the possible contenders. Just two days earlier, amid speculation that he would be named, Jerry had said, 'It would be presumptuous of me to say whether I'd accept it before I know whether it's going to be offered.'

He returned to his familiar theme of neighbourhood rights and responsibilities in his inaugural address to the council. 'There are only three geographical entities to which we can relate,' he said. 'Our country, our region and our immediate neighbourhood, the eight blocks around our house. It is this last one that determines more than anything whether we choose to stay in the city or move out and take our contribution to the tax base with us. We have invested many dollars, much time and effort, in the beautiful development of our downtown. It has done much good for our entire community and we must work to keep that momentum going. But at the same time we must recognise that if a person's immediate neighbourhood is deteriorating — if the houses are boarded up and the streets are unlit — it does us no good to tell him, "Hey, but downtown is beautiful." He'll merely get up, leave the city and enjoy downtown while living in Indian Hill (a small town on the outskirts of Cincinnati).

'If we start giving people more control over their local neighbourhood in terms of budget decisions, setting priorities, zoning and development, then they are more likely to be satisfied with their neighbourhood, and, consequently, more likely to stay. We then solidify the tax base, and the ethnic and cultural diversity that is the lifeblood of our city remains.'

Later he launched the Urban Arts Corps, a volunteer body assigned to run street parties and parades and arrange local activities like painting walls. Further on in his term he called for the city to subsidise low-interest mortgage rates, fixed at eight per cent, to attract middle-class housebuyers to revitalise depressed areas.

As he settled in to his new position, Jerry was presented with a Christmas crisis — a bus drivers' strike. In the USA unions negotiate fixed-term contracts for pay and conditions, rather than open-ended agreements. Drivers and mechanics at Queen City Metro, the publicly run bus company, hoped to take advantage of the fact that their contracts ran out at the beginning of December to squeeze a better deal out of the local transport authority by threatening disruption to the public and shopkeepers at the busiest time of the year. One of their demands was that their new contract would again expire in December, while management offered them a deal that would end in March, to prevent Christmas blackmail in the future.

Jerry talked privately to leaders on both sides, and encouraged them to talk. He publicly criticised both sides for not reaching a quick settlement. As the dispute dragged on he urged the Southwest Ohio Regional Transit Authority to stand firm in refusing another December contract. Intervening in the strike was a tricky matter for Jerry, because his predecessor, Mayor Luken, was a career union organiser and much more experienced in the delicacies of labour relations.

Ironically, he won praise from the head of the local branch of the Amalgamated Transit Union for his call for an end to the December contract. 'He's mayor of all the people,' said Gene Metz. 'If I had been in his place I would probably have done the same.' As well as encouraging a settlement, Jerry, with the help of Charterite councillor Kenneth Blackwell, produced a contingency plan to help members of the public, dealing with the combination of Christmas crowds, congested traffic and winter weather. They threw open city-owned car parks in the evenings and at weekends, paying for the service with money that would normally have gone to subsidise Queen City Metro. They set up an emergency phone number where the elderly, poor or sick could call voluntary agencies like the Council on Aging and the Red Cross to arrange emergency transport. And Jerry called on residents to help their neighbours: 'I am urging every member of this community to take up the spirit of the season and some time in your day to check up on your next-door neighbours. See if they want a ride. See if you can run an errand for them. To the young, here's our chance to show what kind of a contribution we can make to our city. This is the time for help.' And he called on the strikers and management alike to let a little Christmas spirit into their negotiations: 'Leaving a city of nearly half a million people hanging and twisting in the wind seems highly inconsistent with that tradition.' As it happened, the strikers rejected four contracts before the strike was finally settled at the end of the year, with the new contract expiring on 7 January. Jerry was later to say that settling the strike was his greatest achievement as mayor.

Jerry would again call for concerted voluntary efforts later that winter, when another strike, this time a nationwide coal strike, brought an energy crisis to the city. He asked for energy conservation, and his citizens responded so well that Cincinnati could afford to light freeways at night, when other cities were forced to leave them dark despite the snow and ice that made driving dangerous. The city was so successful at cutting back demands for gas and electricity that when the state brought in a plan to allocate coal, for a time it looked as if it would be penalised by getting less than other places.

While Jerry was getting used to the strains of office during his first month as mayor in December 1977, at home Micki was also becoming accustomed to her new role, although she was not at all sure what it was. 'My role as the mayor's wife?' she told the *Cincinnati Enquirer* in a rare interview. 'I wasn't aware there was any statute, or that the City Charter defined a role for a mayor's wife. I think it's something you grow into. When I married Jerry in 1973 I knew of his political aspirations and I wholeheartedly agreed with him. My role as a wife, and I would suspect his role as a husband, is always to be supportive. I support his self-fulfilment and I expect Jerry to support my self-fulfilment. In marriage two people can't be happy unless they are happy independently. I give Jerry my total support to allow him to get himself into situations that are both challenging and rewarding.'

She made it plain that Katie, now 17 months old, was still her first priority, but that because of her experiences with Katie she wanted to let the world, or at least her fellow Cincinnatians, know what opportunities there were for the disabled. 'I think it is important, at least to me, to be home with Katie in her first years. I did this by choice because of those beliefs. But that doesn't mean I won't change later and do different things. One of the things I think I am most interested in now, because of our Katie's handicap, is telling the public how fine the Cincinnati Public School programme for the visually handicapped is.

'Katie is enrolled in what is called early childhood education for handicapped children. She has home video every Monday and Thursday by an instructor in the department. Later, when she's three, she'll be able to enrol in the nursery programme for the visually handicapped. And the infant stimulation programme is fine, too. You don't really know how many good programmes the school system has got until you're in need of one of them personally.'

With what appeared to include a veiled reference to abortion rights — a highly controversial topic in the American heartland, since abortion had only been legalised in the USA in 1973 and was still a hot political issue — she went on: 'I hope all other women have the opportunity of choices to make. That's what the women's movement is all about, women having the right to make their own choices. That's why I decided to stay at home with Katie. I think it is an important contribution to send out into the world a well-adjusted, secure child. And I think that begins early in life. I totally support the woman's movement. I think it is immoral in 1977 that we are still trying to decide whether women should have equality, the right to make choices, the right to their own decisions.'

Micki reiterated her earlier nervousness about making public appearances, although she was more confident about overcoming her fears than she had been three years earlier. However, she was still happy to let Jerry take most of the limelight. 'Today I feel I'm not yet comfortable speaking before large groups because I'm not used to that yet,' she went on. 'But I feel I can grow into the role. Jerry's only been mayor a few days and part of that time he's been out of town. Until we sit down and talk about it, I won't know. If I find something that appeals to me I'll pick it up.' And she laughed, 'Actually, I'm quite happy with all the publicity Jerry gets. He's quite a public person. When someone describes him as a charismatic, electric personality, I have to agree. Most people say you either love him or hate him!'

In early 1978 Jerry walked straight into an emotional row when he declared Sunday 22 January — the fifth anniversary of the landmark Supreme Court decision on Roe versus Wade, which legalised abortion in the USA — Respect Life Day at the request of anti-abortion activists. The original request came from Jerry Schutzman, president of the Greater Cincinnati branch of Life Is For Everyone (LIFE). Schutzman said: 'It marks the fifth anniversary of the Supreme Court's unconstitutional decision to allow the killing of unborn babies by abortion.' Fellow LIFE member Ann Brown added, 'It would be alarming, indeed, if Cincinnati City Council members felt uncomfortable declaring a Respect Life Day.' The pro-life group was planning a candlelit vigil on that Sunday on the steps of the county courthouse, and was to send a delegation of 70 people to an anti-abortion rally in Washington, DC the next day.

As soon as the announcement was made, pro-choice groups responded with fury. Sue Gettys, media representative for the local branch of the National Organisation for Women (NOW), told Jerry: 'This is our day because it is the fifth anniversary of the Supreme Court's decision granting women the right to control their bodies. We are angry and we are outraged that you would proclaim this day in honour of an organisation which would deny women their constitutional rights.'

The NOW pointed out that abortion was an accepted fact in Cincinnati: 'Approximately 12,000 abortions were obtained by women in the city of Cincinnati in 1977. This figure represents the number of women whose lives have been saved from suffering emotional, physical and economical stress that an unwanted pregnancy would have made upon them.' The pro-abortion Freedom of Choice coalition was even planning a rival rally to the pro-lifers, beside a statue of Abraham Lincoln in the city's Lytle Park.

Faced with the protests Jerry, who admitted he was personally pro-life, made a bizarre decision. He declared 22 January Freedom of Choice Day as well! At the time he said he was happy to declare a special day for any organisation that wanted one. 'Either everybody gets a day if they want it, or nobody gets a day,' he said. However, a few months later he did turn down a request for a John Birch Day in honour of an ultra right-wing, anti-communist society named after a Baptist minister and US Intelligence officer who was killed by Chinese communists in 1945 and is regarded by society members as the first victim of the Cold War. 'It's one we just didn't feel comfortable issuing,' was the only explanation he offered.

He did, however, pose happily with an actor dressed up as Chewbacca the Wookie, a huge, hairy creature from outer space who was the co-pilot and pal of Harrison Ford's character Han Solo in the cult, smash-hit movie *Star Wars*, to celebrate the first anniversary of the film's release. And Jerry once even proclaimed an entire week devoted to the tuba, an instrument he had played in high school, and even jokingly challenged Michael Thornton, who played the instrument in the Cincinnati Symphony Orchestra, to a duet of 'Duelling Tubas', based on the country instrumental 'Duelling Banjoes'. 'That spawned requests for every other instrument in the Symphony,' recalled his administrative assistant, Howard Wolkoff.

After the abortion row, Jerry soon ran into another controversy involving two diametrically opposed groups — self-proclaimed Nazis and their detractors. A Nazi group applied for a permit to hold a march in the city and a 'Rally for the Freedom of Rudolf Hess', the last Nazi prisoner held by the Allies, a lone inmate in Germany's Spandau prison. The permit was duly granted in accordance with city laws. Immediately there were cries of protest and a group of banner-wielding demonstrators descended on City Hall. Anti-Nazi spokesman Robert Pouden compared the city to Germany in the 1930s and accused the right-wing extremists of singling out blacks and Jews for attack. 'To support a Nazi march is an affront to every working-class person in Cincinnati,' he said.

Jerry, who was all too well aware of the Nazi shadow that had robbed him of so many family members, but who also championed the right to freedom of speech, was outraged. 'Anybody who suggests that this city government is similar to Hitler's Germany is nuts,' he told the protesters. 'If I insulted anybody, I meant to.'

A rather pathetic march of 18 uniformed Nazis carrying a swastika-emblazoned banner rallied on Fountain Square on 29 April, while up to 100 protesters launched a counter-demonstration. Scuffles broke out and six of the counter-demonstrators were arrested for offences including resisting arrest, disorderly conduct and assault and battery on a police officer. None of the Nazis was arrested. It was a minor incident in the life of Cincinnati, but one that would come back to haunt Jerry years later, when he was controversially and briefly hired to commentate for a Chicago TV station and was accused of exaggerating his role in the affair.

Despite the controversy, Jerry maintained his personal popularity. When he announced a $35-a-head breakfast to help him pay off the $2,300 he still owed from his mayoral campaign, 100 tickets were promptly sold.

As he settled into his year of leadership, Jerry was keen to embrace all his constituents. He was acknowledged as having a broad base of support — the young, the old, minorities, the working class, intellectuals — and he made a point of showing his interest in all of them. One of his first acts was to launch a formal dialogue with the Catholic Archbishop, Joseph Bernardin, already a widely respected churchman who would go on to become the highly influential Cardinal of Chicago. Together they discussed the issues and tensions that affected Catholics and non-Catholics alike, especially the need to improve schools and hospitals.

'He is a very significant person who needs to be tapped for the benefit of all of us,' Jerry said after their first meeting at St Louis's Church in downtown Cincinnati. 'I felt it was a very positive thing to do. We are going to get back together again. I felt it was a good first step. I have nothing but good vibes from it.' Archbishop Bernardin also welcomed the meeting, saying: 'I was very happy to receive him and to discuss the wellbeing of the city with him. If he could think of ways I could be helpful as a citizen and as a churchman, I told him I was willing to help.'

Their partnership helped establish a hospice in Cincinnati, only the fourth independent facility dedicated to easing the terminally ill to a peaceful end in the USA. Both issued statements strongly in favour of the move when the local health agency came to a vote on it. 'Cincinnati has an opportunity to join the pioneers in the USA by being the fourth free-standing hospice,' said Jerry. Bernardin said: 'I wish to recommend strongly approval. Sound leadership, full cooperation of the healthcare community and strong community support all give every indication that the Hospice of Cincinnati will succeed.'

While concerned for people at the end of life, Jerry also reached out to the young, including those not old enough to vote, urging students to become involved in politics to help fight the high unemployment of the era — up to 25 per cent in some areas of Ohio — a problem he called 'the Vietnam of the 1970s'.

'Politicians are running your lives and any time you put decision-making into the hands of a few, you've got trouble,' he declared. 'We want to have a say in what our destiny will be, not only in the field of energy but in the field of poverty, the greatest ill facing our generation today. Unemployment is the Vietnam of the 1970s. You have a right to a job, a right to make a living, a right to live. Unemployment is clearly as moral a cause as getting out of Vietnam and the Civil Rights movement.'

He tapped into the concerns of black residents by setting up a Minority Business Task Force to explore ways of encouraging businesses owned by or employing members of minority races. At the time, minorities, not including women and the disabled as separate categories, made up just over 10 per cent of the private workforce and a little more than 20 per cent of city and Hamilton County employees. But they had higher unemployment rates than whites. The task force concluded that the city was not doing enough to encourage minorities, noting that in 1977 Cincinnati contracted out work worth US$44 million, of which only US$1.7 million went to minority companies, even though 12 per cent of all companies in the city fell into that category.

'This is hardly representative of their availability in Cincinnati,' the task force report read. After studying their recommendations, Jerry proposing a quota system that would give companies owned by minorities, or with more than half the workforce minorities, a minimum of 12 per cent of the value of all city business. It would affect not only work ordered directly by city agencies; any contractor who won a bid to work for the city would have to stipulate how 12 per cent of the successful bid would be spent with minority companies. He also brought in a proposal to encourage local contractors by ruling that out-of town bids had to be at least 5 per cent lower than those from within the city. 'The key to this plan is that for the first time we are trying to establish a policy whereby we use our city budget to influence our economy,' he said as he unveiled his scheme. 'What I'm suggesting is that we start exercising some control over our own economy and put a dent in minority unemployment. I consider this a programme of self-help, a way to get the best use of our dollar.'

Reaction to his proposal was mixed, with some business leaders and the *Cincinnati Enquirer* predicting it would be difficult to carry out and would raise overall costs to the city. Joe Hankerson, executive director of the Business Resource Centre of the Chamber of Commerce, disliked the idea of concessions for local companies but thought the quota could work. 'If out-of-town businesses are going to be penalised by the city then I'm afraid of the consequences,' he said. 'In the final analysis, the out-of-town contractor may take his money home but while he's here he has to pay the same taxes that every other business does. I think the 12 per cent figure is realistic, but I don't know if the assumption that more minorities will be hired is accurate.'

Even local union leader William Sheean, executive secretary of the union umbrella organisation the American Federation of Labour and Congress of Industrial Organisations (AFL-CIO) had doubts: 'Obviously we are helping the economy when we spend our dollars at home,' he said. 'I just don't know if there are enough local minority businesses to fill the contracts.' But Tom Garner, executive director of the Cincinnati Human Relations Committee, was enthusiastic: 'It's a great move in the right direction. It is a commitment on the part of the city to help minority businesses. It will give them a piece of the pie.' Despite the reservations, the bill was passed.

Jerry being Jerry, of course, life as the mayor was far from being all work and no play. Ever the extrovert and the showman, he was delighted to respond to a plea to help out a local nightclub, Bogart's, when one of the regular acts, magician Steve Ferris, was double-booked. Without any previous announcement he bounded on to the stage, casually dressed in slacks, an open-necked shirt and a jumper to keep out the bitter February weather. The surprised audience of around 250 greeted him with applause, cheers and whistles, some of them no doubt remembering his days as a coffee-bar balladeer when he first arrived in town, singing in the duo Linda and Gerry.

That night he tried a combination of not very good stand-up comedy, including an explanation of how a London-born German Jew ended up as mayor of Cincinnati, and a question-and-answer session with the audience. He pieced together part of his unrehearsed act with the help of local radio personality Mark Scheerer in the cocktail bar of the club. Then, sitting on a stool on the stage he came out with quips like, 'I was born in England, but I left when I learned I couldn't be king.' And, 'There are two inches of snow coming to Cincinnati. But that's nothing to worry about. We'll just lower the city two inches. Actually, I'd like to move Cincinnati to Florida '

Things became more serious when a member of the audience asked how they could get rid of county prosecutor Simon Leis. 'There's an election coming up in a couple of years,' he pointed out.

However, he lightened the atmosphere up again when he was asked whether, as an attorney, he would like to be a prosecutor. 'Not really,' he relied. 'I'm too easy. I'd slap them on the wrist and let them go and tell them never to do it again. But I *would* make a good defendant. And I have a good credit rating.' The crowd erupted into roars of laughter at his sly reference to 'the cheque incident'. He also promised his young audience that this year there would finally be a rock concert at the Riverfront Stadium, although he did say there would be a condition. 'The only rules will be no smoking the Astro-Turf!' he laughed. Astro-Turf is the artificial grass most indoor sports arenas lay on the floor.

At the end of his set guitarist Leo Kottke, the star of the evening, joined him on the stage. Jerry pulled from his pocket a six-inch long key, the ceremonial key to the city, and presented it to him, saying: 'It isn't worth much because the city vault is empty.' The vault was not, in fact, empty. But during Jerry's stay in City Hall Cincinnati did run out of keys, because he gave so many of them away. By the time he was halfway through his term he had handed out 60 of them, including gifts to visitors Bob Dylan, Joni Mitchell and Dolly Parton, and at $10 a time that made a considerable dent into the $5,340 budget he had for routine office expenses.

He also had a bit of fun when the Cincinnati Bearcats, a college basketball team, had a crucial game for a place in the national championships. He joined with the mayors of the other cities in the competition in having a light-hearted bet, using trademark products of their city or state, on the outcome. Jerry's wager was a gallon of chilli, Cincinnati's signature dish, which, unlike its Southwestern cousins from Texas and New Mexico, is served over spaghetti with grated cheese and sometimes beans and onions. The other bets were a bushel of peaches from Maynard Jackson of Atlanta, Georgia; a very tall mint julep, the traditional drink of Kentucky gentlemen, from William Stansbury of Louisville; a bale of cotton from Wyeth Chandler of Memphis, Tennessee; a bucket of gulf shrimp from Moon Landrieu of New Orleans, Louisiana; a keg of beer from James Conway of St Louis, Missouri; and a gallon of orange juice from Ben Thompson of Tallahassee, Florida.

Before Jerry could make good on his promise to make Riverfront Stadium rock he had his first taste of national TV fame. Always a popular after-dinner speaker, he addressed a Chamber of Commerce dinner one evening when the guest of honour was Dinah Shore, a top singer of the day and sometime girlfriend of actor Burt Reynolds. After Jerry's speech her manager, Charles Pomerantz, joked that he would make a good guest on her TV talk show. Much to Jerry's surprise, a few weeks later an invitation arrived for him to do just that, appearing on a show with the then mayor of Jerusalem, Teddy Kollek, whom Jerry had met six years earlier during a trip to Jerusalem. He was delighted, but, ironically, he told friends he had no ambitions to break into showbusiness. He was simply glad, he said, to have a chance to give Cincinnati some publicity on national TV.

The Chamber of Commerce were so pleased at the invitation that they paid Jerry's air fare to Los Angeles and put him up in a Beverly Hills hotel.

When he arrived he was limping, the result of an unplanned road race two days earlier. The Cincinnati Heart Association had organised a fund-raising mini-marathon through the streets of Cincinnati. Jerry, as mayor, was named honorary chairman of the event, and was asked to shoot the starting pistol the day of the race. Never much of an athlete, he nevertheless donned spiked running shoes and an official Cincinnati Heart

Mini-Marathon singlet over his regular street clothes of a shirt and slacks. Unluckily for him, he stood in front of the thousands of runners as he fired the gun, and lived to regret it.

'Unfortunately, I learned the hard way that when you are starting 4,000 people off doing anything you don't stand right in front of them,' he later said. 'I just started running to get out of their way, and before I knew it I had gone quite a way. Then somebody said, "Why don't you run the rest of the race?" I guess my macho pride took over and I just couldn't stop then.'

It took Jerry one hour and 46 minutes to complete the 15 kilometre course, with both feet bleeding and blistered and his whole body full of aches and pains. 'Even my hair hurt,' he recalled. 'The winner of the race, Bill Rodgers, finished in about 45 minutes. But I knew I was doing badly because every time I saw a policeman he was saying, "Is there anyone else behind him?"' In fact, Jerry was not the final finisher, and even managed a big grin as he breasted the tape. But he told friends, 'From now on, the only running I'm going to do is for office.'

He rested his weary body and aching feet on the flight to Los Angeles and gingerly walked into the studio for his first national TV appearance. Apart from Mayor Kolleck, also appearing on the show were comedian Robert Klein, who had appeared in films like *The Owl and the Pussycat* with Barbra Streisand and George Segal, and Peter Marshall, the popular host of game show *Hollywood Squares*. Jerry was called on to appear in a cooking segment with Dinah and a culinary expert, and admitted, 'I don't even know how to fry an egg!' And when he was asked how chefs in his home state cooked fish he said the most important factor was that the fish was not from the Ohio River. 'If it is, it probably died before it was caught,' he joked.

Back home he regaled writer Steve Hoffman with tales from his 15 minutes of fame. When he drove his hire car to the CBS studios in Hollywood, he joked, security did not want to let him through the gate marked 'talent'. 'I was the only one not there in a Mercedes,' he said. 'They thought I was there to help clean the studio.' Then when he went in to the make-up room the man working on him refused to believe he could be mayor of a major city because of his youth. 'I let him believe I was a comedian who wouldn't be very funny,' he added.

The four guests found plenty to talk about while they waited to go on air, despite their different occupations, Jerry said. He compared notes with his fellow city leader. 'We joked about our common river problems, the Ohio and the Jordan,' he said later. 'There are comparable issues despite the obvious differences between Cincinnati and Jerusalem. In reality, they get up every day to the same problems as we do, the waterworks have to be working, schools have to be built, streets must be repaired, etc.' Marshall was also a former mayor, although an honorary one, of Burbank, the city next to Los Angeles and home to Warner Bros and Disney studios. He also had a cousin in the Pennsylvania state legislature and his brother was running for governor of New Mexico, so he was able to hold his own on the political front. As for Klein, he was born in the Bronx but went to school in Queens, New York, a rival school to Jerry's, so they swapped stories about high school days. Jerry enjoyed his taste of Hollywood and complained, 'On the way to the airport no one stopped me to sign a movie contract. I kept sticking my head out of the window, looking for talent scouts.'

Jerry's next brush with showbusiness was for a completely different reason. Feminists across the country were campaigning for an amendment to the US constitution guaranteeing women equality with men, and the Equal Rights Amendment had to be ratified by 38 of the 50 states before it could be pass into law. The measure had been introduced to Congress every year since 1923 and finally passed in 1972. There was a 10-year deadline for the states to pass it as well. By 1978 Ohio had ratified the ERA and in February that year former mayor Bobbie Sterne introduced a resolution that would ban the city from sending any officials or employees to conventions held in states that had not agreed to the measure. Jerry was a strong supporter of the move.

So when the annual US Conference of Mayors, where civic leaders discuss their common goals and problems, was set for Atlanta, Georgia, a state that had not endorsed the ERA, he refused to attend. 'I would like to go, but since the city has taken a position to establish a formal protest against the non-ERA states, I don't believe that my presence there is so invaluable that the resolution should be circumvented for my purposes,' he said. He also ruled out accepting private contributions to pay for his trip, adding, 'The protest has no significance if there's no price to pay.' He stood firm, even though Atlanta Mayor Maynard Jackson wrote to him personally, asking him to attend a pro-ERA news conference. 'Join us in Atlanta and impress upon the Georgia Legislature how important passage of this amendment is to the entire nation,' he pleaded. And Lila Cockrell, Mayor of San Antonio, Texas, one of the leaders of the ERA movement in the Lone Star State, asked him to reconsider because Atlanta had been chosen before anyone began boycotting non-ERA states.

When Jerry's protest became public, singer Helen Reddy, whose song 'I Am Woman' had become an anthem for the woman's movement, sent a message of support. And actress Marlo Thomas, who had a bit part in the classic British sex comedy *The Knack* and who years later would play the mother of Jennifer Aniston's character in the TV comedy *Friends*, sent him a telegram of congratulations. 'I want you to know I admire your steadfastness, your courage and your forceful stand on principle in not attending the mayors' convention in the unratified state of Georgia. You are fulfilling the definition of what a great public servant you should be, a human being who is unequivocal in his commitment to human rights.'

Jerry's boycott, in the end, did no good. By the time the 1982 deadline came around only 35 states had ratified the ERA, and it has still not been passed into US law.

Ironically, two years later Marlo, daughter of comedian and philanthropist Danny Thomas, would marry TV personality Phil Donahue, the father of talk TV in the USA. He created the world that Jerry would go on to conquer. In 1996 Donahue hung up his microphone after 29 years on the air, unable to match the ratings of the new king of daytime TV, Jerry Springer. *The Phil Donahue Show* and Jerry's were at the time produced by the same Chicago TV company, and after Donahue retired the limousine that drove him to work every day was reassigned to Jerry!

CHAPTER 10

Finally, the great moment was at hand. Jerry was fulfilling his promise to bring rock to Riverfront Stadium. Not just any rock band but The Eagles, whose *Hotel California*, released the previous year, was their third consecutive chart-topping album in the USA. He made the announcement on 22 June 1978, adding that Steve Miller and Eddy Money would also be performing before a crowd estimated to be 60,000.

Not surprisingly, there were immediate protests about the possibility of troublemakers, rubbish, noise and even damage to the Astro-Turf, or artificial grass, that the Cincinnati Reds baseball team and the Cincinnati Bengals football team played on. Critics also looked back to the trouble at the Led Zeppelin concerts at the Coliseum a couple of years earlier, and complained that once again this show would have 'festival seating', meaning first come, first served. Patrons would also be allowed to stand on the field in front of the stage. There were particular concerns because two people had died in accidents following a concert the previous weekend at Cincinnati's Old Coney amusement park.

Promoter Cal Levy assured the city that he and his Riverfront Concerts group would spend $25,000 from their takings to put three layers of protective covering over the Astro-Turf, and promised a thorough clean-up after the show. Jerry, who said that booze would be banned from the concert, also pointed out that the crowds would be no rowdier or messier than a beer-swilling sell-out crowd for a big baseball game. Once again, he attributed opposition to fear of youth.

'The music seems foreign to a lot of people,' he said. 'It is the media nature, because TV has its roots in the 1960s and learned to get news on the street, to look on a rock audience as a foreign invasion when they're just our kids. We're not preparing for the Russians. We're preparing for our kids. We have learned to survive our music. If someone is hurt going home from a baseball game, no one suggests closing down baseball. Sometimes someone is hurt going home from the symphony, or the library.' And he added, 'We'll clean it up afterwards. There are cans and garbage after a Reds' game. We clean it up.'

He also pointed out the financial benefits for the city. With tickets at $12 a head, the show could gross as much as $720,000. The Eagles's cut was to be 40 per cent of the gross, or $288,000, and after the other acts and the promoters had been paid, and insurance, clean-up and other costs taken care of, the city stood to make $150,000 profit.

Riverfront Stadium was not the only rock sensation in town, however. Before The Eagles 16 August show, British rock star Joe Cocker was to headline a bill that included The Outlaws, Richie Blackmore's Rainbow, the Dixie Dregs and Patti Smith on 4 July at Edgewater Raceway Track in the Cincinnati suburb of Miami. Again there were complaints, with local residents recalling that 10 sheriff's deputies had been injured at the last concert there, three years earlier, leading to 10 arrests, and an overtime bill of more than $40,000 for 242 deputies putting in a total of nearly 4,000 extra hours.

Jerry had also struck up an alliance with WEBN, a rock and roll radio station, and launched his career as a broadcaster, although there was no sign in those early days of the media monster he would one day become. He did a regular commentary on life in the city and political issues, the forerunner of the 'Final Thought' he would later use to end his TV show. But there was no pomp or ceremony about Mr Mayor's broadcasts. John Kiesewetter, TV critic of the *Cincinnati Enquirer* who covered Jerry for years, recalled: 'He used to drive over to the station in the early morning and read his commentary, handwritten on a yellow legal pad. He didn't have a key. He used to call the station manager from a public telephone down the road after he parked, and someone would let him in.'

Ever conscious of people who were not old enough to vote for him, Jerry also decided to provide summer entertainment for school students during the long summer holiday. He approached local business leaders with the idea of setting up a summer basketball league to keep schoolchildren occupied and out of mischief. More than 30 businesses responded enthusiastically, and contributed $56,000 to set up the league, which had 48 teams for boys aged 13 to 18 from all the city's high schools. He also intervened when owners of the local ice hockey team, the Cincinnati Stingers, talked about moving the team to another city, and helped persuade them to stay where they were.

Music was the main focus of Cincinnati that summer in 1978, but as autumn approached Jerry got back to more serious work. Two years earlier Court of Common Pleas Judge Gilbert Brettman had declared that living conditions in the notorious Workhouse prison, where inmates lived in appalling conditions, including having to 'slop out' the buckets they used as crude toilets in the absence of proper plumbing, violated the constitutional rights of prisoners. He ordered a series of improvements to be made and then ruled that the work would be a stop-gap measure and that the jail must be closed.

Jerry had proposed the city should build a 50-bed remand prison for evaluating inmates, at a cost of $3 million, in exchange for Hamilton County building a $25 million, 200-bed facility. Strictly speaking the city-owned Workhouse was for prisoners convicted under city bylaws; prisoners convicted of breaking state laws were the responsibility of Hamilton County. In practice most of the Workhouse inmates were state prisoners because, faced with paying for improvements to an old building that was going to be closed anyway, the city quietly dropped most of its criminal bylaws and told the police to charge people they arrested with violations of state law. After nearly two years of political and financial arguments the county began planning a replacement for the Workhouse. However, by then, the closing deadline of 12 October 1978 was fast approaching. The city applied for court permission to keep the old prison open, and ignore the order to carry out improvements for several years until the new jail was finished.

It must have been very embarrassing for ultra-liberal Jerry to find himself subpoenaed by Legal Aid Society attorney Robert Newman, and grilled about why the city chose to spend millions of dollars on other projects that could more easily be financed privately. Of course, he recalled Jerry's horrified reaction the night he spent pretending to be one of the unfortunates locked up there.

'Isn't it true that the city is subsidising Riverside Stadium to the tune of $1 million a year?' he asked the witness. So much for Jerry's brag that the city would profit from the Eagles concert! Newman also quizzed Jerry about the city spending more than $1 million improving and beautifying Fountain Square, the focal point of downtown. He queried how justified it was to use half a million dollars from the city coffers on the 'skywalks', elevated walkways that created a pedestrian link between major buildings — office blocks, the Convention Centre, hotels, shops and the federal courthouse — to protect downtown visitors and workers from the harsh elements of bitterly cold, snowy winters and hot, humid and rainy summers.

Jerry defended the city's lack of action as best he could, pointing out it would cost hundreds of thousands of dollars to install plumbing in a building that would soon close. 'It would be imprudent if not irresponsible,' he insisted. 'The city has spent substantial amounts of money. The city has not spent more money because it knows the Workhouse will be closed. We are doing many things to make the Workhouse as liveable in as possible. We are not shrugging our shoulders and saying it is not our job. You have to remember that most of the prisoners are not the city's responsibility.' He conceded that with a budget of $5.8 million for recreation the city could have spared some for more leisure facilities for prisoners. However, he also pointed out that projects like Fountain Square and the 'skywalks' had been financed by bonds sold to the public, so the city was committed to carry out the work and repay the investors.

Judge Harry Klusmeier did not seem impressed. He commented: 'I'll agree that the situation sometimes bears a strong resemblance to the Nuremberg Trials. People are saying no, it's not my fault, it's his.'

Work on Fountain Square and the 'skywalks' were not Jerry's only contributions to changing the face of Cincinnati. Although he was clearly a left-leaning liberal, he had a keen appreciation of the importance of capital development to keep a city alive. He backed urban renewal and new development, lobbied Washington for federal grants for inner-city renovation and entered into negotiations with the up-market Saks department store, which would eventually lead to them establishing a shop in the heart of downtown.

A few days after his court appearance, Jerry moved on to a wider stage. He attended the National Conference of Mayors with a radical plan to change the tax structure in the USA. Most American residents pay a two-tier income tax, one payment going to the federal government and on top of that, in the vast majority of states, a state tax. Jerry believed that individual cities should have more money to spend at their own discretion, rather than have to fight to get it from Washington or a state capital, but did not want to increase the tax burden on citizens. He proposed that 10 per cent of federal income taxes should be paid, not to the Internal Revenue Service but to the local community. His idea was well received and the National League of Cities endorsed it, and later called for Congressional hearings on the idea.

Jerry found himself with a national audience for the first time since his appearance on *The Dinah Shore Show*, when he was invited to discuss his tax proposal on a half-hour programme on National Public Radio, the US equivalent of BBC Radio 4, with a group of prominent political journalists. Shortly afterwards he was invited, along with about 100 other Democrats from Ohio to visit the White House for a briefing from President Jimmy Carter and Vice-President Walter Mondale. For once being relatively self-effacing, he did not raise the tax matter during the formal session with the President, but talked about it with a White House staff member and was told to make an appointment to discuss it further with Orin Kramer of Carter's domestic affairs and policy department.

He also discussed it with reporters covering the half-day event, saying, 'We can't operate as a free country if we continue to give our decision-making power to Washington. We can't even budget for next year because we don't know what the federal government are going to do.' Warming to his theme he later told the *Cincinnati Enquirer*: 'I have been in government for seven years and I am convinced that, unless we return control of people's lives to the people, we are going to fall apart. I think my programme of retaining 10 per cent of our personal income taxes in the local government to pay for the needed services that we have to live with every day is a method of putting people in control of their own lives. Taxes are constantly increased. Yet they go other places, while the basic services that we are faced with daily suffer from lack of funds.'

Sadly for Jerry, his proposal was doomed to failure. While the US Government makes changes to the massively complicated federal tax laws every year, Democrats and Republicans alike are keen to keep as much money in Washington as possible.

As the end of his term as mayor approached Jerry knew he would have to take down the poster of John Belushi that adorned his office wall and hand over his keys to Charterite councilwoman Bobbie Sterne, and he admitted that he would do so with regret.

He even joked that he was considering changing his name to Bobbie Sterne and refusing to leave.

Rumours began to circulate once again that Jerry had his eyes set on higher things than his now-familiar role as an ordinary councilman. Sources in Washington told the *Cincinnati Enquirer* that he was quietly sounding out Democrats with a view to challenging Senator John Glenn, the astronaut-turned-politician, for his seat in Congress in the 1980 election.

Jerry denied that he was doing any behind-the-scenes campaigning, but admitted he had heard the rumours and did not rule out the possibility of running. 'I'm apparently in a poll that has been taken along with a number of other people in the state,' he said cagily. 'If you are asking me whether I am running against John Glenn the answer is no. The answer now is no. My instincts tell me that is not a reasonable alternative. That's what I think now. I have no idea what I am going to do. All I can say is that I suspect that I'm going to be on the city council. Nothing I say is irreversible, but if you have to think what is probable, it's that I'll be on the city council.'

In a reflective move as he prepared to return to the backbenches, he told the *Enquirer* that leaving office was going to be a psychological let-down. 'I loved being mayor of Cincinnati,' he said. 'I never realised it could be so much fun. I would love to be mayor for ever. I think I will adjust, just as everyone before me has. I don't think the city will suffer from me leaving the mayor's post.' However, he was quick to point out that he still had work to do on measures he had introduced during his year, and that he had no intention of disappearing on to the sidelines. 'I still have the eight per cent loan programme that I introduced, which I want to push,' he went on. 'I feel there are many ways for people to invest in our city. I am not just talking about investing money. I am talking about living here and working here. No matter what else I do, the 10 per cent tax programme is top priority with me. There are many things I want to see done. Yes, I realise that maybe some of the things I was able to do as mayor cannot be done now, but I still have a profound interest in city government. I will not sit around and mope. I am a part of the system. I can serve as a council member as well as a mayor.'

No interview with Jerry, of course, could fail to mention 'the cheque incident', but he dealt with it cheerfully. 'Hey, I was a kid then,' he laughed. 'Believe me, I have learned a lot since then. I have come a long way. A lot of things have happened to me and they were good. I have a daughter. She means the whole world to me. I have been a good mayor since the north Kentucky incident. Everybody makes mistakes. I made a mistake, but I think what has happened since then has proved my stability.'

Looking back on his term of office, he was asked what his greatest achievement had been. 'In reference to a specific act, probably the settling of the transit strike,' he said. 'But I think in general, my biggest accomplishment was setting a tone for mobility — a rock concert in Riverfront Stadium, a summer basketball league and the eight per cent loan programme, which is still pending. When I came on as mayor I said to the youths of this city, "Hey, there is room for all of us." Run that back eight years when I first ran and I said give the 18-year-olds a chance to vote.'

Surprisingly, Jerry bowed out of office under a cloud. In an unexpected reversal of his previous resolve not to attend official meetings in states that had not ratified the Equal Rights Amendment, in accordance with the city policy refusing to fund such visits, he decided to pay his own way to a meeting of the National League of Cities (NLC) in Kansas City, Missouri, a non-ERA state. The NLC was endorsing his 10 per cent tax idea and he wanted to enjoy his moment of glory. At the meeting Charles Wheeler, mayor of Kansas City and head of an NLC task force on revenue and financing, called it the best idea for urban financing he had heard in 30 years, but added the warning, 'Both Mayor Springer and I think we are talking about two to three years down the road before we can get it worked up in final form.'

Back home, however, Councilman James Luken blasted Jerry and Deputy Mayor Ken Blackwell for attending. 'It's like saying you will not cross the picket lines in front of a building and then sneaking around and entering through the back door,' he sneered. 'I think if you are going to tell city employees, who cannot afford to use their own financial resources that they cannot go, while the top city officials who can afford to use their own funds are able to go, then you are making a mockery of the law.' Jerry could only respond, somewhat unconvincingly in view of his previous stance: 'The law is specifically that city funds not be expended, not that city people can't go.' To which Luken promptly responded, 'When it's in their interest you notice they go!'

Despite that unfortunate ending, however, his term of office met with overall approval. Editorial writer Robert Clerc said in the *Cincinnati Enquirer*: 'One year ago, Jerry Springer set the theme for his mayoralty by lacing his acceptance speech with quips. But in with the humour was a statement of serious purpose that has been carried off to a remarkable extent in so brief a term of office. He laughs now and refers to himself as old "Bricks and Mortar" Springer when he talks about the direction the city has taken since his coming to office. He notes that his reputation before taking office painted him as somewhat less than supportive of capital development. He dismisses those misgivings now, pointing out that Cincinnati has the appearance of one large construction site, with all the renewal projects and construction presently under way. Of course, he would not want the new bricks-and-mortar image to get out of hand.

'He directs attention to his success in effectively promoting the first city rock concert, a venture that proved both peaceful and profitable for Cincinnati despite great misgivings. His work in establishing the city's summer basketball leagues and in keeping the Cincinnati Stingers franchise here are a few of the "people" programmes with which the Springer name is more readily associated. He is candid to the point of insistence about his disappointment with the brevity of his term. He has programmes hanging — the proposed city-sponsored home-loan programme and his tax-sharing programme to name but two —which could benefit from the weight of the mayor's office. Jerry Springer stresses the point that the flamboyance which made his mayoralty unacceptable to a good many Cincinnatians, Republicans and Democrats, has not got in the way of his discharge of his mayoral responsibilities. On that point, and it is an important one, even his sharpest critics would have to agree.

'Jerry Springer jokes now that he will change his name to Bobbie Sterne and retain the mayoralty, a tongue-in-cheek admission of his sadness at giving up office. In that sense he is going out with a laugh, which is exactly the way he came in and most likely will be the way he moves on to higher political office. Between the laughs, though, he didn't do badly for Cincinnati.'

There was one good point about leaving behind the responsibilities of being mayor, and the endless calls on his time to speak at lunches and dinners, attend benefits and perform weddings. He was a very popular choice for people wanting to tie the knot and his office even received requests from people wanting him to act as a marriage counsellor. Perhaps couples in troubled marriages thought that the way he had been able to patch up his own marriage problems after 'the cheque incident' and be seen as a loving husband and father meant he could do the same for them!

Being out of office meant more time for Micki, and, more importantly, his dear Katie.

Father and Mother were delighted at her progress and expected more improvement as the years went on. Admittedly she had been a slow developer because of her sight — 'when you don't see you don't explore, ' Jerry said simply. Also, there was more possible surgery in store for Katie, to correct slightly crossed eyes, or the doctors might simply decide to try her with glasses. But she could see better than anyone had expected when she was first diagnosed and Jerry and Micki had great hopes for her. Jerry said she was a double blessing. Not only was she a joy in herself, she had inspired people outside her family to care. 'Because of my position on city council, so many people heard about it,' Jerry told the *Cincinnati Post*. 'Many sent prayers, told us about doctors, gave us suggestions. We've really appreciated it.' And he joked, 'She's been tested for everything now and I understand the only thing she's really weak in is economics ... no, really, her eyes are her only problem. She's going to be whatever she wants to be, whether it's a bank president or a Cincinnati Bengal!'

CHAPTER 11

Jerry was out of the mayor's office but far from out of the public eye. He threw himself a 'Goodbye Mayor Springer, Hello Jerry' party at a local disco and asked his guests to donate $10 each towards a war chest for his next political campaign. Observers were puzzled — it was a year until the next council election and nearly two years before any state elections. Jerry did not drop anything more than vague hints about what the money was for. 'I am certain that I want to stay in public life and most probably run for public office,' he said. 'That looks like it will be re-election to council or possibly something else, but whatever, that campaign is going to take money. Everybody starts in September and October raising money and I thought here was an opportunity to raise some political funds in a rather enjoyable sort of way.'

He expanded on his theme during a pre-Christmas visit to Cleveland, Ohio, pushing his tax plan, when he said, 'One day I'll be in state politics.' Although he was on a serious political mission, his lighter side came out. Cleveland was reeling from a financial crisis and had just defaulted on $14 million in loans. Jerry played the stand-up comedian during his speech, quipping that he had a cheque for $15 million to give them, and that if the Cincinnati Reds gave their star baseball player Pete Rose to the Cleveland Indians, the city would only owe $12 million.

He was in a similar light-hearted mood the week after Christmas, when he took to the stage with a local rock group, Dusty, once more at Bogart's nightclub.

Despite all his optimism about his tax proposals, and his warm welcome in Cleveland, Jerry found little enthusiasm for the idea when he again went to an NLC conference, this time in Washington. He was just another face in the crowd among hundreds of local government politicians, many of them with their own plans they wanted others to endorse, not the big man that people listened to back home. Frustrated, he returned to Cincinnati, straight into the kind of local political controversy at which he excelled.

While Jerry was in Washington, in the early hours of a chilly March morning two police officers, Dennis Bennington and Robert Seiffert, confronted an armed robbery suspect in the suburb of Walnut Hills, a mixed area of big old houses and smaller, newer homes. Shots rang out and both officers were mortally wounded, although one of them managed to shoot the killer as he fled. The city was stunned and shocked, and crowds poured into two churches where Archbishop Bernardin said requiem Masses for them.

The police, already suffering from low morale and embroiled in deadlocked wage negotiations, complained they received no support from the city when they were asked to put their lives on the line. Facing criminals carrying .375 Magnums, they had to respond with less powerful Smith & Wesson .38 specials. They had to keep their shotguns locked in the boot of their patrol cars, and they were frequently sent to patrol dangerous areas alone. There were also simmering undercurrents of racial tension. Cincinnati Police Department at that time was overwhelmingly white and male, and the black community complained that they were too often the target of unjust suspicion.

On Jerry's return he met a group of policemen's wives and pledged that something should be done to stop such tragedies happening in the future. He immediately proposed new safety measures for all police, including the introduction of two-man patrols in high-crime areas, bulletproof vests for all officers on the street, and floodlights and loudspeakers for patrol cars so the officers could stay locked in their cars while ordering suspects to get out of their vehicles. He also proposed a new committee made up of police and their spouses, city administrators and council members to study the problem of police morale.

'Whether we recognise it or not, the city is faced with what I would term a critical problem of morale among our police officers,' he said. 'We are kidding ourselves if we attribute the current negative feelings simply to the latest killings, for the problem is much deeper than that. Police officers of all ranks believe that they are out there alone, with no support from the city, no support from the administration and no support from the council.'

Some 600 police wives jammed into the council chamber when Jerry formally introduced his proposals, along with about 150 high school students, the biggest turnout for a council meeting anyone could remember. They cheered and clapped as Jerry put forward each point of his plan.

Not everybody was so delighted by his proposals, however. His Democratic rival on the council, Jim Luken, who specialised in police issues, was furious at Jerry for hogging the limelight and announcing details of his proposals before introducing them to the council. 'It was the dirtiest trick in the world,' he stormed. During a party meeting the two men practically came to blows, with Luken storming up to Jerry's desk and challenging him to a fist fight, saying, 'Come on, come on.' Only the intervention of party co-chairman John Wiethe kept the pair's hands off each other. Jerry can't have suspected then that 20 years on he would be witnessing brawls like that, and worse, virtually every day.

While the Police Safety Task Force was considering Jerry's proposals another policeman was killed on duty. Officer Mel Henze, investigating the fatal shooting of a woman in a pool hall, was parked in an alley in his patrol car when a gunman opened fire. Five of the six bullets hit their target. A week later the task force issued their report, recommending that Jerry's proposals be adopted. They also called for the police to be armed with .375 Magnums.

Jerry was unhappy about that idea, as were leaders of the black community, who called it overkill. Even though the city had announced plans for an aggressive hiring campaign to attract blacks and women, some people still saw law and order as a racial matter. Jerry, who thought the Magnums were unnecessary, understood the concerns of black residents but said both blacks and white were to blame for the tension. 'The leadership of both communities has placed the issue in such a light that if you favour law enforcement and protection against violent crime you are anti-black,' he complained. 'And if you happen to be black or liberal, you are automatically anti-police or anti-law enforcement. The fact is that the black community bears the greatest brunt and is most often the victim of violent crime. To frame this issue in terms of law enforcement versus black is not only unfair and untrue, but an invitation to a summer of unrest.'

Despite his disappointment at being largely ignored during his trip to Washington for the NLC meeting, Jerry had attracted national attention. Egyptian President Anwar Sadat and Israeli Prime Minister Menachem Begin, who had shared the Nobel Peace Prize the previous year, had just signed an historic peace treaty, despite the objections of other Arab nations. In particular, the problem of the Palestinians, who had lost their land when Palestine was partitioned in 1948 to create the nation of Israel, was unresolved. Egypt and Israel had agreed the previous year, when they signed the Camp David Accords paving the way to the peace treaty, that they would negotiate with the USA to establish some kind of self-government for the West Bank of the Jordan River and the Gaza Strip.

The American State Department, which runs foreign affairs, was sending a 12-person delegation to the Middle East on a fact-finding tour of Syria, Jordan and Israel to discuss the treaty with government leaders. Five members of the group were chosen by the American Council of Young Political Leaders for their potential for involvement in national politics in the future. Jerry was one of them.

He was the only Jew among the six Democrat and six Republican team, and admitted that the first few days of the 18-day trip were difficult for him, listening to officials in Syria and Jordan complain, 'The Jews did this and the Jews did that.' 'It was tough day after day to just sit there and take that,' he explained on his return. Although Syria, where they spent nine days, was bitterly anti-Israel, it had a small Jewish community. Jerry was able to join one of the families to celebrate the Passover seder, the ritual meal commemorating the flight of the Jews from Egypt, while he was there.

The USA did not recognise the Palestine Liberation Organisation (PLO) then and had no official contact with any of its leaders. So Jerry and his colleagues were shocked when they received a message, passed by a private citizen, that Khalid Fahoum, president of the PLO National Council, wanted to meet them. After checking with security forces that such a meeting would be safe, they visited Fahoum at a flat in the capital, Damascus. The PLO wanted Israel to withdraw from the West Bank and the Golan Heights, territory it won in the Six-Day War of 1967. Jerry asked Fahoum whether the PLO was insisting on withdrawal as a condition of starting negotiations, and was able to report to the US Ambassador and the White House that the organisation wanted the

USA to intercede and urge Israel to pull out to its 1967 borders. They also met the Crown Prince of Jordan, son of King Hussein.

He and the rest of the group were thoroughly debriefed when they returned to Washington, especially in view of their contact with the PLO and Jerry, as usual, was outspoken about the trip. He said he understood the frustrations of Palestinians, especially after talking to refugees, but that creating a new, autonomous Palestine was simply not practical, physically as well as politically. He did not hesitate to let the powers that be know that he had come up with a solution to the thorny problem, which had troubled the world for 30 years and cost thousands of lives.

'I told the State Department that the administration must not pressure Israel into making too many concessions that threaten its very existence,' he said. 'There is no question that all Palestinians believe that what is now Israel belongs to them. But the creation of a separate Palestinian state is not the answer; it would pose a threat to Israel's existence, it would not be economically viable and there would not be enough room to absorb all the refugees. It would be the first major step towards all-out war in the Middle East and would jeopardise the security of the only free and democratic society in that part of the world. The West Bank and Gaza cannot exist as a nation itself. There would have to be an immediate move to expand.

'A better alternative would be to move in the direction of possibly taking part of the West Bank and the Gaza Strip, conveying that over to Jordan and then let Jordan establish within its own border a Palestinian sector. Since 60 per cent of Jordan's population is Palestinian, and what is now Jordan used to be part of the mandate of Palestine, that is the most logical country to deal with the problem. That way the area would be more economically viable and demilitarised. I have reason to believe that such a solution would ultimately be acceptable to King Hussein if, in exchange for Jordan creating a Palestinian sector within it, Israel and Egypt would agree to help Hussein maintain stability in his country.'

A few months after Jerry's Middle Eastern tour, the US Ambassador to the United Nations, Andrew Young, resigned after admitting to President Carter that he had met a leading PLO official in New York. Jerry immediately accused Carter of using the American Jewish community as a scapegoat for putting pressure on him to force Young out of office and causing divisions between Jews and blacks. Ironically Young, who is black, was previously a Georgia congressman and one of Carter's biggest supporters when he ran for the presidency.

'Young wasn't forced from office for talking with the PLO,' said Jerry. 'He and Carter have differed on a whole host of things. Carter wanted to get rid of him and the PLO meeting was only the pretext.' He said that despite official US policy, there were regular talks between American officials and PLO representatives, including three recent meetings with the Ambassador to Austria, Milton Wolf, who was himself Jewish. Recalling his own meeting with Fahoum, Jerry added, 'It was clear we were not the only ones he had spoken to.'

Perhaps it was because of his brief taste of the national limelight and his first tentative steps on the world stage, but small-town Cincinnati politics seemed to be losing their glamour for Jerry. As the autumn progressed he automatically started a re-election campaign, but was half-hearted and told friends this could be his last run. 'Running for the sake of running is no fun, no matter what people might think,' he reflected. 'It's not etched in stone, but this might be it. There comes a time when you have to go on to something else, give someone else a chance.'

Once again Jerry came top of the polls, but the Democratic presence on the council was cut from four to two. Unfortunately for Jerry, the other winner was David Mann, who had first been appointed to the council to replace Jerry when he resigned, and who had backed Jerry in his bid to become mayor. In exchange Jerry had promised him that after the next election he would return the favour. However, after the election he made it plain that he wanted to be mayor again, amid veiled threats that if the Democrats did not choose him he would step down after his next two-year term.

'I intend to stay in politics and I would like a leadership role in the city,' he said. 'If the local Democrats don't want me in that role that's their decision and obviously I'll have to look for something else to do in life. I think running first twice in a row solidifies my position as a political person in this part of the state. I think it just demonstrates that last time wasn't a fluke. There are no new horizons in terms of local politics. You can't do better than keep coming in number one.'

Even though it was up to the Democratic party to choose the mayor, Jerry played on his popular appeal in a *Cincinnati Enquirer* interview. Despite his dominant presence on the council for much of the last eight years, he described himself as an anti-establishment maverick who was attractive to the public who felt they had not got a say in how their city was run.

'There's an awful lot of, "We know what's best" going on in City Hall,' he said. 'Maybe the perception is that even though the voters have lived in this city all their lives they feel just as much on the outside as I do in terms of decision-making. Maybe what they see in me is that they're not part of the establishment either. And it's kind of like, "Go get 'em, Jer." It's pure chemistry. People make up their minds about how they feel about candidates the way they make up their minds about how they feel about other people. It's based on trust, instinct. Just a basic feeling that that person's OK. They act initially on their instincts and then later come to rationalisations. You either like someone or you don't. And I've been very lucky.'

The police wives' association, remembering his support earlier in the year, and the Committee of 50, a group of leading black citizens, both endorsed him. But Jerry's luck was about to run out. He asked Mann to step aside, in view of the fact that he had won 20,000 fewer votes and ended in sixth place. Mann refused.

Clearly disappointed, Jerry announced that he would support Mann as mayor, but would not run for council again. 'Two years ago I told Dave that I would support him for the mayoralty and my word is good,' he told a City Hall press conference two weeks after the election. 'One day politics ends and you are left living with the kind of person you really are. I like to think I can be trusted. I do not anticipate running for Council again. I will serve the two years to which I have been elected and beyond that I will have to decide just what to do with my life.'

Mann had to wait a year, however. Kenneth Blackwell took over from Bobbie Sterne, as the Charterites claimed the first year of the split term.

While he was waiting to learn his political fate Jerry took a night off to see The Eagles performing at Riverfront Stadium. Afterwards he went to a party with the band, and leader Glenn Frey presented him with a cheque for $3,000 towards his campaign expenses, in gratitude for his opposition to expanding nuclear power. It was an uneventful night, which seemed to prove Jerry had been right in pushing so hard to open the arena up for rock bands. However, less than three weeks later all the old concerns about rock concerts and many more serious ones were back in the headlines. This time it was not simply a local Cincinnati problem, but a horror that made headlines around the world.

The Who were 30 minutes into their act in front of a

rowdy, sell-out crowd of 18,000 at the Riverside Coliseum on the cold night of 3 December. Many of the fans had been drinking and smoking dope as they queued up waiting for the doors to open, and now they spilled from seating rows into the aisles, some of them starting fights. The *Cincinnati Post* entertainment editor, Dale Stevens, was so disgusted by the crowd behaviour that he decided that, at 58, he could be getting too old for the hurly-burly of concerts. 'People were sitting in the aisles and fights kept breaking out,' he wrote the next day. 'I sat there thinking that this is the last concert I'll ever attend.' He was lucky. He had a choice.

At 8.45 in the evening Coliseum officials found Bill Curbishley, The Who's business manager, backstage and broke the terrible news. Four young fans had died, two from drug overdoses and two from being trampled in a rush to get through the doors. Curbishley was torn. The concert was in full swing and Pete Townshend, Roger Daltry, John Entwhistle and new drummer Kenny Jones, who had taken over after Keith Moon's tragic death the year before, obviously had no idea of what had happened. Nor, from what he could see of the audience, did anyone in the arena. He talked to fire and safety officials, they consulted Mayor Blackwell, and they all agreed that it would be safer to let the show continue than to infuriate the crowd and possibly panic them by pulling the plug on the show and announcing news of the deaths.

So it was not until after the last encore, as concert-goers started filing out of the Coliseum, that most of them learned about the tragedy, which had stained the banks of the Ohio River with the blood of not four, but 11, Who fans, aged between 15 and 24. For seven young men and four young women, an $11 ticket had turned into a passport to death. At least twelve others were seriously hurt and dozens more had minor injuries in what turned out to be a terrible tragedy unrelated to drugs. First reports of the four being killed, two from drugs, were wrong and totally underestimated what was soon to become apparent.

Tickets for the hotly awaited concert had gone on sale on 28 September and sold out in an hour and a half, the fastest sell-out for a concert in city history. Seats on the floor itself, and the upper balcony, were unreserved, so-called 'festival seating'; the rest of the seats, just 3,578, were pre-assigned.

Fans began milling around the plaza area outside the Coliseum as early as one o'clock in the afternoon, despite the bitterly cold weather and the fact that the doors were not due to open until seven, for the concert at eight. They drank beer and passed joints around, but caused no trouble. By six o'clock there were some 6,000 gathered, with 25 police officers acting as security. Ironically, Lt Dale Menkhaus, in charge of the police detail, would say later that the cops commented among themselves that it was one of the most orderly rock crowds they had ever seen.

However, at seven o'clock, when the doors were due to open, the fans became restive. Someone hurled a bottle at one of the gates, breaking the glass on the door. People rushed forward, trying to force the door open, and Coliseum staff hurriedly opened that gate and two or three others. A surge of bodies pressed towards the narrow entrances and people began to fall. Those who wanted to stop were pressed forward by the crush behind them, couples were separated, friends could not help their fallen companions to get up before they were swept on in the stampede. Screaming and shouting, the mob forced their way into the stadium, those with festival seating tickets rushing for the forward rows, people with reserved places reaching them gratefully, glad to be out of the chaos. But even fans who had seen others fall in front of them and those who inadvertently trampled over the fallen had no idea of the enormity of what had happened.

By the time the last stragglers had made it into the auditorium, and before The Who struck their first chords at around 8.15, the area around the Coliseum was a disaster zone. Crushed bodies, bleeding and beaten survivors crying, piles of shoes and clothes that had been ripped from the victims of mindless, involuntary mob violence, littered the plaza. Police and firefighters frantically gave the kiss of life to injured and even the dead, where they lay on the plaza, because the Coliseum first-aid room was too small to cope with the victims.

Fleets of ambulances ferried the injured to local hospitals and the dead to the Hamilton County Mortuary. Dr Alexander Trott, supervisor of the emergency room at Cincinnati General Hospital said the deaths were caused by multiple cuts and haemorrhages — suffocation would later be ruled the official cause of most deaths — and added grimly that there was, 'some evidence of footprint-like injuries'. As word of the tragedy spread throughout the city, though not to the concert-goers, worried parents started calling the police, asking about the safety of their children.

Mayor Blackwell, in office for only three days, started planning how he would handle the inevitable fallout and rock fan Jerry raced to the scene, breaking the news to *Post* writer Stevens on his way out. 'Not until I was leaving and met Council Member Gerald Springer coming in and heard about the deaths did I realise, with a twinge of undeserved guilt, that I had come to see a concert and in reality, I had been to a funeral,' he wrote.

Police, security officials and fans who had been swept into the mêlée pieced together what had happened. Lt Menkhaus revealed that the police knew people were in trouble but were powerless to do anything about it. 'Some of the people came up to us and said people were down,' he said. 'But we couldn't get to them. It was impossible to get through. I couldn't send my men in individually for fear of them getting hurt. I got them all together and we forced our way through. We found the first body at 7.54pm. The problem lies in such a large crowd attempting to gain entrance through too few doors. Few of those in attendance had any knowledge of the seriousness of this situation.'

Incredulously, officials reported that concert-goers who did realise things were going badly wrong did not seem to care. Fire Marshall Clifford Drury, who arrived on the scene minutes after the alarm was raised, said, 'I appealed to Lt Menkhaus to disperse those people. They weren't concerned about people dying on the plaza. They wanted to get in and hear that damn concert. They were like a crowd of mad bulls.'

Horrifyingly, survivors confirmed what he said. 'People couldn't care less,' said Peggy Matthews, then 27. 'There were broken bottles all over the place. People were kicking and shoving. They would rather see The Who than help someone who was dying.'

Diana Cubert, 20, had a narrow escape when she stumbled at a doorway, fell and was trampled. 'I think my boyfriend walked right over the top of me and didn't know,' she recalled two days later in hospital, where she was treated for badly bruised legs. 'I lay there at least for 15 to 20 minutes. They were laying on and standing on my legs. You could feel their feet move back and forth on your legs. I wanted out so bad but I couldn't move. I was pinned to the ground. I thought I was dead. I didn't think I would make it.'

Her boyfriend, Marty Stonely, who was 24 years old at the time, added, 'It was disgusting. Whoever was the strongest stayed up. I went down about five times. You grab onto somebody and pull yourself up. I was just praying. I didn't think I was going to get out alive.'

Not everyone was completely callous. Terry Thomas, 18, who lost his shoes and cut his feet badly on broken glass, said, 'My girlfriend, she's about 5ft 2in, couldn't breathe. This big guy came pushing through the crowd, picked her up over his head so she could breathe. He held her up for five to ten minutes. We had to fight our way out. I didn't even know about my feet. I started walking away leaving blotches of blood.'

Mark Williams, 20, said, 'I was all the way on the bottom, on the cement. People on the bottom were yelling they were dying. I grabbed this guy by the shirt and said, "wake up". I slapped him in the face. He did not move.'

Not surprisingly, people wanted someone or something to blame. Festival seating was named one of the villains and so were The Who. Lt Menkhaus reported that they had turned up late for their sound check, forcing a delay in opening the doors. Bill Curbishley, the band's business manager, denied that and said the group did their sound check between 6.30 and 7, and that the doors opened only five minutes late. Lt Menkhaus, however, said no doors were open until after the first one was broken at 7.20. He added that he had discussed the possibility of opening more doors because the crowd was so large and restless, but was told the Coliseum did not have any more ticket collectors to man them.

Singer Roger Daltry blamed bad planning for the tragedy. Close to tears the morning after the disaster, he said: 'I'm a performer. You're talking about city officials and promoters who arrange the details of a concert. It's outside the group's control. If the deaths had occurred inside the hall this could be the end of our career. We have an energetic stage act but it's not violent. It's the worst thing that's happened since Keith Moon died. I guess it sounds kind of trite to say that life has to go on. I just hope to hell we can learn something so it doesn't all go to waste. Festival seating's been going on for years and has never been a problem before. That hall had 50 exits and I would guess 50 entrances as well. We know for a fact only three were open even though they tried to say today there were more. The whole thing was ridiculous and totally insane.'

He also pledged to contact the families of the dead: 'I know they're going to feel bitter. I just hope they know anything we could have done to avert it, we would have. There's all this talk about benefits but money won't buy any one of them back.'

That evening, at a concert in Buffalo, New York, which they played to a crowd protected by beefed-up security, he said, 'You all know what happened yesterday. There was nothing we could do about it. We were totally shattered. We lost a lot of family and this show is for them.'

As the inquests on both the dead and the event itself went ahead in Cincinnati, Coliseum concerts by Blue Oyster Cult on 14 December and Aerosmith on 21 December were cancelled. A few weeks later a January concert by ZZ Top was also scrapped.

Jerry wasted no time in getting involved in the aftermath: 'One of the many tragedies of last night is that somebody saw what was happening, had the right remedy and yet didn't believe he had the authority, nor did the people he was talking to believe he had authority, to carry out what might have saved those lives.'

He also spoke out against allowing the tragedy to renew calls to ban rock concerts because of the potential for trouble. In a council meeting two nights after the concert he said, 'I didn't know any of the 11. But then again, I knew them all. They loved and cried and laughed and yelled and felt lonely and sometimes felt insecure and sometimes as if they owned the world. It was all ahead of them, a mere step through the doorway. But the doors wouldn't open and they died in the crush.

'No. People die of failing hearts, colliding cars, fired guns or falling planes. They do not die in human stampedes. No, it can't be. But it is. Death visits us all. It makes no value judgments. The big, the small, rich and poor, even the good die young, but when it happens to 11 so young it constitutes life's toughest punch in the nose. It cries out for explanation. Why? But inevitably finds none.

'Surely we will react. There will be task forces and investigations. We will find out exactly what happened and do whatever is necessary to see that it will never happen again. We will legislate against festival seating, which invited crowds to come early and push in so as to get a good seat, and security and order at the concerts will be beefed up. Certainly one thing seems clear just 36 hours after the tragedy, and that is that if the police had the authority to order all the doors opened, regardless of what else was or wasn't done, the crush would have been averted and those lives saved.

'But beyond all these things that we now know that we will now do, two things stand out in my mind. First, that no matter how long we look for scapegoats, whether it be the Coliseum or the promoters or The Who or the police or whomever, nothing is going to bring those 11 young people back. And second, there is a temptation in light of such tragedy to withdraw, to say no more Coliseum, no more crowd events. I don't believe that that is the answer. We should not shut out the outside world. Nobody died Monday night because of a song or a band. They died because in the chaos and the electricity of the moment, we forgot to care about the human being who was standing in front of us.'

Incredibly, while people were still searching for somewhere to pin the blame, Jerry himself came under fire. Local resident Joan Beck reported that she had written to him on 31 October, complaining about audience behaviour, including heavy drug use, during a Jethro Tull concert attended by her son at the Coliseum. He replied that he had no control over the privately owned Coliseum. After The Who tragedy, she complained he had effectively ignored her warnings.

No controversy concerning Jerry could really be complete without a comment from his *Cincinnati Enquirer* adversary Frank Weikel: 'The committee charged with making a study of the deaths of 11 young people at The Who rock concert will find the problems and concerns about such concerts are not new ... BUT THEY HAVE BEEN IGNORED. On July 10 1977, this column expressed concerns about rock concerts and dealt with a rock concert that was scheduled to be held at Riverfront Stadium. It quoted views of Councilman Jerry Springer and the late Jim Luken, who was mayor of Cincinnati in 1977. Springer favored holding the concert. He gave assurances to the public that "all will be well" and he pointed to the revenues realised by the city by such events. Jim Luken didn't show the same enthusiasm. He said, "We've had enough trouble with festival seating at rock concerts at the Coliseum, which is not totally under the city's control but we SHOULD NOT approve festival seating for a rock concert with a potential of 50,000 in Riverfront Stadium." THIS COLUMN HOPES THAT FESTIVAL SEATING WILL BE ONE OF THE THINGS THE COMMITTEE WILL SUGGEST BANNING.'

Despite Jerry's support for concerts in principle, he agreed with the ban on festival seating. Perhaps because he was the one council member who was actually known to like rock, promoters Electric Factory Concerts chose him to inform that they were proposing a voluntary halt to concerts until at least the end of February 1980, while the investigations continued. Although Mayor Blackwell said that interim safety improvements for large events guaranteed public protection, Jerry disputed this and said he would have proposed a moratorium on concerts if the promoters had not beaten him to it. He told the council, 'I know you are convinced that everything is under control down there, but the public doesn't believe it and I don't believe it.'

CHAPTER 12

After the trauma of The Who tragedy, life went on in Cincinnati, and Jerry appeared to be becoming increasingly disenchanted with political life on the local level. However, he always enjoyed a good political fight, so when the opportunity to take on Charterite Mayor Ken Blackwell in an arena very different from the council chamber came along, he jumped at the chance. Both men agreed to leap into the wrestling ring at a Convention Centre Sports Show, not with each other but with a 27-stone bear called Victor. Not surprisingly, they both lost, with Jerry left nursing a bruised eye and Blackwell a broken little finger.

'I'm a little sore,' Jerry admitted after the fight, joking that he had gone into the ring because Blackwell promised the bear would not harm him. 'Victor turned out to be a Charterite,' he laughed. When he was asked whether Blackwell's fracture meant he was no longer qualified to lead the city he snapped back, 'That question assumes he was qualified to begin with!' Blackwell, who fought second, did claim a moral victory. 'The bear didn't rassle any more that night,' he quipped.

That light-hearted romp must have given Jerry a taste for the spotlight of entertainment as well as politics. He signed up to host a beauty contest for Miss Cincinnati Venus at the Lucy in the Sky Disco and joked that, if he did well at it, he would like to move on to present the Miss America pageant at the end of his political career.

Jerry and Mayor Blackwell were to become strange bedfellows in the spring of 1980, with Jerry performing a major and surprising about-face from his normally predictable liberal viewpoint. On Thursday 1 May a group of about 50 supporters of the Revolutionary Communist Brigade called for a general uprising in a march through the streets of Cincinnati. A host of jeering protestors marched alongside them. Most of the protesters were from the suburb north of downtown where the communists had their headquarters, including the Rev Jack Kerr, pastor of a United Methodist Church. He said: 'I'm glad our country gives people a right to express their views but I don't think their methods are either legal or moral.'

The counter-demonstrators were the biggest troublemakers, with one man ripping up the communists' main banner before the march, forcing them to delay while they patched up a new one. Another grabbed a red flag from a marcher and set it on fire. Still others walked ahead of the parade route, passing out eggs for bystanders to throw at the communists. Overall, however, the 16 police officers assigned to the demonstration kept reasonable order, and other officers handled the inevitable traffic jams.

Ten days later 15 uniformed Nazis, members of the National Socialist Movement, held a rally in Fountain Square, and this time it took 50 police in riot gear to hold back hundreds of counter-protesters. The Nazis, some of whom had travelled from Detroit and Oklahoma, waved placards and preached a hate-filled message of white power, while groups as diverse as the Revolutionary Communist Brigade and Disabled American Veterans tried to shout them down. Under the First Amendment to the American Constitution, freedom of speech, however abhorrent it may be to opponents, is guaranteed, and therefore permits for political rallies, or any other gathering for that matter, could not be easily turned down simply because the people issuing them did not like the message, or feared other people would be offended.

However, after watching the Nazi march from a skywalk, along with Police Chief Myron J Leistler, and then questioning members of the public who had watched the rally teeter on the verge of violence, Mayor Blackwell announced that he would think about banning such demonstrations in future. 'Groups like the Nazis and the Revolutionary Communist Brigade advocate a philosophy that would destroy the basic tenets of American democracy,' he said. 'I think that some community in the Greater Cincinnati area has to suck it up and test the consequences of saying no. We should consider denying some of these demonstrative, disruptive groups permits. I think it can be tested and it should be tested. I would be willing to be a part of a council majority to deny the permit and test the constitutionality on First Amendment grounds.'

At least one onlooker, the Rev Iberus Hacker, agreed, saying, 'Nobody should be able to hide behind the American Constitution in order to preach hatred and murder.'

More to the point, astonishingly in view of his earlier stand on Nazi rallies, so did Jerry. He did not go so far as to call for a total ban on the hatemongers, but he proposed marginalising them by keeping them away from the heart of the city. He said: 'The Constitution may prohibit us from silencing the filth that comes out of their mouths but I can't imagine that we are required to aid their cause by giving them such a prominent platform as Fountain Square and giving them inordinate police protection, which merely magnifies their message or their rally. We should not automatically assume that what these groups are doing is constitutional. I don't think the courts have had their final say yet on these issues. I am not saying they don't have the right to be in Cincinnati, or parade and speak in Cincinnati. I just say why do we have to give them the window of the city, Fountain Square, to do it.'

He proposed a review by the city management on policies concerning the issuing of permits, and a temporary halt to permits for all political rallies except on national public holidays.

'I'm starting off on the assumption that the courts will not let us distinguish between the kind of politics espoused by the Nazis and Communists and the more mainstream political views and that's why I'm saying we may even have to face the possibility of no political rallies on the square,' he went on. 'If the constitution allows us to say we can take them off the square and put them in a booth on the riverfront, that's what we ought to do. Everyone has the right to speak out on whatever they want. And that includes speaking on Fountain Square. That's the First Amendment. But when a permit is requested, one is asking for more than is covered in the First Amendment.'

While Mayor Blackwell heartily endorsed his proposals, other council members were horrified. Jerry's fellow-democrat and mayor-elect David Mann said, 'To say I object to Springer's motion is to put it mildly. How do we decide who is extremist and who is not? I know it's neat politically to jump up and say we've got to stop this, but who are we going to stop next week? It's all right to march down the street in support of the Reds, but not in support of the school system? That's a ludicrous distinction.'

He also pointed out that such a ban would have outlawed,

or at the very least detoured, the civil rights and anti-Vietnam War marches that Jerry had proudly taken part in.

Mayor Blackwell's Charterite colleague, former mayor Bobbie Sterne, was equally blunt. 'Nobody wants to pay the price for freedom and that's one of the prices you pay,' she said. 'If we are not strong enough and convinced enough to be able to defeat an idea like Nazism, we have more trouble than permits on Fountain Square can deal with.'

For once, Jerry realised, he had made a public political mistake. He again raised the spectre of his family losses in German death camps to explain that the sight of Nazi uniforms had made him, 'Perhaps a little insensitive to the subtleties of the Constitution's freedom of speech guarantees.' He revised his proposal simply to give the city power to set the location of any demonstration that would need extra police protection.

Councilman Arnold L Bortz, who was also Jewish, was sympathetic to Jerry's emotions but totally opposed to his plan. 'This forces the most controversial groups to pay the highest price for exercise of that First Amendment right,' he said. He also said, and David Mann backed him, that extremist groups which are allowed to spout their views in public, 'expose themselves to the ridicule they deserve'.

While Jerry was quick to leap into that local controversy, increasingly he was spreading his political net wider, looking to the state, or even national stage for the next transformation of his career. He had briefly flirted with the idea of challenging Ohio Senator John Glenn and after dismissing that thought, began laying the groundwork for a run in the state elections due in 1982, with plans to appoint a full-time, paid campaign staff. Tantalisingly, however, he would not confirm which role he was hoping for. It was widely assumed he would seek the Governorship.

In the meantime his chief political adviser, Mike Ford, was campaigning for Senator Edward Kennedy's attempt to unseat incumbent President Jimmy Carter for the Democratic nomination for the 1980 general election and, despite Jerry's earlier links with Carter, when he went on the Middle East delegation, he also joined Kennedy's backers, although he was not optimistic. 'Basically this is a learning experience for me,' he told the *Cincinnati Enquirer* when he flew to Iowa to help the Kennedy organisation with last-minute campaigning. 'I'm just here to get a taste of the action.' Then, predicting that Carter would win the Iowa caucus, he added with a grin, 'They've promised me Secretary of State if we win.'

Jerry, the only elected official in Cincinnati to support Kennedy, had high hopes of being selected as a delegate to the Democratic National Convention to be held in New York that August, to choose the Presidential candidate. However, when the 161 Ohio delegates were named, he was not among them.

By this time Jerry was firmly the local front runner in the race for the Democratic nomination for governor, even though he had still not formally declared his candidacy. In a statewide opinion poll held in June, 1980, he won 61 per cent of the Cincinnati-area Democratic 'vote'. He started travelling the length and breadth of the state, spending an average of two days a week trying to become better known. At home he had virtually 100 per cent name and face recognition, thanks to his years in local politics and his radio broadcasts; now he needed to boost himself in other major Ohio cities like the state capital, Columbus, Cleveland and Dayton, and build up the money he would need to finance a credible run — estimated by some to be as high as $1.5 million to $2 million, although Springer later said he thought $800,000 was a more realistic figure. The primary elections in which the Democrats and Republicans voted for their choice of candidate were to be held in June 1982, with the election itself the following November.

Cincinnati Enquirer editorial writer Robert Clerc urged him to run. 'The timing could not be better for a Springer run for the governorship,' he wrote. 'During the last decade he staged one of the most impressive political comebacks in area history. He has been a consistent leader among candidates for city office. He has the benefit of his experience as mayor of one of the state's largest cities. And he was candid, after the last election, in stating his belief that he has done all he set out to do here and, therefore, would not seek re-election to council in 1981.

'That announcement, and his proven appeal at the polls, made speculation on Springer's political future a pastime for pundits. For a time there was talk of his challenging Senator John Glenn in this year's democratic primary. Then his support of Senator Edward Kennedy's presidential bid evoked some talk about his seeking a federal appointment. Some persisted in pressing the possibility that he would move to the east side of the city to challenge Congressman Willis D Gradison Jr in the 1st Congressional District.

'Now Springer himself has silenced all but the most dogged rumour-mongers by talking openly and unequivocally about his interest in seeking the governorship in 1982. When asked if it would not be better to seek a lesser state office first, Springer replied with characteristic candour, "But I want to be governor."

'If Springer's organisational support materialises, and if the money begins coming in, he is going to be a formidable candidate. Springer has always been a crowd-pleaser. If he has the funding to mount an effective TV campaign throughout the state, he is going to win a great base of support to add to the 61 per cent the poll showed he has in southwest Ohio.

'One thing that can be said with certainty even at this early date: Springer is enthusiastically committed to making the race. Not since the heady days when he occupied the Cincinnati mayor's office has he been so animated over the possibilities, not only of the campaign, but of the office.

'To that end, he is spending his time these days not only looking for support, but for ideas to round out the priorities he would set for a Springer administration. Solving the troubles of Ohio's schools has top billing. He indicates in conversation even now that he is well along in his thinking on the subject. Certainly, he will have it all together when it is time to make his final decision in 1981.'

Jerry was disappointed not to be named a delegate to the Democratic National Convention but he went along anyway as an observer. By now it had become clear Kennedy's run for the nomination was doomed, because President Carter cunningly called a 'loyalty debate' before the formal opening of the convention, to compel delegates to support the candidate they were initially pledged to.

Jerry, who kept a convention diary for the *Cincinnati Enquirer*, commented, 'By holding this vote prior to the start of the convention, there would be no time for a chemistry to build, which would result in an open revolt and a "dump Carter" movement. So Carter guaranteed himself victory while most of the delegates were still worrying about hotel accommodations, getting floor passes for their relatives and so on.'

With Kennedy out of the running, Jerry devoted the remainder of the convention to working on his own campaign, rubbing shoulders with political powerhouses and drumming up grass-roots support. His two main rivals for the democratic nomination, State Attorney General Billy Joe Brown and former Lieutenant Governor Richard Celeste, who had had an unsuccessful run for the governorship in 1978, were doing the same thing. Even though he was campaigning seriously, and enlisted the support of pro-Kennedy delegate Jene Galvin, from Clermont County, next to Cincinnati, Jerry managed to keep his canvassing light-hearted.

'Jene said he would distribute "Jerry Springer for Governor" buttons to the Ohio delegates,' he said in his diary. 'When I walked into the caucus later in the morning, 30 people were walking around sporting the button. The statewide media converged on me asking for a response. I told them I've never been a governor before and it would look good on my resumé.

'Actually the response among the delegates to my prospective candidacy was encouraging. Our organisation is starting to take shape. Billy Joe Brown and Dick Celeste were holding receptions in New York to promote their candidacy for governor. I was asked whether I would have a party, too. I decided against it. Instead, I figured I'd give each of the delegates a piece of bubble gum to take to their rooms and think about me while they're chewing. It's cheaper that way. Jene Galvin said he would hand out more buttons during the convention. I think I'll promise him the Lieutenant Governor's job. He's real good with buttons.'

While he mainly concentrated on making contact with influential Ohioans, on the last day of the convention he had lunch with one of his political heroes, California Governor Jerry Brown. 'I kept wanting to ask him about Linda Ronstadt but all he wanted to talk about was politics,' he said. 'How boring! I remember when I first became mayor and tried to bring a concert to Riverfront Stadium I wrote Linda a note telling her I thought she was wasting her time with a governor, mayors are where it's at. Apparently, my note was less than persuasive.'

After the convention Jerry concentrated on raising money and goodwill. His campaign manager, Mike Ford, back in Cincinnati after his nine months working on the Kennedy campaign, turned down a Fellowship at the prestigious Harvard University to devote his energies to Jerry's race, and the campaign had four other full-time, paid staff. By October 1980, more than 18 months before the election, Jerry had built up a war chest of $250,000, second only to Attorney General Brown, the acknowledged front runner at that stage. He had amassed so much, so early, he said, to give his run credibility and show the voters he was serious about taking on opponents who were better known at state level. 'The effect of raising that amount is that it convinces people I'm not just positioning myself for secretary of state,' he explained.

When the candidates filed their financial statements, as required by law, Brown had raised $324,000, $117,000 of it in the previous year. Jerry had raised his quarter of a million dollars in just six months. Jerry's campaign manager was delighted. 'The major point is that the attorney general has been saying no one can touch him because he has this amazing war chest,' Ford said. 'He has been raising money for years and only raised $117,00 in the past year. That, to me, says something.'

Jerry was spending at least four days a week outside his home city, making speeches and getting his name and policy known to people who did not know him. Ohio, in a sense, is a state that stretches between two worlds. Cincinnati borders on the Deep South, with Covington, Kentucky, almost an extension of the city with its dozens of restaurants and clubs, including converted ships moored on the Ohio River to give diners a view of downtown Cincinnati. The industrial and manufacturing cities of Toledo and Cleveland in the north sit on Lake Erie and are just a stone's throw, or at least a short boat ride, from Canada. So it was vital for him to become better known among his northern neighbours.

He also made a point of cultivating northern politicians running in various elections around the state that November. Thanks to his substantial campaign funds, he was able to contribute $1,000 to Cuyahoga County Democratic Chairman Timothy Hagen, from Cleveland, towards his campaign for county commissioner, $1,000 to State Representative Dennis Eckhart, from Euclid, a city bordering on Cleveland, and another $1,000 to the Lucas County Democratic Party, in Toledo. They were small amounts, but Jerry hoped the gesture would encourage them to urge their supporters to back him. He also made smaller contributions to friendly candidates across the state.

Unfortunately for Jerry, his financing ran into two hitches. By state law he should have filed a report for every contribution he made to a political campaign, county by county, before the election. However, he did not realise this until early December, and rushed to send in the necessary paperwork. He was reported to the Secretary of State for what was, technically, an election offence. In the event, no action was taken because it was clear Jerry and his advisers had no intention of breaking the law and had set matters straight as soon as he realised what had happened.

Another financial embarrassment was the discovery that one of his supporters, Columbus businessman Larry H Hunt, was accused of investment fraud in West Virginia and Indiana. Jerry immediately returned his $15,000 contribution and said, 'There's no way I can vouch for the life history of everyone who gave to me. If there is any doubt about the validity of this money, I won't deposit it. I don't need this.' Hunt insisted the contribution was made innocently, and that Springer had no idea about the charges. 'I'm just a simple businessman who happens to like Jerry Springer for governor,' he said. 'I expect not one favour if he is elected.'

After four years of a Jimmy Carter administration that seemed to achieve little — though Carter was the first Democratic President of the 20th century not to be involved in a foreign war — the USA took a swing to the right, electing Ronald Reagan for the first of two terms. Jerry was unconcerned and said he had no plans to change the direction of his campaign. He even tried to wrest victory from defeat in the general elections, saying that voters were not so much voting for the right as voting for new faces and new ideas. 'I offer a fresh face and new approaches,' he said, and added, 'I have been the biggest vote-getter in one of the most conservative cities in America. What people want is someone who is honest, not somebody who is out to pretend he is somebody that he isn't.'

Richard Celeste was in a more difficult position. Closely identified with Carter, who had appointed him director of the Peace Corps, in his previous run for governor four years earlier he had counted Carter's mother, Miss Lillian, and the then UN Ambassador Andrew Young among his campaign supporters. Like Jerry, he appeared unworried by the country's right turn and insisted he would win. He also took a side-swipe at Jerry, and Jerry could not resist hitting back.

'I have very high regard for Jerry Springer,' he told a conference on social and economic development at the College of Mount St Joseph. 'But I don't think he's going to be a significant factor in the statewide race in 1982. He will be one of the three or four people that I have to beat. I'd rather not run against him, not because I'm afraid of him but because I like him as a colleague.'

Jerry returned the compliment, saying, 'Dick is a good friend of mine. I think he's a good person. But he's not politically a winner. His comments were just silly.' He also pointed out that Celeste dropped out of sight after losing the 1978 race. 'Every other Democrat won that year but him so he left state politics,' he added. 'He can't come back every four years and say, "I want to be your governor." It doesn't work.'

Never one to underestimate the value of a good gimmick

or a publicity stunt, Jerry took some time off from his campaign to head to a local recording studio. The result was a single, released in Cincinnati. One side was called 'You're Nobody's Darling But My Own', and the other, written by Jerry himself, was called 'Cincinnati'. The lyrics included the lines,

'You can talk about your Texas. You can talk about your Tennessee.
'I've been to all them places and they don't mean a thing to me.
'I was born in a place that lies on the Mason-Dixon line.
'My people love their country music. It's something they won't hide.'

The Mason-Dixon line, technically the border between the states of Maryland and Pennsylvania, was more popularly known as the boundary between the North and the slave-owning South in the years leading up to the American Civil War, in this case the Ohio River. In his zeal to govern his adopted state, Jerry, tongue-in-cheek, had 'forgotten' that he was actually born in London.

Later he also conveniently 'forgot' he was brought up in New York. Recounting his oft-told tale about wanting to go to George Washington's birthday, he recalled that his mother used his confusion over the holiday to give him his first lesson in American history. 'I decided then to become governor of Ohio,' he told the *Cincinnati Enquirer*, even though he had probably never heard of the state as a six-year-old new immigrant.

The other side of his record, a country love song, ended with Jerry telling a woman how beautiful she is and adding, 'Darlin' if when you look in my eyes and believe everything I say to you, you're dumb enough to buy this record.'

The quirky record got air play on the city's radio stations, and WEBN, which also aired his Springer Memorandum, ran an informal telephone poll after it was played, asking listeners whether Jerry should give up politics for a music career. Of the listeners who responded, 77 said he should stick with politics and 48 thought he had a musical future ahead. Jerry laughed, 'I'm not sure whether they wanted me to pursue a record career or just wanted me out of politics.'

To get his name known better outside his home town, his campaigners handed out 50,000 'Jerry Springer for Governor' carrier bags at shopping malls in other cities, during the Christmas rush.

As the long campaign continued, Jerry attracted a large group of young volunteers who knocked on doors drumming up support. One of them, John Pahlgren, recalled years later, 'He had a way of making young people enthusiastic. I wasn't really interested in politics but my girlfriend was, so I tagged along with her. We were young and keen and we really thought he would do it. He really cared about what he was doing, and he cared about the people of Cincinnati, even if they didn't vote for him. When I see him on TV these days I can't believe it's the same man.'

Later in his campaign, Jerry used his army of young workers to study voter registration rolls and compile a list of nearly 400,000 registered Democratic families who always voted, whom he then targeted with letters addressing specific issues like education, taxes and unemployment.

Jerry's campaign coffers continued to swell, and by May 1981, more than a year before the primary elections, he had raised about half a million dollars. He and Ford decided to take a risky decision to raise his profile in the northern part of the state — TV adverts. The risk was that his name and message might register, but that the voters would have forgotten the impact by the time the election came around. Still, they decided to invest about $50,000 on a four-week campaign on the five major TV stations in Cleveland. The 30–60 second spots focused on the economy, unemployment and education as Jerry's three main targets. They also criticised Republican Governor James A Rhodes, who had held the office four times, without actually naming him, for failing to deliver on a pledge for 'jobs and progress'. Ohio had seen the job-market shrinking throughout the 1970s, and only Michigan had suffered worse job losses.

After all his efforts to increase his visibility in northern Ohio, Jerry surprised many of his supporters with his choice for running mate. He picked wealthy Cincinnati businessman Ken Keefe, 42, who had never been involved in politics before. Keefe, a self-made millionaire who had been friendly with Jerry since meeting him and Micki while they were on honeymoon, was already Jerry's biggest campaign contributor, paying $295,000, or more than one-third of the total for 1981, which amounted to $867,000, and was regarded as a good man to raise funds from other people. He absolutely denied buying his way on to the ticket to run for lieutenant governor. 'I believe in Jerry Springer, I am devoted to him,' he insisted. 'There were no discussions of any kind about a deal. I never got involved in any of his council campaigns, but Jerry and I have developed a close relationship in recent months and I really believe in him. He and I share the problem of identity in other parts of the state, but I believe we can overcome it on our merits. My bailiwick of concern is to keep business in Ohio and attract new industry to the state to overcome what we have lost in recent years.'

Although he was a political newcomer, several of his relatives were involved in local Democratic politics. As a businessman with large real estate investments he was seen as more conservative than Jerry. Nevertheless, the two men felt they could work well together.

Campaign manager Ford said, 'As an Irish Catholic and native Ohioan with a solid business background, Ken Keefe provides balance to our ticket in ways that are far more important than geographical considerations. I consider him a heavy hitter in the business world. Ultimately you need money and this is a guy who can raise the bucks.'

Jerry and Keefe decided on a budget of $1.5 million for their campaign, with Keefe agreeing to raise one-third of the total. By the end of the campaign he would have contributed a total of $585,000 of his own money, the largest single contributor ever in an Ohio state campaign.

While the campaign was taking up more and more of his time, true to his word when he was re-elected, Jerry did not neglect his council duties. He dutifully attended the Wednesday evening meetings, even though he was officially a 'lame duck' who was not expected to make any significant contribution as his years as a councilman came to an end.

Trust Jerry to go out on a note of controversy. Just two weeks before it was time to say goodbye to his council colleagues, he proposed an unexpected motion. Echoing his comments when he first became mayor ('Bring on the Rolling Stones') he formally proposed issuing the band an official invitation to perform in the city. Referring to The Who deaths he said, 'It's been nearly two years since the devastating and tragic events of The Who concert at Riverfront Coliseum. It stood as a black mark on our otherwise proud and glorious city. Because of the bad publicity, much of it deserved, this has not been the favourite place for a number of entertainers to come.

'I think it's time to make a statement, saying that Cincinnati has been through a lot, but we now have two years' experience in making such events safe, and the city is now ready to host such entertainment. You can enjoy such entertainment in a safe and peaceful atmosphere. It would be a sign to all who care to watch that our city is again open, that it is alive and well.'

The motion was passed, seven to two, with the proviso that the Stones would be given no special concessions if they did appear, and the Coliseum manager held 7 December open for them. However, the concert did not come off, and the controversy gave the *Cincinnati Enquirer* an excuse to skewer Jerry. 'His motion to involve city council in a half-baked effort to bring the rock group Rolling Stones to the Coliseum was pure silliness,' the newspaper said in an editorial. 'Council surely has more important things to do, even in this transitional period. For that matter, we would hope that Mr Springer, who has prided himself on initiative and imagination during his city service, could come up with more impressive proposals during his waning days as a city official. If he is serious about the Democratic nomination for governor, he'll have to convince Ohioans that he is being more than a rock concert promoter.'

Jerry's council colleagues gave him a rousing send-off, along with a city flag and a Rolling Stones album, at his final council meeting on 25 November 1981. Members of the public crowded the council chamber and the farewells went on for an hour, the longest anyone could remember. Political friends and foes paid tribute to 'the Springer years', with jokes and fond memories. Thomas Luken, who was mayor when Jerry was first elected to the council and now a congressman, remembered, 'I was given the job of taking this irrepressible lad and restraining him. It has been my biggest failure.' Republican Councilman Joseph M DeCourcy commented, 'I've learned from you a very valuable lesson — how to support both sides of an issue.' And Mrs Bobbie Sterne told him, 'I could cheerfully have wrung your neck several times.'

Jerry, with Micki and Katie sitting behind him, was clearly moved by his colleagues' remarks. His voice trembling with emotion, he said his farewells: 'For 10 years I've lived among you, intensely. I experienced the worst moments of my life and the best. You all know that. The compassion, understanding and support that this city has given me through the entire roller-coaster ride of the past 10 years is more than any human being has the right to expect or deserve. I will never forget that. Ever.'

Jerry reflected on his 10 years of city politics in farewell interviews, recalling stunts like his bus hijacking and, of course, 'the cheque incident'. 'When I was on council for the first time it had this concept of being the "city father",' he said. 'I kind of had the idea our government was a three-piece suit. I think it tends to be a more activist city council now and, I hope, a more open one.

'I had to do all my growing up and adjusting in public. Whatever warts I had as a person were front-page news. That made it harder, but it also made the victories and comebacks more satisfying. There's no way to recreate that election night of 1975. The terrible nightmare was just lifted.

'I'm going to dread the emptiness of my Wednesdays. I'm a little bit apprehensive but something inside me tells me to move on. I've been a city councilman longer than I've been anything else.'

Even Jerry's adversaries were gracious about him. Republican Councilman Guy C Guckenberger, the same age as Jerry and first elected at the same time, though he had been appointed to the council a year earlier, said that his initial political animosity had mellowed to respect for Jerry's undoubted abilities. 'I used to get really angry at him debating in front of high school groups,' he admitted. 'My debate tends to be logical and factual. But no matter what you say, he comes out sounding pretty good even though it wasn't always based on fact. He sounded terrific, a real Pied Piper. Jerry brought a lot of levity to council, which helps to break the ice and calm people down. He had a way of demonstrating, in a fairly flamboyant way, the need to pass certain issues. He'd literally embarrass us into doing things.'

William V Donaldson, who was city manager when Jerry was mayor, was more critical, but admitted Jerry's charm was impossible to resist: 'Some people saw Jerry as kind of a whore. I don't think Jerry was ever interested in the issues. I think Jerry was interested in getting elected and having people like him. The substance was much less than the packaging. I could be so mad at him for promising so many things to people, I would go storming across the room, and by the time he explained why he did what he did, I thought it made sense.'

As his council years came to an end and Jerry moved on to the fight for the governorship, he was preparing to make sense of the next stage in his life.

CHAPTER 13

With his life as a Cincinnati councilman behind him, Jerry was now able to devote himself full time to his campaign for the Democratic nomination for governor. At a January 1982 press conference at Cincinnati's Union Terminal, he spelled out his economic goals. Flanked by Micki and Katie, as well as his running mate Ken Keefe, Keefe's wife, Peggy, and their daughter Kelly, he called for industrial regeneration, specifically a revival of the state's coal-mining industry, for the state to invest its pension funds in Ohio institutions, and for more, and better paid, teachers for the state's public schools. Unemployment was approaching 12 per cent, jobs were moving out to other states, especially to the Southern USA where costs were lower, and high school students were dropping out at near-record rates.

The only bright spot for the state amid the gloom of that Ohio winter was the performance of the Cincinnati Bengals, who had won their way to the Superbowl, the equivalent of the FA Cup Final for American Football. They lost 26-21 to the San Francisco 49ers, but their run for the top slot provided plenty of excuses for parties.

'The state of Ohio is in awful shape at this moment,' said Jerry at his press conference just days after Superbowl XVI was played at Pontiac, Michigan. 'The only time Ohio gets national news, except for the Bengals, is when schools close, plants shut down or cities go bankrupt. That is what people know of Ohio. We have all this incredible wealth of natural resources and human resources. Then how come Ohio's broke? Why aren't we using the wealth of the state to start taking care of the economy of our state?'

Ohio had ample supplies of coal, but much of it was soft and sulphurous, and therefore dirty to burn and a major air pollutant, and the state actually imported more expensive coal from other parts of the country to run its power plants. Jerry proposed that the state should buy equipment to wash and crush the coal, which the mines would then sell to power companies, who would pass on their savings to consumers.

'So what have we done?' he asked rhetorically, as his campaign got into full swing and he returned to his key themes time after time. 'We've revived the coal industry in Ohio, making full use of the 200 years' coal supply we have in this state. We've assured jobs for thousands of Ohio miners. We've given Ohio consumers a break with a reduction of 10 per cent or more in their bills. And we've greatly improved the entire Ohio economy by lowering the cost of doing business in this state.'

He claimed that Ohio's $15 billion state pension fund, which was largely invested in other parts of the country, would provide massive benefits if it was brought home, even if the rate of return was lower, because of the knock-on effect such a huge investment would have.

'We're taking the wages of state government workers, investing them in Sun Belt states and in effect subsidising those states to take thousands of jobs away from Ohio,' he thundered. 'We could use this money to buy up mortgages, get the housing industry moving in Ohio again. We could use some of it to provide low-interest loans for Ohio college students. We would use some of it to buy the clean-up equipment for Southeastern Ohio coal.'

He also called for education to be tailored more towards employment, and suggested a return to old-fashioned apprenticeships for students who were not academically able or inclined to go to college, as a way of preventing the high drop-out rate of bored students who did not see the point of high school if they were not going on to higher education. Remarkably for a politician seeking election, he was not afraid of the T-word — tax — and proposed a graduated state income tax specifically to fund education, with a corresponding reduction in property taxes.

It was fairer to fund education from income tax rather than property tax, he said, because raising property taxes hit the retired, the unemployed and people on fixed incomes unfairly. With income tax, he pointed out, 'You have a good year, you pay; you have a bad year, you don't. Education is the most important thing we're going to spend money on in this state. If the choice ever gets down to whether our kids will get educated or whether or not we will pay, we will pay.'

While Jerry was an animated and inspirational speaker who was sometimes accused of having more style than substance, his running mate Keefe was there to back up Jerry's promises with the weight of experience. 'There's not a candidate for governor or lieutenant governor who won't talk about the economy and creating more jobs,' he said. 'But there isn't one of them who has ever created a job, except me. It's been my life.'

Keefe, who developed his father-in-law's fan company from a firm with total annual sales of just $60,000 in the early 1960s to one making $1 million profit selling industrial ventilation systems by the time he sold it in 1979, and who was the majority owner of a 218-acre industrial estate among other commercial property, even appealed to some Republican supporters. 'Many of the Republicans I talk to seem to like our message, that we're going to run the state in a businesslike way and do whatever it takes to get Ohio back on its feet economically,' he told the *Cincinnati Enquirer* as he, too, travelled the length and breadth of the state publicising Jerry's message.

'I had a long discussion with a businessman in Cleveland who requested to talk to me alone,' he went on. 'He expressed some concerns about Jerry's liberal views. But just before I left, he said he was convinced and would write out a cheque for our campaign.

'I talked to a Rotary Club in Portsmouth. Maybe three out of the 160 people who were there were Democrats. But I had some Republicans come up to me after I talked and say they wanted to help Jerry.'

Among the early Republican contributors to Jerry's campaign was property investor Jay C Thompson, who was invited to President Reagan's inauguration and who acted as host at a Republican Lincoln Day dinner in Hamilton County in 1980, where the guests of honour were Virginia Senator John Warner and his wife at the time, screen legend Elizabeth Taylor. He gave $5,000. By the end of the campaign another prominent Cincinnati Republican, Will Radcliff, who made a fortune selling frozen ice cones called Slush Puppies, would give Jerry a total of $140,000.

As he had during his years in local government, Jerry was able to mix a thoughtful approach to his mission with a light-hearted, self-deprecating one. He was serious about his political ambitions, but could never take himself too seriously.

So when the *Cincinnati Enquirer*'s Bob Weston asked him what made him run, he responded: 'I think as long as I could remember, there's always been some sort of influence at home that said I should do something important with my life, something substantive, and this race for governor offers the opportunity to do that. If you have a competitive streak in you, and I recognised I did, the question is, "How do you channel it?" You can go into athletics or entertainment or business. I'm no athlete or businessman. So I tried nightclub singing for a while, but if you had a voice like mine, you'd go into politics, too.'

In the long run, of course, Jerry proved to be a genius at entertaining, and a shrewd businessman as well, long after his political career was behind him.

As well as making personal appearances, Jerry stepped up his TV advertising in the north of the state once again. In a bold move that shocked many political observers, his glossy, four-page media package deliberately included his problems over 'the cheque incident'. 'While in line to become Cincinnati's mayor, Springer's career was driven into eclipse when he acknowledged he had spent time with a prostitute in Fort Mitchell, Kentucky, and that he had paid by cheque,' the press kit baldly stated.

Jerry knew he was taking a risk, but said he wanted to be the first person to raise the issue to show that he did not think it could harm him. 'I hope someone tries to use that against me,' he told the *Columbus Citizen-Journal* newspaper. 'Yes, I admitted it nine years ago and I admit it now. Now stand up Dick Celeste and stand up Bill Brown and tell everybody you never slept with another woman.'

Sex was not the only topic that was a potential minefield in his campaign. So was religion. He unashamedly approached leading members of the Jewish community for support, and cash, in his bid to become the first Jewish governor of Ohio, knowing he could risk an anti-Semitic backlash. But he said, 'There will be some people who vote against me because they may think I'm too liberal, my hair's too long or I'm too Jewish. Those kind of people are beyond my control. The fact is that eight of the ten people who are my largest contributors are not Jewish.'

The candidate from heavily Catholic Cincinnati, with a Catholic running mate, had to think on his feet when he met a group of prominent black Baptist ministers in Cleveland, during a meeting in which one speaker condemned Catholic schools as idolatrous and called on his fellow pastors to discourage their parishioners sending their children to parochial schools, which generally have better academic and safety records than state-run public schools in America and are relatively cheap, by private school standards, because they are generally subsidised by the local diocese. According to the *Cincinnati Enquirer*, Jerry was extremely uneasy listening to men of the cloth tearing into another religion, and was not sure how to play it. When he was finally introduced to the gathering the presiding minister said, 'I hope you're not a Catholic.' He replied, 'Not only am I not a Catholic, but I didn't hear a thing that was said here.' The audience burst out laughing and Jerry launched into his speech.

His joke did not, however, amuse everybody. A few days later the Rev Celsus Griefe, principal of a Catholic school in Cincinnati, wrote an angry letter to the paper, criticising Jerry and accusing him of telling people what they wanted to hear to gain support without necessarily meaning it.

By April, Jerry appeared to be gaining on his main opponent, Richard Celeste. He had spent more on TV exposure months before Celeste and the third runner, William J Brown, started their media blitz, and had gained massive face and name recognition throughout the state. He was perceived as a breath of fresh air, who approached the prospect of being governor with youthful enthusiasm.

Steve Wilson of the Gannett newspaper chain said: 'Springer himself says most people find politics boring. He seems to take a little bit of the boredom away. There's also a perception, at least, that Springer isn't afraid to take on the issues or anything else. His responses to questions don't always seem to be well thought out. It may give the impression that Springer has more charisma than political depth. Whatever the reason, he has an increasing number of people excited about his candidacy.'

Jerry did not simply address large meetings of the party faithful; he went out of his way to meet individuals, greeting them with outrageous comments like, 'Hi, I'm Jerry Springer and I'm running for governor. Vote for me and I promise to make you rich and famous.' Once in Akron, talking to a group of unemployed factory workers upset that jobs were leaving Ohio for southern states he joked, 'That won't happen any more if I'm elected governor, because the first thing I'm going to do is blow up the bridges to Kentucky.' In Cleveland, in the north of the state, he told a group worried about the economy, 'If you elect me I'll turn this state around, then YOU'LL be next to Kentucky!' And in

Cincinnati, when a group of students asked what would happen if they did not vote at all he told them, 'You'll all be arrested.' He also patented what *Cincinnati Post* writer Tim Graham described as the 'extra squeeze', a technique of shaking a woman's hand, then pulling her hand gently towards him and squeezing it again, to show warmth, empathy and sincerity.

When the three Democratic contenders, Jerry, Celeste and Attorney General Brown appeared together at a candidates' debate in the state capital of Columbus, Jerry and Celeste were in broad, liberal agreement on the issues, while Brown came across as more right-wing, supporting increased control over abortion rights and opposing handgun control. As so often in American politics, it was the emotional issues like abortion and firearms that took prominence over the economic and financial matters the candidates pushed when they were campaigning individually.

Celeste opposed parental consent for children to obtain contraceptives and any restrictions on abortions, as well as favouring a handgun ban. Jerry said, 'I am personally opposed to abortion but I am not a woman; I am a politician and I don't believe a politician or the government should interfere in this particular issue. I, too, support the ban of handguns. I also believe whoever commits a crime and uses a handgun should spend time in jail. We worship the guns in society and we have to change that. We have to make our children so scared of guns that they throw up every time they get near one.' He also supported withholding drinks licences to private clubs that discriminated by sex, race or colour when considering membership.

After the debate, Jerry was running virtually neck-and neck with Celeste, according to opinion polls, and old supporter Robert Clerc, editorial writer on the *Cincinnati Enquirer*, speculated that the race would come down to Jerry versus Brown: 'Richard Celeste is still leading most polls, with Springer trailing slightly and state Attorney General William J Brown running third. But since the race has been stamped liberals Springer and Celeste in one corner and moderate/conservative Brown in the other, the only true choice for Democrats if Springer outsells Celeste is Springer or Brown.

'The candidate who was written off a year ago by almost every politics-watcher has established credibility. In the state Democratic organisation, he is a contender and, with a little bit of good luck, could wake up on June 9 as the contender.'

Democrats across the state seemed to be thinking the same

way. Don L Hanni, chairman of the Mahoning County Democratic party in Youngstown, northeastern Ohio, said his county decided not to endorse a candidate, but would have chosen Springer if they had. 'I think he's done very well in the race, this kid,' he said. 'Of course, there is always the problem of peaking too soon, but he's the only guy who seems to be coming on with momentum. A couple of weeks back, the 14 Democratic district leaders in our county met and we had our own informal vote. Twelve of the them supported Springer, two backed Celeste and none of them supported Brown, even though he considers this home territory.'

Even Jerry's adversaries were impressed. In Cleveland, Brown supporter Tim Hagan, chairman of Cuyahoga County Democratic Party, conceded, 'I don't think anyone in the state should underestimate his tenacious effort.'

The debate did, however, cost Jerry some support. The anti-abortion Right to Life group, who had supported him in his last run for city council because of his staunch personal opposition to abortion, called him a turncoat and refused to endorse him. This was a serious rejection because pro-choice candidate Celeste had admitted that opposition by right-to-life supporters had been a factor in his narrow defeat in his run for governor four years earlier.

Dr John C Wilke, a spokesman for Right to Life, said the group had been criticised by some members for the 1979 endorsement of Jerry. He said, 'At the time he seemed very sincere in his opposition to abortion, saying he felt the same way about it as he did about the slaughter of millions of Jews in the Nazi Holocaust. Now his position on abortion is diametrically opposed to ours. There is no way we can endorse him for governor.'

Ironically, with Jerry making such a strong showing in the all-important North, he began to lose ground on his home turf. Celeste moved in to Cincinnati and picked up the support of leading black churchman, the Rev Melvin Jones.

Another prominent black minister, the Rev Fred Shuttlesworth, warned that he would consider supporting Celeste if Jerry, who traditionally had a strong following among the city's black community, did not approach him soon. 'We don't want to wait too long,' he said. 'I hope Jerry isn't taking us for granted. It may be a mistake thus far not getting in touch with us. You always feel the people at home are going to give you support, so you're running out yonder. I think it's going to create a problem. But it's not unsolvable.' Cincinnati financier Marvin Warner, who had himself once considered a run for governor and who was now considered a supporter of Jerry's, switched his alliance as well.

Jerry immediately promised to visit Shuttlesworth and other leaders in the black community within a few days. However, he already had strong home support from Mayor David Mann and was endorsed by the firefighters' union. And he won cheers and votes from young audiences at Xavier University and the University of Cincinnati, with emotional speeches about unemployment and poverty.

'Violence is when a 40-year-old man comes home on a Friday afternoon with a pink slip that says, "Hey, buddy, you're laid off,"' he told the youthful crowd. 'Violence is when a senior citizen has to choose whether this is the month to pay the utility bills or whether this is the month to buy food. If you are 70 years old and sitting in an apartment freezing to death, that is violence. It is violence when a child is hungry and gets tired and falls asleep in class and doesn't learn how to read and drops out of school and ends up in the court system. That is violence.'

Then, with three weeks to go before the 8 June primary election, the fight suddenly became dirty. Brown had commissioned an opinion poll, published on 1 May, which showed Celeste with 35 per cent of the vote, Brown with 34 per cent, and Jerry trailing with just 18 per cent, prompting Celeste to comment: 'I think it is narrowing down to a two-man race between me and Bill Brown and I'm still in front.'

However, the *Akron Beacon Journal* newspaper later revealed that one of the questions in the poll read: 'As you may know, in 1974 Jerry Springer, who had gotten married six months earlier, was arrested on a morals charge with three women in a motel room. He also used a bad cheque to pay for the women's services and subsequently resigned as mayor of Cincinnati. Does this make you much more likely, somewhat more likely, much less likely or somewhat less likely to support Springer for governor?'

Jerry pointed out that he had not been arrested, he had not been in a room with three women, the cheque did not bounce and he was not mayor at the time. 'Other than that, the question was OK,' he said.

Pollster Pat Cadell, who ran Cambridge Survey Research, the polling company used by President Carter in his election campaign, and who wrote the question using information provided by Brown, accepted responsibility for the mistake but denied it had any effect on the results of the poll. Jerry's press secretary, Moss

Murphy, called it, 'A deliberate, dirty attempt to deliberately mislead the voters.'

As rumours circulated that supporters of Brown and Celeste were quietly spreading the word that a vote for Jerry was a vote wasted, because even if he won the primary he would certainly lose the election itself because of the Kentucky affair, Jerry decided to go on the offensive.

He commissioned a series of TV commercials specifically to tell voters what had happened all those years ago in Fort Wright. Campaign manager Mike Ford said the three-week, $320,000 campaign was designed to correct the impression given in the poll and to make the incident so well known it would cease to be an issue. 'What's going down is an inaccurate story,' he said. 'It's difficult enough to deal with it, let alone with the exponentially false things about it that are being spread. But it's part of this man's public life and needs to be dealt with so that we don't have any problems running against Republicans and so he doesn't have to deal with it for the rest of his political life.'

In the ads, which were not shown in Cincinnati because Jerry and Ford felt everyone there knew all about the incident and had long ago decided how, if at all, it affected their opinions, Jerry sat on a stool and talked to the camera. 'Some nine years ago I spent time with a woman I shouldn't have and I paid her with a cheque. I wish I hadn't done that, and the truth is, I wish no one would even know. Perhaps like you, I'm not sure what any of this has to do with being governor, but maybe my talking to you about this makes a point. Ohio is in a world of hurt and the next governor's going to have to take some heavy risks and face some hard truths. I'm prepared to do that. This commercial should be proof. I'm not afraid, even at the truth, even if it hurts. Come on, join me on June 8. We're going to turn this state around.'

When asked why he did not simply ignore the false poll question, he told reporters: 'I'm doing the ad as a human response. Did you read the question? How can I not respond? If they said that about you, you'd hire a lawyer. It has been in the newspaper. If I don't answer I'm slandered as a human being '

The *Washington Post* newspaper wrote: 'No one is sure whether the commercial is the act of a political genius or a fool.' Jerry countered: 'You have to remember, I'm not running for God. What's wrong with the public knowing I'm a human being with warts?'

In any case, the commercials went down well in Cleveland.

On his first visit after they aired, strangers who saw him in the street clamoured to shake his hand and offer him congratulations and their votes. One retired woman who heard him speak at a senior citizen's centre there volunteered to work in his campaign and told the *Cincinnati Post*: 'I think he's a wonderful man. We're all human and anyone can make a mistake. I admire his honesty, for not telling a lie to cover up a lie.'

Back home in Cincinnati, the Rev Shuttlesworth did an about-turn and led the Cincinnati Baptist Ministers Conference in a last-minute endorsement. 'I'm tired of people running for office who parade as angels and turn out to be devils,' he said. 'Because a man once did something wrong I don't think that debilitates him from serving in office.'

Nor did the ad hurt him as far as big business contributors were concerned. Throughout his campaign he had been industrious and ingenious in fund-raising, hiring a man called John O'Leary just to hunt out potential big donors, and trying gimmicks like targeting all the owners of private planes in the state on the grounds that they must have money. He pulled off the biggest coup of all on 26 May, just two weeks before the election.

Toledo stockbroker, land investor and racehorse owner Edward P Wolfram was tempted to back Republican candidate Seth Taft before O'Leary met him and persuaded him to put his weight and his wallet behind Jerry. He obliged with a donation of $30,000 on 30 April. Three weeks later Wolfram invited Jerry for dinner, and the would-be governor, who was in Columbus at the time, quickly chartered a plane and headed to Toledo. There Wolfram and his wife took him out to dinner and asked him how much money he needed.

'If you really want me to win I need $140,000,' he said. Whereupon Mrs Wolfram took out her chequebook, wrote the cheque at the dinner table and gave it to him. That cheque, believed to be the largest single donation ever to a candidate in Ohio, took Jerry's total funds to $2,000,692, raised over two years, and was to be used for last-minute TV spots. At the other end of the spending scale, Jerry's financial disclosure papers showed a gift of $25 from Joseph P Kennedy, son of Bobby Kennedy, the man who had got Jerry into politics in the first place. Incredibly, however, when the dust settled on Jerry's campaign path, he was $300,000 in debt.

Despite the money, the TV commercials and his personal popularity, in the end it was all for nothing. The steam began to run out of Jerry's campaign in the final few days, with last-minute polls showing him still in third place and slipping further back. He put a brave face on predictions that he would get no more than 20 to 30 per cent of the vote, saying: 'First they said I wasn't really running for governor, that I was looking for a lesser state office. Then they said I couldn't get money, and I raised more than anybody else.' However, in his heart he was already convinced he would lose.

The three candidates met for a traditional pre-election dinner the Saturday night before the vote, at the Cleveland City Club. Jerry refused to acknowledge that he was down for the count and actually came out swinging against the Reagan economy, which was squeezing the less fortunate members of society, and once again he called for a tax rise to support social services and welfare programmes. 'There is no one in this society that is so fortunate and so lucky that they can go through life and say, "I made it, why can't they? I'm not going to support that programme because I'm doing well," because tomorrow it can be you. As I've said, there's no way to pay for these services except out of our pockets, and that means an increase in the graduated income tax. There's no way around it.'

On election day Jerry got up and voted for himself and played nine holes of golf before driving, with Micki and Katie who by now was a five-year-old handful, to Columbus. That evening the three of them attended a dinner with their biggest campaign contributors at the Christopher Inn Hotel in downtown Columbus, before the polls closed. Torrential rain and a violent thunderstorm that hit Cincinnati gave Jerry a bad omen; in Hamilton County, where he expected to make a strong showing among his home voters, flooding closed 20 polling places for a while and the downpour kept many voters at home. 'Bill Brown and Dick Celeste must have seeded those clouds,' he joked bitterly.

Still, he danced with Katie for the cameras, smiling, before admitting: 'I'm scared stiff. I've got two years and $2 million in this campaign and it looks like it could all go down the drain.' Even then he could still crack jokes, telling his supporters: 'The reason I brought you here tonight is because if everything doesn't go right, I need a job.' But on a more serious note he added: 'I don't want to sound corny, but this has been a wonderful experience. Whatever happens, it has all been worthwhile.'

Then he went back to his suite at the Imperial House North Motel to watch the results come in on TV. By 10.30pm it was obvious it was all over. State Democratic Party Chairman Paul Tipps called on him to offer his condolences and urge him not to quit politics. 'You did an amazing job,' Tipps told him. 'You were by far the most impressive candidate in the race. Don't get discouraged and please don't get out of politics. Don't quit. We're going to need you running for state office in the future.'

Jerry conceded defeat that night, before the final results were in. By the next morning he was able to put a brave face on the election. 'It could have been worse,' he told reporters. 'I could have been hit by a truck.' And he insisted: 'I'm not giving up politics. That's for sure! I bought a new suit and I've got to get some wear out of it.'

When the final results were in, Jerry was a distant third to Celeste, with just 20 per cent of the statewide Democratic vote, but as a consolation prize at least he knew he was still popular in Cincinnati. He swept every precinct, picking up 72 per cent of the vote.

Suddenly out of politics after 11 years, Jerry was hit by a sense of anti-climax. He pledged to support Celeste throughout the rest of the campaign against the successful Republican primary winner, Clarence J Brown. He then decided to take a break and headed with his wife and daughter to Hilton Head, for a family holiday in the South Carolina resort where he and Micki and honeymooned, leaving Mike Ford behind to start lobbying for a cabinet position for Jerry if Celeste won and to set up a political action committee to raise cash to pay off Jerry's debts and start a war chest for his next campaign, whatever that might be.

Jerry raised the possibility of running for lieutenant governor in 1986, if Celeste was governor and planning to run again. Then, later that June, his name was put forward to run for Congress against Republican Willis D Gradison in the November election, after the original candidate, L Arthur Safer, dropped out.

'Of course it's very flattering,' he said. 'But at this point, no, I'm not interested.'

Cincinnati voters had heard Jerry's protestations that he would not run for this office or that office many times before over the years, and seen him change his mind. But, impossible though it would have been for the people of Cincinnati to believe — and even Jerry did not yet realise — after 11 volatile years, his political life really was over.

Top: A pensive young Councillor Springer during a meeting in Cincinatti, Ohio, 1977.

Bottom: Pressing the flesh: on the campaign trail for governorship in Ohio, 1982.

'Dr Talk' in action – Jerry sings country during a video shoot for his album of the same name.

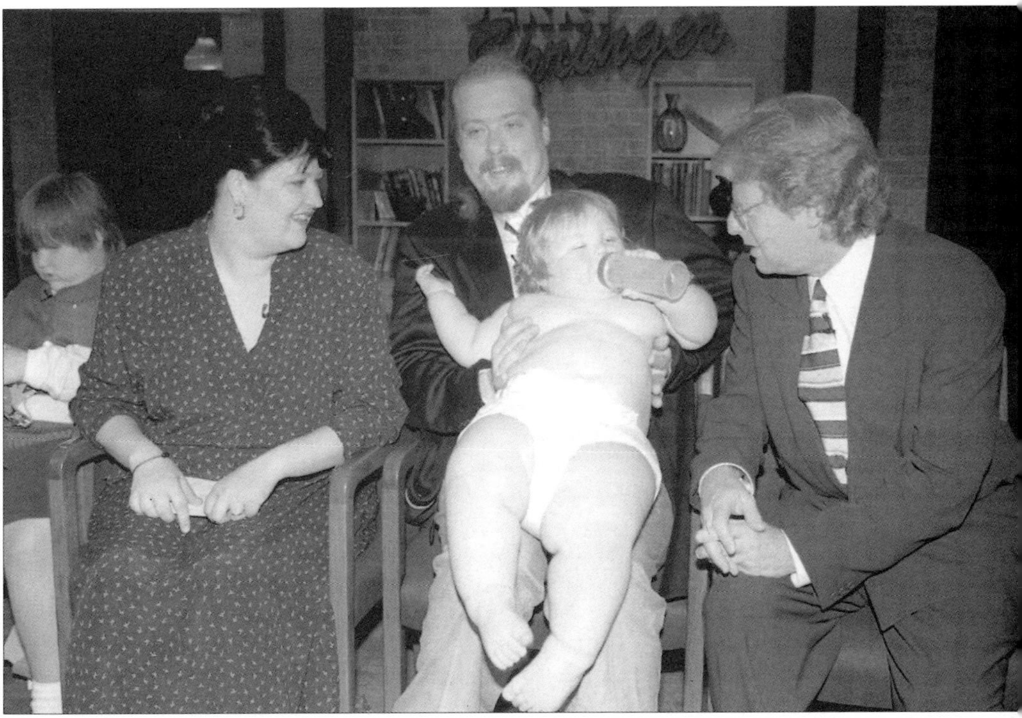

Top: Just another day at the office: meeeting the Strenkerts and 17 month-old-son Zack, suffering from obesity.

Bottom: Jerry inspires devotion from all quarters – especially young and female.

In character – Jerry poses on UK show *The Big Breakfast*.

Top: Outraged protesters march on Fox studios in Chicago to protest about Jerry's show.

Bottom: Fists fly as guests air grievances.

Top: Comics Mini Holmes, Ian Sirota, Johnny Gardhouse and Suzanne Muir appeared on Jerry's show in a fabricated story. They were sued by Multimedia Entertainment and later settled out of court.

Bottom: Jerry takes the UK by storm on *TFI Friday*, with Chris Evans and Will McDonald.

Guaranteed to raise a smile! With porn stars Chandler and Tiffany Mynx.

Jerry Springer – setting a standard for all chat shows!

CHAPTER 14

No sooner had Jerry lost out in his bid to be chosen as the Democratic candidate in the race to become governor of Ohio in 1982 than there was talk of him making a career change. Discreetly, Jerry had discussions with three Cincinnati TV stations — 5, 9 and 12, all affiliated to the big three networks — about the possibilities of getting a job on one of their news shows. However, he would not be able to begin work for any of them until the late autumn, when the election for governor was over, because there might be concerns of ethical conflicts if Jerry were reading an item about the governor's race. Besides, Jerry was not a sore loser. He had committed himself to campaigning for Richard F Celeste, who had beaten him for the Democratic nomination, and did not want to back down on his word.

Nevertheless, only a little more than a month after failing to win the nomination himself, rumours started circulating around the city that he was looking for a job in TV and had been secretly talking to various station managers. This was a surprise because it had been widely expected that Jerry, who was working full-time for the Democratic Party during the run-up to the election, would seek a job in the state government if Celeste was successful in beating Republican candidate Clarence Brown for the governor's seat.

When he was tackled about the rumours at the end of July by the *Cincinnati Post* reporter David Flick, he tried to play down the seriousness of his search for a new on-air job. 'We've done some talking and it's nothing more than that at this point.' Jerry said he would make no decision about his future career plans until after the November election. He added, 'I told them that I wouldn't be getting into anything like that until after November. The important thing for me now is the Celeste campaign.'

Less than a month later he was to switch his priorities.

Despite Jerry making light of his job hunt, three weeks later Joe Lewin, general manager of WLWT Channel 5, the NBC station in town, confirmed that Jerry would be joining the station as a 'showcased contributor' and commentator to its news show as soon as the 2 November election was over. The job offer came after hours of secret negotiations. The discussions were escalated after erroneous reports that Jerry had been approached by the giant ABC network with a job offer as a political analyst on national news started circulating. People immediately started speculating that Jerry's renowned sense of humour, which had made him a favourite of the Ohio media and with many voters, made him well equipped to follow such politicians-turned-TV-analysts as John Lindsay, a former mayor of New York, and Carl Stokes, a former Cleveland mayor. The reports were false but did no harm to Jerry's job search. All three of the local stations were interested in having him work for them but Channel 5 was determined to secure him as he was seen as a well-known and popular character in Cincinnati and therefore likely to attract viewers.

At 38, Jerry was launching a new career in TV. He told *Post* reporters Robert White and Tim Graham that his decision to change jobs meant that he was giving up politics for journalism: 'This is what I'm doing for the foreseeable future. Right now, I'm departing from elective politics. You ask me if that means for ever. For ever is a long time. Ten years ago I wasn't even living in Cincinnati. Right now I'm making a decision to go into TV. This is what I'm going to concentrate on right now.' Jerry's memory seemed a little shaky; he had actually lived in Cincinnati for 13 years by then, the longest time he had ever settled in one place.

Right from the start the career move would have a significant impact on Jerry's life. He was leaping from a salary of $2,500 a month as a consultant and fund-raiser for the Ohio Democratic Party to a TV contract that guaranteed him an income of between $75,000 and $100,000 in his first year on air, at least $10,000 more than he would have made had he become governor of Ohio.

Jerry agreed with the station that his new job would focus on commentaries since he was already comfortable with that format — having done a daily commentary on the WEBN radio station for six years — but he would also include some news reporting on special projects that would not just be limited to political events.

'I don't need to be a candidate to survive,' Jerry said. 'The issues facing the community are larger than partisan politics. I don't feel I'm leaving the subject matter. I'm just leaving the prospect of being a candidate.'

Lewin was pleased to plug his new employee, saying: 'You may be sure that his commentaries and other special subjects will make use of his political savvy. However, we are looking for a broad range of subject material and we expect to explore new areas that will utilise Jerry's experience and insight.'

Jerry's old adversary, columnist Frank Weikel, could not resist a dig at the former mayor's new job. Claiming that Jerry appeared to be 'in a rut for threes', he wrote: 'He finished third in the primary race for governor; now he's with a station that is number three in viewer ratings (during news hours).' He also pointed out that Jerry's law firm was advertising door to door for business in many areas of Cincinnati.

Before Jerry took up his job he had to raise funds for Celeste and himself. Despite his incredible ability to raise money during his abortive run for the nomination, he still managed to be $300,000 in debt when it was all over. The largest outstanding debts were $100,000 to Will Radcliff, owner of the Slush Puppie Corporation, even though he had actually given Jerry $140,000 towards his campaign, and $60,000 which had been loaned to the cause by his brother-in-law, kidney specialist Dr Barry Strauch, who didn't even live in Ohio, but in McLean, Virginia.

Despite the highly paid new job on the horizon, Jerry's financial woes got worse as the year progressed. Even though he had significantly reduced his campaign debts as the summer turned into autumn, he still had creditors chasing him. In October the Internal Revenue Service filed a federal tax lien for $21,736.24 against the Springer Campaign Committee, the financial arm of the organisation that had tried unsuccessfully to win him the Democratic nomination for governor. The lien was part of the approximate $150,000 still owed from the campaign, and represented unpaid payroll taxes, money withheld from campaign workers' salaries, which should have been forwarded to the IRS to pay their federal taxes. Joseph W Budd, the IRS revenue officer who filed the lien at the Hamilton County recorder's office, claimed it was a normal move taken to protect the rights of the federal government with respect to other creditors, meaning the federal government had made a formal move to secure its rights to be paid first. Originally the IRS had been owed $33,000 but that had been reduced. The IRS wanted the remainder of the debt brought down through monthly payments.

Jerry's TV début for Channel 5 news was a baptism of fire. His first appearance came on election night, 2 November, from the state capital of Columbus, where, as a political analyst, he gave blow-by-blow interpretations from 6pm when the show started into the early hours of the following morning, as the results came in. It must have been a bittersweet occasion for Jerry watching his old friend and former political rival Richard F Celeste win the race, and he could only speculate what might have happened if he himself had won the nomination. It must also have been strange being on the other side of the fence on election night, with nobody thrusting microphones and cameras into his face.

However, it was the following week before he took up the mantle as Cincinnati's only full-time news commentator. Just before Jerry was to make his début on Monday 8 November 1982, he appeared on air in a TV teaser (a promotional advert) promising to explain to the viewers of Action 5 News how he came to get his TV job. But he did not live up to his promise. 'A true "how" story would have detailed at least some of the background that caused a highly successful politician of more than 10 years to change careers and move to the TV news department with the lowest ratings in town,' wrote the *Cincinnati Enquirer*'s then TV critic Tom Brinkmoeller. 'He didn't explain that.'

There was no doubt about Jerry's charisma and he was at home in front of the camera. He was clearly a popular and well-recognised character in the town he had called home for so long, and it was understandable that any one of the local TV stations would have regarded him as an asset. He had repeatedly topped the polls in city council elections, and his new lords and masters realised that they could translate that popularity to good viewing figures. According to Brinkmoeller, they looked set to be proved right, from his very first appearance in his *Nightbeat* slot

'His first two-minute commentary contained the kind of easy-to-understand and slightly irreverent style which had previously made him the most refreshing character on Cincinnati City Council,' he wrote. 'The "why" of his change and the "how" of Channel 5's hiring of him were pretty much ignored. Both are more than interesting topics, but ones which aren't being talked about by the former Cincinnati mayor and his new boss.'

In fact, Jerry skirted over the background to his career change and devoted most of his segment to explaining how he saw his new job developing. Instead of being a politician, he told viewers, he now wanted to become a social commentator who could put a fresh interpretation on news events.

Jerry assured the writer that he was not approaching his new job in a frivolous way, but with a firm commitment to TV journalism, even though it was a job in which he had no previous experience. He announced that he had given up his law practice altogether, and that TV was now his full-time career. It was evident Channel 5 had faith in him, because although he would not reveal the length of his contract he added, 'It's a relatively long-term contract for this business, I'm told.'

Always a maverick, he admitted he had opted for the offer from WLWT even though it was running third in the ratings for news programmes because he had confidence in the sort of shows and news it was planning. He also had immense confidence in himself, believing that because he was already so well known that viewers would tune in to watch him if only out of curiosity. A bigger challenge, he thought, was the need for constant new themes and ideas to keep them watching.

He said: 'The biggest problem is being under the discipline of having to write every day. It's really strange to do something new. All my life I've done two things: go to school and be a councilman. On city council if you had one new idea a month you were leading the pack!'

Jerry's first few weeks on air did not go down well with everybody. The *Cincinnati Post* critic David Klein described the fast-talking, wise-cracking new TV commentator as 'really a sheep in wolf's clothing'. He said: 'His furious pace and snarling humour serve mainly to hide the fact that not much is being said. Springer appears to have fallen into a common editorial trap: concentrate on glittering generalities and the little specifics that make everybody mad will never bother you. It's been nearly a month since Springer began his new career as TV commentator, and so far the only difference between his commentaries and those of the traditional wishy-washy local broadcaster is in the wrapping. A long-time politician with a gift for gab, Springer dresses up his otherwise mushy commentaries with some of the most bizarre one-liners this side of *Saturday Night Live*.' *Saturday Night Live* is a long-running satirical TV show which enjoys cult status in the USA and has launched the careers of stars like Bill Murray, Dan Aykroyd, Chevy Chase and John Belushi.

Jerry's topics, not surprisingly, showed his liberal bent — he was opposed to nuclear warfare, wanted hunger and poverty abolished, and praised a new Ohio law banning power companies from cutting off gas and electricity during the harsh winters.

Klein admitted some of Jerry's jokes were funny but added, 'More often they serve only to hide the lack of any real point of view. Indeed, his commentaries were described best by Shakespeare centuries ago — "tales filled with sound and fury, signifying nothing".'

Despite his critics, Jerry went over well with the viewers and his TV bosses and by early in the New Year there was already speculation that he would become more high profile on air, perhaps taking over one of the prime anchor spots on the nightly TV news. Indeed at the end of January 1983, station manager Lewin confirmed that Jerry was to get his first shot at being a news anchor on the last Saturday of the month, when he would sit in for the regular host Robin Phillips. Lewin insisted that this did not mean a shake-up with Jerry assuming a permanent anchor position — yet. 'It's just as a substitute,' he said. He confirmed that Jerry's eventual promotion to a full-time seat in an anchor's chair was possible but not in the foreseeable future, adding, 'Nothing is imminent.'

Jerry was out of politics, but the financial problems concerning his run for governor came back to haunt him early in the New Year of 1983. One of the top contributors to his campaign, Edward 'Ted' Wolfram, a stockbroker who had poured $170,000 into the Springer Primary Campaign fund and had donated $50,000 to the successful Celeste, was being investigated by the Securities and Exchange Commission, the US investment watchdog. All business was suspended at the Toledo-based securities firm of Bell and Beckwith, where Wolfram served as managing partner, when it went bankrupt. Wolfram personally oversaw six accounts that showed debts totalling $41.9 million.

Jerry said that Wolfram's donations, which were made on two personal cheques, were nothing to do with the brokerage firm and were perfectly legal, a claim that turned out to be false, although there was no suggestion that he knew it. It came to light that Wolfram's contributions came about following months of behind-the-scenes work by John O'Leary, the 28-year-old New Jersey native hired by Jerry's campaign to scout Ohio for potential high-roller donors to his political war chest. Jerry successfully distanced himself from Wolfram's problems and insisted once again that he had put politics behind him for his new job in TV.

For his part, Wolfram said he had spent more on a racehorse and a dry oil well than on his contributions to the campaign. 'Jerry owes me absolutely nothing, I took the best shot,' he said. Wolfram was indicted by a federal grand jury on five charges of fraud involving his firm's client accounts that April. The indictment charged that, over a five-year period, Wolfram had defrauded Bell and Beckwith's 7,100 customers by misrepresenting the value and authenticity of the securities used as collateral by his firm. Furthermore, FBI agents confirmed that the money for the contributions made to Jerry and Celeste came from the $36 million lost in the firm's squandered accounts. However, the FBI found no suggestion that either political candidate did anything wrong in accepting the money.

Eventually most of Jerry's campaign cash problems were dealt with in a political payback deal. In Ohio the Bureau of Motor Vehicles, which deals with registering cars and issuing driving licences, was run by politically appointed deputy registrars. These were important posts for the ruling party, not because they wielded any particular political power, but because under Ohio law, 15 cents from the sale of every car registration or driving licence went to the governing party, to be distributed among local party branches.

After Celeste took over as governor on 10 January, Republican deputy registrars were ousted in favour of newly appointed Democrats. An agreement was reached among local and state Democratic leaders that many of the deputy registrars appointed in Hamilton County would use a portion of the revenue from their offices to help retire Jerry's debts. The new governor felt a moral obligation to help Jerry pay off his campaign debts because of the assistance Jerry had given him during the election campaign. He had made numerous campaign appearances on behalf of Celeste during his fight to become governor after he defeated Jerry in the race for the Democratic nomination. It was a case of a political 'you scratch my back and I'll scratch yours', which relieved Jerry of his financial itch.

Despite his protestations that he had turned his back on politics, when a May strike of firemen embroiled in a wages dispute with the city loomed, Jerry could not resist acting as a self-appointed negotiator in a bid to find a compromise. After he made a pro-firemen's union commentary on his nightly show, calling for them to be given a 5.5 per cent wage increase, he received a telephone call from Forrest Buckley, the president of the local Fire Fighters Union. Buckley asked him whether he could help reach a settlement and avoid a strike: 'I think he made a real honest attempt to get something done. He was involved as a person trying to get a settlement, not as a newsperson for Channel 5.'

Jerry's rationale for getting involved was that he was not the reporter covering the story — Jeff Hirsch had been assigned to do that. Jerry merely commented on the strike and was therefore in a position to get involved. He said: 'If I had been covering this as a reporter, I could not have done that. But I'm a commentator. I can't be hypocritical and take a position on the air and then not really mean it. I thought a strike would have been detrimental. I thought I was in a position to help. If one day I'm anchoring the news, that's a different story.'

Behind the scenes he truly was helpful. Fire Fighters Union recording secretary Mark Wilhelm commented: 'He was a busy person and he was going back and forth between the city and us. I think he kept a lot of minds open. He was a good guy.' Jerry tried every trick in the book as he ping-ponged back and forth between various councillors, the city manager and the union, trying to get a compromise.

At one point Jerry ran as fast as he could down the block between City Hall and the union offices, burst into the offices and dramatically announced there was a new deal on offer from City Hall. He said he was passing on a request from City Manager Sylvester Murray that a vote on the latest offer, due to be taken after union president Buckley addressed his members at the nearby convention centre, should be stopped until further talks had taken place. The message was duly relayed and the balloting was postponed.

Murray, however, recalled the incident quite differently. Devious Jerry had come into his office and told him, 'I've heard Buckley wants to talk to you.' To which Murray responded that he would be willing to talk and Jerry had replied, 'I will tell Buckley to call you.' Murray had not objected to the visit from his old boss. He said, 'Jerry was a friend and was genuinely trying to help me and the city.'

By the summer Jerry still had not been appointed as a full-time anchor but, despite the initial criticism he had received, his popularity as a commentator had grown immensely. Even the *Cincinnati Post*'s TV critic David Klein, who had verbally attacked

Jerry during his first few weeks on air, had a complete about-face. He wrote: 'He has become the most impressive single component on Channel 5's 11pm news, primarily because he speaks to viewers in a normal, human kind of voice, without the usual sombre newsman's tones, without the journalistic jargon and without losing sight of the fact that journalism itself is sometimes a pretty laughable affair. Let's face it: after an evening spent listening to professional TV types speak in neutral about the fragmented montages of news they happened to capture that day, it's refreshing to hear Springer come flat out and rail against a city council member, or discuss why TV news is sometimes an insensitive beast. Indeed, one of Springer's strengths is that he is the only TV correspondent in town likely to render opinions about his own business.

'When Springer first began doing these commentaries, he earned catcalls from his competitors and a roasting from the critics, especially me. His commentaries then seemed to be all jokes and no substance. That's no longer true, at least, not usually. On issues involving city hall and local politics, he has become one of Channel 5's major resources. As a former mayor himself, he's well connected to the various power cliques. So far, he seems to have virtually a perfect track record when it comes to predicting what city officials will do on controversial issues.'

Most US TV stations featuring opinion pieces as part of their nightly late news format usually ran the commentary during the last few minutes of the programme when many viewers had fallen asleep. However, Channel 5 recognised the significant contribution Jerry was making to their late-night show and featured him in a prime slot, soon after the first commercial, and within eight minutes of the show's start.

Like him or loathe him, Jerry had quickly established himself as a few minutes of must-watch TV in southern Ohio, at least as far as the critics and a few viewers were concerned. Many nights telephone callers to the station were stacked up on hold, waiting to disagree with the latest *Nightbeat* commentary segment, long before the 11pm programme went off the air. When he picked up the telephone, and Jerry was always willing to talk to people and defend his point of view and, if they were articulate, listen to theirs, Jerry was often greeted by abuse. As he joked: 'There are only so many ways you can call somebody a communist, pinko, fascist pig.'

Still, even though he was popular and made interesting viewing, he had not had the significant effect on the viewership figures that the station, which was still in the third slot in the ratings, had hoped. Jerry could have faced problems. During the year there was a change of general manager at the station and the new man in the hot seat, Robert Gordon, was a staunch Republican who openly admitted he wouldn't have hired Jerry if he'd been the station boss at the time he was appointed. However, he admitted, 'I'll be the first to admit, I would have been wrong. He is an amazingly effective commentator: bright, quick and thoughtful. He adds a unique dimension.'

Jerry graciously responded, 'Bob Gordon doesn't agree with me often, but he's my strongest supporter.' As Jerry celebrated his first anniversary with the station, the *Cincinnati Enquirer*'s Brinkmoeller wrote, 'Springer's style has improved immensely during the past 12 months. His writing ability is sharp, clear, often witty and economical. His nightly messages might infuriate, but they seldom confuse.'

Nevertheless, Jerry felt frustrated. He wanted more. He did not want to move away from Cincinnati to another station in a bigger city — he wanted to be a bigger fish in his comfortable small pond. Nor was he even interested in changing stations within Cincinnati. He wanted to play a bigger role on Channel 5 as a full-time anchorman. He was firmly convinced that if he was allowed more input as an anchor he could be an important member of a team that he believed could move Channel 5 news out of the ratings cellar and to the top.

He had his mind set on challenging the then most popular newsman in town, Channel 12 anchor Nick Clooney, the brother of singer Rosemary Clooney and father of heart-throb actor George Clooney.

CHAPTER 15

Jerry was busy doing what Jerry did best — behind-the-scenes negotiations and making suggestions to get what he wanted. Even so, it took him another four months before he finally achieved his goal. Eventually in March 1984 the early evening news on WLWT reached its lowest ebb. It was actually fourth in a three-way race because more people were tuning in to watch *M*A*S*H* on an independent station than the news on Channel 5. In a bid to halt the slide the station announced the appointment of Cincinnati's newest TV anchor. Jerry was to replace Richard Hull, a former Cable News Network anchor who had been hired by Channel 5 the previous summer on a three-year contract but was now abruptly fired, with his agent negotiating a payoff.

Tom Kuelbs, the station's news director, remembered: 'Jerry ran for anchor the same way he ran for public office, through hard work and exposure to the public.' He gave speeches and attended banquets and award shows day and night.

It was a big jump for Jerry. He was to anchor both the 6pm and 11pm newscast with co-anchor Norma Rashid. In addition, he would continue with his late-night commentaries. This was unique in US TV. Many stations carried commentaries but the cameras always cut away from the newscasters to another personality who only presented his or her personal view on an issue of the day. Now Jerry would remain at the anchor's desk and just turn to the camera for a couple of minutes while presenting his personal perspective on a subject.

Big city TV consultants told the station's general manager, Tony Kiernan, that he was taking too much of a risk. Letting Jerry not only continue to do his commentaries, but do them from his anchor's chair, would give viewers the wrong impression, he said. Anchors should be solid, familiar and objective. They should not be 'warm and fuzzy'. Kiernan remembered, 'They said no ex-mayor had ever succeeded in becoming an anchorman. They said it would be years before Springer was a TV success.' But Kiernan had a hunch and in any case, the station really had nothing to lose.

Jerry recalled: 'You could say they were so low down, so what was the risk? The moves they made were unheard of in the business. They got a partisan politician to do commentary and not give equal time to another side. The got a liberal Democrat in a Republican city to give his point of view. And then they let him anchor!'

However, he insisted he could be objective doing news stories and separate facts from comments. 'That I have a point of view doesn't disqualify me from being honest,' he said. 'The only alternative to not having a point of view is to be an intellectual eunuch. The difference between me and the other anchors in town is that people know where I stand.'

For the two weeks before he was to take over the prime news slots, he was assigned immediately to co-anchor Channel 5's inaptly named 11.30am 'Midday' news with co-host Ann Reskin so that he could get some practice before teaming with Rashid, who had to present the nightly news by herself until Jerry had found his feet. The consummate politician told the *Cincinnati Post* TV critic David Klein: 'Part of me is blown away by it. It was completely unexpected.'

The news of Jerry's appointment came just as Cincinnati's foremost news anchor, Channel 12's Nick Clooney, was packing his bags to take up a new job in Los Angeles as news anchor with KNBC, so Jerry's promotion was seen as Channel 5's bid to fill the vacuum left by Clooney's departure.

The news came as a bitter pill for Hull, who did not learn of the new appointment until the day of the announcement, 12 March, when he returned to the station after a week's holiday: 'I came back from skiing and I didn't have a job.' Stunned by his firing, Hull added, 'I was told Clooney leaving forced them into doing this sooner than they would have done it. In fact, I was told they probably wouldn't have done anything at all if the Clooney move hadn't forced their hand.'

Explaining the decision for the change of faces on the nightly news, Channel 5's news director Bob Yuna admitted that Clooney's departure was one of the determining factors. He said: 'It was Jerry's growth and our judgment that Jerry was the best choice over the long haul. We don't expect miracles inside of six months. The hardest thing we had to do was make a judgment as to whether the current team would do best for us. We decided Jerry joining Norma would give us the best chance over the long haul.' As far as the channel was concerned, the musical chairs had been prompted by three major factors —the station's news ratings had hit a new low in January; Jerry's skills and popularity continued to improve; and Clooney's resignation inevitably meant a new face on TV. Yuna added, 'That opened the window and forced us to make the hard decision.'

There was another factor — Jerry's familiarity among viewers. Native son Nick Clooney's success had spurred the belief that Cincinnati viewers liked to get their TV news from a Cincinnati face and London-born, New York-raised Jerry had had such a high profile in the city for so long that he was regarded as a local. Yuna pointed out, 'It's just a fact of life that viewers in this town place a lot of importance in local people delivering their news.' Nobody was really surprised by the announcement, despite Jerry's ingenuous declaration of surprise. For weeks the media world in Cincinnati had been awash with rumours that his promotion was on the cards, although nobody was speculating when it would happen.

Jerry had been sent to New Hampshire to report on the Democratic primary elections a few weeks earlier, no doubt relishing the opportunity to mix with national politicians. It now turned out that from there he had gone on to New York to be coached in anchoring skills. He recalled: 'There was no cosmetics at all. It was purely delivery. The message was, don't look at other anchors, ever. It gave me confidence that I don't have to change, that I can just continue as Jerry Springer. I don't know an anchor way of speaking, I'm never going to have a deep voice. It changed once, when I was 14, and it's never going to change again.'

Still Jerry insisted that his appointment and Hull's dismissal were totally unexpected, saying: 'It didn't cross my mind they were talking about me taking Rick Hull's place.'

The extra work also meant he renegotiated his financial deal, increasing the $75,000 to $100,000 he was said to be getting for his nightly commentaries. He would not reveal details of his new contract but joked, 'You know, $4 million a year, it was a good package.'

Jerry was ecstatic at his promotion, but he also knew it would put a lot of extra pressure on him to improve the dismal ratings, especially with the departure of Clooney. When he had joined Channel 12 the station was languishing in third place among news programmes, and Clooney had seen it take a commanding lead. Jerry told the *Cincinnati Enquirer*'s Tom Brinkmoeller: 'Here I am, 40 years old, which really isn't old, and I'm doing something new. For one thing, the timing creates more of a spotlight that favours comparison. I know enough about the business now to know that you can't blame the fall on one anchor, and you can't do so with the rise, either. Nick Clooney would be the first person to say that.'

He also talked enthusiastically about his job with WLWT to *Cincinnati Magazine*. He said: 'It's like an election, every single day. I'm incredibly lucky. I keep running into exciting things to do, and I get paid.'

Even though Jerry had now got the job he had wanted for many months, when he attended the Democratic Party's 1984 convention, which was held in San Francisco that July, there was speculation that he was laying the groundwork for a return to politics. Many people recalled the way he had worked the crowd at the 1980 Democratic Convention, joking about giving Ohioan delegates a piece of gum with his name on the wrapper and telling them to chew on the idea of him being governor. Four years later, while Jerry insisted he was purely in California as a journalist covering the event for Channel 5, delegates still remembered that stunt and were now chewing on the idea of seeing his name as the 1986 running mate for Governor Richard F Celeste, who had beaten Jerry for the Democratic nomination in 1982.

The then Lieutenant Governor Myrl Shoemaker was 71 and had been in hospital several times for circulatory problems and cancer treatment. In fact, Shoemaker was so ill that he couldn't attend the San Francisco convention that summer and there was widespread speculation that he would not be on the 1986 ticket. To add to the speculation, in the past Jerry had been vocal in indicating his desire to run with Celeste in 1986, which would put him in a strong position as leading candidate for the Democratic nomination for governor in 1990 — if Celeste won again he could not run for a third term under Ohio state law. Jerry went to great pains to stress that his desire to run with Celeste were expressed before he got his newscasting job.

He was in San Francisco to report the news, not to make it. When asked whether he'd be running for office in 1986, he said: 'Right now, I'm very happy with what I'm doing. I'm not thinking of doing anything other than this.' He did admit there were occasions when he suffered twinges of desire to get back into politics but there were times when other occupations seemed appealing as well. He said, 'If I have a bad day on the air, I'd rather be a cowboy.' Although Jerry seemed to be committed to his TV job, there were many Ohio delegates at the convention who hoped this broadcast cowboy would have a change of heart and re-enter politics, because he had good name recognition and was a proven fund-raiser, two gigantic qualities in the game of US politics.

Even with Jerry as the frontman presenting the news, Channel 5 could not rise from third place in the ratings. So, soon after his return from the convention it was decided to revamp the news format yet again, this time expanding the main evening report from 30 minutes to an hour. 'We want to drop the baggage of the past and start something new,' said Tony Kiernan, the Channel's third general manager in the time Jerry had been working for the station. 'We're putting our people in positions where they do what they do best.'

WLWT was an affiliate of the giant NBC, which is nicknamed the Peacock because of its multicoloured logo. The radical changes came into effect on 17 September, to coincide with the premiere of the Peacock's autumn programming schedule. Action 5 News, as the news programme was called, became News 5. The main news, which had started at 6pm was brought forward by half an hour to 5.30pm, with the first half focusing on what was happening in Cincinnati — reporters would go out on to the streets to interview people about what was important to them and their reactions to local events, and more studio interviews would be done live rather than pre-recorded.

The station designed a new set for that first half-hour to give the show a more modern and lively feel. Behind the anchor desk was a window through which viewers could catch a glimpse of reporters working away on stories in the Channel 5 newsroom, now a commonplace feature of news sets but a relatively new idea back then. Most importantly for Jerry, for the first half of the evening show he was the only presenter on the new set.

While Jerry fronted the first half of the show, co-anchor Rashid did studio interviews on the original news set, which had also been updated by replacing an old backdrop of Cincinnati with a new, more realistic image of the city skyline. She also covered updates of national news. At the end of the first half she and Jerry joined forces on the old set at 6pm and again for the 11pm news.

For the first half of the show Jerry was told to be relaxed and conversational, rather than a conventional, authoritative anchor, while still reading the news rather than commenting on it. That was not seen as much of a stretch for Jerry, by now a seasoned professional. It was still the news but it was also *The Jerry Springer Show*.

The second half of the new show concentrated on major news stories, features and series. By adding 30 minutes as people were arriving home from work, the station's programme was the same length as the early-evening newscasts on its two rival stations WCPO-

TV Channel 9 and WKRC-TV Channel 12, which had both expanded to one hour some time earlier.

The midday news, which still started at 11.30am, was lengthened to an hour and revamped. Even the colour of the cars used for reporters to go out on assignments was changed from silver and black to fire-engine red. Although Jerry was given half an hour of his own, he and Rashid had the kind of on-screen chemistry that meant their team would remain intact for the core parts of the nightly news, international and national reports and the late-night news.

The rock and roll politician turned silk-tie-wearing anchorman confessed that he was a little nervous at sailing into uncharted waters with the revamped broadcast. The truth was that it seemed to outside observers that Jerry would have to walk on water to achieve what the station had assigned him to do — make News 5 number one in the ratings.

The pressure was on and Channel 5 station bosses were convinced that, with an expanded news and Jerry, this time they were in with a chance to attract more viewers. Research had shown that viewers would not wait until 6pm for a half-hour news show when they could get a full hour starting at 5.30pm on the other two rival channels.

Working long hours — 11 hours a day, five days a week — mainly in the studio, meant that, although Jerry was still a high-profile figure in Cincinnati he was not seen out and about, although he was always a popular and much in demand lunchtime speaker for clubs, societies and local organisations when he could spare the time.

In early 1985 he pulled off a major coup for Channel 5, which left their rival stations red-faced and furious and also helped propel Jerry into further local prominence. After he attended a press conference to announce a major charitable airlift of between five and six tons of medical supplies, mainly vaccines, to the drought-plagued East African nation of Ethiopia, he contacted Bob Valentine, one of the organisers, and announced that he would love to accompany the party.

Channel 5 covered the conference and plans for the mercy mission over the following few weeks broadcasting details of where people could send donations, and on 8 February, Jerry devoted his commentary to the plight of the suffering Ethiopians.

As Jerry was so quick off the mark, not only did he get to stretch his wings on his first foreign assignment, Channel 5 was the only local news team that won permission to accompany the airlift.

The airlift was organised by two local Cincinnatians, pharmacist Bob Valentine, president of McMillan Medical Supplies, and Dr Charles Dillard, who worked for McMillan and was also on the staff of the local Bethesda Hospital. They were working with the Rev Joseph Bragotti, a local Roman Catholic missionary who had spent 10 years in Africa with his order, the Comboni Missionaries, to raise money to fund the trip.

At the conference Valentine announced the relief effort and revealed that he, Dr Dillard, Father Bragotti and Ohio Health Commissioner David Jackson were to make a trip to Ethiopia escorting the supplies and would then supervise their distribution throughout the starving nation. Collection of the medicine was being coordinated by the Comboni Mission Centre, which oversaw several missions in Ethiopia.

The Ethiopian government was very sensitive to critical foreign coverage of the country's famine tragedy, and it was believed they would allow only one local news organisation into the country to cover the arrival of the airlift. Thanks to Jerry's quick thinking, that was WLWT.

It also helped that, according to Father Bragotti, more than half of the $8,000 in private donations since the press conference was the direct result of Channel 5 coverage. The organisers were more than happy to help the station cut through the mountains of red tape involved in getting visas to fly to and film in the devastated country.

Executives at Channels 9 and 12 were furious at being upstaged by Jerry. By the time WLWT made the announcement that Jerry was on his way, the station had already obtained visas for him, assistant news director Rick Willis and photographer Paul Mato. In addition to Jerry sending back news reports, it was also planned that he would film a documentary on the Ethiopian situation. Channel 12 booked plane and hotel reservations and contacted the office of US Senator John Glenn, an Ohio Democrat, in the hope that he could help them get visas to go along on the airlift. However, processing the paperwork often took months, especially if the news organisation concerned did not have someone in Ethiopia, preferably someone well connected, to speak on their behalf. Channel 9 conceded defeat without even putting up a fight, announcing they had made an 'editorial decision' not to go on the trip. Jerry had beaten them to the draw.

While Jerry was away in Ethiopia there was renewed talk of his return to politics as Lieutenant Governor Shoemaker's health went further downhill. Political insiders speculated whether Jerry or Charles Luken, mayor of Cincinnati, would be the front-runner in the race for the post in the elections to be held in 1986. Jerry's old council friend David Mann was also tipped as a possible candidate.

When Jerry returned from Africa on Monday 11 March, having spent 10 days in the ravaged country, he was far more interested in promoting his incredible reporting accomplishments from the world stage than in getting involved in local politics.

Just as he had pulled off a coup in getting to the Horn of Africa in the first place, Jerry had an incredible stroke of luck once he got there — one that left more experienced reporters from bigger and more important organisations in the shade.

While the Marxist government had restricted most international news reporting teams to operating within a 30-mile radius of the capital, Jerry had, because he and his crew were escorting medical supplies, managed to sweet-talk the officials into giving him far greater access. While seasoned foreign correspondents kicked their heels in the capital, Addis Ababa, inexperienced Jerry had travelled 250 miles into Ethiopia's southern reaches. He succeeded in getting his scoop even though he discovered: 'The guides the Ethiopian government assigned to the team were in fact secret police officers who travelled everywhere with us and told everybody not to talk to me.' His telephone calls back to the station were monitored and he knew all along that his team's news tapes would be inspected before they left the country. Jerry did not discover until the day of their departure for home that the inspectors did not have a machine on which to view the video tapes.

As they didn't know that, Jerry and his crew worked out a plan. Once they were ready to shoot something potentially controversial or damning, one member of the party distracted the government guide long enough for Jerry to tape three or four sentences of his report. They then filmed tamer material, which the officials were unlikely to object to, making sure the more explosive footage was buried at random. This way, they hoped, whoever inspected the video would not realise the real items could easily be spliced together in the studio to make one coherent piece.

Jerry was horrified by what he witnessed during the trip. It was not simply seeing first-hand the horrors of mass suffering and death. In some ways even worse was the ghastly realisation that so much of it could have been prevented if the Ethiopian culture had not lagged several hundreds of years behind the developed world. He said: 'There is nothing in America that is anything like this. That's not to say some people aren't hurting very badly in America. Everything they're dying from, we know how to cure. We went to one place where six people had recently died from dysentery. They were lacking the medicine to deal with it, medicine the people from Cincinnati were able to give them. We actually saw human beings' lives being saved at that moment.'

The acute hunger he witnessed also affected Jerry. Even

though he was in the south which was better off than the north, the lack of food was severe: 'None of these people have shoes. And yet they walk on hard, rough terrain 20 to 25 miles every day, and they come here and wait. And maybe they get a bowl of soup or a piece of bread. Some of them die along the way.'

Jerry's biggest discovery turned into one of his largest problems when the news crew concluded the drought, devastating though it was, was not the main cause of Ethiopia's problems: 'The government is killing its own people through total incompetence as well as an obscene misalignment of values. Most of the food and medicine the government gets goes right to the soldiers. It's a holocaust without wires, without fences and without guards. I didn't realise the government is such a major part of this problem.' Once he realised what was going on, his biggest problem became that of evading the government guide long enough to tape his report in dribs and drabs.

The material that Jerry got was so explosive for sheltered Cincinnati that Channel 5 editors worked round the clock to get it into a usable form. Only 10 days after his triumphant return Jerry's hour-long documentary was aired to critical acclaim. It took a 'Cincinnati' boy to bring the true gravity of the situation to the well-fed Midwest.

Until then most of the TV coverage had come from overseas, often British, stations and the grainy satellite pictures combined with an accent that, to the American ear, often sounds slow and ponderous, had made the famine seem even more distant, and perhaps easier to blot out from Ohio consciences.

'That psychological shield takes a battering for anyone who watches the hour documentary,' wrote the *Cincinnati Enquirer*'s Brinkmoeller. 'It won't seem as unreal tonight. When it is Springer, the man who served so many years on Cincinnati City Council, who walks into a tent crammed with more than 100 people gathered for a bowl of soup, the Ethiopian tragedy looks much closer than a 19-hour airplane trip.'

Jerry closed his show inside the smoke-filled tent, seated next to a little girl who probably had no idea who he was or what he was doing there. Giving his overview of the Ethiopian tragedy he said, 'We can save some of its children. There is only one child in this world, and she is every child.'

What the viewers did not realise was that it took Jerry three takes to complete that final comment. No hardened newsman used to flying into the world's horror spots, recording a graphic report and moving on, he was deeply and personally affected by the grief he witnessed and the stoicism with which the sufferers bore it. Twice, looking at the child he had chosen to symbolise a nation's agony, he broke down in tears. His passion for his subject spilled over on to the film and gave the documentary a genuinely heartfelt appeal.

Brinkmoeller had nothing but praise for Jerry, who co-wrote the script with assistant news director Rick Williams. The critic ended his review, 'The airlift to Ethiopia was a mercy mission. The Channel 5 news team did more than cover that story. They captured it and brought it home with them.'

Jerry's Ethiopian adventure had an intriguing postscript: he and his travelling companions were invited to Rome to meet Pope John Paul II. Years later, he recalled, 'When the Vatican found out what our group was doing, we got an invitation to have an audience with the Pope. So I went over there, this Jewish guy, and it was pretty inspiring just to see someone who was so religious. I had a 15-minute audience with the Pope.'

When Jerry finally came down from the emotional and euphoric high of his African adventure he found time to address the latest speculation over his possible future in politics. In a letter to the *Cincinnati Enquirer* he made the clearest statement yet that his political career was over and the competition he was most interested in was the ratings race against rival newscasters.

'There have been two articles in your paper recently speculating on my being Governor Richard Celeste's choice for lieutenant governor in 1986,' he wrote. 'The articles were well written. They were flattering. They were also wrong. They were wrong because Lt Gov Myrl Shoemaker is the lieutenant governor, and as soon as he gets better he will run again. He deserves the governor's support, and he'll get it.

'The articles were also wrong because I am not a candidate for lieutenant governor, or governor, or councilman, or mayor, or congressman, or dog warden. Simply put, I'm not in politics, I'm in TV news. I enjoy anchoring on Channel 5. I love being able to write and deliver commentaries every day. I'm working hard at being a journalist; and, thankfully, people are starting to watch us now in growing numbers.

'I haven't lost my love for a good race. But these days I'm running against Al Schottelkotte and Randy Little. That's competition enough! Now, of course, if there's an opening for king, well ...'

Little could he have realised that as the world headed towards the millennium he would reign as the king of trash TV.

CHAPTER 16

Jerry's new role as the prominent anchor seat on the Channel 5 main news had not noticeably increased viewership figures. The station was still number three in the ratings and even general manager Tony Kiernan was having second thoughts about being so positive that Jerry could wave a magic wand and perform the miracle that was needed. A year after teaming Jerry with Norma Rashid on air, Kiernan engaged in secret talks to tried to persuade veteran Channel 9 anchorman Al Schottelkotte to move Channel 5 to see whether he could do any better. He was not interested so Kiernan decided to stick with Jerry, a decision that was eventually to pay off handsomely. Ironically Schottelkotte shortly afterwards decided to step down after 27 years on Channel 9 news.

Although Jerry was not able to boost the figures in his first year, his personal star was in the ascendancy at the Peacock affiliate. In the summer of 1985 his power and responsibility were increased. In addition to being the news co-anchor and still doing his nightly commentaries, Jerry was promoted to managing editor of the news department, a position that was especially created for him. The new job gave him more power over the content of the daily news bulletins and let him put his personal stamp on the programmes. In his new role, which he took up on 15 July, he took a much more active part in deciding which stories to cover and how much air time they were worth. He became involved in briefing reporters before they went on assignments, and reviewed their copy before it was broadcast, rather than just reading the stories blind.

He commented: 'They called me in and offered me the job.

I was really excited about it. This gives me a greater chance to have more of an input.'

No sooner had Jerry been promoted than he came under fire for selling out, turning conservative in a bid to boost the ratings. He leaped to the defence of then President Ronald Reagan when he suffered a brush with cancer and doctors had to remove polyps from his colon. In what observers regarded as a slightly surprising piece, Jerry predicted the Washington press corps would hound the Reagan Presidency for the rest of his term in office looking for indications that his health problems were wearing him down. 'Leave him alone,' urged Jerry. 'Such badgering weakens the nation in the eyes of the world and serves no useful purpose.'

An astonished *Cincinnati Enquirer* asked in amazement: 'Could Jerry Springer be turning conservative in his (relative) old age? The man who had helped 18-year-olds get a vote in Ohio and Riverside Stadium's first rock concert to Cincinnati, the city's one-time liberally Democratic boy mayor, sounded almost Republican.'

TV critic Tom Brinkmoeller asked: 'Could this be the same Springer who lost a bid for the Democratic nomination to become Ohio's governor? Or is this the co-anchor of a last-place newscast whose liberal background is costing him (in the opinion of many) the loyal following of many conservative Cincinnatians?' That week Jerry had already been asked whether he had been told by the WLWT management to mainstream his image in the hopes of kicking up the ratings. He totally denied it. 'They leave my commentaries alone,' he said.

In a commentary made just before his promotion, Jerry demanded armed retaliation against Shiite Moslems who had hijacked a TWA plane and he also called for armed marshals or soldiers on all US flights in the future. He did not see this as a sign that he was moving to the right. Rather, he said, it showed he was an independent who did not automatically follow a set political line: 'I find no inconsistency at all. I don't sense that I've changed my views on anything. Being a liberal doesn't mean you're not practical.'

Jerry insisted he was the same old Jerry, but that the public now saw him differently. In his days on council he had made the headlines as much for what were often seen as publicity grabbing stunts — hijacking the bus, Operation Deep Freeze, calling for a nuclear ban, performing in nightclubs — as he did for policy issues. His public image was largely built on these more outrageous escapades, with reports of routine council matters long since forgotten by most people. Now, however, he was a daily presence on TV, so the public saw and heard a lot more of him, especially through his commentaries, and could not help but know more about his opinions.

Rather tongue in cheek, Brinkmoeller sarcastically pointed out: 'And coincidentally, perhaps, discover he's not such a wild-eyed liberal.'

Whatever double standards the press might perceive, Jerry was on the first few ups-and-downs of what has become an unstoppable roller-coaster career. It did not matter whether the media was knocking him. At the time, it did not even seem to matter that the ratings WLWT so desperately wanted were not being achieved. The viewers that News 5 did have tuned in, at least in part, because of Jerry and the increasingly good on-screen chemistry with his co-anchor Norma Rashid, who was 30 at the time.

When WBBM-TV, the CBS-owned Channel 2 in Chicago, tried to lure Rashid away that October with the offer of a job as a reporter she decided to turn down them down and stay in her anchor's chair. Channel 5 executives were so relieved that both she and Jerry were given new multi-year contracts to ensure they remained with the station in Cincinnati. The new contracts were to last a further two to four years, extending their commitment to the station at least until 1988. WLWT news director Tom Kuelbs and the station's general manager Tony Kiernan were sure that the ratings would eventually improve provided they could keep their dynamic duo intact. 'We didn't want what happened to Channel 12 with Nick Clooney and Ira Joe Fisher to happen to us,' Kuelbs admitted. After Clooney and his co-anchor Fisher took WKRC-TV Channel 12 to No. 1 in local news ratings, they both left the station for more money in bigger markets.

At the close of the 11pm news on Friday 18 October 1985, Jerry used his commentary to announce to his viewers, 'Norma's decided to stay.' He made no mention of the fact that his contract had also been renegotiated.

Not all of Jerry's broadcasting talents were so profitable. The WNKU-FM radio station, an affiliate of National Public Radio, which was supported by donations from listeners rather than advertising, held an on-air fund-raiser trying to raise $10,000 towards its running costs. Jerry and Tom Beehan, the mayor of Covington, the Kentucky town just across the Ohio River from Cincinnati, volunteered to help. They played guitars and sang folk songs between 7.30pm and 7.45pm in the middle of a popular magazine programme, *All Things Considered*. They promised to stop singing as soon as listeners phoned in to promise a total of $100 in 'pledges', the public broadcasting expression for tax-deductible contributions.. However, they had to keep singing for the full 15 minutes and never did reach their goal. 'This is awful, you know, it's really bad,' Jerry told the listeners. Then he made a pledge of his own. He said, 'If anyone has been taping this, I want you to know I'm prepared to buy the tape. I'll buy the tape and burn it.' Well, the station did surpass its $10,000 target by the end of the pledge drive, but with only a little help from Tom and Jerry. By the time they'd finished their set, they'd raised just $35, and Jerry never did reveal whether he handed over any cash to get a bootleg tape!

The WLWT newsroom telephones rang off the hook the night of Monday 14 April 1986 when Channel 5 was set to give a report on a US airforce counter-terrorist bombing raid on Libya. The attack, which resulted in the killing of one of Libyan leader Colonel Muammar Gaddafi's daughters, also hit several camps believed to house terrorists in and around the capital, Tripoli. However, the callers were not expressing their views on the raid. They all wanted to know whether they really had heard Jerry swearing.

The problem was that WLWT had cut away from *The Newlywed Game*, a popular game show, for Jerry to introduce a bulletin about the Libyan strike, which had been ordered by President Ronald Reagan. It was a live report coming direct from the NBC network. However, the feed did not make it on the air and Jerry was left stranded. After the station switched back to the game show, Jerry said to the production staff, 'That made me look like an asshole.' Unfortunately for him, his microphone was still live, and his comment was broadcast over the top of the show's soundtrack.

About 100 people called the station wanting to know, 'Did Jerry Springer say that slang term for a person's posterior on the air?'

Jerry personally spoke to many of the callers, apologising for his comment and explaining how the mistake had happened. However, there was no mention of the slip-up when Jerry presented the late news that night.

During his news reading and commentary years, Jerry settled into a relatively sedentary pattern of working long days in the studio. He usually arrived at the station around 10am and most nights did not leave until midnight or later, staying in the newsroom to take calls from viewers who wanted to discuss his commentaries. He wrote them in longhand on a yellow legal pad, just as he had done during his days at WEBN radio, after dinner each night, once he had seen the main news stories while presenting the 5.30pm news and noting which topics had prompted viewers' telephone calls.

He admitted, 'Every night I'm making a lot of people angry'. Jerry was always very scientific about the timing of his commentary! He confessed: 'When I get two-thirds of the way down the second page, I know I have to bring it home.' Jerry realised that his TV commentaries could achieve far more than any speech he might have made in the council chamber, the Ohio Statehouse or even Washington's Capitol Hill, had he succeeded in his earlier political aspirations, for his commentary was watched in an estimated 98,000 households every night. He admitted: 'The President of the USA isn't on two and a half minutes a night. I'm so happy with what I'm doing. I could do this the rest of my life. I don't know that I will but I could. This is the best job in the world. And they pay me for it, which is absurd, but I'm glad they do.'

Occasionally after work, he hit one of Cincinnati's late-night watering holes, although he was never regarded as a heavy drinker. Sometimes he would drop in to Arnold's Bar and Grill on East Eighth St, Cincinnati's oldest bar dating back to 1861. He used to go to one of the small, discreet rooms on the first floor, complete with creaky floorboards, that sat only a handful of people, where he liked to be served by a ravishing young waitress with flowing, dark hair. Jerry was particularly fond of the busty waitress, who was partially deaf, and showed a lot of patience and kindness towards her.

Jerry spent as much of his spare time as possible with his cherished daughter Katie, watching her grow and bravely overcome the difficulties of her own handicap. He also enjoyed playing with the family dog. He and Micki had moved to a big house in a cul-de-sac in the Cincinnati suburb of Loveland and he drove to work each day in his imported Jaguar car, which he treasured.

In addition to his work at the station, he maintained an active public speaking schedule, just as he had done when he was mayor, making four or five appearances every week, and he was pleased that his audiences finally seemed to have accepted that he had made the transition from politician to TV personality. He now fielded far more questions about his nightly commentaries than about any future political ambitions. He was typically modest about his popularity as a speaker. 'When you speak at a dinner, people come prepared to laugh,' he said. 'Dinners are boring by definition. Most people go because they have to. They're not sitting at home on Saturday night saying, "Hey, instead of going to a movie, let's go to a testimonial dinner!" So anything you give them will be welcome.'

If not on the guest-speaking circuit, lunch was more often than not taken at his desk and was frequently a cheeseburger. Although not an Orthodox Jew or strictly Kosher, Jerry has always followed many of the dietary rules of his faith and stays away from eating pork.

To Jerry the most important part of his job was his nightly two-and-a-half minute personal essay that he delivered from the anchorman's desk. He confessed: 'I have no interest in just being an anchor. Writing commentaries is so intellectually stimulating. In politics, after you develop basic issues, you tend to repeat them day after day. With the commentaries, you're forced to create something new every day. There are not many jobs in the world where you have to create something new, every day, from scratch.'

The on-screen chemistry between Norma Rashid and Jerry was eventually working for viewers. By February 1987 the duo's popularity had finally been able to drag News 5 out of the ratings cellar. The show was a strong second in the ratings. They had been on screen together for three years, the longest continuous tenure among the city's news anchors, when Norma needed to take maternity leave, which left Jerry as the mainstay of Channel 5's nightly news for a while. The station management gave Jerry, who after Nick Clooney's departure had become the oldest TV anchor man in town, yet another new contract, this time committing him to present the news for a further five years. By the time that contract ended, he would have worked as a news anchor at WLWT for eight years, as long as he had spent in council.

Finally in May 1987 Jerry and Norma achieved what many sceptics had regarded as the impossible when Jerry was first given a chance to co-anchor the news. News 5's 11pm broadcast became number one in the ratings and stayed there throughout the remainder of the years Jerry continued as a news presenter.

Channel 5 enjoys a viewership that covered parts of three states — southwest Ohio, southeast Indiana and north Kentucky — and Jerry felt sure that the increased ratings meant that Tri-State viewers had finally accepted him as a newsman instead of a politician between campaigns. He said: 'I don't know when it happened, but sometime in the past year it changed.' He told the *Cincinnati Enquirer's* recently appointed radio and TV critic John Kiesewetter: 'It's grown to be a period of acceptance. No longer do you get people saying, "What's *he* doing on TV?" Now residents ask, "Did you see Springer's commentary last night?"'

Jerry never forgot his past or the fact that he'd been such a political character. He presented a five-night series of commentaries on then-Democratic presidential candidate Gary Hart, the married US senator whose political aspirations were torpedoed when he challenged the press to prove him a scoundrel and lost the bet — he was cheating on his wife with sexy Donna Rice and lied about it. After he laid down his challenge, reporters exposed that he had spent a weekend at his Washington, DC, townhouse home with the beautiful young model. She was also pictured off the coast of Florida sitting on his lap on his yacht, the aptly named *Monkey Business*.

Rather than give his opponents an opportunity to bring up his own past misdeeds with young women, Jerry reminded his viewers of his own dubious involvement in the cheque incident. 'Maybe I should be the last person to speak on this issue, or then again maybe the first,' he told his TV audience. He did not set out to talk so much about the disgraced presidential candidate, but as the week progressed, each evening he thought Hart was the topic everyone had been talking about that day, and he wanted to share his own thoughts on the subject in his commentary, now renamed 'Final Thought'.

'I always started the day out saying, "I'm going to write about something different" but then something happened in the news that day,' he said.

His viewers were becoming increasingly confused by his commentaries. That is because Jerry was, and still is, such a complex character that just when people thought they knew where he stood, he darted off in a different direction. During the summer of 1987, he managed to hold two apparently contradictory opinions on issues of entertainment and freedom of expression. It was no surprise that he spoke in favour of a Beastie Boys and Run DMC. concert, due to be held in Cincinnati, even though there had been violence at some earlier concerts. In a commentary on the concert he said: 'The soul of Cincinnati is not its buildings or its multi-million dollar developments. It's rather in the diversity of its people, its culture, its tastes, its lifestyles, all co-existing. If we start saying no to entertainment that drifts from the mainstream, there is a risk of injury there, too. We could die of boredom.'

Yet at the same time he was strongly opposed to the showing of *Hail Mary*, a controversial French film directed by Jean-Luc Goddard, about a modern-day virgin who inexplicably becomes pregnant. The film, starring Thierry Rhode and Juliette Binoche, was denounced by many people as anti-Catholic. In a commentary Jerry said: 'They do have a right to show the film *Hail Mary*. But that doesn't mean they should do it. We're talking religion here, something very personal and private. People take their religion very seriously. And why for the sake of one movie that we don't have to see, why insult them? Make no mistake, the issue here isn't constitutional rights or artistic licence. It's simply common decency.'

Kiesewetter blasted Jerry in one of his editorials: 'So what's the decent thing to do? Should we ban entertainment that may potentially be physically or morally harmful? Should we permit entertainment that "drifts from the mainstream" and promote diverse cultural opportunities. Or should we ask a bigger question: has the former councilman abandoned philosophical purity for populist positions that garner better TV ratings?'

Everything came back to that God of TV bosses, ratings. Jerry found himself embroiled in a row over allegations that he was playing politics to boost his ratings when the spring sweeps came round in February 1988, which are immensely important for the US TV business.

A bus strike was the talk of the town on the very first day of the sweeps that February. Jerry, who had successfully settled a bus strike during his days as mayor, brought the Queen City Metro management, the company that ran the bus company, and leaders of the striking drivers on to the 11pm news. In a live interview he asked Metro manager Michael Setzer and union president Bob Baker whether they were willing to resume negotiations. Both men agreed that they would call each other the following morning, Friday, and meet later in the day. The next morning Channel 5 issued a statement claiming that Jerry was responsible for bringing both sides back to the bargaining table. The PR plug was picked up by several radio stations and run on their news programmes, even using sound-bites of Jerry's show, giving great publicity for News 5.

The news directors of both of the competing stations cried foul. They claimed that long before Jerry's show both sides in the bus strike had agreed to a proposal by Mayor Charles Luken to renew the negotiations. However, former politician Jerry, who never could resist playing mediator, stuck to his guns and insisted he had brought the two sides together. He acknowledged that Baker and Setzer had agreed to the mayor's suggestion to renew negotiations, but stressed, 'Neither had committed to sitting down and talking at a specific time or date. There was no specific agreement at all.'

Jerry also took credit for the mayor becoming involved in the first place, thanks to his Wednesday night commentary: 'I said the city ought to get involved and the next day the mayor offered to act as mediator. I'm not saying they're related; you can draw your own conclusion.' It was later claimed that Luken had got involved before Jerry's commentary. However, it didn't matter. Jerry had the upper hand, won the PR battle and he basked in the publicity he had successfully manipulated.

However, Jerry's commentaries didn't always land him in hot water. By the end of 1988 he had written and presented around 1,500 short on-air essays, 250 a year for the six years since he'd joined the station. Tish Hauss, News 5's executive producer, came up with the idea of turning his commentaries into a book to help raise funds for a local charity. Jerry liked the idea and was happy to see his often controversial thoughts put to good use. He selected what he regarded as the best of them, a kind of Jerry Springer's greatest hits, which were published and the proceeds went to support the Ruth Lyons Children's Cancer Fund, which raised funds to buy sick children Christmas presents. The limited number of copies were a big hit in Cincinnati and Jerry was pleased to help the kids.

Ruth Lyons was a pioneering Midwestern broadcaster who became a post-World War II phenomenon, turning her no-script talk show into a $2 million-a-year business. Described as 'the most influential housewife in America', she enjoyed a 30-year career, ending up hosting a show called *The 50-50 Club* for WLWT, interviewing guests before a live audience, but she abruptly retired in 1967. At the height of her success an estimated seven million viewers in Ohio, Kentucky, Indiana and West Virginia tuned in. She was also a major philanthropist and received The Great Living Cincinnatian Award in 1987, the year before Jerry donated his book to her cause. She died in 1988.

Jerry admired her because she once credited her success to not talking down to her viewers, eliminating private, showbusiness jokes; considering the housewife an important member of society; believing the average woman was interested in the city and the world; and thinking about the programme every waking moment. Views that Jerry recognised and agreed with, even though he did not know her: 'I never met Ruth Lyons. I never even saw her show. She reigned the daily airwaves before I arrived in Cincinnati, yet I know I've seen her. I've seen her in the smiling faces of the kids who lie in local hospitals, playing with a toy or watching a TV set, rocking with Mom in a rocker that might not have been there if Ruth Lyons hadn't cared and hadn't asked us to care.'

Despite his often bombastic manner, Jerry has always had a way of using words to appear humble and touch other people's hearts and make them feel humble as well.

Jerry dedicated the book to his wife Micki, daughter Katie and sister Evelyn. In the acknowledgements he thanked his parents, who by this time had sadly passed away. He wrote: 'I wish they could see the results of their teachings. But then again, maybe they can.'

The commentaries covered the spectrum of the opinions he had expressed five nights a week, 50 weeks a year — TV personalities do not get much holiday time in the USA — for six years. He talked of the struggles he and others had faced, he remembered people and moments that had played a significant part in his life and the lives of others, he talked about games (he still loved sports) and he opened his heart to discuss the tragedies and celebrations that he and others had faced. Many people in the city still keep a copy at home as a souvenir.

Never afraid to risk making himself look foolish, he put his failure as a folk-singing fund-raiser behind him and turned his attention to country music for a few days. He recorded a spot singing three songs, 'Honky Tonk Angels', 'Bobby McGee' and 'Little Darlin'', which were aired for a week on a local cable station.

The former baby-faced politician, once known by such nicknames as King Kid and the Boy Mayor, had comfortably settled into middle-aged life as the elder statesman of Cincinnati TV anchoring. At the age of 45, he confessed to Kiesewetter: 'It isn't tough being an anchor. If you can get over the nervousness, you can learn it in a month and a half. If the red light is on, you talk. I'm the luckiest person in the world. Look at the job I've got!'

With the confidence that being on top of the TV heap in Cincinnati gave him, Jerry finally confessed that moving into the genre had not been as easy as he had always claimed. Admitting some rare self-doubt, he revealed that at first he found the intimacy of talking to a camera much more intimidating than speaking live to large crowds.

He said: 'At rallies, not everyone pays attention. You can mumble. No one is recording it. In life there are no VCRs. I'd say it took a solid year before I got comfortable anchoring. Then I reached the point where I'd still sweat when things fell apart.' He told Kiesewetter that it was only in the year before their conversation that he had finally realised, 'Hey, it's only television.' Now he was at ease with himself and the camera.

A year earlier on his 44th birthday, the man who was born on the 44th day of the 44th year of the century had realised that his youth was behind him: 'I look at tapes of our newscasts and my face has more lines than my commentary, on certain nights looking like a blue print of Fountain Square West. They're no longer calling me "Boy Mayor" or "Kid Commentator" and since Nick left 12, I'm now the oldest anchor in town. I'm not yet grey, but I'm getting blue, facing the truth of life's only constant — that I'm always older than I've ever been.' But he joked that getting older certainly beat the alternative.

Jerry's old TV rival but personal friend Nick Clooney briefly returned from Los Angeles to Cincinnati airwaves but even he could not shake Jerry's now iron grip on the number one ratings spot. When Clooney quit Cincinnati TV for the second time early in 1988, Jerry paid tribute to his adversary. Jerry described him as 'a very good, hard-working journalist who gets up in the morning, goes to work, tries to find out what happened that day, and tells you about it at night. He's simply an excellent newsman who changed the shape of local TV news over the past 10 years, I think for the better.'

It was not only Clooney who found Jerry impossible to beat. By February 1989 Channel 5's early evening news, hosted by Jerry and Norma Rashid, achieved number one in the ratings for that segment, beating Channel 9's early news for the first time in several years. Jerry also marked 20 years of living in Cincinnati, making him the TV anchor who had lived there for the longest period.

After enjoying uninterrupted years of support for his commentaries and no interference from management, relations between Jerry and Kiernan came to a sudden head in May 1989 when for the first time the station manager ordered one of Jerry's commentaries to be pulled off the air. Kiernan was not even in the studio at the time. He was at home watching the news when

Norma Rashid announced that after the final commercial break of the show, Jerry's commentary would be on the made-for-TV film *Roe v Wade*, the landmark court case that led to abortion being legalised in the USA.

He immediately called the station and ordered the adverts to be extended over the time allotted for Jerry's comments. After the break there was no time for the anchors to do anything but sign off for the night

Ironically, as it turned out, Jerry was not planning to comment on the film itself, but on the right of the NBC network, of which WLWT is an affiliate, to air it at all. NBC had decided to air the film despite heavy opposition from pro-life activists and worries from advertisers who were wary of being associated with such emotional and controversial topics.

It was such a sensitive topic that WLWT received more than 1,000 telephone calls about it before it aired.

Jerry was understandably furious that, after six and a half years and some 1,500 commentaries, his own freedom of expression on Channel 5 had been denied.

He arrived at work the next morning fully prepared to resign, clear his desk and go. After a heated discussion, Kiernan backed down. Later that day he said the commentary was not killed because of what Jerry intended to say but because he hadn't informed him of what he was planning to say. Kiernan told the press: 'Jerry and I have an agreement that on issues of extreme sensitivity we discuss the nature and content of the commentary. We've never forbidden Jerry from doing a commentary. But on issues of extraordinary sensitivity, I have requested that there be some discussion before the fact. This is not an attempt to censor or take editorial control out of Jerry's hands.'

Kiernan said he had wanted to talk to Jerry before the commentary because of the incredible interest in it and the high volume of viewer phone calls on both sides of the abortion issue. He also claimed he had told Jerry the previous Friday that a comment relating to *Roe v Wade* would have to be discussed in advance.

Jerry had a different view of the events that led to the showdown between the two of them. He said he had simply been asked to telephone Kiernan about the movie, and that when he called there was no reply. He said that the last-minute pulling of his commentary 'was sloppily handled and I didn't like the way it was handled by management. The station was under a lot of heat and he was sitting at home watching the news and he said, "Oh no, not a commentary."'

He did, however, acknowledge that the station's management had the right to review what he said on air. 'And if they don't like it, they have every right to fire me.'

After the row and all the resulting publicity, the next day his commentary ran word for word as he had written it, not only in the usual time slot but during the early evening news broadcast as well. In it, Jerry, who is personally opposed to abortion, said: 'NBC or this station isn't pro-choice or right to life. It's simply a company that provides entertainment, information and news. And some of it is good, and some of it isn't, and the debate over whether the movie adequately reflects the truth about Roe v Wade is legitimate. But arguing that it shouldn't be shown is not. Abortion is a divisive enough issue as is, without having to abort the principle of free expression in the process.'

In all the time he had been presenting his evening essay he had only ever discussed the content of his commentaries on hot topics on four occasions. Jerry asked: 'After six years what could I possibly say that would do as much damage as this treatment has done? They've never changed any words.' In the only placatory words he spoke, Jerry added, 'I have more leeway than any person on TV has a right to expect.'

Jerry had proved that at the end of the day his pen was mightier than the station manager's sword. Much of his appeal to viewers was attributed to the commentaries that distinguished him from the anchors of his competitors. To lose Jerry would have almost certainly meant losing ratings and Kiernan could have been shown the door as well.

CHAPTER 17

The Jaguar had been traded in for a Bentley by the time Jerry became homeless. With only $10 in his pocket, he shuffled around downtown in the city where he once reigned as mayor. He ate at soup kitchens in the Over-the-Rhine district of Cincinnati, took catnaps in the public library and slept in the Drop Inn Centre for down-and-outs and under makeshift cardboard homes on the city streets and in the parks. Gone were his trademark silk ties and immaculate suits; in their place were tattered rags, a long beard and a Quaker hat. He looked like Fagin on a bad day. What had happened to the slick TV celebrity? He was chasing that other God, of course: better TV ratings!

For six days and nights Jerry bummed around Cincinnati posing as a homeless destitute for a mind-provoking *When The Streets Are Home* series of reports, which ran on the late-night news. Many of his adversaries had often referred to him as a bum as a politician and news commentator; now he had come up with the idea of being one for real.

The man with the most recognisable nose on TV had put on an elaborate disguise and taken to the streets followed by two undercover colleagues, TV editor Jim Connelly and photographer Rob Busby, carrying a discreet, tiny camera to record the events that unfolded. Amazingly, only one person recognised Jerry during the entire 144 hours he was roughing it for real, disguised in a fake beard and wearing worn-out hand-me-downs.

Jerry's 'ordeal' started at 3pm on Tuesday 9 April in the Mount Adams Playhouse in the Park, when make-up artist Kelly Yurko began applying the cosmetics that would change him into a tramp. He cheerfully admitted that part of him always enjoyed being recognised but it was Kelly's job to destroy that possibility. To take his mind off what was happening Jerry started to recite the famous Gettysburg Address, President Abraham Lincoln's most famous speech, as Kelly added bags under his eyes. Jerry recalled: 'I wasn't even tired but I sure looked it.' He swapped his suit for a scruffy jacket, shirt and a cap, loaned to him by the people at the Playhouse, and he was ready to give the performance of a lifetime. He had also insisted on being given a sleeping bag to carry on his back to add more realism to his portrayal.

It was 4.30pm when, for a chilling moment, Jerry was overcome with self-doubt. He completely lost his usual self-confidence and was sure that people would recognise him. Producer Shannon Reichley shook him out of his brooding. 'It's time to hit the road,' she said as she handed him $10. She added, 'That's it for the week.' That was it. From that moment on the trio's only contact with their station was a daily rendezvous with a TV producer and Kelly for make-up repairs, especially to Jerry's beard.

By 6.15pm Jerry had made his way to the Drop Inn Centre on 12th Street. A lot of people were just standing around outside and Jerry found himself fitting right in, although he kept being haunted by the nagging doubt that they must all be staring at him and that he would quickly be found out. He kept his head down in a desperate bid to avoid making eye contact with any of the other hobos. When he was asked to sign in at the centre he quickly discovered that the lies came easily. He told them he was 43, when, in fact, he was 47, and he gave his name as Charlie Silvera. Luckily for Jerry the assistants at the centre weren't the baseball aficionados that he was — Charlie Silvera was the name of a former back-up catcher who played for the Yankees in the early 1950s.

Jerry had been at the Drop Inn for little more than an hour when he decided to experience more of life on the streets. He started to walk around downtown and kept walking and walking. By now the tension he had first felt had gone and he was more relaxed but he quickly discovered that he was also bored. For the first time he realised that, far from being recognised, no one even noticed him. It felt strange. He was invisible to people in the city where he was king.

The first light-hearted moment he experienced was when he returned to the Drop Inn to stay the night. He went into the recreation area where many of the other 'residents' were watching the late news on Channel 5. In a diary he kept for the *Cincinnati*

Post he recalled: 'A voice in the crowd says, "Hey, where's Springer?" I can't believe my ears.'

As soon as the news ended at 11.30pm it was time for lights out. Jerry's diary recorded: 'I'm assigned mat number 115 in the sleeping room. It's wall-to-wall mats here, each 3ft by 6ft, one touching against the other. No modesty here, either, just a large group of people having blessedly found safe shelter for at least the night. Can't sleep though. Many are snoring, one guy's getting sick, another appears quite drunk and bent on picking a fight. The turmoil subsides somewhat, but not the stench. It's indescribable, beer and body odour?'

As he lay there in the dark, Jerry's thoughts must have strayed to his wife and daughter tucked up clean and warm in bed in their respectable, two-storey house in the suburbs.

By the time Jerry left the Drop Inn the following morning at 6am he was already running out of money and feeling hungry. His lack of cash was the significant factor influencing his decision to skip breakfast. As he walked down Vine Street in the heart of downtown Cincinnati, Jerry noticed that people walking towards him, suddenly stepped to the other side of the pavement and every one of them turned their gaze elsewhere to avoid looking at him. He was beginning to gain the understanding that in the eyes of many the homeless are non-people.

He found sanctuary in the public library soon after it opened for the day. Inside one of the main reading rooms he noticed 10 long wooden tables at which a number of other down-and-outs were seated. He took a book from the shelves, sat down at one of the tables and promptly fell asleep. No one bothered him. Even today the modern central library is a haven for down-and-outs who seek its warmth in winter and air-conditioning in summer. They are tolerated by the staff and library users who realise how much more fortunate they are.

Thanks to word of mouth on the streets Jerry learned that in the late afternoon every Monday, Wednesday and Friday, St Francis Seraph School opened its doors and, more importantly, its kitchen to the homeless. The school let the homeless in for the free hot meals at 4.30pm. Jerry arrived on the corner of Liberty Street and Vine Street, where the school was located, at 4.15pm and already there were about 150 people waiting outside the doors. It struck Jerry that everybody looked old, even the young. Late in the evening, he made his way to the Greyhound Bus Station hoping to get some much needed sleep on a bench. To his horror, he discovered that the old benches he remembered had long gone and there was nowhere for him to stretch out.

Despite there being no bench on which to sleep, Jerry was in desperate need of rest so he slumped down in a corner to ease his aching body and weary mind. But his rest was to be short-lived.

He recalled: 'Just before 1.30am I'm awakened by a portable radio of some sort. My fellow "passengers" have apparently left for their departure gate and I am virtually alone with a security guard who is speaking into what appears to be a police walkie-talkie. "I've got a suspicious character here," he says. With a degree of fear, but a sense of aplomb, I bid a hasty farewell to the bus terminal.' He clearly did not relish the thought of another night in jail, this time for real.

A little later Jerry found the benches he had been seeking outside the Seasongood Pavilion in the city's Eden Park. At last he could stretch out and relax. He couldn't believe the joy he felt and soon he was fast asleep. But once again the grim reality of the law was to intrude into his sleep.

'An eternity later, though probably only an hour,' he went on. 'Someone nudges me. My eyes half open and there's a flashlight pouring a beam of light into my face. "You can't stay here!" a stern voice warns. I see a uniform, probably park police. My first instinct is to tell him, "Hey, I'm Jerry Springer," but I resist that temptation.'

For the first couple of days Jerry felt self-conscious and was convinced he would be recognised as a fake: 'I kept feeling that this was absurd, that somebody would say, "Hey, Springer! Get off that park bench!"'

Midday Thursday found Jerry outside the Bank Cafe. Money was running desperately short but Jerry still hadn't stooped to begging. Nevertheless, regardless of his cash crisis he had to buy something for lunch. Soon after eating, Jerry bumped into Jack, a Korean War veteran, who was his first friend on the street. They got talking and Jerry asked Jack whether he could recommend somewhere to stay for the night. Jack recommended the Drop Inn, the only shelter in town. After they had talked a bit, Jerry learned that Jack, a man in his fifties, received around $300 a month in military pension and social security payments to live off. 'Why don't you get a room of your own?' Jerry asked him. 'I don't want to live alone because they rob you,' came the reply. 'At least at the Drop Inn, I can be with other people.'

That evening Jerry was walking down Gest Street, heading towards the railway sidings. He walked under a freeway overpass. It should have been a road that was familiar to him but he was so disoriented from looking at life from such a different perspective that he did not recognise it. 'Is it I-71?' he asked himself. 'I-75? Does it matter?'

He headed towards a fire he saw burning in the distance, and met up with 43-year-old Bill, a mechanic by trade, now down on his luck and living out of a battered supermarket trolley.

'The blaze is burning in an old steel drum, like something out of a Depression-era movie,' he wrote in his diary. He is thoroughly depressed by the tale Bill, who looks two decades older than his years, has to tell him. He had moved to Cincinnati from Florida in search of his brother but could not find him or a job. He had asthma and a heart condition, which made him virtually unemployable. A few weeks earlier he had suffered a heart attack, and was lucky enough to be taken in by one of the city hospitals. Even though that probably saved his life he had already forgotten the name.

'I asked him, "How do you make it on the street?" and he said, "Well, if you're willing to rob people or deal drugs you can make it on the streets, but I wasn't brought up that way." So by day Bill shuffles around the underside of our city, pushing a once-abandoned shopping cart that contains his only worldly possession, save the worn clothes on his back, an old mattress. Honour-filled but body-afflicted, Bill is a victim, someone who's fallen through cracks our society has made no effort to patch up.'

By Friday, Jerry was more than halfway through his self-inflicted ordeal. He made up his mind, 'Today I must find a job ... or I must beg.' At 9am he was at a place on 12th Street, near the Drop Inn, which found day labour work but he was already too late. As it happened there was no work for anyone that morning but if there had been it would have been filled long before then. Only the earliest of birds caught a worm's worth of work. 'Can I at least fill out an application?' Jerry asked. 'Do you have ID?' he was asked. Jerry said he hadn't and was promptly told, 'No ID, no job.' He resigned himself to spending the day begging.

'"Can you spare a quarter?" I ask a man in a well-tailored suit,' he recalled. 'He doesn't see me, no acknowledgement whatsoever. The man just stares straight ahead.'

Over the course of the day he became hardened to rejection and began to understand why some street people have such an aggressive, threatening approach when they are begging — because they are desperate and being nice doesn't work. Mild-mannered Jerry forced himself to be more aggressive but still he had no luck.

Then he had a moment of triumph. 'Finally, one man gives me a dollar bill and I'm all at once and altogether excited, relieved and genuinely moved by his generosity. There's hope for me yet. The begging continues for a couple of hours and I finally stop to count my bounty. Four dollars!'

Jerry was back in the Cincinnati Public Library Saturday lunchtime when a young man struck up a conversation. This was the first person in four days, other than fellow tramps, who had spoken to him. The young man had been staring at him long and hard before finally approaching and asking, 'Where are you headed?' Jerry was shocked and gave him some non-committal reply.

Then he recalled, 'He blurts out, "Ya know, you look a lot like Jerry Springer." I'm a little taken aback but manage a, "Yeah, I get that all the time." Fifteen minutes later, same guy approaches. "Are you sure you're not Jerry Springer?" he asks. Well, I got to tell someone. I rationalise. It's been a long week. I proceed to tell "Dan" what I'm up to, and evoke from him a pledge to keep my "little secret".'

Sunday could not come quickly enough for Jerry. By the end of the experiment, even though he knew he was playing and would soon be able to shower, change into respectable clothes and eat a decent meal, he felt as much of a bum as he looked. He told the *Cincinnati Enquirer*'s John Kiesewetter: 'By the end of the week, it wore me down. You didn't care what you looked like or smelt like. What you find is surprisingly little anger or bitterness. What you find is resignation. And the question, "Why can't these people get a job?" is just absurd. When you're down at this point, these people have to get their lives together. If they've got an alcohol or drug or mental problem, who's going to hire them? You can't even get a shower, or clean clothes, for a job interview.'

He went home and off came the beard and moustache, the dirty clothes were discarded on the floor and Jerry leaped into the shower. The water rained down on him, washing away the horror of his experience but not the memories. A hug from his precious daughter Katie and a meal were followed by him collapsing into his own bed for a long, sound sleep. Jerry thought to himself and later relayed to his viewers, 'Home. What a word that is, what a wonderful, wonderful word.'

Despite what he'd been through, Jerry still didn't feel that he truly knew what it was like to be homeless: 'No matter what discomfort I'd felt for a week, I always knew there'd be that hot shower, the warm bed, lots to eat. I suffered physically for a time, but I didn't experience any of the emotional or psychological trauma of realising that the abject poverty might never end.'

He later recalled: 'I was like a non-person. No one looked at me. It made me realise that I do the same thing. We don't look at the street people. We don't want to deal with them.'

Kiesewetter enquired whether the experience meant that Jerry found himself giving more money to beggars after having lived as a homeless person. Ever the politician he told him: 'I was always reasonably good about giving money. I guess that's the Democrat in me.'

Cynics dismissed Jerry's experiences as nothing more than begging for better TV ratings. However, Jerry was adamant that he was trying to highlight a real problem that should concern the people of Cincinnati. He said, 'This isn't Ethiopia. This is four blocks from Fountain Square. This is in the shadow of the skyline we brag about.'

Experiencing life on the streets was just one of a number of news coups that Jerry pulled off during the years he served as Cincinnati's leading newscaster.

Jerry successfully secured an interview with disgraced hometown superstar, baseball hero Pete Rose in the federal prison camp in Illinois where he was serving his sentence for illegal gambling on baseball. In the interview, Rose revealed that when he was released he planned to quit his hometown and move to Florida to start a new life running a restaurant. He had previously dabbled in the restaurant business in Cincinnati and one of his closest friends, Jeff Ruby, was a prominent Cincinnati restaurateur. Breaking the news that Rose would leave his home town was a major feather in Jerry's cap and shocked Cincinnati.

During his years with WLWT, Jerry also won seven Emmy awards, TV's top accolade, for his work and was voted TV Best Anchor for five consecutive years.

CHAPTER 18

Jane Purvis wept so hard she could hardly speak as she grasped the hand of a woman she had not seen for 35 years — her daughter, Sandy Mrasak. Many of the 150 people in the studio audience on the fifth floor of the WLWT TV studio in downtown Cincinnati wept along with her as she recounted a harrowing tale of how she had lost her two children, a son and a daughter, one aged four years and the other just four months, after her husband shot her six times before fatally turning the gun on himself. Back in 1956 when she was shot, because she was so seriously injured and had no money, a Georgia court took her children away. Then a man in the audience stood up and said, 'Do you have any idea what your son looks like? Hi, Mom!'

As the boy joined her on stage for a big hug and more tears, Jerry Springer, nattily dressed in a dull olive-gold suit, red tie and brown glasses, unfolded his arms from their now-familiar position, folded across his chest and said: 'Well, it's time to go to the Kleenex. We're going to take a break. We'll be right back.'

That was the tear-jerking start of *The Jerry Springer Show*, aired to just five cities in the USA — Cincinnati and Cleveland, Ohio in the Midwest, Mobile, Alabama in the Deep South, Dallas Texas, in the Southwest, and Los Angeles, California, in the West, on Monday 30 September 1991. A Detroit, Michigan, station was originally scheduled to carry it, but in the end did not.

Three nights later he offered up more standard chat show fare, talking to two women who had been abused by their husbands and an author who had written about the reasons women stay with men who abuse them. Their talk was followed by a bizarre sequel —

a makeover by beauty experts while Jerry chatted about how making victims look beautiful on the outside helped them feel beautiful on the inside. Other shows during his first week covered the sexual appetites of blacks and hispanics, the plight of children whose parents die and telephone addiction. The shows were the culmination of months of planning, and an investment of some $300,000 by Multimedia Entertainment, owners of WLWT, in a bid to launch a new national star.

In 1991 daytime talk shows were hot in the USA. Generally produced by independent companies and sold to the highest bidder in TV markets that might have seven or eight stations, not counting cable and satellite, the ones that took off made fortunes for both the producers and the stars. As they were not committed to one of the big three networks, ABC, CBS and NBC, the makers could switch channels at the end of a contract if they got a higher price. Leading the pack was Oprah Winfrey, whose Chicago-based show started in 1984 and went nationwide two years later. By 1989 she was the richest woman in TV, and in 1991 her show was aired on 220 stations, reaching 8,500,000 households every day. Following her were Phil Donahue, the father of talk TV, with 5,710,000 households watching 230 stations, and Sally Jessy Raphael, who appeared on 194 stations and attracted 4,330,000 households. Both Donahue and Raphael were produced by Multimedia, who thought Jerry had the same potential. Also, Donahue was 55, and had been doing a daily show for 23 years, and there were rumours that he might be thinking of retiring.

The idea to give Jerry a shot at his own show was the brainchild of Multimedia chairman Walter E Bartlett, who had discussed it with him over lunch the previous December. He had been impressed by the ratings rise at the local NBC affiliate after Jerry was appointed co-anchor. The show was announced the following June, with Burt Dubrow, executive producer of the *Sally Jessy Raphael Show* and the man who had masterminded her rise from a radio chat show host to local and then national TV stardom, brought in to supervise the show. Jerry was later to say, when even the early incarnation of his show was criticised for being outrageous, that he did not ask for the job but was ordered to do it by his ultimate boss.

'One day they took me to lunch,' he recalled. 'We were pretty much number one in the news. They said, "We're going to start a new talk show and you're going to host it!" They didn't ask, they assigned me to it.'

Since Multimedia owned both WLWT and a sister station, WKYC in Cleveland, they did not face the risk of making shows and not being able to sell them, and decided to go for an initial run of 200 daily programmes, to be shown over 40 weeks. To hedge his bets, Jerry decided to remain as news anchor for the 5.30pm and 11pm broadcasts, even though that would mean very long working days.

'I have no interest in giving up my role as an anchorman and commentator,' he said when the show was first announced. 'That's my bread and butter.' Nor was he worried that two and a half hours of Jerry every weekday might be too much for even his biggest fans. 'We'll find out,' he said. 'But think about it. To get all of that you'd really have to be glued to the set 20 hours a day. Someone who is going to watch me that much obviously wants to.'

Although chat shows in the early 1990s were tame compared to what they would become by the end of the decade, largely thanks to Jerry, they were already regarded as sleazy and sensational. Phil Donahue, regarded as a sensitive soul who empathised with his guests and covered serious topics, nevertheless once donned a skirt during a show about men who enjoy dressing in women's clothing, and put a flesh-coloured skullcap over his trademark thick, grey hair for a segment about men going bald. Most shows kept their really outrageous topics for the three times a year 'sweeps weeks'. In the most recent sweeps Sally Jessy Raphael, then considered the most outrageous talk-show host, had covered topics like *I Sold My Body To Feed My Kids*, *Transsexual Lesbians*, *Klan Moms and Daughters* and *Truckstop Trixies*.

Jerry insisted he would keep to higher ground. He told *Cincinnati Enquirer* TV critic John Kiesewetter: 'I'm not suicidal. I'm not going to foul it up by doing something absolutely stupid. Would I do things that are probably going to be uncomfortable? Yeah. But I do news stories that sometimes I'm not comfortable with. I'm very conscious of the subject matter that some of these other hosts have done and there are some things that I probably would say, "I just can't do it!" I will not be dancing with The Chippendales. I can tell you that because I have been promised that I would not have to do that. I would object to that.'

However, as he did so often, Jerry gave himself a let out, just in case he changed his mind. 'It isn't as if the public has only seen me as this staid, conservative person,' he added. 'You're talking to a guy who sang with the Beach Boys at Riverfront Stadium, who drove a bus, and who took his shirt off in Fountain Square when the Mr America contest was held there. I sing with local rock groups in town once in a while. My history in Cincinnati is that people have seen me in all kinds of roles. I really do think I've got some latitude here.'

In fact, Kiesewetter was not convinced about the purity of Jerry's intentions and suggested some possible topics for the new show: *Congressmen Who Date Full-Figured Women*, *Lawmen Who Arrest Truckstop Trixies*, and, unable to resist a gentle jab at Jerry's past, *Cash Is Best*.

As it happened, the show ran into the kind of controversy it was destined to become famous for before it even aired. Then, as now, it was standard practice for TV stations to advertise upcoming chat show topics and ask viewers whether they fitted any of the categories or knew someone who did. That August WLWT ran a series of adverts looking for 'High School Tramps', and another for 'People Who Have Had Sex In Weird Places' for the upcoming *Jerry Springer Show*.

Cincinnati was outraged and executive producer Dubrow launched an immediate campaign of damage control to protect Jerry's good name as a serious news anchor. Although around 50 callers to the station had confessed to being tramps, or at least being called tramps, while they were at school, Dubrow insisted it was never a serious prospect for a show.

'All we were doing was exploring some things out of an initial meeting and most of that, *none of that*, are things you'll never see,' he told Kiesewetter, somewhat plaintively. 'We were laughing around the office one day saying, "Didn't everybody go to school, and wasn't there always one loose kind of girl? Where is she now, I wonder? And wouldn't it be neat if she were successful and a corporate executive and the people who made fun of her aren't doing so great? And wouldn't that be great or fun to bring those people together?" So we put some announcements on the air, never for a moment saying it is a show or it isn't a show. It's a thought, but you're not going to see the show, I don't think.

'We're not going to go out of our way to do anything that is dirty or in bad taste. It has nothing to do with Jerry's presence on the news. Jerry is a good person and a solid citizen. He's not going to want to go on the air and do something that doesn't have some sort of value, in some way, shape or form. We're not going to do anything intentionally that's in bad taste. That would be silly.'

One question hovering over the show right from the start was how to differentiate it from the reams of chat already pouring from the TV at all hours of night and day. Comedienne Joan Rivers had a show in those days, as did President Reagan's son, Ron Reagan Jr. Geraldo Rivera, a former ABC newsman who gained international fame in his abortive excavation of mobster Al Capone's Chicago vaults in a live TV special in 1986, and black comedian Arsenio Hall, who co-starred with Eddie Murphy in the film *Coming to America*, were also in the top 10 talk shows.

Dubrow was confident from the start, although he admitted the programme would ease its way gently into the highly competitive marketplace. 'Just by Jerry being there it will be different,' he insisted. 'As we go along we will find our own niche. We're just not going to do anything different in the beginning than anybody else. They don't give you any medals for being different or trying to be different. But Jerry will approach them differently, because he's not Oprah or Sally or Phil. The approach is sometimes more important than the topic itself. There will be some topics that people will say, "Oh my goodness! Why are they doing that?" There are always people who are going to criticise you. We've got to do what we feel is best and good for a national audience.'

In the weeks before the launch of the show, Multimedia renovated the studio where it was to be recorded and Cincinnati was abuzz with expectations. Jerry, who as a boy-wonder politician dressed daringly in jeans and casual sweaters, was going through fittings for more than 25 new suits, and choosing matching shirts and ties to give him a smooth new image. Jerry, who is now famous for his trendy, trademark Armani suits, later recalled: 'The truth is, I didn't know about Armani till my first producer said, "Here, put this on."'

Dubrow pointed to the company's commitment to the show, and said they would back Jerry all the way.

'This is not a shoestring operation,' he went on. 'We have not done a talk show since Sally, so we're very picky about what we do. Money doesn't make a successful talk show. It's the guests, the hosts and the topics. The Phils and Sallys took years to get to the point they are today. We're giving the show time, and it needs time to find itself. Time is what makes the show successful because it gives Jerry the time to get comfortable, gives the staff the time to get known and do better things.

'I'm a believer that with Jerry, if we do everything properly and all the pieces fit into place, we have the next major talk show person here and that means we have an investment in all of our futures and I'm real excited about that. I don't think there is anybody on TV doing a talk show who has what Jerry has. Jerry has vulnerability, a real compassion that I believe is coming though on air. A softness, yet keeping a certain masculinity, which I think is very important, and, God knows, an intelligence, a guy who's lived a life, and it comes through.'

Jerry, excited about the change in his life, was, for once, more diffident. He told Greg Paeth of the *Cincinnati Post*: 'The only way that

I'm going to be able to do what I have to do is be who I am. At the age of 47 I can't suddenly become an actor. In the end, they are going to turn on the cameras and it's going to be me with 150 people in the room and we're going to talk about life, and people are going to respond to that and, ultimately, the viewers will decide whether they like me or they don't and there's nothing I can correct. All I can do is react naturally. You can't fake it every day for an hour. If we're different, it's because we're different from Sally or Phil.'

He was nervous when he recorded his first show, pacing up and down anxiously off-stage, peering at the studio audience. During the first show he was stiff, and looked exhausted, physically and emotionally, by the time it was over.

However, he was also elated and clearly on an adrenalin rush when he spoke to John Kiesewetter, who was in the studio audience for this momentous event, 'How many rushes in a life can a person have? I felt today like the day I was sworn in to be mayor, or the day I did my first commentary or newscast. I'm lucky, I'm really lucky.

'I've never done this before. You can practise the physical stuff, the running up and down the aisles and how you hold the mike. But there is no way for you to rehearse for this until you stand out there. It isn't like you've got to memorise your lines. There are no lines. But this is amazing. It's like you're in a room with 150 people and you're working a lounge. If they gave me a band, I could sing! All I've got to worry about is handling a nice one hour of human relationships. All the other people will handle the TV show.

'I'm either likeable or I'm not. I'm not going to worry about that. I can't control it. I can't say, "How am I going to look in LA?" They're going to see me talking to a bunch of people, hopefully being very sincere and honest and emoting as I would. They're either going to like it or they're not.'

Remarkably, that very first show sowed seeds whose fruit would still be evident years later. Capitalising on his already established reputation as a commentator, the producers decided right from the start that Jerry would add a mini-commentary about the show at the end of each taping. He signed of on night one with his now familiar, 'Till next time, take care of yourself, and each other.'

Looking back at his review of that first show, Kiesewetter must wince. 'Don't give up your desk job,' was his advice to Jerry. He doubted whether the show could maintain the emotions of the first programme and, while he acknowledged the initial tear-jerker was a likely audience puller, he also cast doubt on Jerry's ability to hold the audience. Also he made dire predictions that Jerry's dual role could cost

Channel 5 dearly in its audience ratings for news.

'It's fair to say that the reunion, a TV talk show staple, couldn't have been staged much better by Oprah Winfrey or his Multimedia cousins Phil Donahue and Sally Jessy Raphael,' he wrote the day the show débuted. 'Burt Dubrow, executive producer for *Sally* and *Springer*, stretched the drama over an hour, surprising Purvis with the topic, then with her daughter and later her son. The WLWT studio audience also proved to be a wonderful supporting cast for *Springer*, with several women choking on tears as they talked to Purvis. It shows we could do a national show from Cincinnati.

'Where *Springer* needs help is with Springer. There were some obvious flubs, such as the host's head blocking cameras or the overuse of the phrase "tell me a story". Granted, he'll warm up to playing Phil Donahue Jr. But will we ever warm up to Springer in the role? Will the rest of America, already overdosing on Ron Reagan Jr, Jenny Jones, Chuck Woolery and others, care about this show sprung from Cincinnati? I have grave doubts. And if I ran Channel 5 I'd also worry about the negative impact *Springer* will have on my top-rated newscast, which may be headed down a slippery slope from which it may never recover.'

He was closer to the mark, however, when he predicted that Jerry would not for long feel at home with his early topics. 'Will he present the topics with enough flair to win viewers in Texas, California and Michigan?' he went on. 'I doubt it (though he might prove me wrong). I just can't imagine Jerry Springer being *passionate* about ethnic lovers, telephone addiction, fashion or other daytime TV talk show topics. Frankly, I don't care about his observations about ethnic lovers or high telephone usage. And I winced hearing Springer, who spearheaded medical relief for Ethiopia from his anchor chair, tell today's audience that the reunion was "the kind of thing that TV, I think, ought to be doing".

'Here's my bottom line: Springer can't keep his day job and his desk job. Will he still be the No. 1 newsman by the time Multimedia determines whether *Springer* will succeed nationally? What will it be: fashion or passion?'

Despite Kiesewetter's criticisms, Jerry was a runaway success in Cincinnati. Nearly one-third of all households with TV switched on from 10am to 11am that first Monday were tuned to Jerry — twice as many who watched quiz shows *Let's Make a Deal* and *Wheel of Fortune*, and three times the viewership of another new talk show, *Jenny Jones*. His show followed Phil Donahue, and new shows usually benefit from viewers who simply stay on the same channel after an established, popular programme. But Jerry actually pulled a bigger audience than the then king of daytime TV, and was only marginally behind Oprah Winfrey.

He did not command the same following elsewhere, however. In Cleveland he pulled in only 12 per cent of the viewers in his first week and *Cleveland Plain Dealer* TV critic Tom Feran was dismissive. 'Springer, resembling a trusted family doctor or high school teacher, need only paint his glasses red to be the male Sally Jessy Raphael.' Raphael's trademark is her bright-red spectacle frames. In Los Angeles just seven per cent of viewers turned to him on the Disney-owned KCAL, while in Dallas he had a derisory one per cent on KDFI.

Jerry drew up a rigid schedule to help him juggle his three daily commitments. He arrived at the office at 9am, rather than his usual 10am, to catch up on the news and prepare for the talk show. Taping of the show started at 11, and it normally took an hour and a half. This was then trimmed of pauses and retakes to run for an hour. After lunch he headed to the newsroom at 2.45pm to write his commentary of the day. Then he anchored the 5.30 news and headed home for a late siesta to be refreshed for the 11pm newscast and his commentary. It was a hard routine, but Jerry knew he had to be disciplined if he was going to make his dual roles work.

As the show settled into its second month, and saw a slight dip in its local ratings, some viewers started complaining about the sleazy subject matter. The *Cincinnati Enquirer* asked readers for their opinion of Jerry's performance. By a two-to-one majority they loved the show, and many of the people who did not objected to the format but thought Jerry was great.

'The show is fresh, informative, educative and a show the total family can enjoy together,' said reader Esther Suggs. 'It's a show that, given time, will run toe-to-toe with some of the best talk shows.'

Jeannette Witsken agreed, writing: 'It's really great. I think it's about time that something local is on the air like this. People in Cincinnati have problems, too, and it's great to see a national show being done here.'

It was not only women who liked Jerry. Jim Hall said: 'Jerry Springer has a lot to be proud of. I really enjoy the show and I'm tired of critics making decisions as to what stays on the air and who should be watching what.'

Among his critics, Vivian Ankenbauer wrote: 'The thing I don't like about Jerry's new programme is the lack of his pixy humour. The whole subject matter has been sad and weepy, and that's not Jerry.'

Several people who objected to the show thought Jerry was

being cramped by sticking to an established talk show format. 'He would be the most interesting talk show on TV if they'd just turn him loose, and not do this *Dating Game* stuff, finding lost members of families and all those things that everyone else is doing,' said Claire Butler.

Melissa Satchwell added: 'The shows I've seen have been another attempt to wallow in the grief and dirty laundry of other people. If pertinent political and interesting topics were to be discussed, perhaps it would have a chance. It's like all the other shows.'

Nick Dabado said: 'They should let Jerry be himself, a really funny person as well as intelligent.'

Then a Cincinnati heavyweight weighed into the debate. Jerry's rival anchorman, Nick Clooney, the man he had dethroned from the top spot on local TV, devoted his weekly column in the *Cincinnati Post* to Jerry, praising him and show. 'I'm very glad to see Jerry Springer with his own TV talk show originating in Cincinnati,' he wrote. 'Not only is it good for Jerry, it's good for the city. I've had a hectic few weeks, so I haven't had a chance to sit down and watch the programme yet, but the few short glimpses I've had certainly indicate that Jerry is comfortable in the format and is handling a variety of topics with aplomb. I'm not at all surprised. I've admired his communication skills even before I tried to hire him at Channel 12, 10 years ago.

'As you're probably aware, Cincinnati was for 50 years a mecca for local live broadcasting, a stubborn holdout against the national trend to let New York and Los Angeles do it. The Cincinnati broadcasting stations produced dozens of shows, and Cincinnati audiences supported them long after much larger cities had given up the expensive and chancy form. If Jerry's show can lead to a resurgence in Cincinnati of local TV, which had become bland and predictable like that of every other city in the country, then I'm for it.'

Jerry also got backing from his stablemate, Sally Jessy Raphael, who went to Cincinnati to record a couple of her shows at a local shopping mall, and appeared as a guest on his show. She frankly admitted that talk shows had to be entertaining and give viewers what they want to watch. But she also insisted that despite the lurid-sounding topics, shows like hers and Jerry's could help and educate as well as titillate, as long as it was done in an entertaining way.

'We have to entertain,' she said. 'The initial impact of the box is people will watch you if they're enjoying you. Beyond that, I am committed to try to feel like I did something good in the world. I will cop a plea to a fashion show being entertainment and the

Chippendales being entertainment. But that does not represent the body of our work. Eighty-five per cent of what we do every day is sexual abuse, child molestation, children, morals. I'm a reporter who saw a different kind of reporting. I woke up and I didn't care who the secretary of state was and I'm not so sure the American public does.

'Is the game played the way I'd like it to be played? No. You would want everybody to watch public broadcasting and read the *New York Times*. Now, get real. Therefore we try to find out what people want and give it to them so that they will visit with us every day.'

Jerry's first 'sweeps' week, in November 1991, was disappointing after his strong start. In his home market he just lost first place to Channel 9, tying with *Jeopardy* with 20 per cent of sets switched on at 10 am but falling behind *Family Feud*, which picked up 25 per cent from 10.30 am to 11 am. However, he had a consolation prize because his Channel 5 news at 11 pm ranked first.

In addition, he got an early Christmas present from Multimedia when they announced they were so pleased with the show they had sold it to five more markets, including Washington, DC, Milwaukee, Wisconsin, and Detroit, Michigan.

Jerry was thriving on his dual career. He told John Kiesewetter, who had admitted expecting to see him worn out by the pressure of taping the show, doing two news broadcasts and his commentaries: 'It's just so much fun! I figured it out that I'm still awake the same number of hours; I'm just working during all of them.'

In January 1992 Jerry went to New Orleans to sell himself and his show at the annual convention of the National Association of TV Program Executives, where shows, new and old, are marketed to TV stations around the country. Multimedia struck a three-year, $75 million deal to sell Jerry in a package that included Phil Donahue and Sally Jessy Raphael. His show was to be aired on 16 stations starting the following month and up to 40 by the end of the year, which would mean he would be broadcast over half of the USA. However, he was still well behind Raphael, who appeared on 195 stations covering 95 per cent of the country.

Still, he was elated at the thought of a wider audience. 'I'm just really excited, but I also feel the pressure. I have to be good and I have to get better. By the time we start in those markets and around the country, I have to be up to speed.' He also said he had no plans to give up his news work, not that he could walk away from his contract, which ran until 1994, in any case. 'I love doing it,' he said. 'I admit I get tired but as long as I can do both I will continue to do both.

However, within days of his return from New Orleans, there

were rumours that *The Jerry Springer Show* was moving to Chicago. WLWT general manager Gary Robinson discounted them, saying: 'There are no plans to move the show in the near future. My own view is that we're doing fine with it based here.'

Burt Dubrow was less definite. 'There's no arrangement at this point in time to move the show. That's not to say we might not some day move the show. I think we will. When and where? That hasn't been decided yet.'

Jerry, caught in the middle, admitted he could eventually lose his news job but repeated his commitment to his nightly commentaries. 'I assume I'll be commuting,' he said when asked what would happen if the show moved to Chicago, a 55-minute flight away. 'I can see at some point they'll cut my anchoring, but I don't want to give up the commentary.' However, doing double duty was perhaps beginning to take its toll — in the February sweeps and again in May, Channel 9 beat the Channel 5 11 pm newscast, knocking it from first place after four and a half years.

The show went on, with Jerry continuing to do double duty, as an army of producers scouted round for guests. They combed newspapers, magazines and other TV shows, contacted self-help groups, placed classified advertisements and dreamed up topics for Jerry to announce during the shows, hoping viewers would call or write. Many subjects approached the show by themselves, asking to appear. Even though some of the topics were intensely personal and potentially embarrassing, guests appeared happy to air their dirty linen to the studio audience and viewers across the country.

As Jerry's first year rolled on, topics covered confessions about everything from sex to shopping habits, with segments about missing and neglected children. The top-rated *Jerry Springer Show*, according to the Nielsen Organisation which tracks the TV viewing figures, was *I Want My Wife to Look Sexier*, followed by *Police Psychics Look for Missing Children*, *Street Kids* and *How To Spice Up Your Love Life*. *Albino Children* rounded out the top 10.

'What they're doing is almost like a confession,' senior producer Terry Murphy said of the guests. 'They are saying, "I'm sorry I've been through this. If there's something I can do to keep someone from the pain, I'm gonna do it and say it." It's either healing for them, or they feel like they're going to help someone else. Since we started the show our viewer mail probably has quadrupled. People saying, "This is going on in my life. Can you help me?"'

Not all the guests had sordid secrets to spill. One viewer who wrote in was a former dancer on the 1970s TV series *Soul Train*, who had lost a leg to cancer. 'She's young. She's vibrant,' said Murphy. 'She said, "Hey, I'm getting on with my life. I'd like to give hope to other people who are going through this."'

Jerry recalled his days 'living rough' on the streets of Cincinnati with a well-received segment where he interviewed a 19-year-old homeless youth, 'Tweaky Dave', who was living rough on the streets of Hollywood, still faithful to his liberal credentials. He revisited Dave two years later, when he was trying to get help for street kids even younger than him.

John Kiesewetter was gracious enough to eat his early words about Jerry. He wrote: 'We thought Springer needed help — heck, we knew he was *crazy*! — to try a national TV show. Admit it: we were wrong. Cincinnati's lovable liberal city council member and news commentator is thriving in his third career.'

Guests were not paid to go on the show, but were flown in to Cincinnati, put up at a hotel and reimbursed for any lost wages. However, Cincinnati was not a destination people were automatically attracted to, and the bookers found it increasingly hard to get guests from other parts of the country. As the show was sold in more and more marketplaces — by midsummer it had been picked up in 82 for the beginning of the new season in September and Multimedia were predicting 100 by the beginning of autumn — having guests from the whole of the USA became even more important. So in May it was announced that Jerry would start recording the show in Chicago, starting the following September, but that he would keep his anchorman job and continue to do his commentaries.

'Jerry will remain doing the news,' announced Burt Dubrow. 'We'll arrange a production schedule so he can stay on the air here. At a minimum it would seem to me that he could do four nights of news a week. The reason we're leaving has nothing to do with the city of Cincinnati. It has to do with getting guests. We love the audience here. We love the city. It's a tough decision but it's what we have to do. It's impossible to do a major talk show anywhere but in a major city. The guests are not here. But they're always coming to New York, Chicago or Los Angeles.'

The move to Chicago was traumatic for Jerry as well as exciting. After years of being one of the best-known faces in town, he was suddenly a nobody, a newcomer, even though his photograph hung on the walls of station WMAQ-TV, Chicago's Channel 5, along with nationally known NBC stars like Shelly Long from *Cheers*. He arrived in mid-August to start taping shows for the beginning of the season — a truly nationwide season, with 93 cities carrying the show

— on 14 September. To encourage people to join the studio audience of this programme, which Chicagoans had never seen, he did TV promotions, joking about his days as a graduate law student at Northwestern, when his lecturers had warned him he would never make being a lawyer his career. 'They were right,' he said. 'So I got this talk show and I hope you come and see it.'

John Kiesewetter flew to Chicago to watch one of the early tapings and to chat with Jerry about the differences and similarities between working in the two cities, and his hopes for the show when it went nationwide. Jerry had to dream up new ways of keeping the audience entertained during the inevitable lulls in production, as joking about local personalities would not do. So he cracked jokes about Elvis and sang to the crowd. He found it strange being an unknown again, although he was given a warm welcome.

'It's interesting being in another city,' Jerry told him. 'You can't take for granted what they know here. Everybody here is very nice. They were friendly in the audience, particularly when you consider that we're not on the air here yet. There is a friendliness and openness. To that extent, this is a lot like Cincinnati.'

He admitted, 'When I ran for political office I wasn't scared. I knew what I was talking about. But this is scary. I'm competing against some pretty major people. I don't want to screw up.'

However, in other ways there was a huge gulf between the show he had finished taping in June in Ohio and the new one he was making two states over in Illinois. A nationwide show meant a bigger showcase for his guests and he was determined to make the most of that. It was a general election year, and Jerry hoped to boost his viewer figures by pulling in some big political names, such as Hillary Clinton, Barbara Bush, Tipper Gore, Marilyn Quayle and Margot Perot.

'It's one thing when it's your hometown,' he told Kiesewetter. 'But when it's in all these cities, it's like it's real. Last year I was saying the same thing and believing it but part of me was trying to convince myself. And now we've reached the point where we're a show like everybody else. Even more than the fact that we're in Chicago, it's now that we're legitimately a national talk show. As we're making calls now, it's not, "Who? What's his name?"

'I think we're pretty close to getting some of the wives from the presidential race, and before we wouldn't even have had a return call. Now they are literally looking at tapes of the show. We are seriously on their list to have them as guests. To ask them to come to Cincinnati is an inconvenience because it would mean taking a whole day out of their schedule to come there. But they're always going to those major media markets.'

Jerry's dreams of chatting to a potential presidential wife did not come true, however. Although six years later, when he had long abandoned any pretence of hosting heavyweight political shows, he must have fantasied about a very different programme featuring Hillary Clinton locked in a cat fight with Monica Lewinsky!

He did, none the less, discover he had a presidential fan. During the campaign he met George Bush, who was running for re-election, and was stunned when the leader of the free world asked him about Siamese twins who had appeared on the show.

'It struck me then,' he recalled later, 'What is the President of the USA doing watching MY show? He's got a country to run. I guess the president has more time than you think. It's kind of scary.'

For all his breezy self-confidence, however, and his casual dropping of presidential names, Jerry was still the star-struck new kid on the block. In his first October in Chicago he was invited, along with other talk show hosts, to appear on Phil Donahue's 25th anniversary special. He met Oprah Winfrey, who offered to show him around the Windy City. He was so astonished he responded by stammeringly asking her for her autograph.

Despite Multimedia's confidence in him and their track record at standing by shows like Donahue's and Raphael's, giving them time to find and build their audience, he was also well aware of how quickly TV shows could be cancelled. Ron Reagan Jr had seen his show cancelled after just six months, as had veteran game-show host Chuck Woolery, both men with far greater national name recognition than Jerry. 'I wake up every morning thinking it will be my last,' he admitted. 'That's how I live my life. I've been on so many roller-coasters. I know I'm really lucky. I've got a national talk show and tonight I'm getting on a plane to do the news. I keep thinking, "Boy, one day, I'm really going to pay for all of this, you know?"'

Just as he had drawn up a strict timetable for living when he was juggling the show with two newscasts and his commentaries back home, Jerry worked out an even more complex schedule for shuttling between Cincinnati and Chicago. His original plan was literally to commute several times a week, flying to Chicago in the morning, taping two shows and flying home for the 5.30pm news. It was a logistical nightmare. Covington International Airport was an easy, 15-minute drive from his home in Ohio, but the freeway from Chicago O'Hare International Airport, on the western outskirts of the city, to the studios overlooking Lake Michigan could be a disaster, especially since the freeway was undergoing extensive road works. On top of that the unpredictable Midwestern weather, where hurricanes, tornadoes and thunderstorms are regular occurrences, made flight delays and even cancellations a very real worry. The one-hour time difference, since Ohio is in the Eastern time zone and Illinois in Central, was an added confusion.

'I came up here at 7 o'clock in the morning,' Jerry recalled of his first day in Chicago. 'Which means I got up at 5.30am. I did two shows then got on a plane and went back to do the news. By that time it was midnight, and I had been up since 5.30am and I was jet-lagged twice. I can say, "Oh, I can do it." But it's exhausting. It's very, very tiring.'

After a panic in his first week when the traffic in Chicago was so bad he almost missed his plane, he decided to think again. He changed his schedule to tape two shows each Saturday, then flew to Chicago two other days, taping one show on one and two on the second.

'We're not going to start a week and then decide, "Oh, I can't make it." We know exactly the newscasts I'm on. I want to make it very clear that that's my livelihood. I take it very seriously. And when I'm supposed to be there, at WLWT, I'm there. There will be no sloughing off. News will get the same importance that it's been getting. The truth is, I love doing both talk and news and I'm in no hurry to leave.'

Despite his high-minded talk about interviewing presidential wives, Jerry's national show quickly became a haven for people many in the audience regarded as freaks and weirdos. A 21-stone stripper paraded around the stage for him wearing a leopard-skin bikini, and an elderly man strutted his stuff wearing bikini bottoms while his pet monkey did a striptease. On another occasion a building worker revealed that he had had breast implants so that he could get a night job as a stripping drag queen.

A couple of years later Jerry admitted regretting one segment of that first season — men with a nappy fetish, who rolled around the studio floor dressed like babies, shaking rattles. 'Afterwards, I wondered why we did that,' he pondered.

But there was one show he steadfastly refused to make — one featuring his beloved Katie. Now a lively teenager who was making good progress in school and in life despite her disabilities, the producers naturally thought she was a glowing example of someone who had overcome immense difficulties. But Jerry was adamant. 'They want me to put her on the show,' he said. 'I didn't use her to get elected; I wouldn't use her here.' That pressure has continued over the years, and even though Katie is a regular in the studio and knows all Jerry's team, that is a decision he has always stuck to firmly.

Then, as now, there were always people ready to criticise Jerry for his subject matter, and the *Cincinnati Post*'s Greg Paeth was no exception: 'To butcher and then steal a great line by a wonderful writer, Multimedia Entertainment never went broke underestimating the taste of American TV viewers,' he wrote. 'That couldn't ring any truer than it does right now with *The Jerry Springer Show*, the syndicated talk show that moved out of Cincinnati during the summer and relocated in Chicago. Springer has made the world a little better in the last couple of weeks for obese gay men, drag queens and their lovers, gay twins, dwarf twins, obese women, obese strippers, twins who strip, a construction worker who had breast implant surgery and now works nights as a stripper and adults who enjoy dressing in diapers and acting like infants.'

He questioned how long Cincinnati viewers would continue to take Jerry seriously as anchorman and commentator, and warned that they already seemed disillusioned. 'Until he started his talk show last fall, Springer's newscast was the undisputed ratings leader at 11pm for four years. But Channel 5 lost the last two ratings sweeps to Channel 9 and the November ratings sweeps seem to be developing into a three-way race between Channels 5, 9 and 12.

'Five years at the top, of course, is a long time for any station and any anchor to dominate the news ratings. But it's certainly plausible that Springer at 10am, 5.30pm and 11pm, two and a half hours a day, add up to a Springer overdose for some viewers. Equally plausible is the argument that Springer's credibility as a newsman has been damaged by the talk show role. When you're asking a female impersonator about breast implants at 10am, how can anyone take your comments about Ross Perot seriously at 5.30pm?'

After the all-important November sweeps, *The Jerry Springer Show* was called 'one of the fastest-growing talk shows of the new season'. The numbers were small; 10 per cent of the sets in use were tuned to his show, but that was a 25 per cent increase over the previous year. On the downside, however, his 11pm newscast slipped to third place.

The die was cast, and in January 1993 it was announced that Jerry was leaving WLWT to work full-time in Chicago. Another Jerry era was over in Cincinnati.

Naturally, he did not go quietly, nor did Cincinnati let him go without regrets. More than 100 readers flooded the *Cincinnati Enquirer* with letters saying how much they would miss him.

'He came into my living room every night and he felt like family,' said fan Josephine Thackery. 'The news will never be the same,' said Marjorie Martin, who was dubious about Jerry when he first started on TV. 'I had thought, "What would a former councilman know about presenting the news?" It didn't take me long to change my mind.'

Readers also said they would miss his nightly commentaries. Charlotte Cundy wrote: 'Even when I knew the topic and thought, "Boy, am I going to disagree with what he's going to say," I was always swayed towards his view or made to really consider the other side by his honest, in-depth look at the issue.' Rima Milsky agreed: 'Before each commentary I try to determine my position on his subject *du jour* because I know that after he presents his views I will have to agree with his deductions.'

John Kiesewetter gave Jerry a gracious send-off. 'For two and a half minutes, time stood still every night in my house,' he wrote. 'When Jerry Springer read his commentary I listened to every word. I didn't always agree with the lovable liberal. But his eloquent essays, sometimes bordering on the poetic, made Channel 5's newscast No. 1 from 1987 to 1992. He made me think, laugh, cry or scream in anger at the TV. He stimulated my mind, a destination seldom reached by the typical TV anchor. He told me the news, then he told me his views. Nobody else did that on local TV; few others have done both successfully for any TV station or network.

'He never claimed that reading the nightly news was brain surgery. "If the red light's on you talk," he told me over lunch in 1989. And he never took himself too seriously.

'Most of all, I'll miss his commentary. Whether I agreed with him or not, often his words, a twist of phrase, a summary zinger, would leave me in awe of his writing skill. That's what made it so difficult for me to accept him as Sally Jessy Raphael and just another TV freak show host. Having seen his passion for 20 years it's uncomfortable to watch him waste his national forum on drag queens, strippers, psychics, pornography buyers, nudists, faith healers and cross-dressers.

'What I'll miss about Springer the talk show host is the intelligence he brought into our lives. Now that he'll be devoting his full energy and attention to *The Jerry Springer Show*, maybe he'll be able to take a higher road. Maybe America will finally see the thought-provoking, passionate Springer that many of us have come to admire, respect or love. The man is so powerful he makes the world stand still every night.'

Jerry had mixed feelings about the move. He was delighted at the faith Multimedia had in him, but was sad to be leaving the city that had treated him so well and smiled at his eccentricities over the years. He was astonished at the reaction to his departure, from both the public and his bosses. 'The station is putting together Jerry Springer retrospectives,' he said in amazement. 'It's not my idea, I swear it isn't. I can't handle it. Most people don't get to read about what happens when they die. This week I'm starting to see it, getting a sense of what it will be like around here when I'm gone.

'I dread it. The scary thing is that I'm leaving home. Cincinnati is home. I will never again be in a place for 25 years. I will never go to another city and become mayor and commentator and news anchor. This is the only place I've ever been an adult ... although a lot of people would say I haven't been an adult here.'

One thing Jerry hoped to be able to do once he was permanently in Chicago was to move away from the freak-show image. In fact, he claimed, the show was already devoting more time to serious issues, and he hoped to use it as a force for good.

'Contrary to the digs, if you look at any 20 consecutive shows in the past two months, it's impossible to say there are more than two where you'd think, "Boy, that's sleazy." Look at any 20, and not just the titles because the title is often misleading, but look at the subject matter. You will find we are nowhere near being a sleazy show any more. I have no unfulfilled ambitions beyond the success of the show. Every job I've had has had a social consciousness. I always want to be doing something that has some redeeming social value.

'Don't get me wrong, I don't mind making money. But whatever I do, I want it to be something where I can have an impact on social issues. I'd feel funny making money for no other purpose than making money.'

Jerry gave an emotional goodbye to Cincinnati in his final commentary on Friday 22 January 1993. He was close to tears as he focused on perhaps an unlikely subject — the Kentucky 'cheque incident'. He told his viewers he was so upset at the time he thought about 'ending it all' or fleeing the city, but was glad he had decided to stick it out and grateful to the city for forgiving him. 'For all this that you have given me I can't possibly have given enough back, which is the reason I have been so sad this week, why it is so hard to say goodbye.'

And he signed off with, 'Take care of yourself, and each other. God bless you, and goodbye.'

CHAPTER 19

By now it was a familiar sight on *The Jerry Springer Show*, a woman weeping in disbelief and Jerry, his expression bemused, looking on, arms folded across his chest, microphone in hand. This time the woman who cringed and twisted in her chair as if she had been hit was Shannon, whose husband of 12 years had just confessed he was having an affair with Cindy, the babysitter who looked after their children, aged four and nine.

'I don't even know what to say to you,' she stammered after her husband, John, repeated what he had already told the studio audience while she waited off-stage in a soundproof room. As the studio audience roared approval, she lifted a trembling hand to her mouth and groaned, 'I don't even understand where this is coming from. Oh, Jesus, no!'

Then Jerry brought out Cindy, who elaborated on the affair and bragged that John still called her and was still in love with her, although she was bored with him and wanted to get him off her back. Her new boyfriend also appeared, jeering at Shannon.

During a commercial break in the show, which aired on 7 February 1995, the couple left, saying they could not stand being in front of the cameras any more. As they were filmed walking away Jerry commented, 'This was very hard, obviously. There is no purpose in keeping them on the show anymore.' And at the close of the show, entitled *Honey, Have I Got A Secret For You*, he talked about the unhappy family, saying that bad news can be painful, but that it pays to tell the truth in the end.

The *real* truth came out the next day, when sharp-eyed Canadian viewers recognised 'Shannon', and 'John', as Suzanne Muir,

27, and Johnny Gardhouse, 23, two members of a Toronto comedy team called Blockheads. 'Cindy' was actually Mimi Holmes, 28, a Toronto stand-up comedienne, and her 'boyfriend' was another comic, Ian Sirota, 29.

Jerry and his producers went ballistic. 'All I have to sell is my honesty,' he stormed. 'The only thing that makes a talk show work is that the viewer can sit back, scratch his or her head and say, "I can't believe these people are real."' Complaining of the foursome's 'blatant abuse of trust and faith', he threatened to sue them for breaching the terms of a release they signed before their appearance on the show, in which they promised to tell the truth.

The quartet admitted they had contacted the show as a joke, after watching an episode the previous December in which Jerry asked to hear from people who had slept with their children's babysitters. They did not expect to make it to the air, but said when they were accepted they were so shocked by what they claimed were lies and deceptions on the part of Jerry's staff they decided to go ahead with it to expose the show as a fraud.

'The Springer people just go for it hook, line and sinker,' said Holmes. 'They never checked our references. It was just too easy. We just kept thinking, "They're gonna catch on," but the next thing we know we're at the airport, flying to Chicago.'

Muir said that when she was contacted by producers she was told the show was about bringing the romance back to her marriage, with no mention of any secrets about infidelity or babysitters. 'If I had really been this woman they would have ruined my life,' she complained. 'We were doing this for a reason, which was to prove that these people are not honest in their dealings with the American public and on the level when they try to encourage them to come on. The producers were thinking, "Yahoo, this is great! We've got some great white trash out here and exploit their misery." Look at this whole industry.'

After the pranksters arrived in Chicago on 9 January for the taping, Gardhouse tried to back out. He said he wanted, 'To show them how somebody could really react to something like this, letting them know this could really devastate my family, devastate my wife. They talked me out of it.' He said producers told him he would be safer making a public confession because his wife could turn violent if he told her privately. He later claimed that when Jerry asked him, on the air, why he chose to confess in front of millions of viewers he replied that the producers had told him to and that his response was edited out of the tape that was eventually seen.

Holmes said that while she was waiting to go on, a staff member encouraged her to be aggressive, saying, 'You're gonna let him have it, you're gonna let him have it.' 'It was a big joke to them,' she said.

Five months after the show aired, the four were sued for $50,000 each for defrauding Multimedia Entertainment.

'And that's American money,' said a staggered Muir, who was used to thinking in Canadian dollars which are worth about 20 per cent less than the American greenback, when she received the federal suit. 'Put us all together and we don't even begin to have that much.'

The comedians claimed Multimedia's lawyers had offered to drop the whole matter quietly, in return for a confession that they had committed fraud, a token settlement of US$10 and an undertaking not to discuss the incident in public. That would have let Multimedia give the impression that they had won, by stating truthfully that they had collected both an apology and unspecified damages. But the four decided to tough it out.

'We have nothing to lose,' pointed out Sirota, who said he earned $400 (Canadian dollars) in a good week and had grand savings of $7.14. He said, 'Jerry put us into his circus. But if he wants to fight us in court, we'll show him what a real circus is.'

Added Muir, 'By trying to make an example out of us, they've laid themselves bare.'

Eric Zorn of the *Chicago Tribune* newspaper was disgusted by the suit. 'Jerry Springer does not want to cheat his audience with fake pain!' he wrote. 'The emotional wreckage must be real. You'd think Springer and his coterie would have fallen to their knees in gratitude to learn after the show aired that the whole thing had been a hoax. Had it been real, it would have been one of the most vile, inhumane spectacles ever offered up to the public in the name of entertainment, an emotional beating gratuitously administered to an innocent woman.'

The beleaguered four quickly found two lawyers, one American, one Canadian, willing to represent them for free.

The tables were turned a few days later, when a guest slapped Jerry and the show with a lawsuit, demanding $6 million compensation for misrepresentation when they lured him on to a show in which he was attacked by another guest.

Joseph Pemerton, then 24, from Eagleville, Tennessee, claimed in his federal suit that he had been asked to appear on the show with his girlfriend's sister, Jocelyn McCrary, to talk about patching up family feuds. McCrary's husband, Lester, hated Pemerton with a passion, and Pemerton felt the same way. Relations between them were very hostile. Pemerton said that when the show first called he refused to appear, but the producers hounded him and promised that if he appeared they would help him reach a legal settlement of his long-running feud. They also promised that Lester McCrary, 34, a paroled prisoner who Pemerton said terrified him, would not appear.

Instead the show, called *I'll Do Anything To Kill Your Relationship*, which aired on 17 February, just 10 days after the Canadian débâcle, opened with Jocelyn McCrary bad-mouthing Pemerton and him promptly hurling insults back. As their quarrel reached screaming pitch Jerry announced, 'Lester's here.' McCrary stormed in from the wings with his arms flailing and rushed Pemerton, hitting him twice and hurling him to the floor before security guards grabbed both men and broke up the fight.

Jerry told off Lester McCrary: 'You can't come on the show and hit people. This is a talk show.'

But the damage was done. Pemerton claimed he became stiff and sore and was left with ongoing injuries and persistent anxiety and depression from the traumatic experience. He said he had called one of the producers who had pushed him to appear, to ask for medical advice, and the producer hung up on him.

Worse, not only did his appearance do nothing to iron out his problems with McCrary, but his girlfriend, Nina York, Jocelyn's sister, had left him.

By the time the two lawsuits had been filed, however, the little local fuss over *The Jerry Springer Show* had been overshadowed by a genuine tragedy sparked by one of its competitors, *The Jenny Jones Show*. On 6 March a 24-year-old waiter called Jonathan Schmitz appeared to tape a show about secret crushes. He knew that an acquaintance was going to be revealed as a secret admirer on the show. What he did not know was that the neighbour who fancied him from Orion Township, Michigan, was a man, Scott Amedure, 32. When Schmitz walked on to the set he saw Amedure, whom he knew slightly, and his upstairs neighbour, Donna Riley. Assuming it was Riley who had the crush, he smiled, hugged her and planted a kiss on her cheek. Then Amedure stood up, took his hand and pulled him into a hug. Schmitz did not respond and said, 'I'm a heterosexual; I'm not interested.' He squirmed as he was shown footage shot earlier, of Amedure fantasising about tying him up in a hammock. 'It entails, like, whipped cream and champagne, stuff like that,' Amedure said. When the camera cut back to Schmitz he had his hands over his face.

Although he managed a smile at the initial confrontation, Schmitz sat through the show, taped in the same NBC Tower where Jerry's show was produced, clearly uncomfortable. Towards the end of the segment Jones asked whether he was all right and he said, 'Oh, yeah, I'm fine about it,' though he did not look it.

Three days later, he found an unsigned, sexually suggestive note pinned to his front door. Convinced it was a come-on from Amedure, he went first to a hardware store to buy five rounds of buckshot, then to a gun shop where he paid $249 for a 12-bore shotgun. He drove to Amedure's mobile home and confronted him with the note while his house-mate looked on. Amedure denied writing it. Schmitz returned to his car, came back with the shotgun and shot him twice in the chest, killing him.

A shocked Jones and her distributors insisted that Schmitz had been warned in advance that his secret admirer could be a man or a woman. 'No one was lied to, no one was misled,' said Jim Paratore, president of Telepictures Productions, makers of the show, who have never aired this episode. In a 17 March statement Jones said that Schmitz, 'Like every other guest on the show, he was told that his secret admirer could be a person of the same sex or opposite sex.'

But Oakland County, Michigan, prosecutor, Richard Thompson, who charged Schmitz with murder, said: 'Our evidence shows that he was not aware of the gay angle until he got onstage with the cameras running. Jenny Jones's producer's cynical pursuit of ratings and total insensitivity to what could occur here left one person dead and Mr Schmitz now facing life in prison.'

There was a nationwide outcry against talk shows, calling them intrusive, abusive and invasive. Even the annual convention of the American Psychological Association accepted a report that such shows could be harmful, particularly to children, and included a recommendation that the shows should make sure guests are offered counselling if they want it after making public confessions or facing public confrontations.

Jerry, who these days does offer troubled guests professional help, though few of them accept it, leaped in to the fray, saying that guests should always be warned of the full list of possibilities before any shows promising a surprise. He also said that he did not believe in 1995 that a straight guest discovering someone had a gay crush on them was particularly shocking or surprising. 'You can't blame the show if Schmitz didn't like it that Amedure was gay,' he said. 'Everyone has to take responsibility for his own actions.'

In fact, guests on *The Jerry Springer Show* are told that as a condition of appearing on the show they must sign a release form that lists 21 possible secrets they might learn on the show. In addition, by 1998, they were also asked to sign a document saying that Jerry's production company could sue them for $80,000, the cost of producing a show these days, should they lie. Guests are videotaped signing the form in which they pledge that they will be truthful on the show.

Amedure's family sued Schmitz and the *Jenny Jones* production company for $25 million for negligence, claiming Amedure was plied with vodka before the show and encouraged to hug and kiss Schmitz to heighten the dramatic impact of his 'confession'. 'Although Schmitz actually pulled the trigger, we believe *The Jenny Jones Show* is as guilty as Schmitz for creating the scenario in which, finally, Scott was gunned down,' said their lawyer, Geoffrey Fieger, best known for representing 'Dr Death,' Jack Kevorkian, the controversial pathologist who has helped more than 100 Americans commit suicide. Fieger found additional fame in the summer of 1998, when he won the Democratic nomination to run as governor of Michigan.

Hate mail poured into the *Jenny Jones* studio, including death threats against the host, and she was even given bodyguards to protect her as the threats were taken very seriously.

As the controversy raged on, Dick Robertson, president of Warner Bros Domestic TV Distribution, defended the premise of the show in the prestigious *Hollywood Reporter*, one of the most influential trade newspapers for the Hollywood entertainment industry, clearly holding the same opinion as Jerry about outrageous subjects — that many of the people who slam the shows are élitist snobs who look down on the guests, while the makers of the programmes actually care about their guests and are happy to offer them a public forum they would not otherwise have.

'While certain people make fun of the people who come on these shows and laugh at their dilemmas, I can tell you as a producer and distributor that these people come on to get help,' he said. 'They don't have answers and they are looking for advice. It's real easy for somebody writing for a magazine or newspaper who is college-educated and can afford private therapy, or who just had a nice life as a child, to make fun of these people and call these freak shows. Yes, it's entertaining to watch these shows because it's real life and you could not make this stuff up.

'These people who write these magazine articles may find talk shows distasteful, but fortunately TV is a very democratic medium and if the majority of viewers out there are not watching them over and over again, then the shows will not survive. Who are these people who are writing these articles to say that their values are better than the people who vote with their clickers? Are they saying people should not be allowed to watch them? Should they be the censors of programming? Isn't this like burning books?'

Jones tried to distance herself from the killing saying, in a legal deposition she was required to give lawyers before Schmitz went to trial, that she had little personal involvement with preparations for her own show. However, she told *People* magazine that Schmitz had been warned his secret admirer could be gay. 'He was asked how he'd react and he answered,' she said. 'This was not an ambush.'

She and Warner Bros also launched a battle over the civil suit, arguing that the case should be thrown out because the show was protected under the First Amendment, and that the family had only added it to the lawsuit because Schmitz had few assets while the show had 'deep pockets' — American legal jargon for a person or company brought into a lawsuit they have little connection with because they have lots of money or assets. They argued that letting the case go to trial could have a 'chilling effect' on freedom of speech.

However, in Michigan, Oakland County Circuit Judge Gene Schnelz disagreed and said the case should go ahead.

It was in this atmosphere, in the new knowledge that talk shows could be taken to task legally and not automatically depend on First Amendment rights to free speech to keep them out of the courtroom, that Multimedia quietly opened talks with the Toronto Four to settle their suit against Jerry rather than face a highly publicised and possibly embarrassing trial.

A delighted Suzanne Muir said the Jenny Jones decision, 'Just changed the stakes for talk shows completely.'

In the criminal trial, which was broadcast live on *Court TV* and ended in November 1996, Schmitz was found guilty of second-degree murder after his defence team argued he had a history of depression and suicide attempts, and had been pushed over the edge by the show to the extent that he could not form the intent necessary for a first-degree murder conviction, and was sentenced to 25–50 years in prison. If he had been convicted of first-degree murder the sentence would have been life without the possibility of parole.

During the trial a former *Jenny Jones* producer, Karen Campbell, admitted she had lied to Schmitz when she told him the admirer could be a man or a woman, and gave Jenny a note which read, 'I think Jonathan is going to die when he sees it's Scott.'

Jones herself was called to the stand and said she had never been told Schmitz had told producers he would be uncomfortable if his admirer was a man. She was forced to concede that Schmitz was deceived when he was told his admirer could be a woman. 'The premise of the show was that it was a surprise,' she said. 'I don't produce the show. I don't book the show.' She also reiterated earlier comments that the shows were put together by producers and she was really unaware of the details of the topics or the guests until show-time.

Her testimony earned scathing reviews from American publications. *People* magazine commented: 'Apparently your average Russian Czar was better informed about the condition of the serfs than Jones is about the show that bears her name. Jones, practising what in White House scandals is called deniability, explained from the stand that the only information she usually receives is what is contained in a folder of background material prepared by her staff and often presented to her just before airtime. She did not come off as terribly on the ball.'

However, a source close to the show told another publication: 'Jenny does not read ANYTHING on the air unless she agrees with it ahead of time.'

In September 1998 Schmitz's conviction was overturned by the Michigan Court of Appeals, because during jury selection his defence lawyer had been refused permission to change his mind and exclude a juror he had previously accepted. However, the prosecution said they would appeal the decision, and the appeals court judges added a footnote saying that if they had been the jury in the original trial they might have convicted him of first-degree murder. He was ordered to be held in prison until the prosecution appeals were exhausted.

Around the same time that Jenny Jones was taping the Schmitz-Amedure show, Jerry's viewers thrilled to another sex spectacle — a woman confessing to her husband, John, that she was having an affair, with another woman. He was devastated and stammered, 'You bring me out to Chicago to find this out on TV?' Then the lesbian lover appeared and the three engaged in a heated row. The studio audience erupted in cheers and jeers, and the show's ratings leaped an impressive 15 per cent from the previous day.

However, the killing sparked calls for talk shows to tone down their content. An opinion poll by the prestigious NBC news magazine show *Dateline* showed that 40 per cent of respondents blamed the show for the Amedure tragedy. Robert Gould, a psychiatrist and head of the National Coalition on TV Violence, said: 'These shows are absolute trash, cheap sensationalism, reaching out for the lowest of the low. And unfortunately, they are becoming a big part of our culture. America is becoming a much less civilised country because of them.'

Even some of the presenters themselves seemed to admit that down-and-dirty fights on the air were going too far. Host Rolanda Watts, a younger version of Oprah Winfrey, whose show, *Rolanda*, had débuted the previous season, said: 'This is a challenge, a wake-up call. We've got to find new and creative ways of treating our subjects.'

Oprah herself, the acknowledged queen of talk, called many of her rivals 'base' and said: 'Our intentions are much better. People see that. I'm telling you, I know the difference. They may choose to watch the spectacle for a while. But it will have a short lifespan.'

Three years later she would be forced to eat her words when she was toppled from her pedestal by none other than Jerry.

The problem facing all the daytime chat shows was that the format had proved to be so successful and so financially rewarding, for both the hosts and the production companies, that TV was being flooded with more and more, all desperate to make names for themselves. By early 1995 there were some 20 syndicated shows fighting for viewers and advertising dollars. As well as Jerry, his stablemates Sally Jessy Raphael and Phil Donahue, Oprah Winfrey and Rolanda Watts, the others included Geraldo Rivera, Montel Williams, Ricki Lake, Maury Povich, Jane Whitney, Charles Perez, Richard Bey, Marilyn Kagan, Gordon Elliott, Regis Philbin and Kathie Lee Gifford, Leeza Gibbons, once married to *Coronation Street* star Chris Quinten, and Marilu Henner.

Due to hit the airwaves that autumn were a clutch of minor stars hoping to make a second career in talk TV — rapper-turned-movie actor Mark Wahlberg, who was formerly known as Marky Mark, Gabrielle Carteris of *Beverly Hills 90210*, Carnie Wilson, daughter of Beach Boy Brian Wilson and a member of the second-generation pop group Wilson Phillips, *The Partridge Family*'s Danny Bonaduce, former model Lauren Hutton, divorced chums George and Alana Hamilton and one-time *Cosby* kid Tempestt Bledsoe.

Despite the shock of the *Jenny Jones* shooting, Jerry was unapologetic about his shows and pledged to continue in the same vein. He insisted his guests knew pretty much what they were in for when they agreed to go on the air, although later many were to claim that they, like Amedure on *The Jenny Jones Show*, had been allowed access to more than ample quantities of alcohol before going on the stage. 'We explain to people the parameters, so they don't walk off the show during taping, because we've got lots of other people who are willing to come on the show,' he told his old Cincinnati friend John Kiesewetter, who continued to follow Jerry's TV career. 'We get thousands of letters a week and they pitch us their stories. Everybody wants to get on TV. The talk show may be the last bastion of free speech, where you can say something without being censored.'

Jerry was riding high in the ratings, despite the Canadian hoax, showing a rise of 40 per cent over the previous year by May 1995. He had risen to number five among daytime talk shows, behind *The Oprah Winfrey Show*, *Live With Regis and Kathie Lee*, *Sally Jessy Raphael* and *The Maury Povich Show*, and was seen in 84 per cent of the USA, with women aged 18–34 particularly avid viewers. According to *Entertainment Weekly*, the show was earning $400 million a year.

Regardless of critics who complained that the audience, like the guests, were losers with nothing better to do, Jerry was able to counter gleefully: 'Every day Cher tapes our show and exercises to it the next day. She missed a show and called to see if we'd send her the tape.' His other celebrity fans include Madonna, actor Leslie Nielsen, rocker Jon Bon Jovi, Roseanne, who launched her own talk show in 1998, and baseball great Yogi Berra, who sent Jerry a shirt he once wore. Jerry's assistant, baseball-loving Brenda You, revealed: 'Jerry cried when he got that shirt. Yogi wrote on it, "Dear Jerry, I'm one of your biggest fans, love Yogi Berra."'

Jerry was convinced the shock format was the secret of his success. 'I may love having Oliver North and Jesse Jackson on, but I was the only one watching,' he went on. 'Look, people watch TV during the day to be entertained. It has to be entertaining and interesting.'

He also appeared to be genuinely puzzled that people took 'trash TV' so seriously. 'It's only TV,' he said. 'I just don't see it as a heavy thing. This is just one element of my life. My passion for politics hasn't ebbed at all. It's just not how I make my living. It doesn't mean I've given up my religion, my political passion or my philosophy on life.'

That did not, however, prevent his old station, WLWT in Cincinnati, along with other stations across the country, refusing to show some of the episodes he supplied during the May 'sweeps' of 1995. They included one called *I Slept With 251 Men in 10 Hours*, which Jerry justified by pointing out he criticised the girl throughout the show, another called *I'll Do Anything For One Night With You*, in which a besotted man set himself on fire to impress the object of his affections, and *Hello, I Love You*, in which viewers met returning guests, including one calling himself 'Danny the Wonder Pony,' who specialised in strapping himself into a saddle and giving rides to women from the audience.

Jim Clayton, manager of WLWT, said sex was the main reason for pre-empting shows and airing re-runs in their place. In the case of the serial sex show, he said, 'I watched about 10 minutes and said, "This is a new low. This is disgusting." We pre-screen the show to see whether it reflects community standards and to determine if they're appropriate for the market. We've been doing this for a while this year. We've not had this problem with other shows. We've asked them to eliminate the nudity, and they have. I've told Multimedia Entertainment that we'd be willing to accept a lower rating, if that's what occurs if they clean up the show.'

Unconcerned about criticism, Jerry decided to branch out into other enterprises during his summer break. Multimedia launched a range of Jerry Springer clothes and merchandise — T-shirts, baseball caps, sweat shirts and pants, tote bags, jackets and even disposable cameras emblazoned with his logo. They were sold at the TV Store at the NBC Tower in Chicago, and through college book stores across the USA.

However much Jerry glossed over the outcry over confrontational shows, it was an issue that refused to go away. He was among a number of daytime hosts invited to attend a 'Talk Summit', a two-day conference organised by Population Communications International, with US Secretary of Health and Human Services Donna E Shalala. It was a measure of how influential talk shows were considered that the hosts were invited to join in serious discussions on how their shows could make a positive impact on health and social issues such as birth control.

If that invitation gave daytime talkers a measure of respect, they got none from the next group to try to get involved with their programming. Former US Secretary of Education and drug czar William J Bennett and two Democratic Senators, Joseph L Lieberman of Connecticut and Sam Nunn of Georgia, announced a campaign to clean up the screen.

'In these shows, indecent exposure is celebrated as a virtue,' said Bennett, head of an organisation called Empower America. 'It is hard to remember now, but there was once a time when personal or marital failure were accompanied by guilt or embarrassment. But today, these conditions are a ticket to appear as a guest on *The Sally*

Jessy Raphael Show, *The Ricki Lake Show*, *The Jerry Springer Show*, or one of the dozen or so like him.' He picked out a recent show of Jerry's about a man who confessed to sleeping with his girlfriend's mother, and called on viewers and advertisers to 'reconsider their viewership and sponsorship' of the shows.

Lieberman commented: 'This is the revolt of the revolted. It's about citizenship, not censorship. We're not advocating government censors, but just making the owners and producers of these shows face the moral consequences of what they're doing to our country.'

A few days later the Rev Donald Wildmon, a United Methodist minister, leader of the conservative American Family Association and a long-time campaigner about sex and violence in the media, announced a planned boycott of advertisers who bought time on the targeted shows.

Lieberman and Republican Senator Dan Coats, from Indiana, were to tackle Jerry again, when in 1998 they called for the show to be dropped from a government-subsidised system called closed captioning, which lets deaf viewers read encrypted subtitles.

One of the complaints about all the shows was that they were watched by a large number of children — a survey earlier in the year had shown that 11 per cent of Jerry's audience were under 18.

Jerry was quick to leap to his own and his competitors' defence, claiming the clampdown was a blatant and cynical political ploy to help candidates in the following year's presidential election and that if children watched it they could learn from other people's mistakes.

'A presidential race is coming up and bashing talk shows is a great fund-raising tool,' he said. 'They'll wind up getting a great mailing-list out of this. The studio audience is always on the right side of the moral issue being discussed. I've never once heard an audience cheer a rapist or a wife-beater or a woman who cheats on her husband or a child abuser. So kids learn good lessons from what we do. They are morality plays, admittedly wild ones, but morality plays none the less. More damage has been done to the youth of America by the politicians in Washington in one piece of legislation than in 20 years of talk shows. When they cut AIDS education, when they cut aid to the inner cities and school lunch programmes and Medicare [the American health-care programme for the elderly], that's where the real damage is done.'

Burt Dubrow, by then vice-president of programming for Multimedia, backed Jerry and called on viewers who disliked the show, or objected to their children watching, to reach for the remote control.

'That's part of the parents' job,' he said. 'We should not be faulted if you are allowing your child to watch something that is not intended for a child. I have two kids, ages six and eleven, and I don't let them watch. We certainly feature outrageous people and outrageous situations but they represent very real problems. We don't make this stuff up. And I have trouble understanding how this has had a negative effect on the country. Who are these guys to tell us what people should and should not be watching? Next thing you know they're going to tell us there's a little too much blood on *ER* and we shouldn't watch that either. I can go to bed and close my eyes and feel good, because I know what we're doing isn't bad for anyone. Not that we won't continue to change our product. But it will happen as we see fit, not as someone in Washington does. This isn't Cuba, last time I checked.'

When TV viewing guidelines, warning parents about unsuitable material, were introduced in 1997, *The Jerry Springer Show* was rated TV-M, deeming it unsuitable for viewers under 17. Today it is rated TV-14 in the USA, and is introduced by heavy written warnings across the screen that the content might be offensive.

Proctor & Gamble, the Cincinnati-based manufacturing giant, makers of cleaning products and toiletries and the biggest TV advertiser in America, also the former employer of Jerry's wife, pulled commercials from four daytime shows, including Jerry's, protesting sex and bad language, and companies like Unilever, department store Sears, Roebuck and Co and the country's biggest telephone company, AT&T, also boycotted some shows.

Jerry, as always, came out swinging. He wrote an article for the *Cincinnati Post*, reiterating his belief that his show actually promoted family values by spotlighting and condemning the worst elements of society. But, ever able to laugh at himself, he also talked about the 'silliness' of talk shows and self-deprecatingly added, 'And mine's as silly as any.'

He wrote: 'Some say these shows celebrate immoral behaviour. I disagree. It's just the opposite. I've done almost 1,000 shows in five years, most of them absolutely outrageous. Without exception, the audience verbally condemns, sometimes to the point of booing, anyone who exhibits or preaches immoral or anti-social behaviour. The kids get it every time. Indeed it is virtually impossible to watch our show and not be aware of what is appropriate and what is not.

'Now, some argue that these shows give an inaccurate picture of what America is really like. Well, by that standard virtually everything on TV should be banned. If we let our kids watch the news, they must think the only thing Americans do is murder, rob and rape. Shall we eliminate soap operas because they make people believe that everyone is promiscuous and unfaithful? How about prime-time TV, which makes violence seem so natural? The point is, nothing on TV is the way most people live.

'My answer to the argument that these shows exploit people? Wrong again! It's the news that invades people's lives by jamming microphones into the faces of people who would rather be left alone. It happens to the man coming out of the courthouse and to the family in the middle of a horrible family tragedy. There is never worry whether the story will hurt or embarrass the people being talked about. At least on the talk shows, no one ever comes on who doesn't desperately want to be there. Our guests don't even get paid. This is hardly exploitation!'

When the February sweeps rolled round in 1996 it was obvious the chat show backlash had had some effect. A combination of viewer distaste for the ongoing sleaze and just too many hosts chasing the same format led to generally grim ratings. Oprah Winfrey, who had always taken the highest road, showed an increase, as did Regis Philbin and Kathie Lee Gifford, another gentler show. Jerry's figures stayed flat compared with the previous year.

There was talk that the days of trash TV were numbered, as hosts like Gabrielle Carteris, Danny Bonaduce and Charles Perez were shown the door and others were under threat. Even Phil Donahue, the doyen of the pack, was talking about quitting.

In the end, ironically, Donahue was pushed out as much as he went voluntarily, driven from the top of the ratings heap by the genre he created. He was dropped by the New York TV station which had aired his show for 18 years, and his national ratings slumped. Stations in San Francisco and Los Angeles followed suit, and the domino effect was unstoppable.

Multimedia Executive Vice-President Dick Coveny, acknowledged the 'Springer effect' on the decision to cancel the show after 29 years. He said: 'Some other shows today are pushing the envelope in terms of titillation. Daytime-TV viewers want to be more entertained than informed. When we did shows on child abuse on *Jerry Springer*, nobody watched.'

'When people aren't watching, advertisers aren't buying and Washington is crying, you'd better look for a different kind of show,' said Mort Marcus, President of Buena Vista TV. Jim Paratore of Telepictures Productions concurred: 'The single-issue, relationship-driven talk show market is saturated. The pie isn't any bigger than when Oprah, Phil, Sally and Geraldo were the only ones splitting it.'

Characteristically, Jerry was unconcerned, and vowed to give his audiences more of the same. The numbers might be disappointing, but he knew he had his loyal viewers and knew how to deliver what they wanted.

'The shows are wild shows,' he told *Parade* magazine. 'They're always on the cutting edge. But when moral questions are involved we've got to come out on the right side. We get 3,000 to 4,000 calls a day, both suggestions for shows and people who want to be on. Our producers are told, "Pick out the ones that are the most outrageous but also truthful." It has to be truthful and interesting and, for our show, it must be outrageous. If it's normal living, that's not what our show is about.'

The show's makers felt the same way. By this time Multimedia had been bought out by the nationwide newspaper publishing group Gannett, and Jerry got a new six-year contract, guaranteeing him airtime until 2002, at a reported $3 million a year. And Jerry began to find an international following, on Living TV in the UK and some 30 other countries around the word. The tactics worked. While other shows steered away from the more outrageous subjects, and more and more were cancelled, Jerry suddenly found himself alone at his end of the market, rather than in a crowded field. His ratings shot up, climbing a staggering 200 per cent from 1997 to 1998 and doing what had long seemed the impossible — stealing Oprah Winfrey's crown as top talker in the February sweeps of that year.

That aroused the interest of new advertisers, including Global Insurance and Universal Studios. They bought time on the show, a bargain at $30,000 for 30 seconds, compared with $85,000 for Oprah Winfrey and $60,000 for Rosie O'Donnell. Proctor & Gamble were still disdainful, however. 'Nothing has changed,' said spokeswoman Wendy Jacques. 'The content of the *Springer* programme is not consistent with the guidelines we use to evaluate programmes we think are a suitable environment for our brands.'

It appeared after the Jenny Jones tragedy that shows checked out their guests more carefully, for the issue of fake guests and fake topics slipped into the background.

Even so, it was still on viewers' minds. In an online chat at the beginning of 1998, when Jerry was visiting the West Coast to film a sitcom, one of the first questions he was asked was, 'How are your guests screened to ensure that they are genuine?'

He replied, 'Well that's the job of the producers. The way

people come on our show is to call up to tell us their story. As long as the story is outrageous and truthful they get to be on. The producers make sure they can get whatever evidence they can to verify their story. That can be witnesses, doctors' records, court records. We do our best.' But he also admitted, 'Sometimes I've started the show and I know they aren't telling the truth. So I'll stop the show.'

Then, in April 1998, new allegations of faking came up. The TV magazine show *Extra* produced a string of guests who claimed they were encouraged to make up lurid stories — and that the now-famous fights were actually choreographed.

'We acted everything,' claimed one guest identified as Gary, a bodybuilder. 'When you have to do this. When you have to say this. When you have to punch. When you have to push. They wanted us to wrestle and throw each other around. They said, "We want four fights."'

Another, a model called Kelly, 'revealed' on air that she was two-timing her boyfriend. But on *Extra* she claimed: 'I was supposed to be with someone for two years and I was cheating with my photographer. I didn't even know the two guys.'

Extra reporter Diane Dimond said guests were given 'cheat-sheets, which gave them bullet-point reminders. It's more of a script. We also have pictures of producers with the guests, helping them rehearse, including fights. We have documents, photographs and the good word of 16 people saying the same thing.'

The story was picked up by the major news programmes *20/20* and *Dateline NBC*, as well as the *New York Post* newspaper. In the *Post*, aspiring actor Lonnie Barnett, 27, claimed he had appeared on Jerry's show 17 times, in 1994, 1995 and 1996 in different guises, from a tap-dancer to an anti-Ku Klux Klan campaigner. He even claimed to have gone through a gay marriage on air once. Another guest who asked not to be identified, claimed he had posed as a male escort. He said, 'We knew all the questions before Jerry asked them. We were told. They said I needed a girlfriend but my real girlfriend couldn't go, so I got another girl I just met to pretend.'

On *20/20* stand-up comedian Doug Sandhope and two other men talked about being coached before they went on the air. However, *Dateline* presenter Maria Shriver, superstar Arnold Schwarzenegger's wife and a member of the all-powerful Kennedy family, said she had interviewed a number of guests, none of whom claimed they had been coached.

Instantly denials flowed from Jerry's camp. Executive producer Richard Dominick issued a statement: 'The programme has the strictest production policies and guidelines in place. If, in fact, we find there are violations of these policies, involving either guests who lie or producers who coach them to lie, *The Jerry Springer Show* will take immediate action to rectify the situation.'

However, the day the *Extra* show aired Jerry, on a flying visit to Manhattan, he admitted that there was no way they guaranteed the absolute truthfulness of every guest. He told 150 fans: 'Absolutely silly, outrageous and stupid, that's all it is. We have no obligation to make the show truthful. It's being covered like Watergate. Lighten up!

'I believe that 99 per cent of our guests are absolutely legitimate, that 99 per cent of the people that work for our show are honourable. The fights are not faked. I wouldn't bet my life that everybody I've interviewed has always told me the truth. Overwhelmingly the stories on the show are true. The emotions are sometimes embellished.'

In another interview he said, 'The whole show could be a spoof. There's nothing against the law that says this couldn't be a script.' Then to emphasise the point he was making, he shouted: 'We've found out that a guest on *The Jerry Springer Show* really isn't a transvestite.'

Although he appeared to be shrugging off the claims, Jerry was actually more concerned than he appeared. The company contacted former guests to interview them about how they were approached, and claimed to have discovered a common thread of deceit. Several of them signed affidavits that a former freelance recruiter for the show tried to bribe them into lying to *Extra* that *The Jerry Springer Show* was a set-up. However, a spokesman for Warner Bros, who syndicated the *Extra* show, said none of the people who signed affidavits for Jerry were actually involved in the exposé show. Jerry also claimed some former guests had banded together to set up a company to exploit their appearances on the show by selling book, film and TV rights to their stories.

It was not a good week for Jerry. The NBC channel in Chicago, WMAQ, bowed to pressure from religious and community groups and announced they no longer wanted to air the show. The following evening, Friday 24 April, Jerry appeared on *Late Night With David Letterman* and appeared to be uncomfortable when David asked him about the North Kentucky 'cheque incident'. On the Sunday night's *Dateline*, although Shriver did not unearth any evidence of cheating, she got Jerry to repeat his admission that some of the 14,000 guests who had appeared on the show could have lied.

Then, the next night, *Inside Edition*, another TV news

magazine, trotted out Pamela Jean Knight, calling herself Marsha, one of the two prostitutes who had had trysts with Jerry nearly 25 years earlier.

The Jerry Springer Show was then dealt another blow. *New York Post* gossip columnist Cindy Adams claimed one of the producers of Jerry's show, Norm Lubow, was a self-confessed drug dealer who had sold speed to Kato Kaelin, OJ Simpson's famous houseguest, on behalf of Simpson the night Nicole Brown Simpson and Ron Goldman were murdered. The drug dealer called himself Ron X, but when he signed with Hollywood talent agent Sherri Spillane, ex-wife of crime writer Mickey Spillane, he asked for cheques to be made out to Norm Lubow. She hired top celebrity private eye Don Crutchfield to look into his background, and he deduced the two men were the same. Lubow, who had already denied encouraging guests to fight and coaching them on what to say, also denied he was the mysterious Ron X.

Ironically, growing controversy over the frequent fist fights had already prompted Studios USA to warn Jerry to calm things down. However, that was too late for one unfortunate woman who became a victim of a Jerry-style beating without even going on the show. Teacher Aishah Ahmad told her class at a Brooklyn primary school they would be watching an educational show on TV. Instead the class demanded the set be tuned to *The Jerry Springer Show*, where the subject of the day was *Bisexual Relationships Spell Disaster For Married Couples.* When she refused to change channels four girls, three aged 12 and one 11-year-old, attacked her, punching, slapping and kicking her and even spitting on her. The rest of the class looked on in the true style of Jerry's fans — cheering.

There were no security guards to step in, but Ahmad, 44, was eventually able to fight the girls off and march them to the principal's office. The girls were suspended from school but Ahmad, who was treated in hospital for bruises on her face, neck, back and leg did not press charges.

'I'm on medication and I'm in a lot of pain,' she told the *New York Post*. 'How would you like it if people you have been caring about attacked you for a TV programme that has no educational value? It was not a fun ordeal.'

Jerry may have denied encouraging anyone to incite his guests to violence on the show. But his critics interpreted the incident as obviously having that effect in real life on children who were too young even to watch it under current TV guidelines.

CHAPTER 20

Although Jerry is the unquestioned star of his show several other characters have found fame, if not fortune, by appearing on the programme. For most people, one appearance on *The Jerry Springer Show* must surely be enough, or possibly one too many. But some of the most outrageous guests have made repeat appearances and are greeted with extra-loud cheers by the avid fans in the studio audience who recognise them.

Probably the most recognisable of all the supporting characters in Jerry's life is 6ft 3in tall, shaven-headed Steve Wilkos. Wilkos, who is a serving officer with the Chicago Police Department, moonlights as *The Jerry Springer Show*'s chief security officer and since the fights have heated up and are no longer edited out spends so much time on the screen he now has his own fan club. When the fists are flying, the hair is being tugged and the insults are being hurled, it is big Steve, who weighs in at just over 16 stone (225lb), who is in the thick of it. On an average week, he gets more bruises than most boxers.

Jerry joked: 'Steve gets more airtime than I do. I just ask the questions. He breaks up the fights.' Over the years, Wilkos has learned that the cost of fame in his case is pain. He has been scratched, kicked, punched and even suffered a groin injury separating two sparring women who came to blows over a mutual boyfriend.

The son of a now-retired Chicago police officer, Wilkos followed in his father's footsteps after a stint in the US Marines. The discipline and physical training of both jobs, and years of experience breaking up fights on the mean streets of Chicago, served him in good stead when he found his second job working with Jerry, purely by accident. A fellow officer was working on the show when, in 1994, he asked Wilkos whether he would like to make a bit of extra cash and help out as a muscleman enforcing peace and calm on an episode of the show about the Ku Klux Klan.

He loved his brief experience in the studio, even though in those days most of his action was edited out before the taped show was aired. He was delighted to realise he could turn TV into a second career without jeopardising his day job, which is actually a night job. Six episodes of the show are shot each week, two a day on three days. Each episode, which is cut to an hour for airing, takes about two hours to shoot, depending on how unruly the guests are and how many fights Wilkos and his cohorts have to break up. Since his regular shift is from 4pm to midnight, that gives him plenty of time to clock in for work.

Not only does the show make him extra money, it has won him a fair measure of fame. He is particularly popular among women viewers, who make up the majority of his fan club. When he is not dodging bullets on the beat in the Windy City or stepping between screaming TV guests out for blood, he is travelling the world as one of Jerry's personal bodyguards and has even surfaced in cameo roles on other TV programmes in which Jerry has appeared.

It was not always evident that Wilkos would end up working for law and order, even among the sometimes topsy-turvy standards of life on *The Jerry Springer Show*. The third of four children of Stanley and Jeanette, a beauty-school teacher, as a child he was always getting into trouble and fights. Fortunately for him his no-nonsense father was a tough disciplinarian without whom, he admits, 'I'd probably be in jail today.'

After leaving high school in 1982, when he was 18 he joined the tough Marine Corps. It was while serving in the Marines in Quantico, Virginia, that he met his first wife Rosae, who was also in the service. They married in 1985 but divorced two years later. He subsequently married second wife Hannah but they have also split up. When he left the Marines in 1989 he applied to the Chicago Police Department and joined their ranks in March 1990.

Even though Wilkos loved his moonlighting job right from the start, his parents became very worried about him the first time they tuned in to *The Jerry Springer Show* to see their son on TV. One of Wilkos' first encounters prising people apart was when fists started to fly during a segment on cross-dressers, who have a reputation for being extremely volatile in confrontations. The first thing Wilkos' parents saw was him on stage in the middle of this fight. He remembered: 'They called and said, "You're not gay, are you?"'

Although the punches are real, and a fair few have landed on him, Wilkos insists nobody is really hurt. 'Somebody gets a bruise or a scratch, to me that's not getting hurt,' he said. 'If somebody broke their nose or got their teeth knocked out or broke a finger, a hand, a wrist, an arm, that's getting hurt.'

He says that women are dirtier fighters than men, who aim to land punches but let themselves be separated relatively easily most of the time. Women are more likely to dig their claws into their rival's hair and refuse to let go.

'I come up from behind because just like in a bar fight, if you step in the middle you're likely to get hurt,' he said, describing his anti-brawl techniques. 'With girls it's difficult because they're usually pulling each other's hair. You've got to peel their fingers back or get a pressure point. Men take a few swings and wait for you to break it up. Women claw, scratch, pull hair and won't stop.'

Dealing with dysfunctional guests has made Wilkos grateful for what he has got. He said: 'It makes me realise how lucky I am. I have two good parents, two good jobs and good friends. My life's not bad at all.'

He has no plans at the moment to share that good luck with his adoring female fans, however, because of the hours he works holding down two demanding jobs: 'I work so much, I don't have time for a social life.'

Wilkos' bosses do not mind him becoming a star in his spare time, although they worry about the dangers the tough cop faces on the show as well as those he confronts in the line of duty. His supervisor, Sgt William Johnston, said, 'My main concern is that he doesn't get bit.' So far Wilkos has avoided guests' gnashers.

The fact is working on the show has probably made his job on the beat slightly easier and less dangerous. Often when he turns up to deal with a domestic dispute or other incident someone will recognise him, the tense situation will calm down and the participants end up asking him to get them tickets for the show. Fellow cop Dave Johnsen, who splits the rent of an apartment with Wilkos, said his friend has 'a face that stops people in their tracks'. Often when Wilkos arrives at an incident he is greeted with,

'You're Steve from *The Jerry Springer Show*?' Then things calm down and they try to hit him up for tickets.

Wilkos, who has had the opportunity to meet other TV personalities during his visits to the NBC tower, is a great fan of his boss. 'A lot of people that are on TV or in the movies, they think they're something special. The nice thing about Jerry, he doesn't.'

Accompanying Wilkos into many of those fracas is Todd Schultz, who probably has the worst stage manager's job in the TV industry. In fact, there is always one security guard for each guest on hand during each taping of *The Jerry Springer Show*, but it seems that it is Wilkos and Schultz who are always the two most prominent. In addition to having their own fans clubs, both men also have pages on the Internet devoted to them.

Schultz said: 'I have the most dangerous job on TV. I'm not only the stage manager, I'm a professional referee!' He became Jerry's right-hand man in 1995 when he was just 25 years old, and like Wilkos, he is a big man at 6ft 2in tall and weighing 17st 2lb. (240 lb). He remembered: 'One time, a Klan member nearly smashed my head into a chair, I fell flat on my face trying to catch a flying stool and a young lady tried to kick me where it counts, fortunately she missed! I've been scratched by transsexuals, smacked by mothers and abused by strippers.'

Like Wilkos, Schultz quickly discovered that the most savage fights aren't between macho men but angry women: 'I'm physically bigger but women's adrenalin is all pumped up and even if I hold them back they'll still get in a kick or a slap. Worst of all is hair pulling. Thank God I've got a crew-cut. I've left the stage with clumps of hair on my clothes, fake fingernails down my shirt and teeth marks on my collar!'

But muscular Schultz, who is worshipped by women watchers, had a good training for his job. Born in Scales Mound, Illinois, he studied broadcasting at the University of Wisconsin, Platteville, where he played American football, basketball and baseball. He recalled, 'I hoped to become the next Jerry Springer.' Although he didn't study self-defence or boxing, he has become an expert in crowd control. 'I don't need to learn how to hurt anybody,' he said. 'My job isn't to hurt anybody, but to keep them from hurting each other. I never know what will happen next. We've had mothers fighting daughters, two or more women fighting over the same man and prostitutes fighting over pimps. I wouldn't want to work for any other talk show.' Jerry is delighted to have Schultz working for him: 'Todd's been a lifesaver on more than one occasion. He's definitely got the toughest job on TV.'

It's not just people who work on the programme who have found fame; many guests have gained notoriety as a result of being on *The Jerry Springer Show*.

Bisexual lovers Rufus and Trenae have repeatedly appeared on the show and in Jerry's *Too Hot For TV!* video series. Fans of the show have become intrigued by their relationship and are anxious to keep up with their relationship, which plays out more like a soap opera than a genuine human drama. When they first appeared on the show Trenae was cheating on Rufus with another man. By the time they were invited to return Trenae was seeing a woman, who dumped him when she learned about Rufus. On a subsequent appearance, Rufus had become engaged to Trenae but he was also engaged to a woman at the same time. They were still engaged on another visit to the Chicago set and their mixed-up romance showed no signs of simplifying itself.

Brunette beauty Monique was aghast when her boyfriend Reno admitted that he was really a girl when they appeared on an episode of the show that first aired in 1997. Jerry joked: 'He claimed to have male parts, only he bought his through a catalogue.' Before the programme was over humiliated Monique had ditched her deceiving date but the couple later returned to be married on the show. Jerry explained to the audience, 'She decided she could accept Reno as is.'

It was Jerry whose breath was taken away when bouffant-haired Coco made the first of her many guest appearances. The exhibitionist, who wears low-cut, figure-hugging outfits that show off her ample cleavage, confessed that she was actually in love with Jerry and got turned on by tuning in to *The Jerry Springer Show*. She made her first appearance in 1992 and has since become a regular who also appears on Jerry's videos.

However, there was nothing to be amused about when Siamese twins Lori and Dori Schappell, who are joined at the head, went on the show to talk about their lives and overcoming their handicap. When they appeared on the show they were just turning 30. Lori had a job working in a hospital linen department and her modest wage was enough for the twins to support themselves in a modest apartment in Reading, Pennsylvania. Dori's greatest enjoyment in life was playing her guitar.

The twins manage to lead surprisingly different lives. Dori, who suffers from spina bifida, takes a book to read when she goes to work with Lori. Lori, in turn happily takes country music trips with Dori. 'We are two people with two lives,' said Lori. 'We're not just one person with two heads.'

Their enthusiasm for life not only touched the hearts of the audience but it also touched Jerry's as well. Kind-hearted Jerry later helped Dori fulfil her dream of being a country singer by arranging for her to sing on the show and also at a nightclub.

Brittany, a hunky, 6ft 3in transsexual, had the audience in fits when he admitted getting his girlfriend Dee pregnant. Dee's mother was a guest who wanted to beg Brittany to hang up his dresses and start wearing men's clothes. Even though dark-skinned Brittany said he planned to marry Dee, he still preferred his bra to britches.

Jasmin St Claire first appeared on the show to tell her boyfriend that she wanted to become a stripper. By the time she made her second appearance, she had decided that she wanted to become a porno movie star. And she later returned to tell Jerry about her wild on-screen orgies having sex with 350 men in 10 hours.

Some of Jerry's guests did not merely become famous, they became infamous. Gargantuan Denny Welch, who came from Jerry's old stomping ground in Hamilton, just north of Cincinnati, first appeared on *The Jerry Springer Show* as a cross-dressing entertainer and was to return at least five more times to discuss his weight or perform. The 36-year-old hit the headlines when his weight hit a staggering 61st 6lb (860lb) and he couldn't even leave his home to visit a doctor.

Jerry and 12 of his production staff turned up at Welch's modest house on Molser Avenue in a working-class neighbourhood of Hamilton, East Side in September 1996 to help him get immediate medical treatment for obesity. Welch, who is 6ft 3in tall, could not walk out of his home and faced breaking bones, heart problems or even a stroke. He had not left his bed for four weeks before Jerry turned up to the rescue. The talk show host even hired local building contractor Bob Jackson to tear down an exterior wall to the house and build a platform to enable ambulancemen and helpers to lift Welch out of his sparsely furnished house and get him to hospital. It took eight muscle-bound trainers to carry him across the platform to the waiting ambulance.

Ironically, on their way to Riverfront Diet Clinic and Christ Hospital in Covington, Kentucky, the ambulance went via a truck scale at Valley Asphalt in Sharonville, where Welch was weighed. Astonishingly, the man who claimed to eat only once a day and blamed his weight problems on genetics and depression yet admitted to being able to consume a half gallon of ice cream or a huge bag of crisps at one sitting, was relieved to weigh just 61st (854lb). 'I thought I was going to weigh 1,000lb,' he said.

Jerry pledged to help Denny. 'He doesn't need a talk show host. Right now he needs a doctor.' When he was released from hospital to continue his treatment at home, Jerry's show sent him a present — a special new bed to make his weight control programme more comfortable. Welch went on a rigid diet regime and a personal trainer helped him with an exercise programme. Jerry later presented a show entitled *Jerry Rescues an Obese Man*.

However, Welch's life quickly became uncomfortable and the reason had nothing to do with his weight. In 1998 police charged him with disseminating material harmful to a juvenile. Detectives alleged that the previous year Welch had shown three boys, between the ages of 10 and 13, pornographic videos at his home. He was back up to 57st 2lb (800lb) and once again was bedridden. Welch blamed his reversal in weight loss on suffering respiratory failure, which almost killed him. He told authorities: 'Since then, I've gained all the weight back.'

The weighty problem facing law enforcement was that he was so big he could not fit through the doors of the Butler Juvenile Court building to get into the juvenile court to face trial. It was decided the trial should be moved to the Hamilton Municipal Building. However, the events that followed had all the makings of a drama that could have unfolded on an episode of *The Jerry Springer Show*.

Before the trial Welch, who was a diabetic, was rushed to Fort Hamilton-Hughes Memorial Hospital suffering from heart problems. Welch claimed through his lawyer, Leslie Rauh, that he was so handicapped that he could not control what anyone did in his house. She said: 'He can't even roll over. If juveniles come into his house and decide to watch videos, he can't stop them. The responsibility isn't with Dennis. It's with the parents of the kids. They're the ones who should be cited in court.'

His mother, Rosemary Welch, blamed his heart problems on the stress of the impending trial. She said the boys were frequent visitors who cheered Denny up, and that they had found pornographic videos hidden in a cupboard. Denny, she said, was powerless to stop them watching.

In the end Welch's weight and health problems prevented

him going to court so the trial was moved to his home. He pleaded no contest to the charges. The plea meant that he did not contest the evidence presented against him, but did not admit guilt. Welch said he did not know the boys were in the house, as, at the time of the incident, he was bedridden and groggy from the medication he was taking. Judge David Niehaus ordered him to have no contact with the boys, to receive counselling in his home and to pay the court costs and lawyers' fees.

A vicious fistfight erupted on *The Jerry Springer Show* when young mum Dawn Marie Eaves, who was 24 at the time of her appearance, bragged about her sex life with a 16-year-old boy. 'Everyone's going to say I'm robbing the cradle but I'm having a good time,' she said defiantly, just after her young lover, Josh, started brawling with her live-in boyfriend, Michael Griffith. Dawn escaped injury in the fracas but ended up in jail facing rape charges. The episode, named *Homewreckers*, caught the attention of detectives in Dawn's home town of Geneva, New York. They charged her with rape and endangering the welfare of a child. Her three tiny children, aged between two and five, were placed in care and she was forbidden from having any further contact with her teenage lover. Prosecutor William Hart said: 'God only knows what effect her conduct has had in respect to these children when she's running around with a 16-year-old.'

Another guest arrested for bragging about his sex life was Edward Jeffords, who went on the show with three friends to promote sex with under-age girls in 1995. He pleaded guilty to having sex with a 15-year-old and was sentenced to five years in jail.

Probably topping the list of *The Jerry Springer Show*'s most daring guests was Jeffrey Durham, who appeared on an episode entitled *Men Living as Women*. What Jerry and the producers didn't know was that Durham was also living a subterfuge. For he was a *Man Living on the Run*, a dangerous fugitive from the law wanted for armed robbery who was so sure of himself that he was amused to appear boldly on a TV show seen all around the world.

Durham claimed he was shocked to discover his lover 'Amber', whom he said he had met in a launderette, was actually a man. However, the real person to get a shock was Jerry when he learned the truth: 'I can't believe he had the nerve to come on my show.'

Astonished detectives watching the show spotted Durham, who was a hardened 33-year-old criminal wanted for a 15-year-crime spree that included at least six bank robberies, 40 burglaries and attempted murder. Jerry's show had been taped while he was on location in sun-drenched Daytona Beach, Florida. Durham was a career criminal in South Florida, who carried out most of his crimes in and around Tampa. He decided it would be a hoot to appear brazenly on a TV show there while the cops were hunting him. Shortly after his appearance, Durham allegedly robbed two banks in nearby Melbourne. He had actually met 'Amber' when he was in jail serving a prison sentence for possessing stolen property.

Jerry himself made a guest appearance on *America's Most Wanted: America Fights Back*, a show that highlights the cases of fugitives on the run and asks for the public's help in tracking them down. The show is hosted by John Walsh, who got involved with TV and helped develop the show when his own son was abducted and murdered. Walsh asked Jerry to appear to help persuade Durham to turn himself in. Jerry was happy to oblige. He appealed to Durham to do the right thing and give himself up to the authorities.

Zachary Strenkert is a gentle giant. Zack, as his mother called him, was the world's largest baby according to the *Guinness Book of Records* when he was 17 months old, tipping the scales at a staggering 5 stone (70lb). He was just a slightly larger-than-average bonny baby, weighing 10lb 6oz, when he was born on 25 January 1995. However, he was suffering from a rare, incurable genetic disorder called Golabi Behemel Syndrome, which causes excessive growth. Doctors estimate that Zack, who before his 4th birthday was already 3ft 10in tall and weighed 9st 4lb (130lb), would be more that 7 feet tall and weigh more than 21 stone (301lb) by the time he was fully grown.

Zack and his family appeared on *The Jerry Springer Show* twice when he was a baby, and as a three-year-old he was also featured on *The Oprah Winfrey Show*. As a result Jerry received an unexpected compliment. For many critics regard Jerry as the uncrowned king of sleaze while perceiving Oprah to be the queen of kind hearts. Not so, claimed Zack's mother, Laurie Strenkert. She alleged that her family were not treated particularly warmly by Oprah when they appeared on Oprah's show which aired in the USA on 5 February 1998. Jerry, she said, was just the opposite and rolled out the red carpet for Zack and his parents.

Laurie said: 'When we were off the air, she spoke to us very little. She just kept getting her hair done and had an assistant fetch her drinks. When the cameras started rolling again, she kicked my shoe to get my attention.' To make matters worse, Laurie claimed that the family photographs and videotapes of Zack growing up that she lent the show were never returned. The last straw was an impersonal standard letter from Oprah's Harpo production company, which produces the show, thanking her for being on the programme.

Two years earlier, however, after the Strenkerts twice appeared on Jerry's show, he could not have been nicer. He took them on a personal tour of his office, gave them plenty of food to eat, helped them locate the finest specialists to look at young Zack and wrote them a personal thank-you note. Laurie said: 'Jerry was very cordial to us. But I was so frustrated about what happened on Oprah that I lost sleep.'

To his critics Jerry is a monster incarnate who relishes in exposing freaks and weirdos to the world, but to many of the unfortunates or disadvantaged he comes in contact with, Jerry is not preying on them. In fact, he is one of the few people who treats them as human beings and holds out his hand in friendship.

CHAPTER 21

His show has made Jerry the undisputed sultan of salaciousness, while his behind-the-scenes love life could just as easily get him on to *The Jerry Springer Show* as a guest on: *Top TV Titan Who Can't Give Up His Wife But Dates Other Women, Who Mainly Strip For A Living.*

For the one-time politician has maintained his liking for good-time girls and has dated a string of sexy strippers, pouting porno stars, alluring cover girls and busty beauties — including many women who have appeared as guests on his show — despite still being married to his long-suffering wife, Micki, whom he now tries to keep a secret.

Jerry, who persuades his guests to reveal the most intimate and indiscreet details of their mostly dysfunctional lives, is perfectly prepared to own up to having a lurid love life and is often seen in public escorted by bleached blondes and amorous Amazons. Yet when it comes to Micki, the woman he married in 1973 and the mother of his only daughter, he becomes uncomfortably coy.

When quizzed about the women he has dated, he is happy to confess: 'Yes, I have dated strippers and had sex with girlfriends who were strippers. I have dated women who were accountants, too.' He says: 'You shouldn't assume that because I have dinner with someone or go to a basketball game with someone there is some kind of sexual relationship.'

However, don't dare ask him about his wife of more than 25 years. When he attended an adult education seminar in New York in 1998 and a member of the audience asked him about his wife, he answered: 'I have a wonderful life.' Thinking he must have misheard her, the women corrected him. 'No, your wife,' she said. To which the usually affable Jerry testily replied: 'I know what you said but I never discuss my personal life. When I took this job, I never signed a contract saying I give up being a human being.'

Other people in the 150-strong audience cheered him, but the journalists who witnessed Jerry put the woman down thought it was the height of hypocrisy from the TV maestro who makes his money out of misery and misbehaviour but would not even reveal whether he was married. Those who knew most about him found it particularly galling as this dismissal was coming from the same man who sent out 1997 Christmas cards claiming HE KNOWS WHEN YOU ARE SLEEPING ... AND WITH WHOM!

Journalists who are granted interviews with Jerry are told by his assistants in advance that questions about three subjects are taboo: his marital status, the home he *may* own away from Chicago in another state, and his daughter.

The truth is the wild tales told by his guests on the air are nothing compared to his own off-screen antics. He lusts for hookers, lap dancers and erotic models yet, deep in his heart, still loves Micki and is desperately scared of losing her completely.

Jerry's and Micki's marriage had had its ups and downs for many years and was seriously in trouble by the late 1980s. They split up in the summer of 1990 although they always maintained contact, partly because of their daughter, Katie, who has always been very close to her father.

Since their break-up both Jerry and Micki have filed for divorce but never completed the deed. The woman who stood by her man in his darkest political hour when he confessed to trysts with hookers in a seedy massage parlour still has not completely turned her back on their relationship. She now rarely sees him, however, and lives in semi-seclusion in a luxurious home in a discreet, upmarket Florida suburb, a home he does not want anyone to know he owns.

Jerry claims the marriage came to an end simply because, 'My heart just wasn't in it any more.' But he and Micki still spend some time together and appear to have come to an arrangement.

Micki is just as secretive about their arrangement as her

estranged husband. She lives 1,000 miles away from Chicago in a $1.1 million ocean-front mansion in sleepy Sarasota, Florida. The luxury home is in a high-security neighbourhood and there are a Rolls-Royce, a BMW convertible and a Chevy Suburban parked in the driveway. At the back of the house are a swimming pool and private boat dock.

When asked what her husband does for a living, Micki tells people: 'He's a big shot TV producer.' Jerry and Micki are never seen in public together, although rare photographs do exist, and seldom speak each other's name to their friends. A neighbour who asked about Micki's husband was told by her: 'He lives in Chicago and I live here with Katie and that suits everyone. I keep my days full with a great social life and looking after Katie. And Jerry does what Jerry does.' At her coffee parties and all-girl get-togethers mentioning Jerry is strictly forbidden.

But those closest to Micki maintain that she has always been 'madly in love' with him. That was obvious from the very early days when he publicly confessed to having been with prostitutes just months after marrying Micki.

Until the summer of 1998 Micki still spent part of her time at the last home she and Jerry had lived in together, in the ironically named Loveland on the outskirts of Cincinnati. She told a friend she kept it 'just for the memories' even though most of the rooms were unfurnished. The sons of neighbours were asked to watch the house and keep the garden tidy and the lawns mown for her visits. She even kept a car parked at the Covington International Airport and made once-a-month visits back to the Ohio and Kentucky area. The grey-painted house on a secluded cul-de-sac, registered in Jerry's name, was sold in July 1998.

'It's a place where Micki can be Micki, not Jerry Springer's wife,' a friend said before it was sold. 'Some of the happiest years of her life were spent there.' Just like her roots, so Micki has clung to Jerry through thick and thin. The friend added: 'She made a commitment to him and she's going to stick to it. There's no question in Micki's mind — he is her husband.'

Throughout it all, Jerry desperately tries to keep his private life shrouded in mystery. After his 1974 confession he kept out of trouble, no doubt because he lived such a public life as councilman, candidate and commentator. However, after his separation from Micki, and as his show became so popular, Jerry was a prime target to be linked with other women and his fans and foes alike took great interest in his love life.

Despite his denials, many scandalous stories about the man have suggested that a powerful sex-drive is an all-important part of his make-up. Even though he had long moved on to pastures new the *Cincinnati Post* found it necessary to write about his sex life in June 1998. *Post* columnist David Wecker wrote: 'Jerry long ago established that he has an active libido.'

The American magazine the *National Enquirer* accused Jerry of keeping a mistress, dating plenty of busty young strippers and a porn star behind her back and hiding all of the women from his wife.

'Now he's terrified that the girls will all find out about each other,' the *Enquirer* wrote in February 1998. 'Maybe they'll all meet on a future episode of the show, complete with a fist fight.'

A source told the magazine: 'Jerry is out of control. He's on a date with his young bimbos in Chicago just about every night while his wife Micki sits at home in Florida and doesn't know what's going on. When Jerry's on the road, he has women all over the place. His bodyguard takes him to sleazy clubs and ends up driving Jerry to his hotel with a carload of women. Jerry goes for any woman who has a 40 triple D bra size and he gets up to 10 calls a day from girlfriends in New York and Los Angeles. Advisers told him not to be seen with all these women, but he doesn't pay any attention. He can't stop himself.'

Jerry appeared to have a very casual attitude towards his romantic relationships if all the rumours and reported sightings are to be believed. He turned up at a Chicago Bulls basketball game one Saturday night with a stunning 23-year-old beauty by his side, only to be seen at the same arena three nights later with a lovely 19-year-old who earned her living as a luscious lap dancer.

Despite his indiscretions, to some extent Jerry has patched up his relationship with Micki and according to those around him he is desperate not to lose her permanently, even though he cannot control himself when it comes to women.

'He is paranoid about losing his wife and he is paranoid about each of his girlfriends finding out about one another,' an associate revealed. 'He doesn't want to lose any of them. He wants them all.'

One relationship Jerry has consistently denied is with a woman known as the 'Black Widow' of Cincinnati, Della Dante

Sutorious, currently serving 24 years in prison for murdering her fifth husband, heart surgeon Darryl Sutorious. Born Della Hall in 1950, the daughter of a US soldier stationed in England and Liverpool-born Olga Brown, who moved to Ohio after they married, she was a gold-digger whose husbands and boyfriends reported a bizarre series of attacks if they got on the wrong side of her. She allegedly set one boyfriend's bed on fire with a paraffin lamp, and another man suspected she burned down his house when they had a row. She was said to have trashed men's homes, destroyed electrical appliances, stolen wallets and other possessions, and killed tropical fish by breaking their tanks. Fourth husband David Britteon, a Briton who admitted marrying her to win permanent residency in the USA, recalled waking up once to find her holding a gun to his head.

By the late 1980s Della, who changed her name to Dante because she thought it sounded more high-class, was bragging to boyfriends that she had dated former councilman Jerry.

According to author Aphrodite Jones, who wrote about her bizarre life and eventual murder conviction in the book *Della's Web*, Della and Jerry both attended a black-tie party thrown in Cincinnati in the run-up to the Cincinnati Bengals' appearance at the Superbowl, the American Football equivalent of the cup final, in 1982. Bizarrely, it was held at the swimming pool at a major office building, and Della was quickly asked to leave after she got her escort to push an ex-boyfriend into the pool. After that she talked incessantly about her friendship with Jerry, and was even said to carry around a 'special' photograph of him. For his part, he always denied knowing the woman who was nicknamed 'Notorious Sutorius' when she went to trial.

Della, who had a vivid fantasy life that included outlandish accounts of abuse when she was a child, regaled another husband, Grant Basset, with stories about Jerry. 'Jerry would do it this way,' she told him when they argued. 'Jerry is the smartest man on the face of the earth.' Then she would laugh, 'You should see his legs when he's in his underwear. They're so skinny. He does the funniest things when he's walking around half naked.'

Later, when his show went nationwide, friends and relatives reported she talked to his image on the screen. 'Oh, Jerry, that tie doesn't go with that jacket, ' she would say. 'You know better than to dress like that.'

When a scandal broke out in the USA over the controversial movie *Primary Colors*, which starred John Travolta as a randy American presidential candidate cheating on his wife, who was played by British Oscar-winning actress Emma Thompson, people back in Cincinnati were laughing all the way to the cinema. The film is based on the book of the same title by Joe Klein, a fictional account of then-Arkansas Governor Bill Clinton's real-life run for the White House in 1992. Not surprisingly the 'president' as portrayed in the film reminded people in southwest Ohio as much of Jerry Springer as it did of Bill Clinton.

'That's Jerry,' declared former Cincinnati mayor and Democratic congressman Tom Luken. After watching the movie he said: 'It was really more like Jerry Springer than Bill Clinton. He went to a house of ill repute, and paid with a cheque. None the less, he ran well, got re-elected to council and then he was elected mayor. Nobody could ever figure out how Jerry Springer did it. It was the same situation as Clinton.'

Jerry's former aide Tim Burke, who went on to become Hamilton County Democratic chairman, agreed: 'That scene in the factory, where candidate Clinton turns a group of surly factory workers into supporters, especially reminded me of Jerry; the way he used humour and self-denigration to bring people to his side. It was Jerry.'

The laughter reverberated so loudly around the Queen City that the *Cincinnati Post* even ran a story that saying that locals thought Travolta's character was more like Jerry than Clinton.

Probably the biggest Jerry-related scandal to hit the headlines was when the British multi-million circulation newspaper the *News of the World* published video pictures of Jerry enjoying a sex-romp with a porn-queen and her mother just hours before they took part in one of his shows on serial sex.

Blonde Kendra Jade, 21, and her 28-year-old stepmother, Kelly, confessed to their sordid sex session in Room 906 of the Executive Plaza in Chicago, where show guests usually stay, with their one-night-stand partner, widely described as the sleaziest man on TV. Kendra said: 'He sneaked into our hotel and got on the bed with both of us. I've met weird men, but none like him. He's a hypocrite.'

Kendra had agreed to appear on the show about having

multiple sex partners because she was one of six porn queens attempting to set a record by bedding more than 350 men. She had sex with 80 men on film while taking part in the contest, which was organised by John T Bone, a fat, middle-aged Lancastrian who now lives in Los Angeles. Kendra's stepmother, who was in the audience when the show was taped, was also her manager. They had appeared on the show before so Jerry knew all about their outrageous sex lives.

True to Kendra's opinion about his hypocrisy, on the programme, which aired before the *News of the World* made its shocking revelations, Jerry launched into a lecture on the sanctity of love. Just hours after their squalid sex session, he had the astonishing audacity to rebuke them on air for their promiscuity: 'Sex should be confined to loving couples in a special relationship.'

The *News of the World* wrote: 'Even they sat open-mouthed in shock as Springer sanctimoniously confronted a Blackpool pornographer organising the record attempt and spouted on air, "Doesn't this perpetuate the myth that women are nothing but sex objects? If you had a daughter is this something you would want her to do?" Then Springer turned to the camera, his face a mask of pious concern, and intoned to a starstruck audience, "Sex is to do with an emotional relationship with each other."'

Kelly, from Massachusetts, had first appeared on *The Jerry Springer Show* on a programme about unfit mothers. She had revealed she was married at 18 to Kendra's father. Kendra was 10 at the time. Kelly went from taking her to school to watching her become a dancer, get into the porn business and eventually managing her career.

Jerry was smitten with Kendra from the start. She recalled: 'As I shook his hand at that first meeting, I could see that his eyes were mentally undressing me. I knew right away he wanted me, and I figured that sooner or later we'd end up in bed together. He didn't especially turn me on, he's old enough to be my grandfather. But it was cool knowing that somebody famous was interested in sleeping with me.'

Six weeks after their first appearance they were invited back to appear in another show about sex.

During that interim period, Jerry had spoken to Kendra on the telephone many times, she claimed. She said that Jerry seemed lonely and unhappy. He told her that despite his tremendous worldwide success, he was ashamed of his sleazy reputation. Kendra said he told her, 'I hate the fact that I've become known for my show. It's just a silly, stupid show.' She added, 'It's funny how a guy like Jerry Springer, who seems to have everything in the world going for him, could be so lonely and sad.'

It was easy for the randy ringmaster to arrange his last liaison with the dubious duo long before arriving at their room that fateful night. He had telephoned them to say he might drop by. Then he had pondered the idea of meeting them somewhere else and at one point he had even made a telephone call to them in which he said, 'I also have a limo so maybe we could go round in the limo for a bit.'

He was desperately worried about being spotted by journalists but soon after midnight he showed up at their hotel room dressed casually in a jacket, green sweatshirt and jeans. Upon entering the room, he saw Kendra, who has a rose-coloured tattoo on her shoulder, lying on one of the twin beds wearing skimpy black lingerie. Her stepmother took off her own white top and trousers revealing that she also was wearing erotic underwear. Everything that was going on in the room was captured on tape by a video camera hidden in Kendra's handbag, sitting on a dressing table.

He threw off his jacket, hugged the two women and sat down beside them on the bed. Then as he chatted about his show, in a video obtained by the *News of the World*, Jerry could clearly be seen stroking Kendra's peroxide-blonde hair.

The women told Jerry that some of his production staff encouraged guests to lie to make the show more sensational. Their comments seemed to go over Jerry's head. He simply replied: 'I never talk to the guests beforehand.' It appeared not to register with him that in fact he was in a hotel bedroom with two of his show's guests, just hours before they were scheduled to make an appearance on his programme.

In the tape recording, Jerry seemed to have forgotten what his next show was about and when Kelly, who has starred in porn movies with her stepdaughter, reminded him it was about multiple sex sessions, he appeared bored and asked Kendra, who was caressing his body, to give him a massage.

Kendra later told the *News of the World*: 'I took off his trousers and started to do things to him. Then he took off my underwear. I remember he loved my pierced navel.'

Jerry and Kendra continued their frolic for about an hour, including performing sex acts, with Kelly watching, before he finally left around 2am because he had a radio interview scheduled for 7am.

Kendra, who had engaged in the filmed sex marathon just 24 hours before her liaison with Jerry, recalled: 'He knew that I had sexual intercourse with 80 men. He didn't care. But I still wouldn't let him have unprotected sex. It wouldn't have mattered anyway, because he had a problem and was always quick to apologise for it.'

The next morning nobody in his audience, with the exception of Kelly, had any idea how intimate he had been with Kendra when he set about her on the show. He told her: 'Three hundred and fifty men is not sex, that's assault. What do you say to the majority of people who say this is highly immoral?' Unflustered, she replied, 'I love sex.' Well, Jerry already knew that from personal experience.

'It's supposed to be something intimate, something personal," he went on. 'Having sex with someone you're mad about is special. Having sex for money, which is what you did, how is that different from prostitution?' To which Kendra stated, 'I love it.'

Jerry appeared bemused, scratched his head and said, 'I'm running out of questions.' Even in his 'Final Thought', Jerry had to take a holier than thou stand. He told his viewers: 'Our show is about the outrageous and I can't imagine anything else more outrageous. Sex is to do with an emotional relationship with each other. When sex is involved, make sure you have at least some feeling with the person with whom you are having sex.'

Kendra was just as adamant about her feelings towards Jerry. She told a *News of the World* reporter, 'He's just a hypocrite.' And in her later interview with *Globe*, she seemed surprised when she admitted that Jerry's telephone calls to her came to an abrupt halt once she had helped set him up. 'He just stopped calling me. I knew he was hurt.' Amazingly, Kendra appeared to think she had been good for Jerry: 'I know in the months I knew him, I helped him fulfil his needs. In my own way, I gave him the affection he needed.'

As part of his damage control Jerry appeared on the highly popular and much-regarded CNN talk show *Larry King Live*. He tried to convey the message that if his viewers liked him, they had to accept him for what he was, warts and all. He had already been scheduled to appear with Larry and decided to go ahead with the interview, even though he had been approached by *News of the World* reporters just hours earlier and confronted with the information they had obtained from the steamy videos. He hoped against hope that no one would call the show — viewers from around the world can telephone in and put their own questions to guests — and ask about the sordid episode, and his gamble paid off. On the show, he confessed to veteran interviewer King that he was not perfect. He insisted, 'I'm trying to be the best person that I can.'

Privately, he confessed to a friend: 'I screwed up. I may have lost everything I've worked so hard to achieve. I guess I'm as stupid as some of my guests.'

As part of his battle to prevent the sordid story making headlines on his home turf, Jerry threatened to sue any US publication that printed the photographs and report. His team of high-powered and highly paid legal eagles sent out sharply worded letters to CNN and such tabloid TV shows as *Hard Copy*, *Extra* and *Inside Edition*, warning that he would sue if they 'violated his privacy' by airing the video. He feared the tape might end up being sold through mail order and video stores, as had happened with a sexually explicit tape of former *Baywatch* TV series actress Pamela Anderson having intercourse with her husband, rock star Tommy Lee.

Jerry's lawyer Michael Plonsker announced: 'Mr Springer does not comment on his personal life. And if somebody violates his right of privacy, he will pursue his legal rights and remedies to the fullest extent.' Jerry believed that he was set up in the hotel room so he hired top Los Angeles-based, private detective-to-the-stars Anthony Pellicano — previously employed by Michael Jackson, Steven Seagal, Sylvester Stallone, Kevin Costner, James Wood, Roseanne and Mark Fuhrman, the disgraced Los Angeles police detective who investigated OJ Simpson on charges that he murdered his ex-wife, to name but a few of this Hollywood tough guy's client list — to investigate. Pellicano announced, 'A crime has been committed and we're looking into it.' Employing Pellicano is supposed to put the fear of God into any potential 'victim'. However, despite Illinois law forbidding the taping of anyone without their knowledge or consent, Jerry has so far not sued anyone over the embarrassing incident.

Meanwhile Kendra was delighted by the publicity. 'This

tape is going to make me more famous than Monica Lewinsky.' She announced her next role was to star in a new porn movie entitled *Too Hot For Porno*, a take-off of Jerry's best-selling video series *Too Hot For TV!* There was speculation that Jerry's sex tryst with Kendra might have exposed him to the risk of contracting AIDS. But she countered the AIDS speculation by saying that as an active member of the pornography industry she is tested for HIV every 30 days and has always turned in a negative result.

Kendra could not get enough of the limelight. Only weeks after hitting the headlines she announced: 'I'm pregnant with Jerry Springer's baby.' Jerry was furious. He said: 'I don't believe she's pregnant — and even if she is, there's no way I'm the father.' He stressed that she had had sex with multiple partners on a single day, so how could she possibly be certain who the father was? Strangely, no one else was able to confirm her 'pregnancy' and the phantom soon passed away, although the ghost haunted Jerry for a while.

His sexual indiscretions heightened speculation that his boss, multi-millionaire entrepreneur businessman Barry Diller, whose Studios USA by this time owned Jerry's production, might scrap *The Jerry Springer Show*. He was already unhappy with the violence and Jerry being at the centre of a sex scandal might have given him the excuse he needed to pull the plug. There was even speculation that Phil Donahue, the man Jerry had deposed, or comedian-turned movie and TV star Tom Arnold, once married to Roseanne, might be brought in to replace Jerry.

Jerry retreated to another home he owns in Florida until the smoke cleared and, strange as it might seem, spent hours on the telephone talking with his estranged wife about his problems. His efforts over the past couple of years to reconcile with Micki suffered a major setback thanks to the latest episode in his life, which might have been the subject of his own show, *Porn Star Busts Up My Shaky Marriage.*

After his unwanted publicity with Kendra his bosses had demanded that Jerry improve his image. A confidante disclosed, 'Executives ordered him to clean up his sex life.'

As usual no long-term damage was done and Jerry lived to date another day. When parallels are drawn between him and the guests on his show, Jerry still maintains, 'Compared with these people, I'm really dull.' Others might not agree with him.

CHAPTER 22

Although Jerry is worshipped by his legion of fans around the world, he is also loathed by many others, especially at home in the USA. It seems that whatever he gets involved with quickly becomes as controversial as his own outrageous talk show.

So it was when he agreed to return to presenting TV news commentaries. There might seem to have been no doubt that Jerry had the credentials to deliver a nightly commentary for a Chicago news programme. After all, he had done it for years in Cincinnati. However, when he was invited to present editorial essays for Chicago NBC affiliate WMAQ, starting on 5 May 1997, it was as if someone had thrown a hand grenade into the news room.

Joel Cheatwood, the station's then newly appointed vice-president of news, was very upbeat when Jerry's appointment was announced on 23 April that year. He obviously had no idea about what was shortly to unfold. 'I think people are going to see a side of Jerry Springer they've never seen before. His insight and perspective on the issues of the day is reminiscent of a time when news commentary was a major part of service provided by broadcasters.'

However, Cheatwood — one of the most influential innovators in American TV's journalism, had made a name for himself at WSVN, Fox Television's Miami affiliate, where he added tightly cut, rapid reports, visual pyrotechnics and sensational stories, leading the station's newscast from third to first place in the ratings — was soon running for cover as the grenade exploded and the shrapnel started flying in all directions. The irony of it was that it had all started out as an April Fool's joke that quickly backfired and by the end no one was laughing. Jerry's appointment caused a backlash that would have been worthy of an episode of *The Jerry Springer Show*.

Respected Chicago news anchorwoman Carol Marin, who had worked for WMAQ for many years and was arguably the most admired TV journalist in the city, resigned on air in protest over Jerry's appointment and her tearful farewell to colleagues gained national publicity. The débâcle had the whole of the Windy City talking and taking sides. Although Cheatwood's highly successful techniques had been widely copied in other American cities, strait-laced Marin was not a fan of his style or liking for stunts. 'There was a sense that style was increasingly winning out over substance. Springer was simply the last straw,' Marin said.

'Jerry offered to come on as an anchor as an April Fool's joke,' admitted WMAQ-TV station manager Lyle Banks, recalling a January chat over dinner in New Orleans. He had said he was looking for ways to spice up the newscasts and Jerry quipped that he would be available on 1 April. There were laughs all around the table, including from executives at Universal Television, the studio that then produced the show, 'But then everybody was quiet and it was like, "Maybe that's not such a bad idea,"' Banks remembered. That joke led to a serious discussion about him doing news commentaries. When the notion was leaked to the local press the following month, the touch paper was lit and people with any sense should have known to stand well back.

As soon as Marin resigned, after weeks of feuding over Jerry's appointment, journalist Martha T Moore wrote in *USA Today*, one of only a handful of US newspapers that has a national circulation: 'The city is in an uproar. And everyone is jumping in with comments on the Commentator Controversy.'

Marin, an Emmy-award winning reporter who joined station WMAQ in 1978 and had been a news anchor since 1985, described her resignation as drawing a line in the sand. She said: 'It's about the credibility and validity of news. Jerry Springer was for me the final kind of push point of "What are we telling our viewers about who we are and what we are involved in?"' She described Jerry as 'the poster child for the worst TV has to offer'.

The controversy was interpreted as touching on one of the most sensitive nerves in journalism — the quality of local TV news in the face of intense financial pressure to win ratings. This was not, of course, the first time had Jerry found himself at the centre of a row over ratings. Critics of his hiring viewed his appointment as a move by a station that seemed stuck in the number two slot in the ratings in the country's third-largest TV market to win viewers during a sweeps period. In this case the buck was stopping with Jerry. High ratings equalled high advertising prices; as in every year before and since stations across the USA target their most sensational stories or publicity stunts for sweeps.

'I don't think having Jerry Springer on a newscast, in a role that is traditionally performed by a journalist, adds any credibility to the newscast,' announced Patricia Dean, chair of the broadcast division at Northwestern University's Medill School of Journalism and a former colleague of Marin's. 'Instead, it lends credence to the argument that the newscast is going to go more tabloid.'

Marin's departure from the station was front page news in the city's two leading newspapers, the *Chicago Tribune* and the *Chicago Sun-Times*. Callers jammed the telephone lines of radio call-in shows. 'It's a shame for the city,' said one caller. 'She's a good lady with a lot of integrity.' Others vowed to remain loyal to Marin and not WMAQ. Still, Jerry wasn't without his supporters. The *Sun-Times* described Marin as 'élitist' for objecting to him; after all he had also won his fair share of Emmys, seven in all. It was also suggested that Marin's contract was about to expire and she knew it was not going to be renewed so she decided to turn Jerry's appointment to her advantage, gain maximum publicity for herself and, in the process, probably get new job offers flooding in. Jerry said: 'No one can honestly believe she's giving up a million-dollar job because I'm doing a minute and a half a week.'

Marin's resignation certainly was not a complete surprise to her bosses. On 6 March 1997, seven weeks before Jerry's appointment was announced, she had asked to be released from her contract. Marin, who had won 15 Emmy awards and was a member of the Chicago Journalism Hall of Fame, had been embroiled in a long-running feud with the station's management over journalistic ethics and the direction of the TV news show stretching back for a couple of years. WMAQ's management rejected her request, which led to speculation that they timed the inevitable showdown to maximise publicity during the May ratings sweeps. General manager Banks later admitted that Marin had been told her multi-million dollar contract was not going to be renewed. 'She had been told the station was going in another direction. I regret the misperception of her departure.' When the heat was finally to get too hot for Jerry to bear, Banks added: 'It was truly unfortunate that the beginning of his tenure as a guest commentator was unfairly associated with the departure of Carol Marin. The headlines were filled with insinuation that we had chosen Mr Springer over her. That simply was not the case. Carol had discussed her desired departure with us several months preceding this turn of events.'

Most people did not know about the behind-the-scenes intricacies as this very public drama was unfolding, but it did not matter. Marin had tremendous support from other members of the media and from the public. There was, however, some criticism about the timing of her decision to quit, since she had been arguing with her bosses for months. She and her co-anchor Ron Magers, who had been an on-screen team for 12 years, had a meeting with management in which they asked for the decision to hire Jerry to be reversed and said that if that scheme went ahead they would not introduce him. This was not her first row with WMAQ. When the station launched a series of community projects in conjunction with some of the advertisers, she was asked to take part and do on-air promotions of the advertisers in slots called public service announcements rather than commercials, but she and Magers refused to cooperate.

Matters came to a head when she refused to participate in a report about fire safety after discovering one of the broadcast's advertisers was a smoke-detector company. As a result she was suspended from her duties for three days in 1996. Marin had been outraged over what she considered to be the trivialisation of the news because of such stunts as Chicago Bulls basketball star Dennis Rodman presenting a sports report wearing a velvet dress.

Before her resignation both she and Magers stuck to their decision to refuse to introduce Jerry's commentaries. *Time* magazine wrote: 'To the two news anchors, sharing a show with the unabashed chronicler of America's most tawdry domestic dramas was like being asked to drink battery acid.'

The controversy was so fierce that the president of NBC TV stations, John Rohrbeck, found it necessary to make a few comments of his own: 'Station management did not view bringing Jerry Springer on to do commentaries as an endorsement of his talk show. I don't find that having someone who is an award-winning commentator coming on WMAQ is in any way reducing the standards of what we represent.'

Whether or not Jerry would do a good job presenting his own editorial commentaries was beside the point to his detractors. Marin said: 'His legacy in Chicago is a number of years of doing the worst kind of TV. I understand free enterprise and I understand free speech. But I have a right to defend something I've invested 19 years in if I think it will undermine the integrity of the broadcast.'

TV viewers and critics in Chicago had a completely different perception of Jerry from audiences in Cincinnati. Viewers 300 miles to the southeast of Chicago regarded him as a serious TV news anchorman and commentator, a former mayor, good city politician and would-be Ohio governor. However, in America's second city he was known only for hosting a show that dealt with such topics as *My Boyfriend Is A Girl, I'm A Teen Call Girl, My Sister's Pregnant By My Ex* and *Seven Months Pregnant And Still Stripping*. He was the self-confessed ringmaster of an 'admittedly wild and crazy show'. People seemed incapable of disassociating him from the presenter of a parade of strippers, hookers, porno-junkies, Klan thugs and women who slept with their sisters' husbands. His critics could only associate him with a motley assortment of dysfunctional losers, malcontents and borderline psychotics.

John Callaway, the host of *Chicago Tonight*, a nightly programme, talked of watching a Jerry show in which a woman confessed to her fiancé that she had had a year-long lesbian affair. Callaway described Jerry's 'Final Thought' on that show as 'brilliant, thoughtful, compassionate, psychologically sound'. But he added, 'He's taken the money and run. He worked very, very hard at destroying his journalistic credentials and his show, and he succeeded.' Jerry's arrival in the commentary chair came just six days after the death of Chicago's most famous columnist, Mike Royko, who wrote widely read syndicated columns. Callaway said that it was 'a truly sad week in the history of Chicago journalism'.

During the day that Jerry was due to make his first commentary, Monday 5 May, it was business as usual, at least as far as he was concerned. Jerry went to the NBC Tower in the normal way and recorded his talk show. That day's subject: *Pregnant Women Who Work in the Sex Industry*. While he was in the studio bathing in the glory of his adoring fans screaming 'JER-RY! JER-RY!' about 70 women and children were outside marching up and down, carrying banners protesting in support of Marin.

WMAQ's newsroom was usually buzzing with excitement as the journalists rushed to prepare the nightly bulletins. However, as Jerry entered the studio to present his first *Another Point of View* news segment it was tensely silent and he suddenly realised how genuinely unpopular he was there. There had been a rumour circulating that there was a plot to sabotage his Teleprompter so precautions were taken to see that nothing unexpected happened. Before going on air he shared an uncomfortable handshake with Magers, the remaining anchor.

Magers recalled: 'I had only met Jerry once, prior to the blow up in our newsroom. He had been taping the show for only a couple of months. I passed him in the hall, and we shook hands. He leaned forward as if he was sharing a great secret, and he whispered, "I know I'm going to hell for this." I was quite taken aback. Apparently, Jerry wasn't proud of what he was doing. Maybe he is now. I don't know.'

In his return to TV news commentaries, after a break of four years, Jerry, who was not even being paid for all the aggravation he was having to face — 'it was purely voluntary' — lashed out at his critics. Although it had been business as usual, his anger over the constant criticism of his return to making commentaries had been brewing all day. He told his viewers: 'This elitist snobbery that only people who meet an anchor's approval to share the set is now being hidden in the self-righteous cries of journalistic integrity. Bull ... and you can fill in the rest of that word. Please understand, we have no journalism in a free society unless we have commentary from all parts of the community — from the poor, the disenfranchised, the right, the left, the outrageous and, yes, the different. Not just from the endless array of Walter Cronkite wannabes that populate every newscast in the country so that virtually every news programme looks alike.' He accused Carol Marin of using the incident as a 'stepping stone to martyrdom'.

Jerry wove his commentary around a story about a tough decision he faced as mayor of Cincinnati when he was asked to sign a parade permit for a group of neo-Nazis. He told his viewers that he sought the advice of his parents, who had escaped the Holocaust but lost several close relatives and friends to Hitler's extermination of the Jews. They told him to allow the march to go ahead as they believed in the concept of free speech, a right that was squashed under the Nazis.

Marin got her chance to respond to Jerry on *The Late Late Show With Tom Snyder*, a show that aired in the early hours of the morning after all the late-night newscasts were finished and was hosted, as the title suggested by Tom Snyder, a highly rated veteran TV personality in the USA. Referring to Jerry, Marin told Snyder, 'He is a grenade in that newscast. And once you do something to disrupt totally the trust of the viewers, you can't just get that trust back. This is not about Jerry Springer. It's about all sorts of elements, in what I fear is, in the public's view, the dumbing down of news. Jerry Springer doesn't represent even a paragraph of this huge discussion of what is news. I don't see this as a movement or a crusade. I'm not a martyr. I'm not the Mother Teresa of journalism. I'm just a reporter with strong feelings and strong commitment about this.'

Jerry called Marin's comments 'tremendously rude'. He told the *New York Times*: 'When she's alone in a dark room sometime, she ought to write me an apology. What kind of lesson is this for her children?' He confessed to his old friend John Kiesewetter that he was stunned by the 'unwarranted, vicious assaults' from journalists who otherwise staunchly defend the First Amendment. 'I'm used to being beat up in the press, sometimes deservedly so, but it's never been national,' he said. 'And it's more vicious because it's the reporters' profession. This story isn't about me. The story is the arrogance of those of us who make a living in front of the cameras believing we can dictate who else gets to talk.'

The normally self-effacing Jerry was steaming by the time he granted *TV Guide* magazine writer J Max Robins an interview to reply to those who had maligned him. As he sat in his office filled with baseball memorabilia, smoking a king-size cigar and rocking back and forth in the chair behind his desk, he let both barrels go as he fired a salvo across his critics: 'I've been pilloried for no good reason. I've been used as a step in Marin's martyrdom and contract negotiations. The personal attacks have been brutal — she called me a "poster child for the worst TV has to offer", that all I was about was talking about women and their watermelon-size breasts. Doesn't anybody know I was an anchor and did commentary for 10 years and won seven Emmys doing it? So I do a silly talk show that I love. That's not all I'm about.'

Cincinnati's WLWT, the station where Jerry launched his TV career, devoted much of its newscast that Monday evening to Jerry and the controversy surrounding his return to making TV commentaries. Norma Rashid, his former co-anchor, even flew to Chicago on that day to interview Jerry in his luxury 91st-floor apartment in the prestigious John Hancock Centre, where he looks out on spectacular views over the city and Lake Michigan, before he made his first commentary. In addition to her news reports, WLWT also carried his entire commentary on its 11pm news programme.

A review of Jerry's début commentary was splashed across the front page of the following morning's *Chicago Sun-Times*. The headline announced: SPRINGER FIGHTS BACK, FIRST COMMENTARY BLASTS MARIN. The story got more prominence than the arrival from Portland, Oregon, of the city's new archbishop — the replacement for Jerry's former Cincinnati colleague Archbishop Joseph Bernardin, who had recently died — who was to be installed later that week, and the execution-style murder of a prominent local property developer. The *Chicago Tribune* review said that Jerry had used 'wild and extreme imagery', which it suggested 'brought Monday's 10pm newscast on the NBC affiliate closer to the level of the talk show he hosts'.

The WMAQ viewers' feedback telephone line was jammed within minutes of Jerry going on air. Of the 3,762 calls received only 46 were in support of him.

Surprisingly, despite the intense hype generated by Jerry's arrival in the newsroom, WMAQ did not see the gigantic ratings surge on Monday night that observers had anticipated, although the figures did rise slightly. The rival ABC affiliate managed to maintain its lead. His début drew about half the audience that Marin attracted for her on-air resignation a week earlier.

Even some of Jerry's legion of young fans who were in the audience for a taping of his show the following morning, an episode entitled *My Mom's Boyfriend is 17*, questioned his credibility to comment on news issues. Christine Pabin, an 18-year-old university student who was in the audience, told an interviewer: 'I don't believe I can take him seriously.'

Jerry stuck by his guns and his precious First Amendment right, 'The station thinks I have a point of view that's worth listening to. The worst thing that can happen is that you'll disagree with me. God bless America!' He regarded his appearance in itself to be a victory. He said: 'It's successful because I had the right to speak. Free speech is never dependent on what is said; it's a matter of the right to say it.'

Jerry's daughter Katie, who was then 21, was by his side after he came off air, as he unwound with a group of reporters who had travelled to witness him make his first commentary. She asked him whether he would have returned to the job had he known the brutal backlash it had prompted. He told her and those around them: 'I probably wouldn't have. But once it became an issue, I couldn't back down, because I'd have to admit they were right.' He added: 'Ultimately, it will be the audience who decides whether to buy it or not.'

It seemed that everything Jerry did concerning these commentaries landed him in hot water. That was especially true of his very first one. No sooner had he made it than he found himself at the centre of yet another controversy.

The banner headline across the front page of the *Cincinnati Post* screamed TODAY'S SPRINGER: TALK SHOW HOSTS WHO FIB. Reporter Sharon Moloney wrote: 'Former Cincinnati mayor turned Chicago talk show host Jerry Springer remembers his valiant stand for free speech in Cincinnati nearly 20 years ago. Trouble is, it didn't happen.' In his first commentary Jerry had recalled the story of the Nazi march and seeking his parents' advice. He claimed that as a result of their advice he had defended free speech even for his enemies: 'Much of my family was exterminated in the concentration camps in Germany during World War II. I didn't think, in respect of my parents who were survivors of it all, that I could go along with the permit, and yet I knew my constitutional obligation as mayor.'

Moloney explained to her readers: 'The fact is neither Springer nor any Cincinnati mayor under the city charter has ever had the authority to grant or refuse or sign permits for parades or marches or demonstrations. It isn't up to the mayor, or city council. It's up to the city administration, ultimately the city manager. In addition, the weak mayor system under which

Cincinnati's government operates gives the mayor no more power than any other city council member to do anything. According to past and present city solicitors, under the city's administrative code the Safety Director is the authority who must approve parade permits, and the head of the Public Works Department approves permits for the use of Fountain Square, which is where the Nazis demonstrated in 1978, when Springer was mayor.'

Moloney looked back into the issue of the Nazis demonstration in 1978 and discovered that the council had discussed the issue but that the members had been told by the city's lawyers that the council had no authority to approve or deny the permits. She also recalled the fact that in 1980, when the Nazis again wanted to demonstrate in Fountain Square, Jerry, who was no longer mayor but was still a sitting council member at the time, had, in fact, tried to limit their speech rights. He attempted in a motion, supported by some other council members, to change the city administrative code to give the city Safety Director authority to limit demonstrations, by specifying where and when groups could demonstrate. Moloney said: 'His avowed purpose, cited in published articles at the time, was to try to reduce the influence of "extremist" group demonstrations by forcing them to demonstrate somewhere other than the heart of the city.' Specifically, Jerry's motion would have allowed the city administration far more leeway to impose demonstration sites and times.

Along with the Nazis, the Revolutionary Communist Party, which was also a part of the political demonstrations scene then, also objected to Jerry's proposal, saying they needed to demonstrate in an area where they would be seen and their message conveyed to those they were trying to reach. His motion went nowhere after city lawyers again agreed with civil rights attorneys that forbidding certain groups the use of the public square would amount to a violation of free speech, a violation of the First Amendment that Jerry has throughout the years been so vocal about being the right of every American.

The *Post* did not let the issue lie there. In an editorial the newspaper expressed its belief that Jerry had 'twisted his controversial return to news commentary into an issue of free speech'. The paper wrote: 'In a free society, commentary should come "from all parts of the community", including the poor, disenfranchised, outrageous and different, argued Springer, who primarily speaks for the weird and sleazy. In reality, Springer's flip-flop from sleaze journalism has nothing to do with a news station's desire to provide a voice for Everyman. It's only about publicity, controversy and TV ratings.'

The controversy over Jerry doing commentaries had whipped the Windy City into a frenzy, meaning that Jerry found himself swapping places — answering the questions rather than asking them on a slew of TV chat shows and news programmes. He appeared on the American shows *The Tonight Show*, *Today*, *ABC World News Tonight*, *Crossfire*, *The Howard Stern Show* and *The Late Late Show with Tom Snyder*. Among the newspapers and magazines that interviewed him were *Time*, the *New York Times*, the *Los Angeles Times*, *Washington Post*, the *Cincinnati Enquirer* and *USA Today*. During the first few days there seemed no chance of the controversy subsiding.

Jerry was extremely upset that he found himself having to defend his first commentary, especially to the residents in his old adopted home town of Cincinnati. He was hurt that he had been accused of 'fibbing' over his involvement in granting a permit for the 1978 Nazi march. He told his close confidant Kiesewetter: 'Obviously, the city manager is the one who puts his signature on it. But it was a sensitive issue, a hot issue. So Bill Donaldson and Henry Sandman came to me in my office and said: "What do you want to do with this?" I told Donaldson, who was the city manager, and Sandman, the safety director, that I wanted to consult my father. If my parents were offended then, I told the two city officials, "You will have to find someone else for your mayor." I was the mayor of the city. I didn't want to be party to marching without talking to my parents. That's exactly what happened. I've spoken about it for years.'

A year after the controversy Kiesewetter still believed Jerry's version of events: 'The *Post* went to the current mayor who basically said, "That's not the way it happens now, so it couldn't have happened like that then." But back then, I think Jerry's explanation was plausible. The mayor and the city manager shared an office. I really think Springer felt strongly about this and would have told him how deeply he felt.'

Jerry devoted his second night's commentary to the new archbishop's installation and chastised Americans for choosing their religious doctrines à la carte. At least one of the people who had disapproved of his commentary over his row with

Marin called in to say that she approved of his second commentary. Mary Ann Staszewski said: 'He won some points and proved what he could do. It's too bad he didn't do something like that the first night.'

The row just would not go away. In protest at Jerry's addition to the news programme, best-selling author and Catholic priest the Rev Andrew Greeley, whose novels include *The Cardinal Sins*, *An Occasion of Sin* and *Irish Gold*, and the Rev Don Senior, president of the Catholic Theological Union, refused to appear as commentators on WMAQ-TV reports that Wednesday night covering the installation of Archbishop Francis George.

The petulant priests need not have worried. The controversy over Jerry's alleged exaggeration of his role in the Nazi permit incident kept him off the air that Wednesday night. WMAQ management decided not to run his commentary during the same newscast in which it carried a story about the alleged discrepancies being reported and talked about in Cincinnati. Lyle Banks, who in addition to being WMAQ's general manager was also the station's president, said: 'As a news station, we have an obligation to ask Jerry about the situation. We asked him about it, he answered it and we believe him.'

That was that as a TV commentator in Chicago, Jerry went out like he came in — surrounded by contention. He had been at centre stage but in the end he gave only three performances. On the Thursday Jerry quit, saying in a handwritten note to Banks: 'I'll be on tonight, but no more for a while. OK? It's gotten too personal.' He added that for the few times he was going to do his commentaries: 'It's probably not worth the flak.' Even Jerry was feeling the deep cuts caused by the flying shrapnel. 'This is my happiest day in a week. Enough is enough.' Banks, probably relieved because he had witnessed his viewer ratings take a nosedive that week, accepted Jerry's decision saying: 'He regrets the personal attacks he has endured. Over the last few days we have heard from a number of viewers, many of whom disagreed with our decision to put Mr Springer on the air. We appreciate the feedback and feel we are being responsive to it.' Banks admitted: 'We never imagined this would create this kind of firestorm. But maybe it's a good thing that all this controversy has pushed us to examine what news is about.'

Putting on a brave face, Jerry did not discount the possibility of doing opinion pieces for another station. However, it would have to be: 'One with a less hostile environment. I walked into a civil war. I've got a contract for six years at my regular job, and I think I'm blessed by having my talk show.'

Jerry later admitted that agreeing to do the TV commentaries had turned him into something of a national joke in the USA, 'I became a target. I was caught up in the heat of the moment. I was naïve. I let my ego get in the way. I didn't pick the fight. I didn't belong in that newsroom. I wasn't an employee. If they didn't want to let me in, how was I going to win? I have no problem with the position I took. Who is any anchor to say whom he or she is going to share the dais with? That's absurd. I don't back down from that position at all. But how many other people were going to lose their jobs? Suddenly I wondered why I was taking all the crap. By the middle of the week it became clear that with one or two exceptions, no one in the media was listening to me. I was determined to have a serious commentary, no jokes in it, no one-liners, boom — make the point. And of course the media were saying the story was, "Do transvestites who sleep with their uncles belong on the local news? Or the national news?" Of course not. That never was my position. I never thought crazy talk show subjects belonged on the news. I was asked to do commentaries on serious news items.'

Less than two weeks after his departure Magers also quit, despite having a three-year contract. In the fall-out over the rows over Jerry and the loss of their respected anchor team, WMAQ saw its ratings slide 25 per cent over the next few months.

The American media had watched every twist and turn of the unfolding drama and reported it with relish. Their viewers and readers had gobbled up every morsel, not in a dissimilar way to Jerry's fans, whom they regarded as piranhas, consuming their daily dish of dirt.

Pundits postulated on the long-term effect of his demise from the commentator's chair on news programmes. 'Something like this forces them to re-evaluate the coverage that they do provide and the elements of entertainment that they build into their newscasts,' said Michael Marsden, co-editor of the *Journal of Popular Film and TV* in Washington, DC, and dean of the School of Arts and Sciences at Northern Michigan University in Marquette. 'The Marin-Springer controversy forces them to ask what is news, and every newscast I've seen contains certain elements of entertainment.'

Jerry told Kiesewetter: 'I asked myself, "Why am I going through this?" This is not my career. So I'm not doing any more. If this was my career, or my full-time job, I'd say this was a fight worth fighting.' Kiesewetter was disappointed: 'When I heard Jerry Springer was going to do commentaries for Chicago's WMAQ-TV, I hoped it was a sign that he had come to his senses. That he was trying to go legit. That he was trying to exorcise the daytime talk-show demons that have seized the stimulating nightly news commentator we had watched for 11 years on WLWT.' Incredibly, he even wondered whether Jerry was planning to quit his talk show and return to news but that was never his intention.

Jerry said: 'I have been consistent and honest about this show, telling you the show is silly and crazy. A lot of the people we have on have deplorable lifestyles. I don't approve of what goes on. This is the only national show I'm going to have, and I'm not going to screw it up.'

He complained: 'Every time I move on to something else, there's always this justification. When I went from mayor to doing the news, they said, "You can't do the news, you're a politician." Then they said, "You can't be an anchor and be a commentator because you can't be opinionated." With the talk show, they said, "What does he know about being an entertainer?" Why can't you go to your job, do it the best you can, and just be judged on the job you do?'

Despite everything that Jerry says, Kiesewetter has a different perspective on what he really feels, 'In my opinion, the WMAQ-TV commentaries were his first attempts to restore some credibility. He desperately wants to be seen as a serious social commentator, not a trash talker. His talk show millions have put him in Armani suits and a 91st-floor condo in the John Hancock Building with an awesome view of The Loop and Lake Michigan. And yet everybody in the Windy City, maybe the whole world, is looking down on him. It was his choice. And ours, too.'

The débâcle may have damaged WMAQ's news programme but it certainly didn't harm *The Jerry Springer Show*. The show's viewership skyrocketed. It enjoyed the biggest increase in viewership of all talk shows watched during the daytime that week in May. Despite future criticisms of Jerry's show that lay ahead, there would to be no stopping him. Jerry was on the fast track to the top. The controversy over his commentaries, which were only supposed to be seen on the news in the Chicago area, had propelled Jerry and his *The Jerry Springer Show* truly into the limelight. The show was increasingly finding new markets across the USA. He was too hot not to watch. Soon his would be the hottest show on US TV.

CHAPTER 23

The boycott of the Chicago TV station by priest-turned-author the Rev Andrew Greeley and the Rev Don Senior, Catholic Theological Union President, over Jerry's appointment as a news commentator was not the only unholy row in which Jerry found himself as his show shot up the US TV ratings and he was becoming ever increasingly a major international celebrity.

A tough-talking pastor who had spent years battling drug dealers on the crime-ridden streets of Chicago vowed to exorcise him from the airwaves. At the same time as Jerry was appearing on the cover of *Rolling Stone* magazine with tiny horns and a forked tail painted on his photograph characterising him as the devil, he was coming under fierce attack from the Rev Michael Pfleger, an outspoken Catholic priest who described himself as an 'errand boy for Jesus'.

Pfleger fumed: 'He has raised the bathtub ring to a new level.' The crusading cleric, adoptive father of two black sons, claimed that the show 'markets violence to kids'. He launched his campaign after watching a few minutes of *The Jerry Springer Show* while visiting a sick friend in hospital and he was convinced of his mission when he saw Jerry jokingly dressed as Satan in the magazine.

'I'd be perfectly happy to deal with issues that only affect my parish,' said Pfleger. 'The problem is, Jerry Springer affects the kids in my parish just as much as he affects kids in the rest of the country. As long as they show fights and kids keep watching, I'll be on his case.'

As soon as Jerry's show became high profile it was almost inevitable that Jerry and Pfleger, a charismatic religious activist with a history of taking on and beating powerful opponents, were destined to lock horns in a battle worthy of an episode of *The Jerry Springer Show*.

However, even Jerry seemed surprised by the zealous reaction of the battling brother, who, while describing the fights on Jerry's show as immoral, came out of his corner with both fists flying. He urged an end to the fights, set up and coordinated a Dump Springer Coalition, made up of religious leaders and concerned citizens, and organised an advertising boycott that prompted several large companies to drop their commercials from being aired during the show.

None of Pfleger's supporters was surprised by his almost Rocky-like body blow to his opponent. 'He's just an ordinary guy but led by God,' said Gerald Stewart, one of his parishioners. 'That's all that sets him apart.'

Chicago-born Pfleger — Father Mike to the parishioners who flock to his cavernous St Sabina's church on the city's run-down South Side to hear his stirring sermons each Sunday — is an articulate blond, blue-eyed enthusiast who stands in marked contrast to the mainly working-class black community he has served for nearly 20 years.

In his eyes the fight against Jerry was no less worthy than the struggle in support of the civil rights movement had been in the 1960s, a great irony since Jerry had been so active in supporting that cause. Pfleger attacked his foe, saying: 'He is glorifying violence every day. Calling a woman a ho and a bitch every day is sick. This is not normal behaviour.'

Pfleger, whose critics say he is as much of a publicity-seeker as Jerry, tried to force a face-to-face confrontation, but Pfleger said he would not speak to him: 'He thinks I ought to mind my own business and stay in my church. I never understand when they say, "Why don't you just stay in your church?" This is the job of the church. It is the moral voice.'

Although he was unable to force Jerry to the debating table, the two men did have a brief street confrontation. Jerry ignored the priest as he shouted: 'We are not going to sit back and allow violence, pornography, obscenity and degrading of women on your show.' Pfleger later said: 'When women are constantly called derogatory names on a TV show, how can we wonder why kids hit their sisters. Anything that presents it as normal behaviour shares the blame. My concern with *Springer* is that the audience is youth-oriented. And we're seeing that the number one increase in violence in the country is with the youth. The brawls on the show teach this as the normal way to handle a disagreement. When you disagree with someone, you hit them.'

The belligerent brother was well practised in setting his sights on high-profile targets. Previously he had warred with the Chicago City Council for 14 years to get them to ban the advertising of spirits and tobacco on billboards in residential areas. Arguing that those advertising billboards were especially prominent in minority neighbourhoods, he was eventually victorious in the autumn of 1997. He also forced the G Heilman Brewing Co. to stop production of their PowerMaster malt beer, which was heavily marketed to young blacks, by threatening a nationwide boycott in 1991. Fuelled by these successes, he set his sights on Jerry.

'Pfleger has always been seen within the archdiocese as a rebel,' said Laura Washington, publisher of the *Chicago Reporter*, a magazine that focuses on urban issues. 'That gives him some additional cachet as someone who's willing to take on the establishment. His decision to target the advertisers rather than the format of the show was a brilliant strategic move.'

As *The Jerry Springer Show* became increasingly popular, it became blatantly obvious that people either loved Jerry or hated him — there was no middle ground. When the National Association of TV Programme Executives Convention was held in February 1998, Jerry, who also attended the gathering, found himself being pilloried and praised. Grant Tinker, the ever-powerful former NBC chairman and ex-husband of actress Mary Tyler Moore, was telling delegates to the convention in New Orleans that *The Jerry Springer Show* had set a new low for TV that 'debases all of us'. ABC President Robert Iger said *The Jerry Springer Show* 'embarrasses the TV industry'.

However, at the same conference, Roseanne, who was there to speak to the gathering about her own eagerly awaited syndicated talk show, due to start in September of that year, told them that she adored Jerry and watched his show all the time.

Jerry was there, always the seasoned politician, working the convention floor, defending himself. He described his show as 'an idiom for outrageousness. It's a cultural cartoon, and people have a good time with it.' The trouble for Tinker, and others who agreed with him, was that the cartoon that sprang into their minds was *Tom and Jerry*, where the cat and mouse chase each other around bashing the hell out of each other.

'There's almost like an anger for the show's success from a certain element of the TV industry,' said Jerry. 'It reminds me of politics. The same issues apply. I was a populist, liberal politician, and my show is populist. It's something the hoity-toity don't like. I'm speaking to the same crowd on a power, cultural, educational and style level.'

Opposition to *The Jerry Springer Show* was growing all over the USA. As a result some strange bedfellows joined forces. Two irate senators from opposing political persuasions, Joseph Lieberman, a Democrat from Connecticut, and Dan Coast, a Republican from Indiana, demanded that Jerry's show be denied use of the government subsidy that provides subtitles for deaf and hearing-impaired viewers.

'*The Jerry Springer Show* is the closest thing to pornography on broadcast TV,' the senators said in a statement. 'It regularly features such perverse subject matter as pregnant strippers, teenage prostitutes and undertaker sex, and characteristically exploits and revels in the problems of its guests.'

Lieberman said: 'The popularity of Jerry Springer has been disappointing, to say the least. We took a lot of encouragement that many of the worst talk shows went off the air. How, in the midst of this, Springer comes along and is so successful is a mystery. It's an awful commentary on our culture and our country.' Lieberman and former US Education Secretary William J Bennett lashed into the show when they attended the National Association of Broadcasters convention in Las Vegas, Nevada. According to Empower America, a conservative advocacy group of which Bennett was a co-founder and co-director, one million American children watched *The Jerry Springer Show* daily. Bennett said: 'I am concerned about children who watch the show and learn that anything goes, that any form of behaviour is acceptable, and that the best way to settle a conflict is with a fist to the face.' Lieberman and Bennett asked broadcasting executives to halt the spread of 'must sleaze TV' by re-establishing an industry-wide code of conduct. They even presented their first 'Silver Sewer' award to the show's former owner, Seagram, 'for underwriting the cultural pollution of the *Jerry Springer* talk show'.

Other politicians and groups also regarded Jerry as the anti-Christ of chat. The Sacramento County Board of Supervisors tried unsuccessfully in March 1998 to pressure executives at KOVR-TV in central California to move his show from its 4pm time slot, claiming schoolchildren were being exposed to the fights and name-calling. Parents in Detroit, Michigan, picketed station WDIV-TV for putting the show on in the afternoon, again to no avail. Parents in other communities complained of children engaging in *Jerry Springer Show*-style fights in school playgrounds.

A critic for the *Newsday* newspaper described *The Jerry Springer Show* as 'very possibly the worst programme in the history of TV'. The Atlanta Journal-Constitution described the show as 'an emotional snuff movie that debases the people who are on it, the people who watch it, even the TVs on which it airs'. US TV personality Geraldo Rivera, who once had his nose broken in a fight with a guest on his talk show but had made a significant effort to go upmarket with a news programme, said: 'If that's the level that the daytime business has sunk to, I'm so pleased not to be part of it any more.' Later in the year Rivera launched an even more vicious attack on Jerry. In the October issue of *Playboy* magazine he said: 'I think Jerry Springer is the most shameful man in America. I look at him and see Geraldo at his worst, times ten. It's appalling that it still exists, that people advertise on that programme. It's disgusting.' A surprisingly sanctimonious Rivera explained why he had got out of the trash end of talk shows: 'We all started trying to out-low-ball the other guy. I'd do *My Daughter Is A Hooker And So Am I*, so you'd do *My Daughter Is A Hooker, So Am I And So Is My Mother.* It just got crazy. But when I started losing my advertiser support, I pulled out of the death dive just to save myself and whatever remained of my reputation.'

Robert Peters, spokesman for Morality In Media, a New York-based organisation that monitors the content of TV shows, said: 'He exploits every human vulnerability and every debased human behaviour for the sake of ratings. The show focuses on the kind of behaviour that civilised people have been trying to curb since the beginning of civilisation. How much lower can you go? Obviously, mortal injury is the next step.'

Despite his success in rocketing up the ratings, Jerry was definitely facing a spring of discontent. His opponents were growing increasingly vocal and the show's producer and distributor, Studios USA, was getting cold feet. Fearing a firestorm of protests, Jerry's bosses demanded that he turn down the heat by a few degrees. Studios USA's executive vice-president in charge of talk shows, Henry Schleiff, said: 'We have listened to our critics. We do try to be responsible, good corporate citizens. We think we can tweak the show in a way that will allow guests to be in one another's faces without getting into physical contact. We can tone it down by a matter of degrees without losing the fundamental craziness of the show.'

Jerry's old friend and observer John Kiesewetter carried out a survey of five randomly selected shows that had been shown during the February ratings sweeps for the *Cincinnati Enquirer* in an attempt to see whether Jerry was living up to his reputation as the Don King of TV. He found that an average of 129 expletives were 'bleeped' from each show and that as many as 12 fights took place during the average hour-long programme, which actually meant about 42 minutes on the air in the USA because of the time spent for commercial breaks.

Kiesewetter said: 'Jerry is right about one thing: his programme should not be called a "talk" show. His guests don't talk. They scream, yell, punch, slap, kick and throw things. Call it unprofessional wrestling or really amateur boxing. Or call it TV's hottest new spectator sport, as the audience revels in the anguish of others learning their lovers have been cheating and lying.' Jerry explained to Kiesewetter that on his show, 'we do surprises'. Being the sceptical seasoned journalist he is, Kiesewetter said: 'Other words come to my mind, like "brawls" or "free-for-alls." Maybe the best description is "sucker punch", an unexpected blow below the belt, on national TV. Then the fists, flowers, chairs and profanities start to fly.'

Jerry just doesn't see it that way: 'We'll let anyone on the show as long as their story is outrageous. We'll bleep out the foul language, but we won't censor their ideas or positions even though we may find them distasteful.'

One wag suggested that if Studio USA truly wanted to tone things down, Jerry should fit his studio guests with strait-jackets.

During his survey Kiesewetter never found an occasion where Jerry, a self-confessed coward, got involved in breaking up a fight. However hard Kiesewetter may have tried he would never have uncovered one of the rare occasions where Jerry did intervene because it never made it on to the air. The show's executive producer Richard Dominick ruled it was: too soft for TV!

The show was never aired, not because it was out of control, but because Jerry abandoned his spectator role and stepped in to protect a guest. Dennis, a 28-year-old estranged husband, was trying to reconcile with his wife of six years, Liz, but she had a new boyfriend Dave, 25, who wanted her to dump Dennis once and for all. Dennis was desperate to patch things up with Liz for the sake of their three children.

It looked like a normal show, with Dennis and Dave fighting over Liz. Then she dropped a bombshell, not an unusual event on the show, but this one was different. She told the audience she had let Dennis move back home with her and the children because he had tried to kill himself. She became verbally abusive and Dennis looked confused and upset, unsure of what was going on.

Jerry abandoned his usual place in the audience, went on stage and sat down between the married couple. Gently he calmed the atmosphere down, congratulating Liz on her compassion for taking him in, and encouraging Dennis to concentrate more on sorting out his personal problems before trying for a reconciliation.

The producers were horrified by this turn of events. All guests are interviewed at least three times before they are invited to a taping, partly to screen out people with severe psychological problems as well as to make sure they are telling the truth, and they had had no hint of the suicide attempt.

Dominick admitted that the unusual segment had its moving moments, but he was not happy with Jerry's conciliatory approach. He said later, 'That's not our show.'

Steve Rosenberg, Studios USA's president of distribution, might have disagreed. He was ecstatic over the show's ratings but he also understood the critics' concerns: 'We want to be responsible producers. We have to take a good, hard look at what people see, but we also look at the numbers that say a large part of the population likes what the show is doing right now.' To try to placate the situation, Studios USA voluntarily announced in April that it would attempt to cut down on the catfighting and punch-throwing among the guests. The new measures included increased security and a warning to guests that they could be booted from the show if they got violent. In addition Studios USA gave the show a TV-M rating, meaning it was suitable only for mature audiences, under the US TV ratings system introduced in 1997. They had previously rated it TV-14, meaning it was only suitable to be seen by children of 14 or over. Rosenberg added: 'It's not for everyone. It's not for children.'

A few days later Studios USA executives went even further. From promising to 'minimise further altercations' the executives made the quantum leap to pledging that 'all the physical violence' would end. The backlash against the chair-throwing, fist-fighting and hair-pulling was too much for the company to bear. Executives feared that the backlash threatened to turn TV's biggest money maker into a public relations disaster. The pledge followed a meeting between Studios USA chief executive Greg Meidel and representatives of Pfleger's Dump Springer Coalition, which Jerry and his people were not invited to attend. Before the battle of the to-brawl-or-not-to-brawl was over Meidel could not take the punches any more and announced he was stepping down as chairman of Studios USA.

Jerry did not agree that his show was 'too hot for kids!' or 'for TV!' A confrontation appeared to be looming on the horizon. Jerry believes that his show 'should be shown to kids at home'. He constantly returns to his old theme that soap operas and prime-time shows glamorise sex and violence and that it is laden with negative behaviour: 'No one says *that* behaviour is bad. They glamorise it, make it look beautiful and sexy. That's what's enticing to kids. There's nothing on our show to make them say, "I want to try this." Kids watch other shows, see muggings, robberies and rape, and it's all done to beautiful music. In our show, you look at what's going on, and you say, "YECCH!" We make it clear that violence is no good. We make it clear that infidelity, promiscuity, drugs and prostitution are bad.'

TV critics predicted that if Studios USA followed through on their pledge to purge the on-air fights the show's ratings would sink rapidly. Eric Mink wrote in the *Los Angeles Daily News*: 'It's the fighting that allows viewers to tell the difference between Springer's show and the essentially identical exhibitions hosted by Sally, Montel, Jenny and Ricki. It's the fighting scenes that are used as viewer bait in on-air promos for upcoming Springer shows. It's the fighting that gets the studio audience on its feet, grinning and whooping with delight and that gives the buzz-generating high-schoolers and college kids watching at home something to laugh at and talk about. It's the fighting and the non-bleeped verbiage that has made the Springer videotape one of the hottest commodities in home video. It's the fighting that has pumped Springer's ratings past those of Oprah Winfrey's high-road talk show, and Rosie O'Donnell's easygoing, show-bizzy gabfest. In other words, it's the fighting that has turned *Springer* from just another modestly successful dumb-and-dumber daytime talk show into a frenzied cash-cow phenomenon for its producer-syndicator.'

Ironically the fist fights could not come to an abrupt end because there were some eight weeks' worth of pre-taped fisticuffs already in the can waiting to be aired. This meant that the earliest the American people would see the new *Jerry Springer Show* would be on 8 June 1998, conveniently after the May sweeps, which meant that the advertising rates would already have been set right up until that November.

Mink concluded that Studios USA's decision 'to change the show's direction so soon after the current approach started bearing financial fruit is as astounding as it is admirable'. Referring to the decision by Barry Diller, the head of Studios USA, to tone down *The Jerry Springer Show*, Mink concluded: 'Diller and his colleagues deserve enormous credit for being sufficiently embarrassed by the Springer spectacle to take a shot at it.'

As the battle over whether the fights should stay or go raged on, so Americans started analysing why the programme was so popular with viewers. Psychiatrists and other mental and social therapists started spouting off theories. The show had become such a surprising success, so the experts explained, because it provided an escape valve for people's pent-up anger and frustrations.

Dr Lois Mueller, a clinical psychologist based in Tampa, Florida, said: 'We all know at least one person we'd like to throw a pie at Springer's guests help us release aggression. We should be grateful that the outrageous antics on the show help us let off steam non-violently and legally. We might get the urge to walk around naked, like one of his more uninhibited guests and thanks to Springer we can fulfil those desires by watching the show. Most of us have felt like letting it all hang out at one time or another. We'd love to get down and dirty and wrestle in the mud, but don't because we're afraid of what other folks will think.'

Dr Jamie Turndorf, a New York-based psychotherapist, concluded that Jerry's popularity was caused by everyone identifying with the outrageous sentiments expressed by his guests: 'We get a thrill out of watching Springer and his guests. Most of us are too civilised to haul off and sock someone, but we all have bottled up aggression. Watching Springer releases this aggression.'

Jerry thought they were all taking his popularity far too seriously. He had a far simpler explanation: 'It's like chewing gum in between class at school. It's just a momentary escape from your life and shouldn't be taken seriously.'

Some TV stations in the USA were feeling the heat more than others. At exactly the same time as Studios USA was promising to tone down and eventually stop the violence, WMAQ in Chicago, which had been feeling the brunt of the pressure from religious groups like that organised by Pfleger and other community groups, asked Studios USA to release them from the remaining three years of their contract. Management at the station had changed in the year since Jerry was at the centre of a controversy after his short-lived stint reading commentaries on WMAQ's nightly news, which led to the resignation of the programme's two most popular anchors. The new management was nowhere near as enamoured by Jerry.

Larry Wert, WMAQ's new president and general manager, suggested in a statement that Jerry's standards were not in line with the station's or in keeping with community standards. Publicly Wert was not saying much about his decision to scrap the show but privately the month before he had told some colleagues that he had misgivings about the programme 'from a moral viewpoint, if you are going to claim to be a responsible, community-serving TV studio'.

As it happened Studios USA executives were delighted. The show was immediately picked up by Fox's Chicago station WFLD Channel 32 for a hefty licence fee increase, an average of $60,000 a week for a three-year contract, which was about three times what WMAQ were paying.

Father Pfleger demanded a meeting with the show's producers and the management at WFLD and organised protests outside both stations. He had declared an instant victory when Studios USA said it was eliminating violence from the show. His 'victory' appeared rather hollow as part of WFLD's deal allowed it to air Jerry's show twice a day instead of once as had been the arrangement with WMAQ. The station needed to air it twice a day, once at 9am and again at 11pm, to help recoup its costs by bringing in more advertising dollars. That in itself was a gamble because in the USA controversy is a trait that usually does not attract advertisers.

Marge Navolio, president and chief executive of the Chicago-based advertising agency CPM Inc., said: 'We have clients who absolutely will have nothing to do with the show because they don't want to catch flak from the public. To them, it's just too much damn trouble.' Other CPM clients were more tolerant and said they would continue to advertise during the show as long as people kept watching it. She added: 'The hipper and less conservative the market, the more they will say "live and let live". They look at it and ask, "How different is it from World Wrestling Federation? They're just not in trunks."'

Even Jerry's old station WLWT in Cincinnati was

distancing itself from its one-time star TV journalist. There the show was aired with a disclaimer about its controversial content. WLWT general manager Rick Rogala said at the time: 'We're contracted to run the show and we'll continue to honour the contract. He's number one in America, right or wrong, and I'm not necessarily sure that that's a good thing.'

The city that had loved and laughed at Jerry for 20 years seemed to heartily disapprove of his third career. A lobby group called Citizens for Community Values called on WLWT to stop the show altogether, and when it would not, circulated a petition to advertisers urging them not to support it. They said: '*The Jerry Springer Show* mocks our culture, preys upon and exploits dysfunctional people, and sends a message that disagreement should be resolved with violence. Jerry Springer's response to his critics is an insult! He says, "If you don't like it, don't watch."'

They invoked their own rights under the First Amendment to the US Constitution, so precious to Jerry, to justify their call to take the show off the air. 'In reference to indecent broadcasting the USA Supreme Court has said, "To say that one may avoid further offence by turning the dial is like saying that the remedy for an assault is to run away after the first blow. Patently offensive, indecent material presented over the airwaves confronts the citizen, not only in public, but also in the privacy of the home, where the individual's right to be let alone plainly outweighs the First Amendment rights of the intruder. Second, broadcasting is uniquely accessible to children, even those too young to read."'

Jerry was coming under a more fierce attack than any of his guests ever had to face. Along with the national outburst of condemnation and criticism came the reports about alleged phoney guests and probes into Jerry's sex life, even dragging up the cheque incident with the hookers of 25 years before. Some in the entertainment business were wondering whether America's best known sideshow barker could survive the April showers that had turned into torrential thunderstorms. Resilient Jerry appeared to be protected by a strong umbrella. Bill Carroll, vice-president of programming for the Katz TV Group, which represents local TV stations all over the USA in their negotiations with national advertisers, said confidently: 'As long as it's distinctive and outrageous, people will continue to tune in.' But he was equally sure that if the outrageousness diminished because Jerry and his producers were demanding absolute honesty from every guest on the show, then viewers might lose interest. *The Jerry Springer Show* was facing the biggest dilemma of its life. Carroll, whose New York-based firm is the largest of its type in America, added: 'The people who are watching are the younger folks and they are the most fickle. It's the flavour of the month.'

Most people in the entertainment industry were sceptical that Jerry would change his ways. They deduced, correctly as it was to turn out, that a leopard does not change his spots or, in this case, a populist politician doesn't turn his back on the popular vote. Hollywood has two bibles of the entertainment industry, which are must reads every day for every executive, the *Hollywood Reporter* and *Daily Variety*. *Variety*'s Cynthia Littleton concluded: 'Not since Joseph Stalin cut his short-lived deal with the devil Nazis in 1939 has a non-aggression pact provoked so much controversy, not to mention headlines.'

As had been widely expected, defiant Jerry said that he had no plans to live up to Studios USA executives' pledge to stop the fights. 'I'm not going to buckle. I don't want to tone it down. That's absurd. I don't know why they issued that statement.'

However, Jerry conceded that the ultimate decision about the show's future rested with Diller, chairman of Studios USA's parent company USA Networks Inc., who took over *The Jerry Springer Show* in a buy-out of Universal Studio's domestic TV operation early in 1998. He dismissed speculation about resigning, but there was a veiled hint that he might be preparing to walk when he added, 'It's ultimately going to be Diller's decision and whoever the people are under him, they'll decide whether they want to have me or not. And if they don't want to have me, then I assume maybe someone else will.'

Jerry and executive producer Dominick vowed to resist, claiming they would set out to produce the 'wildest weeks of TV ever shown'. Dominick said: 'We intend to become even wilder, sexier and more outrageous than ever. Nothing is taboo for us. The only thing we rule out is normal behaviour. If people want that then they should tune into Oprah and the others.' Dominick quietly slated subjects such as *Men Who Want To Be Babies*, *People Who Refuse To Wear Clothes*, *The Attack Of The Ex-Lovers* and *Gals Confess To Husbands And Boyfriends: I'm Secretly A Prostitute*. He said: 'The way Jerry sees it, we live in a pure democracy and if people don't like what we air they can turn it off.'

Throughout early May Jerry was flip-flopping over whether or not he would jettison the violent mêlées that had propelled his show to the top of the ratings and gained him international fame.

After telling outrageous radio shock jock Howard Stern he would battle his Studio USA bosses, he told CNN's Larry King: 'You'll see some adjustments, not much. There'll be less blows to the head, we'll keep people further apart.' Extra security people were employed part-time from the Chicago police force to add more muscle to the show's security squad. He said to King: 'Obviously, I can't sit here and predict to you how many fights there are going to be, but we're going to make sure nobody gets hurt.' Jerry told King that he had come to an understanding with his studio bosses after being caught by surprise by the announcement that the violence was to be eliminated from the show. But in the next breath he was telling *Tonight Show* host Jay Leno the fighting would be 'up to the people on the show'.

While all this was going on Jerry was also having to deal with a new scandal — pictures of him having a tryst with pouting porno star Kendra Jade and her stepmother were appearing in the UK's *News of the World* and the *Globe* in the USA. It was turning into one hell of a year for Jerry, a man who was quickly becoming regarded as the satan of sleaze rather than the ringmaster of raunchy TV.

However, not all the news was bad for Jerry. A new deal signed between Universal International TV, which handled international syndication, and the British broadcasting group Flextech TV ensured that UK TV audiences would continue to get a daily double dose of *The Jerry Springer Show* on Flextech's cable channel Living TV. The deal covered the period from the start of January 1998 through the lifetime of the show's production. The show had already been sold to ITV, which meant that it aired twice a day. During a 'Springer' weekend aired on Living TV early in 1998 the show had outperformed BBC2, Channel 4, Channel 5 and all other cable and satellite channels. In fact, *The Jerry Springer Show* had developed into one of Living TV's most successful programmes since it was launched in 1995.

Very soon there was much industry speculation in the USA that, despite the profitability of *The Jerry Springer Show*, the continuing controversy over violence could hinder his corporate bosses' longer-term plans. It transpired that shortly after taking charge of Studios USA in February that year, Diller had promised Senator Lieberman, who had been unrelenting in his criticism of the show, that it would be cleaned up. Lieberman admitted: 'Diller told me he would accept responsibility for *Springer* and that he was going to draw some lines about the show's content. I applaud the move to take out the violence. I guess what it will be now is trash without violence. In the world of TV, progress comes in small steps.' Diller, who helped create Rupert Murdoch's highly successful Fox TV network, was ambitiously attempting to build another empire through his control of the USA Network, the Home Shopping Network and a chain of TV stations. His aspirations required some friends, like Lieberman, in Washington, DC.

There were all sorts of issues that the US Congress and the Federal Communications Commission (the FCC) were looking into that would have a direct impact on the growth of Diller's business empire. It was believed that he felt that toning down *The Jerry Springer Show* might lead to a drop in ratings and short-term revenue but could have far-reaching political benefits and it seemed he thought it was worth the gamble. Lieberman confirmed: 'Certainly Diller's willingness to draw lines will increase his credibility in Washington.'

Jerry and Studios USA executives met for a secret discussion about toning down the show. They remained tight-lipped about what went on behind closed doors but it appeared that a compromise might have been reached. Then, just as it looked like Jerry was rolling over like a whipped dog, he taped what was probably, even by *Jerry Springer* standards, his most outrageous show ever. For an episode entitled *I Married A Horse* Jerry introduced to his audience a man who claimed to love his horse in ways that would make Mr Ed blush.

Other guests talked about their pet paramours. They revealed how they loved, and they meant *loved*, their pets. A man and a woman both told how they enjoyed having sex with their dogs. The man even confessed that he was turned on only by canines, not by people. One humourist suggested that if Catherine the Great had been alive she would have been booked as a guest on the show. During the show's taping Jerry told his audience, 'When the bosses see this, they'll beg me to bring back the fights.'

Criticism rained down on Jerry, who argued that he'd been told to cut out the violence and on that show at least nobody threw a punch. No, the punches were coming from TV station managers all over the country who refused to air the programme. Even in ultra-liberal Los Angeles, the management at KCAL-TV Channel 9, which showed the *Springer Show* twice daily, announced that bestiality would not be broadcast on their airwaves. A spokesman for WLWT in Cincinnati, which also refused to air the show, described it as 'brutal'.

Violence had been given the heave-ho but obviously cruelty to animals had not. Studios USA screamed 'Hold your horses' at the 11th hour and the episode was pulled altogether. Anticipating a problem Studios USA had already offered TV stations across the country an alternative episode, *Past Guests Do Battle*, and that was aired in its place.

Jerry had long joked about doing a show on bestiality. At the end of his show, he often asks people who might be involved in upcoming subjects to give his producers a call in case they qualify as potential guests. At one show's taping, as part of a closing which was never actually aired on TV Jerry asked: 'Are you the black sheep of the family or are you dating someone who is a black sheep? In fact, if you are dating a sheep give us a call on 1-800-29-JERRY.' Then Jerry broke into laughter, turned to his audience and confessed with a smirk on his face, 'I would *love* to do that!' Although Jerry's TV audience never saw his hint of things to come, the hilarious moment did eventually find its way on to one of his *Too Hot For TV!* videos.

The summer of 1998 was shaping up to be a hot one for Jerry and his distributors. If he could not be tamed there was talk that Studios USA would sell the show to another syndicator, one that might be a little less skittish about shows on topics such as animal love.

Diller was embarrassed by the show and wanted to distance his company from Jerry. 'When you're in businesses that are regulated, you don't need enemies in Washington,' a source told top *TV Guide* writer J Max Robins at the end of May. 'But he's in a jam because the show makes so much money, and he doesn't want to send the wrong signal to Wall Street.' Worried about the power of Wall Street investors, Diller started downplaying the importance to his company of *The Jerry Springer Show*'s revenue. Savvy investment brokers were telling him that, none the less, the revenue was substantial, even if plenty of blue-chip advertisers would not go near the show. Diller countered that despite licensing fees, advertising and video sales, which were bringing in more than $40 million, his company would sell off the show without adversely affecting its stock price. Diller's money men were telling anyone who would listen that USA Networks Inc., which also had the Home Shopping Network, cable networks, TV stations and Ticketmaster, a giant company selling tickets for concerts, theatres and sports events nationwide and had an annual estimated cash flow of $455 million, could easily survive without *Springer*.

American money men widely regarded Diller's desire to banish Jerry's show from his stable as a financial decision and not a moral one. Although he would lose $40 million in revenue by letting *The Jerry Springer Show* go elsewhere, he stood to make many times that amount by keeping his image free of sleaze. Richard Read, media analyst for Credit Lyonnais Securities said, '*Springer* is not vital to what Barry's doing.' Diller had a dream of reformatting TV into a giant direct-sales vehicle, with ads pitching goods and services directly to viewers in much the same way as the Home Shopping Network. Credit Lyonnais saw good prospects in his vision. He had already made a fortune through selling cheap imitation diamond jewellery on his shopping network and supported such lowbrow TV shows as *Hercules: The Legendary Journey* and *Xena: Warrior Princess* because they were good vehicles for commercials. He was also selling merchandise based on the shows' characters on the shopping network. With Jerry, there were no such cross-marketing opportunities, only headaches caused by complaints over the fights, swearing, sexual content and deviant behaviour of the guests.

It was felt that the most logical buyer would be a major TV station group that could guarantee the show's distribution.

The war of words had all been waged up to and around the all-important May sweeps. Ironically, Jerry came out unscathed. Once again *The Jerry Springer Show* was the big winner in the influential Nielsen household ratings far ahead of his major competitor Oprah Winfrey. Nationally *Oprah* was down 15 percent on the May 1997 figures while *Springer* was up a whopping 152 percent. It was going to be hard to argue against the top-rated daytime syndicated talk show in the country.

TV watchdogs waited with bated breath for 8 June to arrive to witness the new *Springer*. When would the first fist connect or the first chair be thrown? Topics that first week indicated volatility rather than violence. They included *You're Too Fat To Do Porn, My Lover Has A Secret* and *You're A Man, Dress Like One*! The fights were, in fact, edited out during that first sanitised week and Jerry revealed: 'If we see that viewers are unhappy that we're editing stuff out, then we won't edit it out anymore. This week, the fights are going to be edited out. Whether we continue this policy or not ... we'll see.'

Whatever happened, it seemed, the show remained a lightning rod for controversy. As widely predicted by TV industry observers the week that the non-violence pledge took effect saw

The Jerry Springer Show plunge in the ratings to its lowest Nielsen figures since January 1998. It was still strong enough to be head of the daytime pack but viewership fell by seven per cent. Viewers were calling TV stations all over the country asking: 'Where are the fist fights?' *The Jerry Springer Show*'s top spin doctor, executive producer Dominick, tried to put the situation into perspective, blaming the drop in viewers on it being summer: 'I don't think there's going to be a permanent drop-off. Besides the policy is not no violence, the policy is that if anybody gets hit, it will be our security people. We won't let guests get punched in the face, or wrestle on the ground. It's still controlled chaos.'

When Jerry had a face-to-face meeting with management, the executives at USA Networks did not seem as displeased with the show as they had stated publicly. Jerry disclosed: 'I got nothing out of those meetings except a lot of money. They came out and said, "God bless you and here's a bonus." It was amazing. They said, "Keep doing the show, God bless you, couldn't be happier." Their concern was that no one get hurt.'

Playboy magazine wrote in July in a preface to a candid interview Jerry had granted the publication, 'Jerry Springer may well be one of the most despised men in America, blamed for a surprising percentage of America's ills and often called, by otherwise smart people, a harbinger of the end of civilisation as we know it. It's easy to see why. No show in the history of TV has ever sunk quite so low.'

If the battle on the home front wasn't enough, Jerry's show and shows like his suddenly found themselves coming under attack in the UK. A government watchdog committee described confessional TV shows like Jerry's as the modern equivalent of placing offenders in the stocks. In its first annual report, the Broadcasting Standards Commission (BSC) described the genre as 'victim entertainment' and accused daytime chat shows of making 'the abnormal normal'.

Commission chairman Lady Howe of Aberavon warned: 'Is it worth asking whether this rapidly increasing section of the broadcast menu is to be welcomed? Some would argue that the exploitation of the misfortunes of others is not an endearing human trait. There is a limit to trial by TV. A society which has long since abandoned the stocks should think twice about the modern version, designed to titillate and entertain rather than inform.' In its report the BSC stated that it believed guests may need protection for their own good. Although the BSC could have little, if not no authority over US chat shows, it certainly could have an influence on the homegrown variety. The commission, a statutory body set up to represent the viewer on issues of taste, decency, fairness and privacy, had adjudicated on a significant number of complaints about talk shows in the months coming up to its first report from participants who felt they were unfairly treated and viewers unhappy with the subjects discussed.

Lady Howe expressed concern for the guests in the shows who were exploited and felt distressed after their appearances. 'There are times when it all goes too far and as this genre is growing, it involves people who may know nothing about broadcasting. We need to be concerned about participants because there's plenty of evidence that they don't realise what they're getting into. There is little doubt that many who take part are happy to be included. But it is sometimes easy for broadcasting professionals for whom TV is a daily experience to forget that, for many others, contact with the production process and appearance on the screen is a once-in-a-lifetime experience that they might live to regret.'

The Independent TV Commission (ITC), a fellow watchdog organisation, had already called for greater responsibility from confessional show producers when it published its own annual review of ITV and Channel 4 earlier in the year. In August, by which time the show had been moved to a 9.25am time slot, it declared Jerry's show as being too violent for daytime TV when children might be watching. The commission said it had received 86 complaints, an unusually high number, since the commercial ITV network had begun airing it weekdays at 1.30pm in March 1998. It upheld 15 complaints against one particular episode entitled *I'm Here To Stop Your Wedding*, which was aired on 31 May in Britain, saying that it breached the family viewing requirement of the programme code. The ITC ruled that the 'violent behaviour' of Jerry's guests made the show unsuitable for viewing before the 9pm watershed. At LWT, the station that airs the show for the entire ITV network, executives promised that violent scenes would not be shown again before the 9pm cut-off. However, they insisted that they had no plans to drop the show altogether because it was so popular with British viewers. Dianne Nelmes, the controller of daytime TV, admitted that it was an uphill task to find enough shows that were not too sexually explicit and did not contain too many fights for the 1.30pm slot. The ITC also complained about two episodes of *Springer* that were shown on the Living TV channel.

However, in the USA putting a petticoat on a pit bull could not last long. The general feeling of many experts in the US TV industry was that the physical as well as emotional conflicts would have to return if the show wished to maintain its popularity with viewers.

So it came as no surprise that less than a month after the self-imposed ban on fights they started to appear again. While it was not an out-and-out free-for-all as in the show's more heady fight days, mêlées were definitely back in by the middle of July. People were shoving and pushing each other and headlocking and brawling, with the beefy on-set security guards back in the middle of it all. They only thing missing were actual punches, which were still being edited out. The fight-filled episodes started to air hot on the heels of news from the Nielsen ratings that the show had lost 10 per cent of its viewers across the USA since it had begun cleaning up its act. Instead of being the clear leader of the pack, Jerry's show was still No. 1 but tied with Oprah. For a few weeks the guests had been kept further apart on stage, reducing the potential for physical confrontations, but as the summer progressed they were once again sitting side by side.

To maintain its lead, the gloves had to come off and the guests had to come out fighting. Faster than a guest could say 'I'm sleeping with my daughter's boyfriend' the battles came back rapidly. Jerry fought his way back to the top of the heap. The hardcore fans applauded the show's return to form. 'Yippeeee!' posted 'Phyliss' on the alt.fan.jerry-springer newsgroup in cyberspace. Diller ordered his executives to make no further comments about the brouhaha and he seemed to have lost his interest in shedding the show from his empire. WFLD in Chicago had a special deal with Studios USA allowing it to edit out the fights from the show, even though as a general rule individual stations are not allowed to edit syndicated shows that they buy. The station's general manager, Stacey Marks-Bonner, was keeping her end of a bargain with the Dump Springer Coalition to cut out the worst of the violence.

The coalition's organiser, pacifist pastor Pfleger, promised his fight would continue and set about organising protests outside Studios USA's Los Angeles offices. In addition, he singled out the 19 companies whose commercials appeared on the show in the USA and organised a campaign trying to persuade the firms, which ranged from Sony and Seagram to the drug company Glaxo Wellcome, to stop advertising there. However, when protestors did picket Studios USA in Los Angeles they were met by an opposing group, organised by local rock radio station KROQ-FM, sporting banners expressing such thoughts as 'Jesus Loves Jerry'. Studios USA top brass refused to meet Pfleger and his group, who were turned away by security guards. The guards gave them a letter from Robert Fleming, group president of the company, that read in part: 'The fact is, we have substantially toned down *The Jerry Springer Show*.' Pfleger countered that Studios USA had reneged on its promise to reduce the violence.

A confident Richard Dominick was revelling in the new shows he was producing that autumn, 'They are wilder and crazier than ever before.'

The fights were not now even restricted to the TV guests. In the USA potential jurors wait in a separate room where they can watch TV until they are called upon to be seated and adjudicate on a criminal case. However, court officials in Los Angeles and Long Beach, California, banned jurors from watching *The Jerry Springer Show* when it was discovered the jurors were getting into too many arguments and fights over who was right and who was wrong on the show.

The jury was well and truly out on *The Jerry Springer Show*. Only 1999 would reveal whether Jerry's show would last in its most popular format through into the new millennium.

CHAPTER 24

Moving to Chicago did not mean Jerry cut all his links with Cincinnati. Although he was separated from Micki, he was in regular contact with her because of Katie, who was now a lively teenager looking forward to going to college, despite her disabilities. Besides, Cincinnati still regarded him as a favourite, if somewhat madcap, son.

He was still far from being the national and later international superstar he was to become and was happy to maintain ties with the city that had been his home for so long. As his fame spread, he branched out into other areas of showbusiness, making guest appearances on other shows and eventually signing book and movie deals. He maintained his interest in politics throughout, and even though he once joked he was making so much money, 'I'm just two paycheques away from being a Republican', he was still a staunchly liberal Democrat.

Three months after his emotional departure from Cincinnati, he was invited back to be Grand Marshal of the 73rd annual Findlay Market Opening Day parade, marking the start of the baseball season. The parade, which featured 155 colourful floats and displays, preceded the first game of the 1993 season, with the Cincinnati Reds hosting the Montreal Expos.

Later that year he was back again, to be 'roasted' at a fund-raising dinner for the Society of Professional Journalists' college scholarship fund. Roasts are an American tradition whereby the guest of honour is roundly abused and insulted, reminded of past embarrassments and generally verbally battered by a selection of friends and colleagues. In Jerry's case, one of his tormentors at the $50-

a-head dinner at the Omni Netherland Plaza hotel was former Hamilton Country prosecutor Simon Leis, now sheriff of the county, who had been involved in the investigation of the Northern Kentucky 'cheque incident'. The roasters, who also included old council colleagues Charles Luken and Kenneth Blackwell, and Jerry's long-time TV co-anchor, Norma Rashid, were clearly not short of material.

He also went back to his roots to host a TV special for teenagers to mark Law Day USA, a theme day dedicated to the rule of law. He led a panel of high school students, lawyers, judges and clergy to discuss legal and ethical problems facing teenagers. In the show, *Just Solutions: It May Be Legal But Is It Right?* broadcast on local cable TV, he discussed topics such as: should a school athletics coach ask a doctor to give an injured star athlete painkillers to help him compete? And is it really wrong to cheat on a maths test if your report card has already been marked and cheating will not affect your grade in school?

Jerry was by now getting national attention. Clips from his programme featured regularly on *Talk Soup*, a daily cable TV roundup of the best and worst moments from talk shows. Among the segments chosen from his shows were an interview with a blissfully married happy couple, she was 44, he was 14; a woman coping with her husband's death by exposing herself to strange men; and an insomniac who needed pain to send himself to sleep, so he used a lighted cigarette to burn himself to sleep. He had so far managed to avoid setting fire to the bed when he appeared on *The Jerry Springer Show*.

In September 1993 Jerry was asked to stand in for *Talk Soup* host Greg Kinnear, now an actor who was nominated for an Oscar in the 1997 film *As Good As It Gets*, for a long weekend. He hosted three half-hour versions of the show on Friday and hour-long episodes on Saturday and Sunday. That was his first taste of national TV other than his own show since he appeared with Dinah Shore years earlier, but it was not to be his last.

Later that year he appeared as a thinly disguised version of himself in an episode of the raunchy and raucous sitcom *Married ... With Children*. He played the host of *The Masculine Feminist*, character Peg Bundy's favourite talk show, who encouraged women to take over the local bowling alley, thus depriving her loud-mouthed lout of a husband, Al Bundy, of his weekly night out with the boys. Al and his buddies, wearing masks and T-shirts emblazoned with the symbol for a woman crossed out and the words 'No Ma'am', invaded the talk show set and bound and gagged the hapless Jerry for most of the episode.

Jerry explained how he ended up with his first acting role, and admitted he did not have to stretch himself for the job. 'They needed someone who's kind of a feminist,' he said. 'What really ticks Al Bundy off is a guy who supports women's causes. So maybe it was a bit of typecasting. It's a funny script. They have good writers. It would be funny without me. No one is going to confuse me with an actor. I managed to do 10 years on the TV news without being mistaken for a journalist.'

The exposure helped promote the show, as did an appearance hosting *Evening At The Improv*, a popular cable programme showcasing new stand-up comedians at a trendy club and restaurant in West Hollywood, California. Jerry also appeared as a guest on *Larry King Live*, talking about his show to the Cable News Network celebrity.

He was his normal, self-deprecating self when he played a one-night stand at West Hollywood's trendy Viper Room, where actor River Phoenix had died of a drugs overdose the previous year. He joined rockabilly group Rattled Roosters on stage and belted out 'I Saw Her Standing There', 'I Want You, I Need You, I Love You' and, wearing an Elvis-style cape over his leather jacket, 'Love Me Tender'.

'I will never convince myself I'm any good,' admitted Jerry. 'My theory is that people will tolerate almost anything when they're drinking.'

In 1995 he went back into the music studio for the first time since his run for governor, releasing a country music CD, *Dr Talk*, on the Fiddle Fish Music label. After months of controversy over the *Jenny Jones* shooting, the tongue-in-cheek release provided some much-appreciated light relief.

Jerry wrote the title song himself, paralleling the subjects of country music and chat shows, with the less-than-immortal chorus,

There's Oprah, Phil and Sally
And Jerry Springer too
A little dose of a talk show host
You won't seem quite as blue.

He also sang 'Please Help Me I'm Falling', 'Cold, Cold Heart', 'Talk Back Trembling Lips' and 'Mr Tambourine Man'.

Jerry got the idea when he took his beloved Katie to the country music capital of Nashville, Tennessee, for a holiday and to escape the constant chatter about talk shows in May 1995. 'Traditional country songs are invariably about broken relationships and divorce and cheating, who slept with whom, etc.,' he recalled, explaining his decision. 'So I was at the Grand Ole Opry with my daughter, and we're listening to the music, and it dawned on me that the themes are consistent. So I wrote the song, which kind of makes fun of talk shows.'

The Grand Ole Opry is the major concert hall in Nashville — actually in Opryland, a giant entertainment centre on the outskirts of the city — and a magnet for country music fans.

During the same trip he met 'Achy Breaky Heart' singer Billy Ray Cyrus, who later invited Jerry to open shows for him. Cyrus said he asked Jerry to share the stage because he seemed willing to try anything. 'He is a real person and people love him no matter what he does,' Cyrus said.

The album certainly did not win rave reviews. *Entertainment Weekly* wrote: 'To say that Springer's voice is thin is like observing that Kate Moss ain't too chubby,' and in California, the *Orange County Register* writer Kinny Littlefield said: 'Tony Bennett he ain't. But exuberance spikes his scratchy delivery. Talk show host Jerry Springer can't sing at all.' Nevertheless, it did win him the chance to open concerts for Cyrus in Cleveland, Ohio; Philadelphia, Pennsylvania; and Miami, Florida.

At the concerts he was accompanied by a five-piece band and two women backing singers, and the crowds went wild when he appeared on stage, dressed for the part in jeans and black boots. He also opened for the country band Alabama and, of course, he performed on his own show.

Jerry was refreshingly frank about his abilities. 'OK, I stink,' he admitted. 'I'm no threat to Sinatra, but what the heck? Like, what do I know about country music? This has taken off with a life of its own and I'm going for the ride. I'm having a blast! Everyone understands what this is. We are having fun. I was not playing with a full deck when I did this.' He appreciated the cheers and applause that concert fans gave him, but was under no illusions about a career in music. 'Everyone knows what it is,' he went on. 'They're not sitting there saying, "Oh, he's going to be a great musician." It's just fun. It's entertainment. We go on, we tell a few jokes, then I sing. But that's all it is. It's just the guy who lives next door to you singing, nothing more than that.'

On a more serious note, he joined forces with veteran comedian Jerry Lewis to take part in a TV fund-raising show on behalf of the Muscular Dystrophy Association. The annual show, broadcast every year on the Labor Day holiday weekend, the public holiday which marks the end of summer and the return to school is an American institution. Lewis has worked tirelessly at it since the early 1950s and has raised more than $1.6 billion dollars for research over the years. Jerry was happy to help out, and returned to the show for the next three years.

This was by no means Jerry's only contribution to charity, although he does not like to make a fuss about his work for good causes. Spurred on by his love for Katie, and his pride in her accomplishments, he enjoys helping other children in need. He is vice-president on the board of the National Muscular Dystrophy Association, and says, 'It is a privilege to help raise funds for this vital research on behalf of children stricken with these life-threatening illnesses.'

He is also on the advisory board of the Audrey Hepburn Hollywood for Children Fund, a foundation dedicated to continuing the late actress's tireless work to help underprivileged children around the world. Closer to home, recognising the importance of education, he has set up a scholarship fund at the inner-city Kellman School in Chicago to help struggling children.

Jerry maintained his interest in politics and was delighted that the Democratic party chose Chicago for their 1996 convention. His attendance there was very different from his last one in 1968. Then he had been just another unknown struggling student, watching anti-Vietnam War campaigners being beaten up. Now he was a millionaire, one of the best-known faces in the country, living in style in his skyscraper apartment in the luxurious John Hancock Building, named for the first man to put his signature to the American Declaration of Independence, with sweeping views over Lake Michigan.

He got himself media credentials and took in a film crew with a view to taping a segment about wacky Presidential candidates. However, he was the one who came across as wacky, hugging former vice-presidential candidate Geraldine Ferraro, Walter Mondale's running mate in 1984 and announcing, 'I'm running for vice-president in the year 2000. I think we need a talk show host for vice-president.'

In reality Jerry has pledged never to return to politics as a career, 'I'd never have a career in politics again, because it makes you dishonest. If you make a living in politics then inevitably you have to compromise.'

He attended A-list parties, including a Planet Hollywood bash and one thrown by John F Kennedy Jr's political magazine *George*, but pompous Kennedy opted to be interviewed by Oprah Winfrey, not Jerry. Soul legend Aretha Franklin, in town at the same time to give a concert, also turned him down, backing out of a promised chat with two days' notice.

Jerry was, however, able to console himself with the knowledge that he had friends in high places; a month earlier he had been among guests at a birthday party for President Clinton at Radio City Music Hall in New York. Clinton told him: 'I've seen your show.' Jerry's response? 'I'm sorry to hear that.'

Two years later when the Clinton–Lewinsky sex scandal broke humourists speculated that they would make ideal candidates to appear on *The Jerry Springer Show* but the show's producers responded that the President's relationship with his former White House intern was just too tame and not outrageous enough.

Jerry discussed his changed fortunes with old Cincinnati pal John Kiesewetter, reflecting that Cincinnatians who remembered him in his previous jobs had a very different view of him from the rest of the country. He insisted that while his trappings might have changed, he was still the same old Jerry he always was.

'I'm as liberal as I've ever been,' he said. 'I sleep very well at night. I manage to make a very good living without changing my political stripes. My job is to be an entertainer. It doesn't mean what I am as a person. I haven't sold out. It's just that this is my job. But I have never once ever on my show changed my political views. I never once on the show came across as a conservative. This is showbusiness. And for people who knew me in Cincinnati, it's hard to put me in the same category as showbusiness. But that's the job. The rest of the country sees me as a showbusiness personality.'

He did draw parallels between the two sides of his life. 'My best friend says that my audience never changed,' he went on. 'From politics to news to the Harvest Home Parade, it's always been the young people I attract. It has never been "Mr Springer". Whether you're in Mount Adams [Cincinnati's entertainment district] or Los Angeles or Chicago, it's always "Hey, JER-RY!" It's a natural audience for me. I admit I'm a little old for this connection, but I'm not threatening to young people. I'm their uncle. Their crazy uncle.'

The perceived dichotomy between his political beliefs and his showbusiness character caused him one dilemma. He was approached to write a book, but refused to pen his autobiography or a story about his experiences as a talk show host. He said: 'If I write a book I would write a political book and I need more time for that. That's the problem. And I won't do an as-told-to book with someone. If I'm writing a book, I'm *writing* the book.'

However, two years later, ironically, he changed his mind on two of his points and announced that he was co-writing a book,

Ringmaster, about behind-the-scenes secrets from *The Jerry Springer Show*. His co-author was Laura Morton, who had already written books with *Taxi* star Marilu Henner and top US TV newscaster Joan Lunden.

He said: 'From my unique perspective as ringmaster of this circus whose name the show bears, I thought a book might be the best way to share some thoughts about the show, the industry and, to some extent, the culture that to the chagrin of many has embraced it.'

If Jerry's fans were expecting to learn much about his personal life when they bought his book they were in for a disappointment. Although it is packed with photographs, many from the show, and some poignant pictures from his family album, he deliberately does not reveal much about himself or his family.

The first six chapters are bizarrely formatted as an interview with God, as the host of a Heavenly talk show, and in them Jerry gives readers a brief history of his life from his birth in London, emigration to America and career in Cincinnati, both as a politician and businessman.

The book then shifts to a more conventional narrative as he tells the story of the show, along with passages written by assorted members of his staff, including Steve Wilkos, Todd Schultz, Richard Dominick and Burt Dubrow, recalling highlights of various shows.

Micki and Katie, the two most important women in his life, are given a scant four pages, two of them a Father's Day Final Thought from an early *Jerry Springer Show* about his daughter, in which he says, 'I'm happy to report that Katie sees, hears and talks unceasingly on the phone with her boyfriend. She's preparing for college and for anything she wants to be. Katie for President. What hurdles couldn't she overcome? She's a gift to all she meets and for me, the greatest Father's Day gift of all.'

He describes Micki as, 'Simply put, the best woman I've ever known. The truth is, we've always had a wonderful, caring relationship. But I wasn't always a very good husband to her. In my otherwise wonderful life, it's my one regret. She desrved better.'

Jerry flew to Cincinnati to sign copies of his book for fans, but the 273-page volume, fleshed out with his favourite Final Thoughts and lists of show topics, had a hostile reception from the city's two newspapers.

Jim Knippenberg wrote in the *Cincinnati Enquirer*, '*Ringmaster!* is a quick read, with its oversized type and widely spaced lines. It's well written enough, breezy, chatty, occasionally funny and sometimes insightful. It's also whiny, defensive and preachy.'

Knippenberg criticises Jerry for taking verbal swings at critics like conservative William Bennett and the constant repetition of his familiar mantra that the news exploits people more than his show. 'What's missing here is a personal side. True, we get a bio at the beginning, and true, we get a bit about The Cheque Incident, but a current view is missing. Courtship of wife Micki and birth of daughter Katie takes two pages. That's because he says he hates talking publicly about things private.

'In my 30 years in public life, I've always refused to talk about my private life (otherwise, of course, it would no longer be private).

'Yeah, but people want to know. A few details, however trivial, would go a long way to rounding out the picture. It doesn't happen in *Ringmaster!*'

In the *Cincinnati Post*, Keith Herrell wrote, 'Don't look for instrospection — Springer can't remember making a decision about going to law school, but he wound up at Northwestern University's law school and made his way from there to Cincinnati.

'You say he's exploited innocent people? I sure have, he responds, but not on *The Jerry Springer Show*. "You see, I did the news. For 10 years I anchored the news in Cincinnati, and like all newscasts and newspapers, we were often horribly exploitative."

'Springer also defends himself from charges that his show is faked, saying producers take pains to verify guests' stories (including the man who cut off his penis with garden shears).'

Entertainment Weekly rated the book a C: '*The Jerry Springer Show* employs a dentist for the programme's many guests with few or no teeth. That's the most sensational thing you'll learn in *Ringmaster!*, Springer's part-autobiography, part-behind-the-scenes show guide. What's more shocking is the amount of time Springer spends portraying himself as a liberal, civic-minded ex-politician who fights prejudice in all forms because some of his relatives were killed in the Holocaust.

'He takes a nearly-belligerent tone with critics; Why must his show be maligned, Springer asks, when TV news "seriously exploits and hurts people every day?" Once he's rammed that point home, he delivers the good stuff, like the dirt on the guest who had sex with his horse.'

USA Today, however, described the book as 'breezy' and welcomed the brief details about Micki and Katie. Their reveiwer added, 'And there are titbits for fans, like "no older people" are allowed in the front row, in case of furious onstage action; the show has a "drawerful" of leftover engagement rings; and even pets get mascara if a guest requires it.'

Before the book came to fruition he was once again cast as himself, in the 200th episode of *Roseanne*, in which she dreams about parading the dysfunctional Connor family on his show, and *Night Stand With Dick Dietrick*, a spoof of talk shows that routinely took pot-shots at *The Jerry Springer Show*. In that episode Jerry was seen plotting to take his revenge on Dietrick for his constant carping.

He appeared on *The X-Files* in late 1997, again playing himself in a black-and-white episode, in which a woman who watched a *Jerry Springer Show* when a female guest claimed to be the mother of a werewolf gave birth to a Frankenstein's monster-like creature. Writing disparagingly about the episode, Greg Paeth said in the *Cincinnati Post*: 'Of course, Springer would never tackle a topic like that. Not unless the werewolf had really infuriated a vampire who works nights as a stripper.' Jerry disagreed with Paeth and laughed later: '*The X-Files* people thought they were doing something really outrageous but we had done that show for real. We found a woman called The Monkey Lady who used to be in the circus; a lovely woman but born covered with hair.'

By this time he had begun to experience foreign adulation. He was huge in Belgium and the UK, where he appeared on *The Ruby Wax Show*, and on a visit to The Netherlands to promote the show he was mobbed like a rock star. He appeared on a talk show there, very different from his own, and reflected: 'Being over there, it's far more open. But their TV is far more conservative. We are clearly the most outrageous show in Holland.'

The Springer steamroller seemed unstoppable. He had another guest appearance on *Talk Soup*, and appeared in a sketch on *The Tonight Show*, hosted by Jay Leno.

Jerry fans also had a new chance to see bolder and better shows with the launch of the video series, *Jerry Springer: Too Hot For TV*. Although his critics could hardly credit it, some guests or fights were simply too outrageous to be aired in the USA, even with a TV-M rating attached. Rather than waste the unusable footage, the producers decided to release them on a home video, available only through mail order. It went on sale in time for Christmas 1997, quickly sold 300,000 copies at $19.95 a time and was said to be the fastest-selling video of all time.

It was the first of a series, all of which sold like hot cakes. For once, however, Jerry made a mistake. He did not think anyone would buy the tape and sold the rights for a flat fee.

'I totally misread it,' he admitted. 'I didn't want to do the tape. I thought it would just increase the heat. I thought every columnist in America would look at the tape and say, "Aha, the trashy Springer is at it again." I also thought no one would buy it. So we'd get all this heat, and for what? I signed off on it for a nominal fee. No percentage of sales. And the video has become an all-time best-seller. What a schmuck.'

He made sure he did not repeat the mistake, and worked out a royalty scheme for the sequels. By October 1998 there were seven on the market and Jerry was raking in the money. In September 1998, *Forbes* magazine, the bible of the American business and financial world, estimated his cut from the videos at $1 million. Their breakdown of his finances for the year reckoned that he had made $4 million from the show, from a gross income of $100 million, $1.5 million for his book, $2 million for the film and a final million from merchandising and personal appearances, for a total of $9.5 million.

Jerry's growing fame began to rub off on his staff. In early 1998 when he appeared, again playing himself, in an episode of the sitcom *Between Brothers*, starring Kadeem Hardison and Dondre T Whitfield, security chief Steve Wilkos and stage manager Todd Schultz also had cameos. Jerry's growing popularity was particularly good for Wilkos, who by now was his part-time personal bodyguard. Whenever Jerry got to travel Wilkos was able to get time off from the Chicago Police Department to tour the world with him.

Jerry also did a guest spot in the spoof series *Mad TV*. 'The premise was very funny,' he recalled. 'Me going crazy because no one on the stage would fight. I grab someone in the audience, pull a gun and snarl, "There'd better be a fight or the old bitch gets it",' and another on the cult cartoon show *Beavis and Butthead*.

Finally he won his first dramatic role, one that promised to be a ratings winner. Former *Baywatch* babe Pamela Anderson was given a new series, *V.I.P.*, in which she stars as the glamorous head of a private investigation agency, and Jerry was delighted to take part in it. The couple met at a TV convention where they were both promoting their shows, and Jerry confessed he was a big fan. She immediately offered him a guest appearance.

In fact Jerry, who once kept a life-size cardboard cutout of her in her skimpy red *Baywatch* bathing costume in his office for months, was said to have made a big play for her during filming. He played a lovesick client who hired Pam's character to help him out. In one scene they were chased across a beach riding a three-wheeled dune buggy, and Jerry made the most of clinging on to Pam, who was driving.

By now the big screen was inevitably beginning to beckon. He played himself in Rodney Dangerfield's 1997 movie *Meet Wally Sparks*, in which Dangerfield played the fictional host of the sleaziest talk show on the air, and had a cameo role, along with baseball slugger Sammy Sosa, in the feature film *Kissing A Fool*, starring *Friends* actor David Schwimmer. Schwimmer is such a huge Jerry fan he even offered him the role of a sleazy photographer in the first film he was to direct, a high-school reunion picture called *Since You've Been Gone*.

Rumours began to fly that Jerry would make a film biography of his wild and crazy life, and in March 1998 it was announced that he had signed a $2 million deal to make a comedy, to be produced by Steve Stabler (one of the producers of the Jim Carrey film *Dumb and Dumber*) and Gary Goldstein.

However, he was quick to deny stories that the film, which was given the working title *Springers*, would be autobiographical. 'When they first approached me I said, "If you're talking about an autobiography, absolutely do not continue the conversation,"' he said. 'It will be a comedy of some sort or a day-in-the-life story. But it's not going to be my life story. That's in the contract.'

When the film opened in the United States in late November 1998 to cash in on the long Thanksgiving holiday weekend, which traditionally attracts large movie audiences, it told a tale of two 'typical' guest groups vying for their moment of fame on the slightly fictionalised *Jerry Show*. The film has Jerry playing Jerry Farrelly, the host of the nationally syndicated chat show, which is a sensational hit in the USA.

One of the two groups is a self-described 'white trash' clan who live in a central Florida trailer park. Molly Hagan plays Connie, who makes a living driving a mobile canteen selling snacks by the roadside and is the mother of motel room cleaner-cum-prostitute Angel, played by Jaime Pressly. At the time, Angel is having an affair with her mother's unemployed second husband, Rusty, played by Michael Dudikoff, who had packed on the pounds since his *American Ninja* movie days.

Connie suspects that her husband and daughter are a twosome and when she catches them in the act, she decides to teach them a lesson; first by sexually servicing Angel's dim-witted fiancé, aptly named Willie (played by Ashley Holbrook, who got the part after being spotted operating the video camera during auditions for the movie) and then by calling Jerry's hotline, since this predicament is just perfect for his forthcoming show, *I Slept With My Stepdaddy*.

Meanwhile, elsewhere in America, black beauty Starletta, played by Wendy Raquel Robinson, has caught her boyfriend Demond, acted by Michael Jai White, in bed with her best friend Vonda, played by Tangie Ambrose. Starletta then discovers that Demond's 'stick it anywhere' policy has extended to another of her friends, Leshawnette, played by Nicki Micheaux. This is ideal fodder for Jerry's segment on *My Traitor Girlfriend*.

Soon both groups are on their way to be guests of *The Jerry Show*, which for the purpose of the movie has been transplanted from Chicago to Los Angeles.

When the two groups meet at a guests' briefing, a mutual dislike between them quickly develops, fuelled mainly by Angel and Demond's instant carnal attraction for one another. Added to this mixture of lust and loathing is a sex-with-transvestites sub-plot, and from there the comedy plays itself out.

The film, directed by Neil Abramson, is, like the book, called *Ringmaster*, although in all the publicity the name was changed to *Jerry Springer's Ringmaster*. It was made in a rush, with Jerry spending less than a month shooting in Los Angeles during his summer break from taping his real show in Chicago.

The movie was completed in double quick time to cash in on Jerry's popularity, as the producers always understood that hanging over their project like the sword of Damocles was the constant possibility that the bubble might burst on a phenomenon like their star.

Talking about Springermania, Jerry told *Los Angeles Daily News* movie critic Bob Strauss, 'I know what this is. This is a fleeting moment, it's a blip on the screen. I'm not going into any time capsule. Right now, I'm part of the pop culture; I understand it has a lifespan.' And he told *USA Today* writer Kevin V Johnson, 'I'm riding a horse. I'm holding on and having a great time.'

Ringmaster, which was widely despised by the critics, narrowly slipped into the box office Top 10 the week it opened, earning a respectable US$5,002,893, but quickly disappeared from sight the following week.

Top of the box office that week was *A Bug's Life*, made by the Walt Disney studio's off-shoot Buena Vista. It had been released the previous week and had already raked in a staggering US$46,111,456.

There were only three other actual new releases that week: *Babe: Pig in the City*, which was widely expected to be a big box office success despite being struck by last-minute technical hitches, *Home Fries* and the much-hyped *Very Bad Things*.

But none of the new releases fared well. *Babe* earned a disastrous US$8,200,515 and came in at the number 5 slot, which led to heads rolling at Universal Studios, the makers of the film. *Home Fries*, which starred Drew Barrymore and Luke Wilson, came in at number 8 earning US$5,313,518. And *Very Bad Things*, which starred Cameron Diaz and Christian Slater, failed to make the Top 10, only managing number 11 with earnings of just US$4,657,574.

Therefore Jerry could console himself with his respectable performance in the ratings and earnings, despite the lashing he was getting from the critics.

Michael Rechtshaffen wrote in the *Hollywood Reporter*, 'The fictionalised account of the events leading up to an appearance on Springer's show, a.k.a. *Lifestyles of the Poor and Trashy*, plays like one of Jerry's *Too Hot for TV* videos, with the added bonus of bad writing and direction.' He offered Jerry a Final Thought: 'Don't quit your day job.'

People magazine said the film was, 'Strictly for would-be guests on Jerry's show.'

Writing in *Daily Variety* newspaper, the bible of the entertainment industry in Los Angeles, Dennis Harvey said, '*Ringmaster* is basically *The Jerry Springer Show* with a script, plus a tad more nudity and hardcore cussing than broadcast standards allow. Wit is on the level of the *bon mot* "To love, honour and obey ... my ass!"'

He described the film as, 'A big screen translation nobody was waiting for.' And Bob Strauss asked in the *Daily News*, 'Are the guests on *The Jerry Springer Show* stupid or moronic? The movie *Ringmaster* answers that burning question. The answer is yes. The level of humour here is, in a word, broad; the level of conversation, loud. The combination makes for a few laughs, markedly more groans and an overall feeling of time and effort wasted.'

Discussing Jerry's acting talents, he said, 'Springer himself comes off as an affable, self-deprecating type. When he's not sporting a "What have I done?" grimace, he's passionately arguing that his show is about people, not trash.

'It would be élitist to claim otherwise about the TV show anyway. But the made-up characters in *Ringmaster* register a few rungs down on the evolutionary scale from the stars of *Babe: Pig in the City*. They don't speak as well, either.'

As the crowd was entering LA's Hollywood Palladium for the party after the film première, one guest said aloud, 'I feel like I'm about to see two-headed babies.' But journalist Bill Higgins, who was covering the event for *Daily Variety* said: 'She was wrong. Just plenty of one-head transvestites, who were described by one woman as "looking like a cross between World Federation wrestlers and Divine."

'Just as every country gets the leader (and the phone company) it deserves, every film gets the party it warrants. Springer got a lot of big men in fishnet stockings, platinum wigs and second-hand Bob Mackie gowns.' Première coordinator Carlotta Florio admitted: 'We asked people to dress "trashy chic".'

Jerry said of his film, 'We all have this cliché about these people when we see them for 15 minutes on what's admittedly a crazy silly show, but in the film we get to see who they really are. By the end of the movie you really relate to these people. All of a sudden it's more than a trailer park. It's a real life to them.'

After Jerry beat Oprah Winfrey in the TV ratings for the first time in February 1998 his critics were enraged. James Collins wrote in *Time* magazine: 'No one who is honest would deny that his show is entertaining. But it is also ... what are the right words? Horrible? Disgusting? It is disgusting because it parades real people before the mob as objects of ridicule.'

Frazier Moore of the *Associated Press* commented: 'We can concede the God-given right of every American to watch *Jerry Springer* and even to appear on it. And as Springer rightly points out, those of us who aren't fans can just go watch something else. But none of that spares Springer from his own disgrace as the host of such effluent. Springer is an opportunist who would shout "Fire!" in a crowded studio and defend it as free speech. He is a voyeur who fans the flames that engulf his guests, then according to his mood, justifies it as righteous discourse or silly entertainment.'

Jerry did not care, nor did his fans. The college kids who were his core audience filled auditoriums when he went on sold-out speaking tours. Much to his delight the girls in the crowd developed a welcoming gimmick, pulling up their T-shirts to bare their breasts, often with his name written on them. Whatever harping comments the critics, priests and politicians cared to make only served to increase his popularity and prominence.

Across the USA Jerry had become a topic of conversation. There was far more chat about him and his programme elsewhere than there was talk on his talk show. He dominated column inches in newspapers and magazines, was the topic of discussions on other chat shows both on radio and TV, everywhere people looked there was Jerry.

The nationwide controversy even spawned a new talk show that was actually billed as the antidote to *Jerry Springer*. Cleveland, Ohio comedian and writer Joanne Hart, known as Mother Love, was given a show called *Forgive Or Forget*, in which guests tearfully apologise for past wrongs and beg the person they have offended to forgive them.

Guests make their confessions before going through a 'forgiveness door'. If their apology has been accepted, the wronged party is waiting behind the door to kiss and make up; if not, there is a videotaped message explaining why they can't put the past behind them.

One early guest was singer Melba Moore, who apologised to her forgiving father for not telling him when she was forced into bankruptcy and for turning to drugs and booze after the collapse of her marriage.

Hart said: 'This is nowhere close to *Jerry Springer*. Jerry does his thing and Mother Love is going to do her thing and that's all about bringing people together to say, "I'm sorry". This isn't a *Springer* crowd that wants to slug it out. These are people who want to make amends.'

He even found himself coming under attack from the usually nicer-than-nice Rosie O'Donnell, who disapproved of her TV rival: 'He's very Teflon. It's almost like he has no responsibility, like it's happening around him and he doesn't understand.' Maybe hoping her prediction will come true, Rosie believes that Jerry's show will eventually lose its popularity. She said, 'It's like wrestling. It's sort of a meteoric, short-lived brightness. I think it's going to fade away.'

So far Jerry's star seems to continue in its ascendancy.

Jerry did not let all the adulation go to his head. On a trip back to Ohio to speak to an enthusiastic crowd of students at the University of Cincinnati, he visited his old stomping ground, City Hall. It was just like old times, except this time people were clamouring for autographs and his every move was captured by cameras for the TV magazine show *Access Hollywood*.

He hugged his long-time friend and occasional political foe Bobbie Sterne, who was still a councillor, the only one of the current nine who had served with him, and sat in the mayor's chair, for old time's sake.

'What incredible, wonderful memories when I walked into this chamber,' he said.

To a group of Girl Scouts visiting the Town Hall to earn government badges, he joked: 'My greatest wish, particularly for the young people, is that they never appear on my show.'

While the storm clouds built up on his new home turf of Chicago, Jerry, accompanied by Steve Wilkos, headed to the UK to promote his show, which was becoming increasingly popular. He was hailed with headlines like, IS THIS THE MAN WHO WILL DESTROY BRITISH TV? and ALIEN NATION.

The main purpose of his visit was to speak on the importance of freedom of speech at Oxford University and again at an evening in London organised by Jewish society L'Chaim, in which he defended his show, even the appearances by neo-Nazis, with his familiar comments about free speech.

'The lesson of the Holocaust is you never, ever judge someone based on what they are,' he said, repeating an old theme that he has expressed many times before. 'You only judge them based on what they do. We Jews cannot now turn around and suddenly discriminate against others. We have to be the most liberal of all faiths. Jews should know more than anyone else about racism and the same things that were once said about Jews in America are now being said about blacks and other minorities.

'It's like with the show. Some of the reasons given by people who don't watch are so élitist it's frightening. They think it is beneath them. They don't want to see 'those' kind of people in their homes. They think these people are 'trash'. They *aren't* trash. They may be poor or poorly educated, but they aren't trash.'

TV's latest defender of free speech, no matter how much it costs, and apologist for the underdog, no matter how offensive he or she may be, takes both the accolades and the attacks in his stride. 'I'm enjoying the ride,' he says. 'It's fun.' His greatest satisfaction is not being Jerry Springer superstar but knowing that his top priority, his daughter Katie, will never have to worry about her future. He says, 'Because of this, my daughter, will be taken care of for ever. That's worth everything. I've accomplished that one thing, and I can enjoy the rest of my life. It's a great life. I mean, who wouldn't want to be me? I'm great, I'm having a great time.'

Through nearly 30 years in the public eye, constantly reinventing himself, shrugging off criticism and complaint, revelling in controversy, he has survived and flourished as the ringmaster in an arena of his own making.

Jerry's star may not always shine as brightly as it does today but no one can deny that he is a living example of the American dream and that he has fulfilled his own dreams for himself and his cherished daughter.

FINAL THOUGHT

Jerry is the talk show host everyone loves to hate and hates to love. He is an easy and frequent target of both critics and comics alike, who relish tearing him and his show to shreds. Yet *The Jerry Springer Show* has discovered a formula that works as well as it offends. Like eating chocolate or having sex when you shouldn't, Jerry and his 'silly' show have become one of its legion of fans' guilty secrets.

Jerry is a true American success story; if not the most controversial, then one of TV's most unlikely superstars. He came from a poor, immigrant background and was on his third career before finding international stardom in his fifties.

The secret of his show, and maybe his life, is his ability to detach himself from the chaos. He is the host who stands there with a bemused grin on his face, shaking his head occasionally when the action gets out of hand, appearing as if he doesn't get it any more than those who criticise his programme for giving a forum to people who, in the mind of his detractors, should not be allowed a voice in polite society.

He revels in the fact that he is giving people on the lower rungs of the ladder an opportunity to bathe in the spotlight, however briefly. He says: 'Celebrities are always going on TV talking about their most intimate moments, who they've slept with, the whole bit, but when regular people do it, we call it trash; it's such a double standard.'

Jerry believes that everyone in the world could appear on his show: 'Everyone has at least one story in their life that would make the rest of the world say, "Whoa, that's strange." The only thing that makes our show different is our guests want to tell their story. Many people wouldn't want to.'

As Jerry proves every day, many others do. He says: 'Volunteering to be on the show is not a minor point. If someone wants to come on and say, "This is what I've done, boy, am I a fool," that's fine.'

Definitely, though, the one person who will never appear on the show is the man whose life would surely warrant it: Jerry Springer himself.

'Would I be a guest on my own show?' he asks rhetorically. 'Never. First, I'm a chicken. Second, I wear rented suits. And third, I believe you have your own life and you leave it at home. But that's just my opinion.' One which his fans, and guests starving for attention, evidently don't share.

Another person he does not want to see on his show is his daughter, Katie: 'My greatest goal is that my child will never be on my show.' He adds, 'This is a ride. Sometimes I feel like my life has been a ride. I have had all these great jobs, totally unrelated to one another, and I'm just passing through, having a great time. Now that I have this show, I want it to be the most successful show on TV. That's my goal.'

Looking at his life he could almost be called a gypsy. He's been a politician, serious news journalist, and now one of the most popular entertainers. He has also called a lot of places home: briefly England, certainly the USA and many cities have been his resting place. First the suburbs of New York, for many years Cincinnati, where he is still regarded as a wayward son, and now Chicago, where he seems to have settled for the time being.

He says: 'Chicago has, in a sense, adopted me. You wouldn't know that from the newspaper reporters; that's their job. But the regular people are great. Everywhere I go I hear, "Come on in." If I felt that people thought I was loathsome, I'd say, "Oh shit, what am I doing?" But I get on airplanes, go to restaurants, and go anywhere, and people are so damn nice to me.'

Possibly that is because if you examine his record Jerry may come across as being reckless in his private life but he also gives the impression of someone who is caring and, quite simply, damn nice.

Off the studio set, he describes his role as a circus ringmaster with no control over the tigers, acrobats and clowns circling around him. Anyone who believes that is as ignorant and ill-informed as many of the show's guests appear to be.

Jerry Springer is a master politician, wordsmith, articulator and manipulator who has been the central figure in helping the show fight its way, literally and figuratively, to the head of the talk show heap. In the USA alone viewership increased from 3 million in 1997 to 11 million in 1998 and is still rising.

Jeanne Heaton, a psychologist at Ohio University who has written about the talk show phenomenon in her book *Tuning in Trouble*, has examined Jerry's popularity. She says: 'Our research indicates that what audiences like are the fights and the really outrageous behaviour. They tell us that straight up. And it's a natural reaction. Think about it. If you're walking along the street and you saw a fight breaking out, you'd stop to look. People are drawn to the commotion.'

However, she is not one of his supporters. She believes that shows like Jerry's have a reckless disregard for the fragility of troubled people. 'It doesn't take much, if you take volatile people and reward them for their violent outrageous behaviour, to flip them over the edge. I don't think these shows do anything to subdue this. Someday soon someone's going to shoot someone on the air.' Of course, one shooting has already happened, though after guests appeared on another chat show and not during the broadcast.

Jerry and his fans dismiss these outbursts as scaremongering and élitist nonsense. For many *The Jerry Springer Show* is the perfect escape after a hard day of work, much more relaxing than watching the news and from Jerry's viewpoint far less violent.

Explaining the fights, he says: 'They see how people behave on this show, and they think that's the way they can behave on the show.'

Jerry adds: 'Nobody comes on our show to get help. I can't believe there's a human being on planet Earth thinking, "This show will solve my problems." Our show is about outrageous people in outrageous situations, and every once in a while they throw furniture. It's crazy. It's wild. And young people get it.

'We're on the edge, and I know that. But our show does not endorse any kind of behaviour. I don't think my show is sleazy. I don't have people screwing on screen. We bleep out the bad language. We never have knives or guns. It's tame compared to most shows. For those who knock it, it's just a headline for them. And that's OK. Apparently people like it. They vote every day. I don't want to be defensive about the show. In time, people will get it. The kids already get it. I don't mind the criticism. If you don't like it, you don't have to watch it. Our show is an hour of escapist TV.

It's like watching a cartoon. It's chewing gum for the mind.'

JoAnn Brown, assistant director of student activities at the University of Tampa, where Jerry was given a hero's welcome when he went to speak there in 1998, said: 'Students like to see it because it makes them feel their lives aren't so bad. They also see the show as total comedy.'

Jerry acknowledges that his name has indeed become an idiom, shorthand for bad behaviour, 'All you have to do is say that and you don't have to define anything else. It's weird, because I don't see myself as that. I make no apologies for the show. I'm having the time of my life. I love it. But I think it's silly when I see myself being defined by my show, the good or the bad.'

He is also surprisingly modest, and hates being mentioned in the same breath as Oprah Winfrey, the talk show queen he dethroned after she spent an unchallenged decade at the top of the TV ratings, but whom he says will live on in memory long after his silly show is forgotten.

'Thirty years from now people will remember Oprah and the impact she's had on our culture and on TV,' he says. 'Oprah deserves to be respected for being a great talent, for running a serious talk show. In terms of talk shows it's not fair to mention Oprah and me in the same sentence.

'I'm a blip on the screen in terms of TV history and I recognise that. I don't need to be remembered. I want my daughter to always know she had a dad who loved her. That is the only memory that counts. Everything else is just vanity. Nobody comes back because they were well remembered. God will do what he does to us when we're gone. My hope is that nobody remembers me.'

Executive producer Richard Dominick, often credited with making the show what it is today, believes that Jerry should take much of the praise, 'He's just as amazed by what's going on as you and I are, and that's the attraction. Jerry's a real nice guy. He's like the uncle you can't wait to have come over. He has a calming influence.'

Summing up his show, Jerry's message is: 'We pride ourselves in showing viewers from time to time the more outrageous people of our society. Those who are either wildly eccentric or in their political and social beings simple defiant of convention. Now while none of these lifestyles or manners are particularly ones we would necessarily choose for ourselves, how boring life would be if there was no outrageousness. That is to say, there were none among us who would push the edges of the envelope. Please understand, because we show it, does not constitute an endorsement of it or any particular view or behaviour, any more than reporting a murder on the news or a prime-time movie about a rape is an endorsement of those horrors. Look, TV does not and must not create values. It's merely a picture of all that's out there. The good, the bad, the ugly, a world upon which we apply our own values, learned and nurtured through family, church and experience. Remember, if we permit only those views which the majority of us hold then you and I are free only so long as we agree with the majority. If you believe nothing else I ever say in my commentaries I offer at the end of every show, believe this: the politicians or companies that seek to control what each of us may watch are a far greater danger to us and our treasured freedoms than any of our guests ever could or will be.'

* * *

Take care of yourself. And each other.

CERTIFIED COPY OF AN ENTRY OF BIRTH

GIVEN AT THE GENERAL REGISTER OFFICE

Application Number W011035

REGISTRATION DISTRICT Hendon

1944 BIRTH in the Sub-district of Hendon in the County of Middlesex

Columns:-	1	2	3	4	5	6	7	8	9	10*
No.	When and where born	Name, if any	Sex	Name and surname of father	Name, surname and maiden surname of mother	Occupation of father	Signature, description and residence of informant	When registered	Signature of registrar	Name entered after registration
364	Thirteenth February 1944 24 Hayes Crescent Golders Green Hendon U.D.	Gerald Norman	Boy	Richard Springer	Margot Springer formerly Kallmann	Bag Manufacturer of 48 Belvedere Court Lyttelton Road Finchley U.D.	M. Springer Mother 48 Belvedere Court Lyttelton Road Finchley N. 2.	Seventh March 1944	Mona F. Taylor Interim Registrar	

CERTIFIED to be a true copy of an entry in the certified copy of a Register of Births in the District above mentioned.

Given at the GENERAL REGISTER OFFICE, under the Seal of the said Office, the 2nd day of October 1998

*See note overleaf

BXBY 494839

CAUTION:- It is an offence to falsify a certificate or to make or knowingly use a false certificate or a copy of a false certificate intending it to be accepted as genuine to the prejudice of any person or to possess a certificate knowing it to be false without lawful authority.

WARNING: THIS CERTIFICATE IS NOT EVIDENCE OF THE IDENTITY OF THE PERSON PRESENTING IT.

Dd.0034 200M 12/97 Mcr(202471)